SPARTA AT WAR

SPARTA AT WAR

STRATEGY, TACTICS, AND CAMPAIGNS, 550–362 BC

SCOTT M. RUSCH

FRONTLINE BOOKS, LONDON

FRONTLINE BOOKS, LONDON

Sparta at War: Strategy, Tactics, and Campaigns, 550–362 BC

First published in 2011 by Frontline Books, an imprint of
Pen & Sword Books Limited, 47 Church Street, Barnsley, S. Yorkshire, S70 2AS
www.frontline-books.com

This paperback edition published in 2014 by Frontline Books

ISBN: 978-1-78303-011-8

For more information on our books, please visit
www.frontline-books.com,
email info@frontline-books.com
or write to us at the above address.

Typeset by JCS Publishing Services Ltd, www.jcs-publishing.co.uk in Jenson Pro font (11.25pt on 13.5pt)
Maps created by Alex Swanston, Pen and Sword Mapping Department
Printed and bound by CPI Group (UK) Ltd, Croydon, CR0 4YY

Contents

ILLUSTRATIONS

Plates AND 133

Figures

Maps

FOREWORD TO THE REVISED EDITION

The publication of this revised edition of *Sparta at War* provides a welcome opportunity to revise my text and correct errors. Since pagination and indexing had to remain the same throughout, revision meant improving what already existed rather than making major alterations. However, in this foreword I can discuss some of the changes made, as well as comment on matters that have arisen since the initial hardcover publication of this book.

I begin with the cover illustration. A reviewer strongly objected to my use of the statuette from the Wadsworth Atheneum, since its provenance is unknown, and it could depict a figure from legend or a non-Spartan. I have altered the text to Plate 6 to make this point clearly. Still, I feel use of the statuette on the cover is proper. It certainly has the appearance of a Spartiate: helmeted, barefooted, hair long and carefully dressed, and wrapped in a long *himation* cloak, called a *tribōn* in Sparta, where it was common attire. Perhaps the artist did not intend to depict a Spartiate, but his figurine can certainly stand in for one.

Plate 10 also required alteration to its text. I had misidentified a figure on the far right in the back as a light-armed man. He is a hoplite – I failed on my initial inspection to detect the presence of two shields. The vase, then, does not depict a light-armed man fighting among hoplites. Moreover, I eventually realised that the actions depicted may not have been typical of early sixth-century hoplite combat. Instead, they may illustrate a tale in which two champion combatants have slain each other, and their fellow soldiers, hitherto sitting and watching the fight, now arise and engage each other. In other words, it may be a variant of the *Seven Against Thebes* story, or even a depiction in miniature of the unexpected result of the Battle of Champions, recounted in Chapter Three. If so, the piece really cannot tell us much about hoplite combat in its era.

Most changes in the main text were meant to simplify my complicated sentences. Two new items do need mention here. On page 18 I now write: 'Most Greek levies were incapable of an immediate second effort on a battlefield, even when victorious.' In my original text I denied the ability of most Greek hoplites to recover after a pursuit. This ignored the Thebans at Coronea, and more importantly the Greek armies at Cunaxa and Marathon.* In all three battles the victorious units had time

---

* Cunaxa: Xenophon, *Anabasis* 1.8.17–20, 10.4–15. Marathon: Herodotus 6.111–13.

to recover, reorganise, and make a second attack. At First Mantinea and the Nemea the Spartans conserved their strength in their first onsets, then quickly turned and attacked victorious enemy units before these could recover and react.

Another change later in the same chapter adds a reference by the Athenian orator Isocrates to the Spartiates' employment of Perioecs in warfare, which I quote here: 'For in the campaigns in which a king is commanding, they station them man by man besides themselves (*kat' andra sumparatattesthai sphisin autois*), some they even station in the first rank, and when need arises to send out a relief force anywhere, if they themselves should fear either the labours or the dangers or the amount of time required, they dispatch these to bear the brunt ahead of the others.'* Isocrates in this speech seeks to denounce the Spartiates, and seems to confuse Perioecs with Neodamodeis here, so he is distrusted. However, Jean Ducat recently argued for the essential accuracy of Isocrates' description of the Perioecs' situation,† and I agree. Here the rhetorical exaggeration lies in attributing long-distance campaigns to the Perioecs alone – although Isocrates may have viewed the Neodamodeis as a class of Perioecs, not Helots – and in seeing their fighting in the front rank in the main army as an imposition instead of an honour, since the front rank of the Spartan army consisted of officers. The statement that the Lacedaemonian units were integrated on a one-for-one basis may not seem credible – Ducat does not believe it – but it should not be dismissed. In Xenophon's time, the inhabitants of Sparta could not fill the ranks by themselves. Peers were counted in the hundreds, not the thousands, while many or most of the 'inferiors' were dependants of the relatively small number of richer Peers,‡ which in turn would have limited their numbers. It seems the mass of craftsmen and merchants did not serve as hoplites, since they were mobilised separately and ordered to provide goods and services to the army.§ Therefore Perioecs were needed to help man the morai or lochoi. Perioecs were not citizens of Sparta, and, Ducat argues, not even citizens of a Lacedaemonian state, raising doubts that they could serve in the same units as Peers. The same objection could be made about the presence of 'inferiors' in Spartiate units, however, and at least Perioecs were Lacedaemonians. Pairing each Perioec with a Peer or an 'inferior' would have guaranteed the highest possible level of control over the Perioecs' actions in battle. In the complete absence of any evidence for separate units of Perioecs in battle, aside from the Sciritae, we must take seriously whatever evidence we do possess.

---

* Isocrates 12.180.

† Jean Ducat, 'Le status de périèques lacédémoinens', *Ktèma* 33, 2008, 1–86, especially 32–6.

‡ Hodkinson 1997b.

§ Xenophon *Lakedaimoniōn Politeia* 11.2; compare Xenophon *Cyropaedia* 6.2.37.

Turning to new matters, a remarkable number of books relevant to this work have been published since it came out in 2011.* Here I wish to mention Donald Kagan and Gregory Viggiano, eds., *Men of Bronze: Hoplite Warfare in Ancient Greece* (Princeton, 2013), and especially the article 'Farmers and Hoplites' by Hans van Wees. In it he argues that the evidence for eighth- through mid-sixth-century Greece shows that hoplites were mostly members of the leisured landowning class, not working farmers. Hired men and slaves worked the land, with the landowners living in town. If true, and surveys of the Greek countryside are entirely in accord (see Lin Foxhall's article in the same work), then the Spartiates can be seen as preserving that era's norms by means of the 'Lycurgan' system. The Spartan conquest of Messenia might have been nothing more than one set of landowners displacing another. The smaller the core of opposition to the Spartans, the easier the conquest of Messenia would have been, and the easier the subsequent preservation of Sparta's rule.

Of even greater interest is Christopher Matthew's *A Storm of Spears* (Pen and Sword, Barnsley, 2012). Matthew argues at length from his re-enactment experience that underarm spear thrusts (as depicted in *Plates 9, 21, 22,* and *23*) were stronger and more effective than overarm thrusts (seen in *Plates 8, 10, 14,* and *25*). He demonstrates that many depictions of hoplites performing overarm thrusts actually show javelin throwing. Matthew also argues that, at least in the fifth and fourth centuries, hoplites generally formed 'shield walls' in which the right edge of each man's shield overlapped the left of his neighbour's shield. Combined with underarm spear thrusts, battles between hoplite formations would have resembled the traditional notion of combat between Macedonian phalanxes, with massed shoving being effected not by shields but by spear-points.

This is a novel model, different from both the 'orthodox' view of hoplite combat consisting chiefly of massed shoving of shields, and the 'heterodox' view of it consisting of thousands of individual combats of the sort usually depicted by Greek artists. How it will fare under criticism remains to be seen. Other hoplite re-enactors, and re-enactors of Dark Age English and Viking combat (which featured use of shield walls), continue to use the spear overarm, or combine overarm and underarm uses.† The validity of the 'shield wall' concept has also been

---

* For example: Nic Fields, *The Spartan Way* (Pen and Sword, Barnsley, 2013); Christopher Matthew and Matthew Trundle, eds, *Beyond the Gates of Fire: New Perspectives on the Battle of Thermopylae* (Pen and Sword, Barnsley, 2013); Paul Cartledge, *After Thermopylae: The Oath of Plataea and the End of the Graeco-Persian Wars* (Oxford University Press, 2013); Boris Rankov, ed., *Trireme Olympias: The Final Report* (Oxbow Books, 2012).

† J. Kim Siddorn, *Viking Weapons & Warfare* (Tempus Publishing, Stroud 2003), 34–8, 54–9 (both stances used). Richard Underwood, *Anglo-Saxon Weapons and Warfare* (Tempus Publishing, Stroud 1999), 45–6 (both stances used). Overarm only: The Hoplite Association www.4hoplites.com/Warfare.htm. Underarm: Nikolas Lloyd, www.lloydianaspects.co.uk/weapons/spear.html.

questioned.* Matthew's analysis of First Mantinea has the Spartans advancing in 'shield wall' formation while their enemies come on in a less-closed one. This is contradicted by Thucydides' account in 5.71, which has both sides contracting and moving rightwards, the Spartans more than their foes. If the 'shield wall' was used at all, then both lines were formed in that way from the start. However, Matthew's thesis does have some explanatory power. The 'shield wall' formation would have caused the phalanx to advance slowly. We find such slow advances in the non-battle of Argos and the First Battle of Mantinea, as well as in the Battle of the Nemea. A running advance, used at Marathon or Cunaxa, required a more open formation. In the first phase of Coronea, the Thebans and Agesilaus' mercenaries and East Greeks did charge their Greek enemies at the run. However, Agesilaus' soldiers were accustomed to charging Asians at the run, while the Thebans were doubtless aiming at the flank of the opposing Orchomenians and so had no need for a tight formation. Still, the shattered shields littering the field after the second phase of Coronea argue for massed shoving of the most 'orthodox' kind. But a desperate effort by one close-formed body of hoplites to force their way through another close-formed body of hoplites was unusual, and must have led to much body-to-body, shield-to-shield contact. Xenophon says Coronea was like no other battle of his time,† so his account of it can tell us what could occur in Greek hoplite battles, but not necessarily what was typical of them.

If I were writing *Sparta at War* today, then, I would have much new material to consider, and would have reason to alter some arguments and depictions. But I am certain this work's analysis of the overall arc of Spartan military history remains valid and useful, as does its detailed coverage of Sparta's wars, campaigns, and battles in the period 550 to 362 BC. I hope readers will agree.

---

* Peter Krentz, article 'Hoplite Hell', in Donald Kagan and Gregory F. Viggiano, eds, *Men of Bronze: Hoplite Warfare in Ancient Greece* (Princeton, 2013), 140.
† Xenophon, *Hellenica* 4.3.16; *Agesilaus* 2.9.

Acknowledgements

I first want to thank Michael Leventhal of Frontline Books for commissioning this title, enduring with godlike patience my repeated delays, and guiding it to publication at long last. My thanks next go to the staff at Frontline for their efforts in seeing this book through to print, with special nods to Deborah Hercun, senior editor, Alex Swanston, mapmaker, and Matthew Gale, compiler of the index. My friends Dr Rob S. Rice and Dr David Conwell deserve kudos for reviewing the first proofs and offering corrections and amendments on rather short notice. I am also grateful to the anonymous reviewer for his kind remarks and helpful observations. Any errors that remain are, of course, my own.

I also want to thank all the staff members of the museums and associations that provided the many images used here, with special thanks to the Photography and Imaging Department of the British Museum for the combined image of blocks 872 and 877 of the Nereid Monument, which I ordered done for this work. On a private note, I would like to thank my family, friends, and co-workers for their help and encouragement over the course of this project, with a special nod to David Conwell for his photos.

Finally, I dedicate this book to my father, Raymond W. Rusch, USCG, and to my *Doktorvater*, A. John Graham. I wish they could have seen it.

~ **One** ~

The Race of Unconquered Heracles

Introduction

From *c*.550 until 371,* the predominant dominant military power in Greece was Sparta. It held the entire southern portion of the Peloponnese, Greece's great southern peninsula, a huge territory for a single Greek city-state. It led an extensive alliance system, which we call the 'Peloponnesian League', and intervened abroad. Its armies fought and won ten major pitched land battles between *c*.550 and 394. Sparta led the successful defence of Greece against the Persian invasion of 480–479, winning undying fame. In the 460s it survived natural disaster, internal revolt, and wars with neighbouring states, and went on to lead opposition to the city-state of Athens and its naval empire in the Aegean Sea. The long Peloponnesian War that followed (431–404) ended with Athens crushed and Sparta dominant in Greece and the Aegean. Resentment of Sparta's empire and war with Persia caused the formation of an anti-Spartan Greek coalition. In the Corinthian War (395–386) the Spartans lost their naval empire, but by winning land battles they remained dominant in Greece. However, in the 370s a series of setbacks ended with the defeat of a Spartan army by the city-state of Thebes in a pitched battle at Leuctra in 371. In winter 370/69 Thebes and its allies invaded Laconia, the Spartan homeland, attacked Sparta itself, and liberated Messenia, the region west of Laconia, long ruled by the Spartans, who subsequently lost their position of leadership. They never regained it, despite two centuries of effort.

In this book we shall examine in detail the period from *c*.550 to 362, to see how the Spartans campaigned and fought during their prime, how they overcame such powerful empires, and why they finally met defeat. We shall also survey a broader period, from *c*.950 to 195, to discover how Sparta became the dominant land power in Greece, and why it never managed to regain that dominance after Leuctra.

---

* All dates are BC unless otherwise noted.

The Rise of Sparta, c.950–c.550[1]

Unfortunately, how Sparta became dominant is a question that cannot be answered in detail. After Greece's Bronze Age civilisation collapsed, literacy in Greece revived only in the eighth century. The earliest major historians, Herodotus and Thucydides, date to the late fifth century. Greek reconstructions of their early history, based on oral traditions and written poems, laws, and oracles, prove varied, imaginative, and questionable.[2]

Tradition held that the Dorians, the Spartans' ancestors, helped the Heraclids, the exiled descendants of Heracles, recover their rightful thrones in the Peloponnese. The Heraclids created kingdoms in the Argolid, the north-eastern region of the Peloponnese, in Messenia in the south-west, and in Laconia in the south-east. The Laconian kingdom, Lacedaemon (*Lakedaimōn*), had as its first Heraclid rulers the twins Eurysthenes and Procles, sires of its two equal royal houses, the Agiads and Eurypontids. Their capital was Sparta (modern Sparti) on the right bank of the Eurotas River in the heart of Laconia (*Figure 1*). The Heraclids and the Spartiates, the full citizen elite of Sparta, ruled the other free Laconians, the Perioecs

1. The Eurotas River and the eastern edge of modern Sparti, seen from the site of the sanctuary of Menelaus and Helen, with the Taÿgetus mountain range in the background (*David Conwell*)

(*Perioikoi*: 'those dwelling around [us]'). Greeks often referred to the two together as Lacedaemonians; we today say Spartans. Tending to the Spartiates' farms and homes were the Helots (*Heilōtai*), slaves or serfs descended from peoples conquered in war or punished for shirking battle.

In fact, archaeologists actually can provide no indisputable evidence of any influx of new people into the Peloponnese at the close of the Bronze Age. Only in the mid-tenth century is it certain that Laconia had any settlements at all, these being at Sparta, at Amyclae six kilometres to its south, and at a few other sites. The 'Return of the Heraclids/Dorian Invasion' is an origins myth, created from many accounts of migration and invasion.[3] The idea of Heraclid ancestry was also a late creation. The ancients themselves noticed that the Agiads and Eurypontids were not named after their supposed ancestors Eurysthenes and Procles.[4] The Spartan royal families probably borrowed the idea of descent from Heracles from the Temenids of Argos, who claimed the Heraclid conqueror Temenus as their ancestor.[5] Asserting Heraclid descent gave these families a legitimate pre-Dorian claim to rule in the Peloponnese. The idea of descent from twins obliged the two Spartan houses to tolerate each other's existence. We do not know what historical accident actually produced Sparta's unusual dual kingship.

Separated from Messenia by the great Taÿgetus mountain range, from Arcadia, the central highlands region of the Peloponnese, by Mount Chelmos and the limestone hills of the Sciritis district, from Laconia's east coast by the Parnon range, and from the Gulf of Laconia by the foothills of the two mountain ranges, Sparta and Laconia seem to have existed in relative isolation from *c.*950 to *c.*750. That isolation ended *c.*750. Sparta came to dominate the large central plain of Laconia, and no other settlement in the region could compete. Habitation at Sparta began on the bank of the Eurotas in the neighbourhood of Limnae, home of the cult of Artemis Orthia. By *c.*700, settlement had expanded west into the district of Mesoa, which lay south of the low acropolis hill where the shrine of Athena Poliouchos, Sparta's patron deity, was situated. Across the river, a shrine of Helen and Menelaus was created no later than this era. Sparta had become a functioning city-state. The next two centuries saw the development of the neighborhoods of Pitana, west of the acropolis to the shrine of Artemis Issoria, and Cynosura, south of Limnae and Mesoa. Also, Amyclae and its sanctuary of Apollo Hyacinthus, situated six kilometres south of Sparta, became a district of the city.

As for early Messenia, it seems to have been as isolated as Laconia. Separated from Laconia by Mount Taÿgetus, Messenia had rich upper and lower plains, called Stenyclarus and Macaria, through which ran the river Pamisus. Mount Ithome, one of the strongest natural fortifications in the Peloponnese, overlooked both plains.[6] Below it, a settlement, Messene, had existed since the ninth century. However, the balance of early habitation lay in the region's west-coast districts, and featured small settlements set on defensible hilltops and ridges. But the Greek revival of the last half of the eighth century passed by Messenia. Many sites were destroyed or abandoned, and no great city-state developed at Messene, even though habitation declined on the west coast and increased in the Pamisus valley. Native pottery styles and art gave way to Laconian ones, and Laconian cults arose.[7]

Clearly Sparta conquered Messenia in the late eighth and early seventh centuries, preventing its further development. Three quotations from the seventh-century Spartan poet Tyrtaeus describe a war with Messene,[8] won by the Eurypontid king Theopompus. It was a major event in what must have been a long process of conquest and settlement:

> (1) Under our king, Theopompus beloved of the gods,
> Through whom we took wide-spaced Messene.
>
> (2) Messene, a good [place] to plough, a good [place] to plant.
>
> (3) Around which for nineteen years they fought
> Unceasingly, always having a stout-hearted will, [these]
> Spearmen fathers of our fathers.
> In the twentieth [year], abandoning their rich farms,
> They [the Messenians] fled from the great Ithomaean mountains.[9]

The need to fight 'unceasingly' around the site probably resulted from the need to protect lands and settlements already held in the region, and to guard the routes around and across Taÿgetus from Messenian raiders. The length of the war is unsurprising. In this era settlements were small, and even Sparta was none too large. However life at Sparta was organised at this time, maintaining a war in Messenia must have been a terrific strain. The inhabitants of Messene had Mount Ithome as a refuge. Judging from the depiction of the Trojan assault on the Achaean wall in Book XII of the *Iliad*, where both sides throw rocks at each other while the Trojans try to force the gates, Greek siegecraft in this era was far too simple for the Spartans to take Ithome by force, barring surprise, treason, or a very weak defence. Things did not change much over the centuries (*Plates 16, 17*). Maintaining a tight investment of Ithome would prove beyond the Spartans' power in the 460s, even though populations were far larger then. Greek city-state armies were militia levies, self-armed, lightly trained, and able to campaign for only several weeks at a time. Sparta's army was no different. Developing sophisticated siegecraft and imposing lengthy blockades were beyond the capabilities of individual city-states. With defensible sites so readily available in Greece, a land four-fifths hill and mountain, and the ability to take fortified sites so limited, Greeks instead attacked the countryside, raiding farms and herds and ravaging crops and trees. The Spartans would have attacked the Messenians by these means, while the Messenians will have harassed

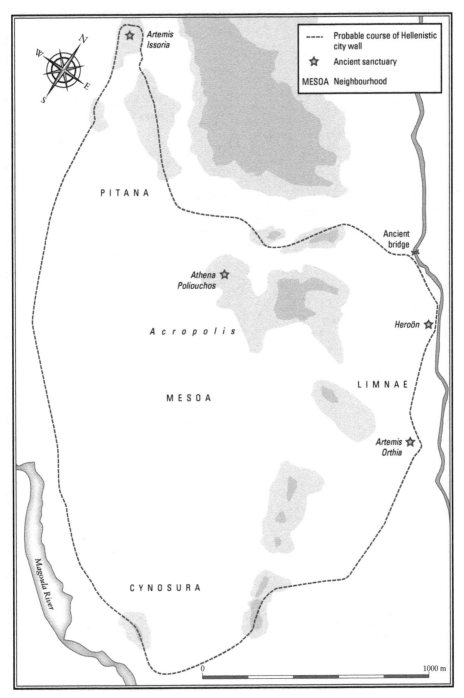

Map 1.1 The city of Sparta

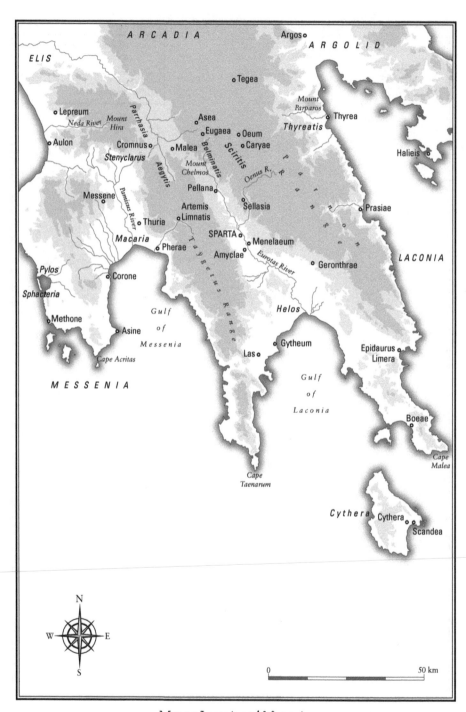

Map 1.2 Laconia and Messenia

the invaders, tried to drive them off by fighting battles, and raided Spartan-held sites in Messenia or crossed Taÿgetus to strike into Laconia. The Messenians endured, until those still resisting could stand no more and fled into exile abroad.

The conquest of Messenia and the incorporation of the island of Cythera and the east coast of Laconia into Lacedaemon, completed by c.550, created a state over three times larger than either Athens or Thebes and its Boeotian Confederation, Sparta's later rivals. The Spartans' unusual aggression probably arose from the atypical dual kingship, which would have set two ruling families against each other in efforts to be acclaimed the best in warfare, manliness, policy, and wealth. That the kings competed in conquest is explained by geography: the inland Spartans were ill-suited to trade or piracy, making war with neighbours the obvious route to martial glory, good farmland, and slave labour.

The conquest of Messenia also demanded a high level of organisation relative to the period. Tyrtaeus' poem 'Eunomia' ('Law and Order') and the 'Great Rhetra', an early law in the form of an oracle, show seventh-century Sparta to have been governed by the Gerousia, a thirty-man council of *gerontes*, elders, that included the two kings. It debated policy and proposed measures to be decided by assemblies of the people, and could reject measures that it had not proposed and would not accept. Still, the people had a voice, and could referee disputes dividing the kings and elders.[10] Another Tyrtaean poem shows the army organised by civic divisions into the three Dorian tribes, the Hylleis, Dymanes, and Pamphyloi.[11] The poems are dated at least two generations after the conquest, but an organisation on these lines would have been required to mobilise and direct the Spartan war effort.

Besides the Messenians, late reports also claim the Spartans attacked the southern Arcadians and, in concert with local allies, fought Argos, the leading city-state of the Argolid. However, the tough Arcadian highlanders and rich, advanced Argives repeatedly defeated the Spartans. These reports may be anachronistic,[12] but the Heraclid ancestry of Sparta's kings gave them a claim on the Argolid, which the aggressive Spartans may have advanced. Moreover, border conflicts were common in Greece, and anyone hard-pressed in war – such as the Messenians – desperately sought allies. Therefore, early conflicts between the Spartans and the Argives and Arcadians seem quite possible.

Conquering is one thing; keeping is another. The surviving fragments of Tyrtaeus appear to refer to a great crisis two generations after the conquest of Messenia, featuring a Messenian revolt, warfare with Argives and Arcadians, and internal political dissension. One of these, in a third-century papyrus from Egypt, has the word *Messēniōn*, 'of Messenians', in a clearly military context.[13] The lines on Theopompus' conquest cited above were perhaps meant to remind Spartans that the Messenians had been defeated before and could be again, even if it took another twenty-year war. Some other passages recalled to listeners the profit and honour of subjecting the Messenians:

> (1) Like asses worn by great burdens,
> By dire necessity bringing to their masters
> Half of all, however much produce the cropland bears.
>
> (2) Bewailing the masters, both their wives and themselves alike,
> As often as the destructive lot of death would fall upon any.[14]

However, since poor farmers typically had large families, a ready source of labour, the Messenians would have been numerous, making them a grave threat in a revolt. And they had allies: another fragment from Egypt has the words for 'of Argives' and perhaps 'Arcadians' (. . . *kades Argeiōnunel* . . .).[15] Possibly this is misleading, but, as already noted, it is certain that the Messenians would have sought help, and it is likely that the neighbours of a state as aggressive as early Sparta had cause to provide it, so aid to the revolt is credible.

Sparta was also threatened from within. The fourth-century philosopher Aristotle, discussing how factional struggles arose in aristocracies, noted that they occurred 'whenever some are too poor, others too rich, and this comes about especially in wars; it also occurred in Lacedaemon at the time of the Messenian War – as is clear from the poem of Tyrtaeus called "Eunomia". For some, distressed because of the war, resolved to make a redistribution of the land.'[16] Calls for redistribution of land, the greatest source of wealth in an agricultural society, indicated civil strife in a Greek city. The fragments of the 'Eunomia' emphasise that Zeus himself gave Sparta to the Heraclid kings,[17] and stress the primacy of the kings and elders in government. The leading men of Sparta will have owned the most land, and must have resisted efforts to redistribute it. More generally, the small size of Greek city-states, and the Greeks' highly competitive culture, meant that conflict among political factions was intense, fed by hostility between different Greek ethnicities, strife between the rich and poor, and disputes over life-and-death political and military decisions. Therefore ancient Greek history was filled with civil strife, often resulting in coups d'état, massacres, seizures of power by dictators (*tyrannoi*, tyrants), and betrayals of cities to enemies. Evidently early Sparta was not immune to such unrest.

Tyrtaeus did not hide the magnitude of the peril, although perhaps he exaggerated it. In one poem he raised the prospect of exile if the Spartans failed to fight hard, seeking to shame young men into fighting among the *promachoi*, the foremost fighters, and not running away, leaving behind older men 'whose knees are no longer nimble'. He depicted one such elder, 'his head already white and beard hoary', left 'holding his bloody genitals in his dear hands' as he breathed his last, stripped naked for trophies by the foe.[18] Greeks usually left the 'oldest and youngest', men over fifty and teenagers, at home to defend the main settlement in wartime,[19] so for this depiction to have seemed credible, the situation must have been desperate. Another poem calls on those of 'the race of unconquered Heracles' to have courage, face the enemy's multitudes, and not flee, 'considering life hateful, death's black evils dear as the rays of the sun'. The young men addressed had hard experience of war, and 'have been among pursued and pursuers', meeting defeat as well as victory. The poet urges each of the heavily armed 'panoplieds' (*panoploi*) to avoid the shame of flight, and to stand by and protect his fellows,

> And not stand outside the range of missiles, for he has a shield;
> But going close, hand-to-hand, stabbing with a long spear
> Or with a sword, let him take his foeman,
> And setting foot by foot, and pressing shield against shield,
> And crest to crest and helmet to helmet
> And chest to chest brought near, let him fight his man ...

The poet ends by urging each light-armed 'naked' (*gymnētes*), crouching here and there under cover of shields, to stay close by the panoplied and throw stones and javelins at the enemy.[20] Whether the shields were their own or those of the panoplied is unclear in the poem. However, light-armed men are depicted in the Homeric poems and early art (*Figures 2, 3*) as fighting behind heavy-armed men, a parallel to the spearman–bowman teams of Near Eastern armies (*Plate 15*).[21] Numerous lead votive figures of shielded spearmen and unshielded archers, dating from 650 to 500, have been found at Sparta (*Plates 1, 2, 3*). Most archers kneel and have helmets, but are otherwise unprotected, so their bodies must have been shielded by others, with only their helmeted heads exposed.

A third poem dismisses all virtues that Greek nobles competed with each other to display save one: 'impetuous might' (*thouris alkē*), a common good for the city, as it allowed one to 'bear the sight of bloody slaughter', stand firm among the foremost men, risk his life, encourage his fellows, and fight his people's foes. A man who did this best, who 'quickly routed the savage ranks of foemen, by his zeal held fast the surge of battle', would be celebrated by the city if he survived, and deeply mourned if he fell.[22]

Judging from the extant poetry of Tyrtaeus, it seems that 'impetuous might' was rather lacking among the Spartan levies in his era. A late commentator on Aristotle even claims that Tyrtaeus mentioned a battle against the Messenians in which the Spartans either stationed a blocking force to threaten their front-line men with beatings if they gave way, or deployed their men in front of a trench.[23] Possibly later Greeks misunderstood a poem that referred to an upcoming assault on a trench and

2. Fragment of a mid-sixth-century moulded pithos from the Heroön at Sparta, showing a slinger, unarmoured aside from a helmet, fighting behind a heavily armed spearman (*Dawkins 1929: plate XV. Reproduced with permission of the British School at Athens*)

wall, warning listeners not to flee from the attack on the wall lest they be trapped by the trench. Still, this is far from certain.[24]

However they managed it, the Spartans overcame their enemies and preserved their realm. But it appears 'impetuous might' was still lacking in the Spartan army of the early sixth century. Herodotus claims the Spartans of that era marched against Tegea bearing fetters to use on the captives they expected to take, only to suffer defeat and wear the fetters themselves as they worked in the Tegeans' fields. Repeated defeats followed, which would have stimulated discord in Sparta and thoughts of revolt among its subjects. Only the discovery by the Spartan agent Lichas of a talisman, the bones of the hero Orestes, ended the defeats at Tegean hands.[25] Herodotus says that 'the greater part of the Peloponnese had been subdued' by the Spartans by the middle of the sixth century.[26]

Sparta's success was probably due less to a talisman than to the adoption of the social and political system attributed to Lycurgus, which authors of the fifth and fourth century saw as the source of Sparta's military effectiveness.[27] Lycurgus was said to have been the guardian of an early Spartan king. Faced with civil strife and lawlessness, he created harmony among the Spartiates and made them into fierce warriors by establishing his laws and seeing that they were obeyed. In fact, no known

3. A line drawing of the Heroön
pithos, showing added material
from a second piece found
in the nineteenth century
(*Dawkins 1929: plate XVI.
Reproduced with permission of
the British School at Athens*)

ancient source for Lycurgus predates the fifth century, suggesting that the story of his lawgiving originated then. The Lycurgus myth, the 'Bones of Orestes' tale, and a rule at Sparta obliging young men to declare the laws perfect and unchanged, with only the elderly allowed to examine them in private,[28] together displaced memory of the system's development as a response to the triple threat revealed by the seventh-century Messenian revolt and raised again by the setbacks at Tegea.

Harmony and Army, c.550–362[29]

'Lycurgan' society addressed the triple threat of internal strife, revolt of subjects, and wars with neighbours by establishing concord among Spartiate men and encouraging them to create a determined and effective militia army. Concord arose from the enforcement of surface equality: adult Spartiates – the *Homoioi*, 'Similars' or 'Peers' – experienced the same upbringing and initiations. They wore the same simple styles of clothing and had the same hairstyles: long hair and beard and shaved moustaches. They ate the same simple foods at the messes, which each Peer had to join and attend regularly if he was to remain a full citizen. They even received the same simple manner of burial. Each Peer owned Helot-worked farms and did not work, save to manage his property and participate in the city's activities. When at peace, Peers passed their time in sports, hunting, athletics, dances, choruses, conversation, and public affairs. This situation did much to keep internal conflicts under control. The conspiracies against the state that did arise were suppressed with little bloodshed, and foreign foes were denied the chance to exploit strife between Spartan factions, although such strife still occurred. The Spartans, by contrast, constantly exploited civil strife in other cities. Thucydides saw this as the chief reason for their power in the Peloponnese.[30]

Official oversight of the system came from the board of five ephors (*ephoroi*, 'overseers'), which does not appear in Tyrtaeus or the 'Great Rhetra'. The board was elected annually by the Spartiates, and any Spartiate could serve, though only once. The ephors presided over the Assembly, ordered mobilisations, decided military commands, held trials with the Gerousia, kept the kings under control, and otherwise oversaw the operations of the Lycurgan system and enforced its laws. The Spartiate Assembly held deliberations, decided on war or peace, voted in officials, and enacted laws, as motions were referred to it by the ephors. The Gerousia continued to deliberate measures, kill improper motions, and act as a capital court in cases involving Spartiates. The kings served in the Gerousia and as judges, commanded the Spartan levy, and acted as sacrificial priests – this last a role suited to aristocrats claiming descent from a hero and a god.

Members of the elite among the ephors, elders, and kings determined Spartan policy. The Spartiate Assembly decided disputes among the elite and sanctioned their decisions.[31] The tight Spartiate oligarchy, the habitual privacy among messmates, periodic expulsions of foreigners from Lacedaemon (*xenēlasia*),[32] and Spartans' devotion to 'laconic' speech – their peculiar form of eloquence, substituting pithy responses for lengthy discussions – produced a security-minded secretiveness unusual in ancient Greece. Spartans could keep their own counsel. This, combined with a native penchant for deceit and craftiness, made the *ruse de guerre* a common feature of Spartan warfare.

Although at home the kings were little more than honoured hereditary magistrates, on campaign they led the massed levies, and had their authority in the field enforced by a curse on those who attempted to hinder them.[33] They usually received firm obedience, although exceptions did occur. Once back in Sparta, however, they could suffer severely for making unpopular decisions on campaign. After *c.*505 only one king led an army. Even before that date, only one king may have commanded, with the other acting as his second-in-command, something seen in forces led by Spartan commoners. At least one of the two royal families produced a competent general in any period, an important factor in the survival of the kingship.

The principle of single command led the Spartans to reject boards of generals, common elsewhere in the Greek world, although their generals did hold councils of war. For major naval commands the Spartans chose a *nauarchos*, 'ship commander', anglicised as 'navarch'. The navarch enjoyed the war powers of a king, but was limited to a single year in office with no second term, to prevent him abusing the position for personal power.[34] It is likely that navarchs were chosen when needed for a year's term, with an extension of a few months possible.[35] To command a specific region abroad Sparta appointed a harmost (*harmostēs*, 'fixer'). Harmosts played a major role from the Peloponnesian War onwards,[36] as did the *xenagoi*, 'leaders of foreigners', Spartan officers sent to direct allied units.[37]

These allied units came most often from Sparta's Peloponnesian League, which in time included every Peloponnesian state except Argos, Sparta's inveterate rival. Cities outside the Peloponnese also joined. The nature of the 'league' is debated,[38] but the allies were consulted at 'league congresses' before wars of aggression or intervention. If they voted for war, the allies followed and Sparta led. The Peloponnesian League helped Sparta face strong enemies such as the Persians and Athenians. However, its member cities were not always obedient or loyal. In fact, disloyal allies often appear among Sparta's enemies. The Spartans needed to be strong to overawe their allies or overcome them in war.

The Perioecs and Helots were another uncertain source of Spartan might. The former inhabited small communities scattered throughout Lacedaemonian territory, especially on its borders and coasts, and so acted as its guards.[39] Helots lived on their masters' estates and in their homes, and perhaps also in small communities of their own. The origin and nature of Helotry and the Helots' actual relationship to Tyrtaeus' Messenians are subjects hotly debated among scholars,[40] but it is clear they had families and spoke Greek. Certainly the ones in Messenia could identify themselves with the old Messenians. Perioecs served alongside the Spartiates as heavy infantry and cavalry. Helots acted as servants and oarsmen, and could fight as light-armed men, but since they were normally prevented from having arms,[41] they were unlikely to be of much use in battle. However, every ancient army had to transport itself, its supplies, and its gear, on ox-carts or the backs of donkeys, mules, or men. Every army also had to forage for water, food, firewood, bedding, and fodder for animals. Moreover, Greek armies sought to ravage enemy farmlands, destroying crops, trees, vines, and houses. Helots performed these vital tasks in the Spartan army. After 424 freed Helots also served as heavy infantrymen as well, though in their own units, not with Spartiates and Perioecs. However, Helots and Perioecs did have the potential to revolt, though scholars disagree how great a threat they posed.[42] Notable revolts and secessions occurred in the 460s and the invasion of 370/69, but on other occasions the two groups proved surprisingly loyal to the Spartiates, even in times of crisis. The perceived balance of power at home and abroad, and the threats facing Perioec and Helot families and the fields and herds that supported them, appear critical in determining their loyalty or disloyalty to Sparta. The Spartiates accordingly needed to remain strong in order to keep them obedient.

Sparta's rule over its allies and subjects, therefore, depended on its military might. This might did not result from the Spartiates being 'professional' soldiers or having a modern-style autonomous military organisation. Sparta relied on its militia levy, as did every Greek city. Greeks trained teenaged ephebes (*ephēbai*) and raised units of *epilektoi*, picked men; so did the Spartiates. The difference was in degree. The upbringing substituted for the ephebate. Boys were inspected by tribal elders at birth and raised communally from age seven onwards. They were organised by age into small bands, each led by a young man and overseen by an elected official. They lived hard and ate little, being encouraged to steal food, supposedly to develop shrewdness and self-discipline. Athletic competitions, a fixture of Greek aristocratic life, occurred often. Slackness was harshly punished. Indoctrination and initiation, not education as such, was stressed. Weapon training is not reported, but the boys would have picked it up anyway.[43] Homosexual friendships between maturing boys and young adults, common among upper-class Greeks, saw the adult partners instructing youths in deportment and skills such as hunting and, perhaps, combat.[44]

On reaching adulthood, a young Spartiate was ready for campaigning. From age twenty to twenty-nine, he lived with his fellows, passing his time at duties, sports, or hunting, but competed with them to be chosen for the *Hippeis* (horsemen), Sparta's standing unit of *epilektoi*. He also had to join a public mess, and eat his dinners there unless abroad or occupied in duties. Herodotus says the messes were one of the things pertaining to war that Lycurgus created,[45] so it seems Spartiates served in wartime alongside men they dined with in peace, an important boost to morale.

At age thirty a Spartiate could establish his own household, but had to remain fit and was liable for military service outside Lacedaemon's borders until the age of sixty.[46] Since relatively few men in other Greek cities kept in constant physical training,[47] this emphasis on athleticism gave the Spartiates an advantage. The Spartans exercised even on campaign.[48] Aristotle felt that Spartan superiority resulted from their exercising their young men while other cities did not. When the latter also began to do so, the Spartans suffered defeats.[49]

Matching this physical conditioning was mental conditioning. Herodotus says that a law ruled Spartans in warfare: 'It always gives the same order, forbidding them to flee from any number of men in battle, but remaining in position (*en tēi taxi*) to conquer or perish.'[50] He gives three instances of picked units of Spartans dying virtually to the last man.[51] Thucydides confirms that Spartan armies fought long and stubbornly until their enemies were routed, and says that when a body of Spartan troops surrendered to the Athenians in 425, all Greeks were shocked, for they 'thought the Lacedaemonians would yield their arms from neither hunger nor any necessity, but grasping them and fighting as long as they were able, would perish'.[52] Spartans could be defeated, even routed, but by and large their reputation was deserved. Tyrtaeus would have been delighted.

Indeed, conditioning provided by learning Tyrtaeus' poems during the Lycurgan upbringing and singing them when on campaign probably contributed to creating this stubbornness in battle.[53] Fear of state punishment may have done so as well, although the record shows that this was more spoken of than done.[54] The real enforcer, and this is true for the entire Lycurgan system, was peer pressure. Spartiates lived highly public lives, competed to be seen as being the best in obeying the laws,[55] and constantly commented on and criticised each other. Anyone who became known as a coward would suffer considerable humiliation. Herodotus tells how one of the two survivors of Thermopylae, who missed the last battle due to eye disease, was called 'Aristodemus the Trembler' back home. No Spartan would speak to him or give him fire. He sought his death in battle at Plataea to clear his name.[56] The other survivor committed suicide. Suicidal actions, or outright suicide, by Spartiates seeking to avoid shame are reported.[57] The fourth-century writer, philosopher, and mercenary general Xenophon, who knew the Spartans well, gives an impressive list of the personal slights and abuse a 'coward' and his family experienced.[58] In contrast, news of the deaths of close family members in a defeat was welcomed by Spartiates, since it meant that they had died well and could not be suspected of cowardice. Relatives of survivors, by contrast, were visibly ashamed, since it had to be assumed that they had fled.[59]

Other factors augmented the effects of these measures. The Spartans impressed their opponents by entering battle with their armour polished to a brilliant shine, garlanded as if taking part in a religious celebration, their bodies anointed with oil as if in an athletic competition, and their long hair – mark of an adult Spartiate male – carefully combed and dressed (*Plates 5, 6*). In the later fifth and early fourth centuries Spartan armies had a uniform appearance. Each man wore a cloak coloured red by dyes made from sea snails found in Laconian waters, and bore on his shield the letter lambda (Λ) for *Lakedaimōn*. Such uniformity did not exist earlier, to judge from Laconian art and Herodotus' reports that Persians had to be told by Greeks whether or not they faced Spartans.[60]

Spartan organisational strengths were well evident at times of mobilisation. Since Spartiates belonged to specific age classes, the ephors mobilised by age. Therefore before Leuctra they mobilised those 'up to thirty-five years from manhood' (twenty to fifty-four), and after the defeat those 'up to forty years from manhood' (twenty to fifty-nine), as well as those in public office who had been left behind. This system made mobilisation far faster and easier than creating and posting lists of names, as was done elsewhere. The ephors next summoned artisans to join the army and requisitioned all necessary gear.[61]

Xenophon notes approvingly how a king would set out with an army, sacrificing animals at home and then at the borders of Lacedaemon, checking each time to see if the omens were favourable before proceeding. Even among the ancients, the Spartans were noted for their careful observance of omens, festivals, and prophecies. Every day before sunrise the king sacrificed, seeking the gods' goodwill before attempting other actions. His chief officers were present, as were two ephors, who observed the proceedings and kept order. When the sacrifices were over, the king called his officers together and passed on his orders for the day. 'So, seeing this, you would think all others are improvisers in military affairs, but the Lacedaemonians are the only craftsmen in the activities of war,' says Xenophon.[62] Camps had a standard circular layout, which varied with terrain, and there were set procedures for day-watches and night-watches in outposts. Camp life had a fixed routine: exercises before breakfast, light pastimes in the afternoon when the heat made strenuous activity inadvisable, and exercises, hymns, dinner, and relaxation in the cool evening.[63] Modest as this level of discipline and organisation seems today, Xenophon thought it superior to the haphazard situation in other Greek militia armies.

The Spartans specialised in serving as *hoplitai*, 'armed men' (anglicised as 'hoplites'), heavy infantrymen of the type Tyrtaeus called the 'panoplieds'. Hoplite armament developed in the late eighth and early seventh centuries, and remained much the same for three centuries (*Plate 7*).[64] The spear was over two metres long and had a leaf-shaped bronze or iron spearhead and heavier bronze butt-spike, and so was balanced about ninety centimetres from the back. A short iron cut-and-thrust or chopping sword acted as backup. Body armour featured a bronze helmet with a horsehair crest, bronze greaves, and a bronze cuirass or leather or linen corselet, although many avoided the last and relied on their shields. The shield was round, almost a metre in diameter, worn on the left arm, and had a shallow bowl shape, a flat rim, a core of poplar, willow, or other flexible wood, an inner lining of leather, and a decoration or thin bronze facing. It was heavy at seven kilograms, and borne by a centre armband and a handgrip. It could also be rested by setting its rim on the hoplite's shoulder. When the hoplite fought in an open, individual fashion, he turned his left side towards his opponent, advanced his left leg and set his right behind; protected by his shield, he struck with his spear at his foe. Re-enactors have identified three shield positions, called 'wards', used in such open combat (*Plates 8, 9, 21*).[65]

However, the shield's size and weight, and its limited range of extension, meant that hoplites fought best in massed, formed combat. There is much scholarly debate on the nature of hoplite combat.[66] In the seventh and sixth centuries, the evidence of Tyrtaeus and art suggests that a line of noble *promachoi* was supported by a mixed group of hoplites and light-armed men, the latter unarmoured and hurling javelins or stones or using bows or slings. A portion of a Corinthian krater from the first quarter of the sixth century appears to show such a battle, depicting two formations in cross-section (*Plate 10*).[67] Fighting has been underway for some time, with bodies drawn back on both sides. Men now press forward towards the *promachoi*, while a body of men in reserve on the right rises from where they have been kneeling. They differ from those ahead of them in colouring and gear, so we know that we are not seeing the same group of men in two actions. The hoplites fight close by each other, yet move freely. However, the image may not depict a typical battle, but rather a story in which duelling champions have slain each other and the warriors watching on either side arise and advance into battle.

Once each side's hoplites had massed at the front, either group or both might have begun shoving. Massed shoving, *ōthismos*, is attested in later hoplite battles, as we shall find. It has been plausibly suggested that the shallow-dome design of the hoplite shield, with its thin front and thick rims, was meant to bear the loads of a pushing crowd and to allow the hoplite to breathe while facing front, with another man's shield pressed to the flat of his back.[68] Since the design of the hoplite shield remained the same for some three centuries, it is possible that massed shoving took place in hoplite warfare from the start, if not necessarily immediately or in every battle. Certainly the entire formation cannot have performed *ōthismos* while it contained light-armed men – they would have been crushed.

In the fifth and fourth centuries, hoplites clearly fought in a formation called a phalanx ('log'). In it hoplites normally were formed eight to twelve ranks deep. Protected by men to his right, left, rear, and front, each hoplite was challenged to hold his position and match their courage. Thucydides, an experienced soldier, says that during a phalanx's advance each man moved right to get under cover of his neighbour's shield, for when facing forward the shield did not protect a hoplite's right side. Men on the right flank of the formation also moved out past the enemy's left flank.[69] This compression and rightward movement would not have happened when formations were more open and unshielded light-armed men fought among the hoplites. In this era, light troops, now called *psiloi* ('bares'), commonly fought outside the phalanx as skirmishers. They may have been forced out by increasing use of massed shoving by hoplites. Certainly individual combat by hoplites was de-emphasised in this era,[70] although it still occurred in any circumstance where hoplites could not be closely formed.[71] Phalanx battles were preceded by implicit challenges, divinatory and propitiatory sacrifices, and speeches by officers; they were followed by the victors giving honours to their bravest men, granting a burial truce to the defeated, and raising a trophy, a sacrosanct memorial decorated with captured arms and placed at the point where the battle turned in their favour. These rituals had an obvious moral impact on militiamen imbued with a strong spirit of competition, accustomed to speech-making, believing in prophecy and omens, and fearing the restless spirits of the unburied dead. They helped get men into battle and keep them there.

In combat the Spartans performed most of these rituals – except for the orations, for which Thucydides says they substituted mutual encouragement and singing of hymns and war-songs as they advanced. He also says that they sought to maintain formation at all times, advancing 'slowly and to [the sound of] many pipers as established by custom, not for the sake of religion, but so that, going on evenly with rhythm, they should advance and their battle-order not break apart, as large armies are likely to do in their onsets'.[72] By maintaining their formation, the Spartans gave enemies no openings to exploit. It cost them the final charge into battle performed by other hoplite armies, which encouraged attackers and caused their rear ranks to push the front ones ahead. The Spartans preferred to maintain control of their forces; they refused to pursue defeated enemies far, and avoided exhausting their men.[73] Most Greek levies were incapable of an immediate second effort on a battlefield, even when victorious. The Spartans could achieve this, and so won battles.

To maintain this control, the Spartan army was organised into a hierarchy of units commanded by officers. Orders went down a chain of command: 'When the king is leading, everything is commanded by him,' Thucydides reports, 'and he indicates to the polemarchs what is needed, they to the lochagoi, those to the pentecosteres, these moreover to the enomotarchs, and these to the enomotia'.[74] Polemarchs (*polemarchoi*: 'war leaders') were general officers who could command independently major citizen units, and shared the king's mess on campaign. The lochagoi (*lochagoi*: 'ambush leaders') led units called lochoi (*lochoi*, literally 'ambushes'). The pentecosters (*pentēkostēres*: 'leaders of fiftieths') are actually called penteconters (*pentēkontēres*: 'leaders of fifty men') in Thucydides' text,[75] but this is probably a manuscript error, because they led pentecostyes (*pentēkostyes*: 'fiftieths'), and pentecosters later appear in Xenophon.[76] The name implies that at one time each unit comprised a fiftieth of the levy. Enomotarchs (*enōmotarchai*: 'leaders of enōmotiai') commanded the basic unit of the army, the enomotia (*enōmotia*: 'sworn band'). The enomotia was a platoon-sized body whose members had to be able to hear their officer's shouted commands. One battle saw enomoties averaging thirty-two men each, another thirty-six.[77] It has been suggested that the enomotia ideally contained a man from every age class,[78] but this is doubtful, as high death rates in antiquity meant that younger age classes significantly outnumbered older ones. The oath sworn is unknown, but may have bound the men to stay with their leader, alive or dead, to obey orders from higher officers, to fight to the death rather than flee, and to see the dead had burial.[79]

Thucydides says that 'very nearly all the army of the Lacedaemonians, except for a bit, consists of officers set over officers, and the duty of executing orders belongs to many.'[80] We do not know any other Greek army that had so many levels of command or unit types. The Athenian levy, for example, was divided into ten tribal regiments, each of which, if the levy was large enough, was further divided into company-sized march units called lochoi.[81] In Sparta the level of command went down to the platoon-sized unit, this being the enomotia, and even below that, to the individual file. All hoplites were formed into ranks and files, but according to Xenophon:

> In the Laconian formation the front rank men are officers, and each file has everything, however much is required to be provided. It is so easy to understand this formation that no one who can recognize men should go wrong. For it is given to some to lead, but commanded to others to follow. The deployment manoeuvres are made clear verbally by the enomotarch as though by a herald, by which means the ranks become thinner or deeper; therefore there is nothing difficult to understand.[82]

Xenophon goes on to describe manoeuvres Greek instructors in tactics viewed as very difficult, but which the Spartan army could perform easily: deploying from column of march into line of battle, reversing the phalanx to face an enemy appearing in the rear, switching the wings of a formed phalanx, and wheeling companies out of line of march to face an enemy to the right or the left.[83] In command and control, then, and in tactical manoeuvre on the battlefield, the Spartans had great advantages over other Greek armies.

Just how the Spartans trained for combat is not reported, although the description in Xenophon's *Cyropaedia* of the training of Persian commoners to fight as heavy infantry in ordered files, each file being led by a Persian officer of the Peer-like *homotimoi* class, seems likely to have been inspired by Spartan examples.[84] In any case, training for fighting with spears must have been easier than that for fighting with pikes or missile weapons. The follow-the-leader Spartan file organisation made manoeuvring easy for the followers to perform, if not for the leaders. This would have been a crucial factor in the incorporation of Perioecic hoplites into the Spartan phalanx. That Perioecs served 'man for man' alongside the Spartiates is stated directly by the fourth-century Athenian orator Isocrates,[85] and may be inferred from the accounts of the battles at Plataea in 479, Mantinea in 418, and Leuctra in 371. In each instance we know Perioecs must have been present, but aside from the Sciritae – men from the Sciritis district in northern Laconia – separate Perioecic units fail to appear in the army organisations reported for Mantinea by Thucydides and for Leuctra by Xenophon. Herodotus mentions no Perioecic dead at Plataea, despite giving detailed reports of casualties and tombs. The simplest explanation is that Perioecs served in the same units as Spartiates, but the latter provided the leaders of files, and generally fought at or near the front. Perioecs did march separately from the Spartiates, but the known instances always occurred in the Peloponnese at times when no immediate threat of combat existed.[86] Given the existence of so many scattered Perioecic communities, Perioecs had to start a march in numerous small, separate bands, but once united with the Spartiates they fought alongside them in the same units.

As for the preparation of the file leaders and higher ranks of officers, that most likely took place among the *Hippeis*. Greek states formed picked units, after all, so they could have solders who were thoroughly drilled and prepared for combat.[87] The fierce competition among young men to be chosen for the *Hippeis* makes sense, if this was the path to officer status. Scholars often write that the *Hippeis* were the royal guards of the kings,[88] but this is an error. The Spartans appointed fifty bodyguards to protect kings when a hoplite battle was expected, believing it would be disgraceful to allow a Heraclid to be slain in battle.[89] Assigning a standing force of armed men in peacetime to the command of two competing leaders would have been begging for civil strife. The *Hippeis* probably originated in the seventh century as a picked band of horsemen, one hundred from each Dorian tribe, but in the fifth and fourth centuries its men fought as hoplites, and at home served the magistrates. At both Mantinea and, perhaps, Leuctra, the kings stood among the *Hippeis*, but that does not mean the unit was a royal guard. It made sense for the kings to place themselves among picked men when in a battle.[90]

The precise organisation of the Spartan army at any time is a subject of great scholarly controversy,[91] as the major ancient sources report five or six different army organisations for the period from the late sixth century to the middle of the fourth. The argument presented in this book is that each report is valid for its era. Sufficient changes occurred over the centuries to Sparta's population and situation to warrant alterations in organisation, and of course the specific circumstances of any particular mobilisation would have affected army size and composition. That some ancient sources explicitly or implicitly denied the validity of descriptions of Spartan army organisation appearing in others can be attributed to the Spartan habit of denying that changes ever occurred in Lycurgus' perfect arrangements.[92]

In all these ways, therefore, Lycurgan Sparta provided Spartans with a highly effective hoplite militia army. However, not every strategic effect of Lycurgan society was positive. Herodotus reports that in 479 the Spartans fielded five thousand Spartiate and five thousand Perioecic hoplites, and forty thousand Helot and Perioecic light-armed. If the report is accurate, this was a mighty host, far stronger than the individual armies of most Greek city-states. In 480 the Spartiates numbered eight thousand, according to Herodotus – a figure consistent with his others for Sparta.[93]

However, it did not last. Aristotle wrote that the total number of full Spartan citizens even before his time, the late fourth century, had dropped to less than a thousand.[94] This he attributed to the defective system of Spartan land tenure, which allowed some Spartiates to own too much property and others too little. Those with too little property could not pay their mess dues; they lost their membership, and therefore their citizenship. Since Greek custom was to split inherited property evenly among men, and in Sparta women also inherited some property, a family with several children and a relatively small amount of land could see every male lose his full citizen status, becoming an 'inferior', a Spartiate lacking the franchise. Efforts were made to limit family sizes, but doing so risked leaving no heirs at all due to the high death rates of antiquity, when only half of the children born reached adulthood.

Various factors increased the downward pressure: losses to warfare and earthquake, damage to rural property from Helot revolts and wartime raids, declining fertility of marginal farmland, and the Spartiates' refusal to recruit new Peers from outside their own circles.[95] Moreover, since wealth married wealth, over time the richest families gained control of most of the land. By the fourth century, Sparta had become a plutocracy, in which poorer Spartiates and 'inferiors' were clients of the rich.[96] Decline in the number of Spartiates of course meant a decline in the size and effectiveness of the levy, as well as a decline in the pool of leadership talent. Thus, Spartiate oliganthropy (*oliganthrōpia*, 'fewness of men') played an important role in Sparta's fall from power.

Lycurgan society also caused the Spartans to focus heavily upon hoplite combat and pitched battle. This strong focus led to Spartan inadequacy in other forms of warfare, such as naval combat, siegecraft, and the use of cavalry and light-armed troops. At times this cost the Spartans dearly in wars with abler opponents.

That said, it was no small thing to have an excellent hoplite army. Greece's rough terrain would seem best suited to armies of skirmishing light infantry, but the need to defend the rich agriculture of the plains and the cities located there, combined with the militia character of Greek city-state armies, led instead to massed armies of hoplites. Unless Greeks lived in ways that encouraged agility and skill with missile weapons, as on the island of Crete or in Aetolia in north-western Greece, they could not produce good skirmishing light infantry. Cavalry, still a developing arm in Greece in the seventh and sixth centuries, could predominate only in regions with large plains, such as Boeotia in central Greece and Thessaly in the north. The defence of mountainous borders did occur, but the existence of multiple routes through the mountains often allowed armies to bypass defences, and the sea provided a way around them. Therefore, fielding armies of heavy-armed spearmen to fight for the plains and cities made military sense. Massed hoplite combat suited armies of part-time soldiers, and placed the burden of defence on the wealthier citizens, justifying their pre-eminence in the state. Militia forces in recent centuries have secured society's 'haves' against its 'have-nots', and this was true in ancient Greece as well. Winning a phalanx battle gave the victors the initiative over the now-weakened and discouraged foe, secured the victors' homeland from major invasions, if not from raids, and opened the losers' territory to invasion and ravaging. Defeat and damage to the countryside encouraged civil strife among the losers, which the victors could try to exploit. Because Sparta consistently won pitched phalanx battles, the Laconian interior remained undevastated for centuries, and its armies ravaged freely and exploited internal strife among its enemies. As a result, Sparta ruled Lacedaemon and dominated the Peloponnese.

To sum up, during its formative period Sparta acquired an unusually large territory and body of subjects, probably in wars arising from competition between the two leading families which became the Heraclid royal houses. A large class – virtually a caste – of landowning Spartiates was created. The threats posed to the Spartiates by foreign foes, Helot and Perioec rebels, and contending Spartiate factions, led to the development of the social and political system attributed to Lycurgus. This system disciplined the Spartiates and enforced harmony among them. In time, it brought about the creation of a superior hoplite militia army, which by 550 had made Sparta leader of the Peloponnese and dominant in mainland Greece. A threat to this dominance, however, required the Spartiates to oppose it in battle, with themselves fighting in the front ranks. The greater the battle, the more Spartiates in action, with the result that every great battle risked the very existence of the Spartiates as a people, to say nothing of their hold on their state. The greater the drop in Spartiate population over time, the greater the risk became. And yet the Spartiates maintained their dominance, in the Peloponnese and sometimes beyond it, for almost two centuries. We shall now see how they managed this feat.

~ Two ~

Leader of the Peloponnese, *c.*550–481

Sparta's strategic circumstances and military operations during the early period of its ascendancy are known principally from Herodotus, who in the third quarter of the fifth century gathered information for his history of the Persian invasion of 480–479 and the events that caused it. Much of his information came from oral traditions tied to temples, festivals, dedications, and oracles. He also used oral history, that is, old men's recollections of their experiences, or what they knew about older family members. These memories reached back at least to the second half of the sixth century, as we shall see, countering to some extent the Spartan habit of attributing current practices to Lycurgus. Herodotus' accounts of Spartan history in this period are episodic and have a strong storytelling flavour, but they seem based upon real events.

Croesus and the Battle of Champions[1]

In strategic terms, in the period *c.*550–481 Sparta secured its leading position in the Peloponnese while cautiously undertaking opportunistic interventions in Greece and the Aegean. Its most radical step came in *c.*550, when it allied with Croesus, King of Lydia in western Asia Minor (modern Turkey), who planned war with Cyrus of Persia, his eastern neighbour. Croesus perhaps hoped that his alliance with Sparta, the strongest power in Greece, would help secure his rear against revolts by his Greek subjects, and facilitate his hiring of mercenaries in the Peloponnese. The Spartans were flattered by Croesus' attentions and pleased by his gift of gold for a statue of Apollo. They doubtless considered being an ally of the famously wealthy and powerful king to be a safe investment. In the event, the Spartans missed Croesus' indecisive summer campaign against Cyrus because of a war with Argos. Cyrus then staged a surprise winter offensive, defeated the Lydians, and besieged Sardis, Croesus' capital. Croesus sent to his allies for relief. Herodotus says that the Spartans wanted to go, 'but when they were already prepared and the ships were ready,'[2] word came that Sardis had fallen.[3]

The Greeks of Asia Minor now sent an embassy to Sparta, asking for aid. The Spartans refused, although Herodotus reports a story in which a lone Spartan envoy from a group sent to assess the situation told Cyrus that 'he must harm no city of the land of Hellas [Greece], as they would not suffer it.'[4] The tale is very suspect at best, but it makes a useful point. From now until 490, the Spartans would refuse to aid those who sought their help against Persia, until the Persians came to mainland Greece itself. Attacking the power that had overthrown Croesus so quickly doubtless seemed foolish to the Spartans.[5]

The war between Sparta and Argos was being fought over the Thyreatis border district in north-eastern Laconia, on the coast between the Parnon range and the southern Argolid – the last defensible ground before reaching Argive home territory on the direct route from Sparta.

> When the Argives came to the rescue of the lost territory, it was agreed in talks there that three hundred of each side should fight; the land would belong to whichever proved superior. The majority of each army was to be dismissed to its own country and not stay with the contenders, since, if the armies remained present, those on either side might try to defend their men if they saw them being beaten. Having agreed, the armies were dismissed, and the picked men of each side stayed behind and fought. Those fighting were so evenly matched that only three were left out of six hundred men, Alcenor and Chromius of the Argives, Othryadas of the Lacedaemonians. These remained alive when night came on. Having seemingly won, the two Argives ran home to Argos; but Othryadas the Lacedaemonian, stripping the Argive dead and taking their arms to his camp, held his position in the battle line [*en tēi taxi eiche heōuton*]. On the second day both sides were present, having learned of events. For a time each side claimed victory, one saying that more of their men had survived, the other proving these had fled, while their man had remained and stripped the enemy dead. At last they went from this arguing to combat; many on both sides perished, but the Lacedaemonians won.[6]

The Argives continued to claim victory in the 'Battle of Champions', saying that Perilaus, a prize-winning wrestler at the Nemean Games, had slain Othryadas. According to Herodotus, Othryadas committed suicide, for he was ashamed to return to Sparta after all his comrades had perished.[7] Later sources asserted that Othryadas despoiled the Argive dead and created a trophy, declaring Sparta's victory by inscribing a shield with his own blood.[8] Battlefield trophies are only attested in Greek art a century after these events, so the tale is probably anachronistic.[9] Certainly Herodotus did not report it. He did, however, stress the importance of Othryadas' holding his position in the formation (*en tēi taxi eiche heōuton*), which certainly expressed the hoplite ideology of his Spartan informants.

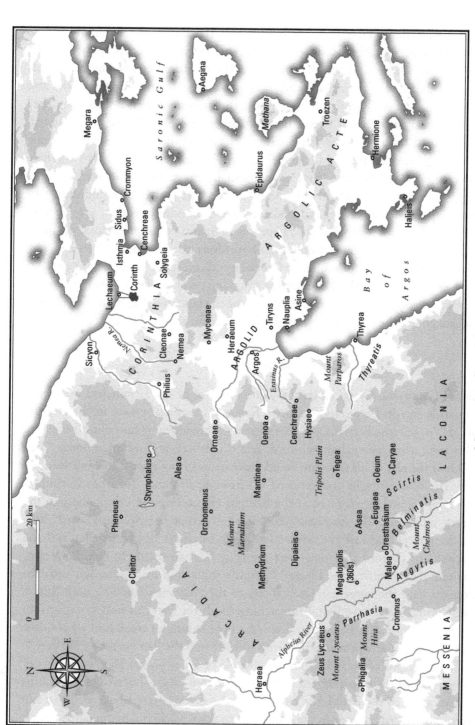

Map 2.1: Arcadia and Argos

A source much later than Herodotus sets the Battle of Champions in the conquest era,[10] but the size of the contingents seems more appropriate for the higher populations of the sixth century, and the situation reported by Herodotus seems well suited to champion combat. The Spartans historically proved reluctant to campaign abroad while an Argive war threatened at home.[11] However, they could expect little from Croesus if they failed to aid him. A champion combat, then, would have benefited the Spartans by ending the conflict swiftly, freeing them to go abroad. It would have helped the Argives, of course, by giving them the chance to recover the Thyreatis without having to fight the entire Spartan army. Herodotus' account of the finding of the Bones of Orestes indicates that the *Hippeis* already existed, so bodies of three hundred *epilektoi* are credible. Herodotus does not say that the *Hippeis* were Sparta's champions, and it is likely that men with sons were chosen for the hazardous task, as would be done in 480. Champion combats appear often in Greek legend and epics,[12] including a legendary Heraclid attempt on the Peloponnese,[13] making combat of this sort appropriate for the Spartans and Argives. It would not be the last time that champion combat was sought by the Argives and, at least in principle, accepted by the Spartans.[14]

Assault on Samos[15]

In 525 Cambyses, Cyrus' successor, gained control of the Levant and was about to invade Egypt. Polycrates, tyrant of Samos and a naval power in the Aegean, decided to join the Persians and sent them a fleet manned by his political enemies. This went awry when they mutinied, seized the fleet, and returned home. They defeated the rest of his navy, but could make no headway against the well-fortified city. The rebels sought and received aid from Sparta and also from Corinth, a powerful trading city located at the isthmus connecting the Peloponnese to the Greek mainland. The Samians told Herodotus that the Spartans owed them for Samian aid against the Messenians. The Spartans denied it; they and the Corinthians claimed that they were avenging Samian thefts. In fact, Polycrates' habitual piracy must have affected Corinth's trade, and his association with the Persians gave the latter increased access to the Aegean, something both Sparta and Corinth must have found threatening. With the Persians heavily engaged in Egypt and Polycrates' fleet neutralized, the opportunity to crush him was evident and enticing. Sparta provided the army, Corinth and the Samian rebels the fleet.[16]

The force probably landed near the temple of Hera several kilometres west of Samos city, where a Spartan-led fleet later anchored in 479. Located on the south-eastern coast of the island, the city itself had a 6,400-metre circuit wall that ran from an enclosed harbour in the south-east to the Kastelli hill in the north-east; it

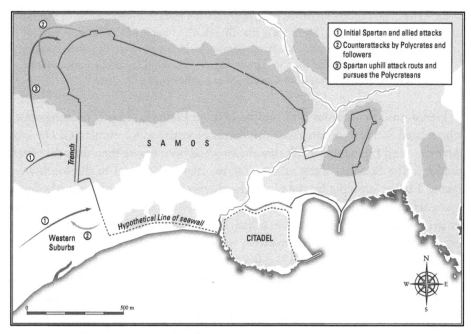

Map 2.2: The city of Samos

then crossed the valley of the Chesios stream, headed north and west over the high ridge of Ampelos hill, and finally curved south to descend the hill and cross the western plain before reaching the seashore. The circuit had several towers, as well as trenches on its western side.[17] Walled cities were normal in the Greek east, and were becoming more common in Greece itself as populations grew. City defences typically featured walls with stone socles (bases) on which sat the mudbrick (adobe) walls and battlements. This was the case at Samos.

When the Lacedaemonians arrived with a great host, they laid siege to Samos. Attacking towards the wall, they made their way into the tower standing by the sea at the suburb of the city, but thereafter they were driven out by Polycrates, who came to the rescue with a large force. His mercenaries and many of the Samians themselves sallied out by the upper tower on the ridge of the hill, but receiving the Lacedaemonians only for a short time they fled back, being pursued and killed. Now if the pursuing Lacedaemonians had been peers [*homoioi*] of Archias and Lycopas on that day, Samos would have been captured. For Archias and Lycopas alone entered the wall with the fleeing Samians, and their return route being blocked were killed in the Samians' city. I have myself met another Archias, third in generation from this Archias, son of Samius son of Archias, in Pitana (for this was his village), who honoured the Samians most of all his foreign guests, and said the name Samius had been given to his father, because his own father Archias had died in Samos, fighting bravely. He said he honoured the Samians because his grandfather was buried at public expense by them.[18]

Herodotus knew Samos well, and had visited Pitana in Sparta, meeting a man who related family tradition about this battle. Note the arch comment on *Homoioi*: Archias – and Herodotus – felt that the two had been braver than the other Peers that day. The Spartans likely attacked across the level ground in the south-west, taking a tower 'standing by the sea at the suburb of the city', although whether it was part of the city wall or a watch-tower in the suburbs is unclear. Polycrates in person counterattacked and expelled them. Assaulting walls disordered and exhausted attackers, making them rather vulnerable to sorties (*Plate 16*).[19] Polycrates' mercenaries and loyalists also sallied from a gate in the wall on the ridge of Ampelos. They deployed on the slopes to threaten the Spartan left. They may have included some of the thousand archers that Herodotus says Polycrates possessed.[20] The Spartans, however, attacked uphill and drove them back into the city, with Archias and Lycopas actually entering the gates with the fleeing enemy. Pursuing men into the gates of a fortification offered the hope of forcing an entry, but only at great risk, as the events here show.

Polycrates made no further attempt to drive off his enemies by force, avoiding a pitched set-piece battle against the Spartans, whom Herodotus describes as numerous. However, after an unsuccessful forty-day siege, the Spartan and Corinthian forces left for home. Herodotus heard a tale, which he thought foolish, that Polycrates had bribed the Spartans to withdraw with lead coins plated with electrum. Such coins have been found.[21] However, Herodotus says that the army was large, which meant it had to be composed of militia levies rather than picked troops. A militia force could not stay for a long siege.

Despite this failure, late accounts say that the Spartans overthrew the tyrant Lygdamis of Naxos, an island in the Cyclades.[22] It occurred either at this time or in the period of Spartan naval power in the Aegean a late source reports for the years 517–515.[23] Even so, the militia levy character of Sparta's army hindered its acceptance of appeals for aid from overseas, a situation that would only change in the late fifth century. In the 550s or 540s, Epizephyrian Locris in southern Italy sought Sparta's aid in a war with its neighbour, Croton. Instead of troops, the Spartans offered the aid of the Dioscuri, Castor and Polydeuces, the twin demigods who were the divine counterparts of Sparta's dual kings. Locris accepted, and won.[24]

Cleomenes[25]

Dominating Herodotus' account of Spartan policy for the decades from *c*.520 to *c*.490 is the Agiad king Cleomenes, son of Anaxandridas. He was evidently one of those Spartan kings who had the charisma and political skills to exploit fully his privileges, and was a controversial character. Herodotus reports tales of Cleomenes' virtue and wit,[26] and of his cruelty and madness.[27] As rivals he had both the Eurypontid king Demaratus and his own eldest half-brother, Dorieus, first among those of his age at Sparta. Unhappy at being ruled by Cleomenes, Dorieus led colonising expeditions abroad in the 510s, and died in Sicily.[28] Cleomenes continued the policy of refusing to help Persia's enemies. In 517, when Maeandrius of Samos came to Sparta to seek aid against the Persians, who had taken over the island after Polycrates' death, Cleomenes had the ephors expel him from Sparta and the Peloponnese.[29] In around 513, Darius I, Cambyses' successor, invaded the Balkans, conquering as far west as Macedon and as far north as the Danube. He failed against the Scythian nomads, who lived in the lands north of the Black Sea. Herodotus says that Cleomenes later negotiated with Scythian envoys. A joint invasion of the Balkans to drive the Persians out of Europe would have made sense, but Herodotus says the proposal was that the Scythians would invade via the Caucasus, the Spartans via the port of Ephesus in western Asia Minor. The idea presumably was for the Spartans to raise Asia Minor in revolt, and provide strong infantry forces to aid the Scythian cavalry. No expeditions occurred, and the story may be a fantasy.[30]

Affairs in Greece certainly distracted the Spartans. At the eastern end of the Isthmus of Corinth lay the Dorian city of Megara. East of Megara and the island of Aegina in the Saronic Gulf was the triangular peninsula of Attica, the land of Athens. An Ionian Greek people, the Athenians were numerous and, in the 510s, ruled by the sons of the tyrant Peisistratus. North of Attica and Megara were the mountain-ringed plains of Boeotia, a populous region as large as Attica, where the city of Thebes was forging a confederation. Recently the Boeotians had driven off the Thessalians, who led a strong confederation in their northern Greek homeland.

In 519,[31] the people of Plataea in southern Boeotia, hard-pressed in a war with their neighbour Thebes over the plain between their cities, offered themselves as subjects to Cleomenes and the Spartans, whom Herodotus says happened to be in the area. The Spartans replied that Plataea was too distant for them to aid effectively, and suggested they go to their neighbour Athens instead. The Athenians told Herodotus that the Spartans did not so much intend to help Plataea with this advice as to set the Athenians against the Boeotians. Plataea submitted to Athens, Thebes fought Athens, and Athens won. The two rising powers were now at each other's throats, and neutralised for the time being.[32]

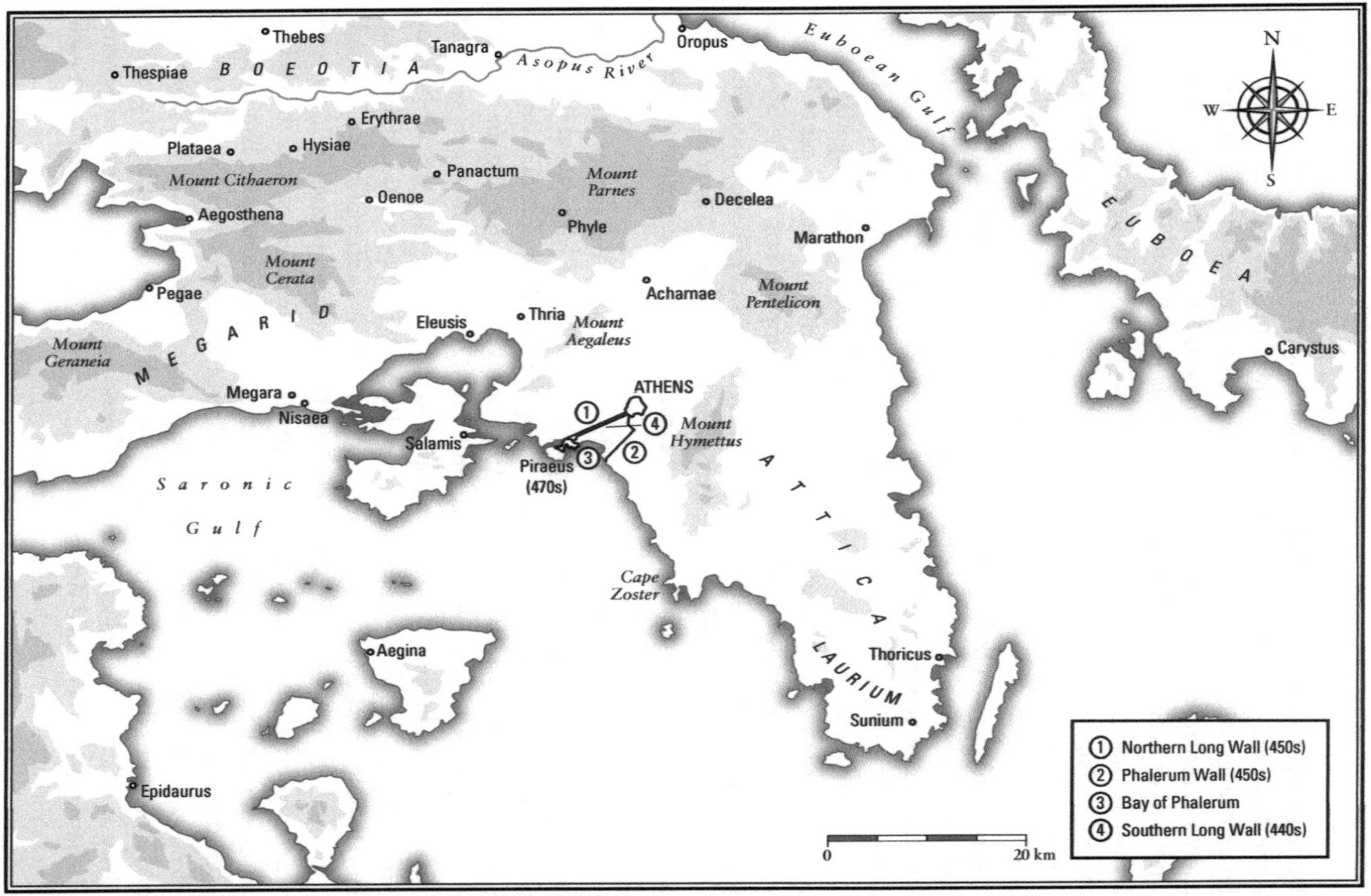

Map 2.3 Attica

The Spartan refusal to intervene may have been due to a renewed threat from Argos, for the second-century AD travel-writer Pausanias reports that Cleomenes at the start of his reign attacked it.[33] However, Herodotus says that Cleomenes only ruled for a short time,[34] and Pausanias may have been operating under the same misconception. We do have reason to date the campaign after the Spartan interventions in Attica, so we shall start with the latter.

In 511 the Spartans invaded Attica in order to overthrow the Peisistratid tyranny. Three years before, the assassination of his brother Hipparchus caused Hippias, the leading Peisistratid, to fear a general uprising. He disarmed the Athenians, began courting Persian aid, and started building a coastal fort at Munichia harbour, in what would later become the port city of the Piraeus. In a revolt, it would be the tyrants' refuge and base of operations, in effect acting as an *epiteichisma*, a 'fort in enemy territory', easily supplied by sea. Herodotus says that the Spartans intervened owing to pressure from the Delphic Oracle, which was friendly to the Alcmaeonids, an exiled clan of Athenian aristocrats.[35] The Aristotelian *Athēnaiōn Politeia*, a study of the constitution of Athens written for Aristotle's school, offers an old Peisistratid friendship with Argos as a reason for the Spartan action,[36] but Argos did not intervene. Herodotus claims that the Peisistratids had become friends with Sparta, a policy that Delphi's advocacy countered. In any case, the desire to keep Athens from becoming a Persian subject may have been foremost in Spartan minds. Thucydides says that Spartan policy was not to exact tribute from the allies, but to establish in them oligarchies: governments in which only the wealthier citizens could vote and hold office, as at Sparta.[37] Overthrowing tyrants was one way for Sparta to create such governments, so attacking the Peisistratids suited this policy. There is a report that Anaxandridas and the ephor Chilon overthrew Aeschines, tyrant of Sicyon.[38] Sparta in fact gained a reputation, arguably undeserved, for detesting tyranny.[39]

Instead of a king and levy army, the Spartans sent a fleet and army led by a non-royal named Anchimolus, whom Herodotus mistakenly calls Anchimolius. He must have been expected to besiege the Munichia fort by land and sea. Since the Athenians had been disarmed, only the loyalists and mercenaries of the tyrants would have been able to offer resistance, so Anchimolus' forces were probably modest, meant to be maintained in the field longer than a mass levy. He landed south of the Piraeus, at Phalerum – its bay being Athens' major port at that time.[40]

Landing at Phalerum he disembarked his men, but the Peisistratids, having learned of these things in advance, summoned aid from Thessaly; for they had made an alliance for themselves there. Receiving their request, the Thessalians came to a common agreement and sent a thousand horsemen and their king, Cineas, a man of Condaeum. When they had these allies, the Peisistratids persuaded them to fight in this fashion: laying waste the plain of Phalerum, and making the place fit for horses, they launched the cavalry against the army [or 'camp': *stratopedōi*], falling upon them, they killed many of the Lacedaemonians, and indeed even Anchimolus, while forcing those who survived back into their ships. The first expedition of the Lacedaemonians departed in this fashion.[41]

Thus reports Herodotus. By the sixth century, some Greek peoples had advanced from riding to battle but fighting on foot to fielding actual cavalry, able to skirmish against formed infantry units and charge disordered ones.[42] Inhabiting the largest plains in Greece, the Thessalians were known for their cavalry, and the Peisistratids themselves were cavalry proponents. The tyrants had Phalerum cleared of trees, field walls, and other obstructions, opening the way for a surprise charge that may have caught the Spartans in camp (*Plate 14*). No Peloponnesian cavalry, as opposed to mounted infantry (the original *Hippeis?*), is attested before the later fifth century,[43] and Anchimolus had no response.

The Spartans responded by sending a larger expedition by land over the Isthmus of Corinth, led by Cleomenes. The Thessalians attacked, but were quickly put to flight, losing more than forty men. The survivors headed home. The Roman stratagem-writer Frontinus claims that Cleomenes had trees felled, obstructing the battlefield so cavalry could not pass – the opposite of what the Peisistratids had done at Phalerum. How this led to his victory is not explained.[44] Perhaps he prepared a site for an ambush and lured the Thessalians into it. The king then besieged the Peisistratids in their citadel, the Athenian Acropolis. Evidently the Munichia fort was unavailable. 'The Lacedaemonians could not have removed the Peisistratids in any way at all (for they had no intention to carry out a siege, and the Peisistratids were well supplied with food and drink),' says Herodotus, 'and after besieging them for a few days would have gone back to Sparta.'[45] Perhaps so, since this must have been a levy army, and could not have remained for a long blockade. Yet Cleomenes must have planned to leave a force behind to defend the city against the Peisistratid garrison, until the Athenians could rearm and undertake a blockade. The tyrants evidently expected a siege, for they tried to smuggle their sons out of Attica. The boys were captured, however, and to secure their return the Peisistratids agreed to depart Attica.[46]

Subsequent events at Athens frustrated Spartan expectations. Civil strife among the Athenian aristocratic factions began, leading in 507 to the Alcmaeonid Cleisthenes extending the right to vote and hold most offices to every adult male citizen, making Athens a democracy, a novelty in Greece in this era.[47] In what perhaps was a private venture, Cleomenes intervened with a small force, aiming to make his 'guest-friend' Isagoras ruler of Athens (guest-friendship being an inherited tie of hospitality between Greek nobles). Initially unopposed, Cleomenes and Isagoras banished seven hundred Alcmaeonid families. However, when they tried to suppress the democratic council, the people rose in revolt.

Herodotus says that Cleomenes and Isagoras seized the Acropolis, but after only two days under siege Cleomenes and his men departed under truce, along with Isagoras, whose followers were bound and condemned to death.[48] The Aristotelian *Athēnaiōn Politeia* claims that the seizure of the Acropolis was unplanned – carried out because the king and his followers fled there after being mobbed – and that the Isagoreans left as well. Another source states that the Isagoreans seized Eleusis, a fortified town and major cult site near the Megarian border, and used it as an *epiteichisma*.[49] It is difficult to see why the king would have left the Acropolis so quickly if he had chosen it as a base, since he would have laid in supplies, so Herodotus was probably misled about the outcome of the revolt.

With the Isagoreans holding open the road to Attica, Cleomenes mobilised a large army of the Spartans and their allies. The Spartiates must have voted for it, as Demaratus joined the expedition. Expecting an invasion, Athens sought Persian aid.[50] Cleomenes co-ordinated his invasion with offensives by Thebes, which seized places in north-western Attica, and by the Chalcidians of Euboea, the large island off the north-eastern coast of Attica. The Athenians ignored these and massed at Eleusis to fight Cleomenes. As the two armies were about to engage, the Corinthians, historically friends of Athens,[51] turned and marched off, saying that the invasion was unjust. Next to go was Demaratus, for the first time openly defying his Agiad colleague. The army broke up, and the Athenians turned against the Boeotians and Chalcidians, defeating both.[52] Later, after further defeats, Thebes sought aid from Aegina, an old foe of Athens. The Aeginetans began a sporadic war of naval raiding that lasted from *c.*505 to 481.[53]

We do not know if Demaratus was tried for desertion, but the Spartans enacted a rule that no longer would both kings lead the army, or both Dioscuri accompany it.[54] A single commander-in-chief was no novelty, since only one commander is named for each of the earlier invasions of Attica, while Tyrtaeus had praised only Theopompus for the conquest of Messene. However, at Plataea in 479 Pausanias had a colleague, perhaps as a second-in-command.[55] Cleomenes for his part later held a meeting of Sparta's allies. Abandoning Isagoras' cause, he sought to convince them to help restore the Peisistratids. He advanced the justification that oracles he had taken from the Acropolis predicted future Spartan wars with Athens. Presumably the allies would have been bound by oath to obey the decision reached, as was done later. Following Corinth's lead, the allies voted him down.[56] Since Athens had a large and vigorous population – put at thirty thousand by Herodotus[57] – the Spartans clearly had reason to avoid undertaking the expedition without their allies.

Momentous events soon drew Cleomenes' attention from Athens. In 499 the Ionian Greeks of western Asia Minor led a great revolt against Persia. Herodotus tells how Aristagoras of the Ionian city of Miletus tried to persuade Cleomenes

to conquer the Persian Empire. On discovering the distances involved, the king
dismissed Aristagoras with the words: 'you are saying nothing acceptable to the
Lacedaemonians, wishing to lead them on a journey of three months away from
the sea.'[58] It is clear that Herodotus understood the factors limiting Spartan
adventurism. At one point he depicts Aristagoras urging the Spartan king to
abandon as unprofitable 'your battles against the Messenians, equal matches for
you, and the Arcadians and Argives'.[59] It would have been poor rhetoric for the
real Aristagoras to have reminded Cleomenes of these potential threats to Sparta,
but it was vital for Herodotus to remind his readers why Sparta had to refuse the
Ionian's pleas. The Athenians did send help to the Ionians, which in turn brought
the Persians to Greece in revenge, or so Herodotus held.[60]

Cleomenes may have been concerned with Argos in any case. Although
Pausanias says that he attacked Argos immediately after becoming king, scholars
generally date his expedition against the city to 494, because Herodotus connects
the event to the so-called 'Epicene Oracle' that threatened destruction to both
Miletus and Argos 'when the female shall defeat the male'.[61] The Persians
destroyed Miletus after their fleet, manned by the nautical peoples of the eastern
Mediterranean littoral, won the great naval battle of Lade in 494. However, some
scholars doubt that the oracle has been reconstructed correctly, or that it even
referred to the Argives of Argos.[62] Nevertheless, the fiasco at Eleusis will have
stimulated resistance to Spartan domination of the Peloponnese, a situation
which would explain some odd features in Herodotus' account.

Herodotus says that Cleomenes received an oracle at Delphi predicting he
would 'take Argos'. He led the Spartan army against the city, but arriving at the
Erasinus River (modern Kelephari) several kilometres south of Argos, his sacrifices
to its god failed to give him favourable omens for a crossing. Remarking that the
god's patriotism would fail to save his fellow citizens, Cleomenes withdrew to
the Thyreatis, where he sacrificed a bull to the sea before boarding ship with his
men and landing on the Argive coast between the port of Nauplia and the town
of Tiryns, then closer to the sea than it is today. The Argives marched out against
him, deploying near Tiryns at a place named Sepeia, very close to the Spartans.
Herodotus says they did not fear open battle, but rather being taken by deceit,
owing to the warning of the 'Epicene Oracle'.[63]

> They resolved to make use of the enemy's herald, and having so decided, did suchlike:
> whenever the Spartiate herald would proclaim anything to the Lacedaemonians, the
> Argives would also do the same thing. Learning that the Argives were doing whatever
> his own herald was proclaiming, Cleomenes passed word along to his men, that when
> the herald would announce it was time to make breakfast, they were then to take up their
> arms and advance against the Argives. These things were done by the Lacedaemonians;

for the attack fell upon the Argives as they were making breakfast in accordance with the proclamation, and many of them they slew, but surrounded and guarded the greater part of them, who had fled for shelter into the grove of Argos.[64]

Unwilling to violate the sacred grove, Cleomenes first tricked some fifty men into coming out by claiming that ransoms had come for them. Instead they were killed. When those still within the grove discovered this and refused to come out, the king had Helots pile brushwood around the grove and burn it down, killing all within. Only after destroying the grove, the story goes, did Cleomenes ask its name. On being told it was 'Argos', he realised that he had now 'taken Argos' and fulfilled the prophecy, and therefore could not expect to take the city. The king then sent most of his army home, but took a thousand of his best men and went to sacrifice at the Heraeum, the great sanctuary of Hera north-east of Argos. When he returned home, his enemies brought him to trial before the ephors on the charge of bribery, proven by his not attempting to take Argos when he could have done so easily. He responded that he had fulfilled the oracle, and that, seeking omens at the Heraeum, one had appeared that showed he would not take the city. He was readily acquitted.[65]

The oracles and omens give this account an uncomfortable fairy-tale aspect. The story of the surprise attack resembles a Greek folk tale, while stories in which a wicked ruler locks foes in a building and sets it afire also raise doubts about the destruction of the Argos Grove. The second-century AD biographer Plutarch gives a variant story in which Cleomenes made a truce for seven days, but attacked on the third night when the Argives were sleeping.[66] However, Herodotus reports six thousand Argive dead, and the later sources give similar figures. The Argives would lose another thousand aiding Aegina against Athens in the 480s.[67] The resultant Argive weakness is shown by the fact that the towns of Mycenae and Tiryns, located within sight of Argos, ignored the latter's pro-Persian neutrality and sent men to aid Sparta against the invading Persians in 480 and 479. We are even told that slaves or Argive subjects took control in Argos, until the sons of the dead Argives came of age and expelled them. Clearly the Argives suffered heavy losses. Since fleeing hoplites normally abandoned their heavy shields and outdistanced their pursuers, how could so many Argives have been slain? They must have been trapped, and their taking refuge in Argos Grove in the belief that the king would respect its sanctity would explain how they were trapped.

Other details are readily explained. Delays before battle were common in Greek warfare, as armies of militia levies sought favourable omens, awaited reinforcements, and worked themselves up for battle.[68] While waiting, armies took up defensive positions, using hillsides, rivers, or other features. The delay and the surprise attack at Sepeia are explained if we assume that the Argives held a defensive position – one in which the grove and other terrain features played roles. In that case, the 'Epicene Oracle' story may have arisen from the Argives' desire to provide a less embarrassing explanation of their cautiousness than a simple fear of Spartan prowess. Cleomenes' earlier withdrawal from the Erasinus may have been due to the Argives' taking position behind it, with the king using the excuse of unfavourable sacrifices to justify his withdrawal. The 'taking Argos' tale, and that of the omens at the Heraeum, won a trial for the king, giving him reason to create them. In spite of its more fabulous features, then, Herodotus' account seems grounded in reality.

Assuming the fulfillment of the oracle was not the real reason Cleomenes failed to exploit his victory by assaulting Argos, what was the cause? Actually, the Argives later claimed that he had assaulted the city, but said its defences had been put in order by the poetess Telesilla, who, like Tyrtaeus, had rallied old men, boys, and young women to its walls and driven off Cleomenes, and so 'the female' did defeat 'the male', as the oracle had predicted.[69] If so, however, it is extremely surprising that Herodotus fails to report it. Had the Spartans been driven off by women, all Greece would have noted it.

Sticking with Herodotus, it is Cleomenes' march with only a thousand men to the Heraeum, the great shrine on the Argive plain, that reveals his mind, as it demonstrated the weakness of Argos and the extent of Cleomenes' victory. Since the Spartans and Argives knew this already, the demonstration must have been for Argos' allies and subjects and for the rest of the Peloponnesians.

Also relevant is the fact that, after withdrawing from the Erasinus, the king could have marched by land to Argos from Arcadian Mantinea in the northern Tripolis valley, from Dorian Phlius north-west of Argos, or from Corinth to the north-east. Instead, he withdrew to Thryea, gathered a fleet, and undertook a landing on a possibly hostile shore. Perhaps the Argives and Spartans had agreed to restrict the fighting to their own territories, in the same way that they had agreed to the Battle of Champions, but it is difficult to see why Sparta would have limited its options in this way.

Finally, Herodotus mentions that the cities of Sicyon, north-west of Corinth, and of the island of Aegina in the Saronic Gulf provided ships for Cleomenes' landing (although the Aeginetans later claimed they did so unwillingly).[70] It has been suggested that the terms of alliance at this time were limited to the defence of Sparta and its allies against invasion, revolts, and coups d'état by would-be tyrants; if so, the aim of taking Argos would not have justified a mobilisation. However, the precise terms of Sparta's alliances are strongly debated among scholars.[71]

The demonstration of victory, the avoidance of allied territory, and the suggestion that only a few, possibly unwilling, allies were present, suggest strong divisions over policy within Sparta and among its allies. Sparta seems to have abandoned efforts to annex lands in the Peloponnese after its failures at Tegea, a restraint that was probably necessary for its diplomacy in the Peloponnesian League. The fall of Argos and Spartan expansion into its rich plain, however, would have upset the entire balance of power in the Peloponnese, raising fears among Sparta's neighbours of further aggression. Opposition to the invasion among the allies must have been strong. But the Heraclids' right to rule the Argolid, and the prize of its lands, must have decided many Spartiates for annexation. It is clear from the earlier attempts on Tegea and Dorieus' colonisation efforts that desire for land remained strong in sixth-century Lacedaemon. Cleomenes' argument that the oracle had been fulfilled blocked any further effort. He was willing to cripple Argos and show reluctant allies that Sparta could not be opposed lightly, but he maintained the policy of Spartan dominance in preference to annexing the Argolid and risking war with the allies. Cleomenes was bloody-handed, ruthless, cynical, and manipulative, but he did have the virtue of prudence.

After defeating the Ionian revolt in 494, and recovering the south-eastern Balkans in 492, Darius sent heralds to Greece to demand 'earth and water', symbols of submission. Herodotus reports that the ones that came to Sparta were thrown down a well and told to get earth and water there. Since the persons of heralds were sacrosanct, their murder was sacrilegious. Perhaps those advocating strong resistance to Persia incited the killing in order to force their fellow Spartans to take action. Later an attempt was made to expiate the sacrilege by offering the lives of two Spartan heralds in return.[72]

Evidence of a split appears soon after this. Cleomenes sought to aid Athens, now threatened by a Persian naval expedition, by demanding the Aeginetans end their war with Athens and give hostages. Demaratus encouraged the Aeginetans to refuse. Cleomenes responded by conspiring to replace Demaratus with the latter's cousin, Leotychidas. Leotychidas accused Demaratus of illegitimacy, and Cleomenes bribed the prophetess at Delphi to confirm it when the Spartans sent to the oracle. Demaratus was deposed, and soon fled, going to the Persian court.[73] Cleomenes and Leotychidas then took the hostages. However, the bribery at Delphi was soon uncovered, and Cleomenes fled into exile. He went first to Thessaly, and then united leaders of the Arcadians behind him. Unnerved, the Spartans recalled him. Herodotus says that he then went entirely mad, was confined by his family, and finally committed a grisly suicide.[74] Leotychidas was condemned also, and handed over to the Aeginetans for punishment, but was returned after attempting unsuccessfully to help them get their hostages back from Athens. He remained the Eurypontid king, though likely in disgrace.[75] It is arguably a tribute to Lycurgan society that the strains revealed by these events did not end in bloody civil strife.

The division and confusion in Sparta's leadership probably explain why Sparta had not mobilised when the Persian naval expedition crossed the Aegean in 490, besieged and took Eretria in Euboea, and landed at Marathon in eastern Attica. When an Athenian messenger was sent to ask for the Spartans' aid he was told that they would help, but had to delay their march, for 'they did not wish to break the law. It was the ninth day of the rising month, and they said that on the ninth they could not march off since the course [of the moon] was not full.'[76] The Greeks told time by the cycles of the moon, and their lunar calendars had months divided into thirds, the ninth therefore occurring in the first (rising) third, and the full moon in the middle third. They also considered many days, or even times of day, lucky or unlucky for certain actions.[77] The prohibition here may have been tied to the Carnea festival month, when the Spartans customarily did not campaign, but this is uncertain.[78] Opponents of sending aid would have insisted on strict observance of the prohibition.

There is another explanation for the delay. The fourth-century philosopher Plato claimed that Spartan aid to Athens was 'hindered by the war then ongoing against Messene and by whatever else may have occurred – for we do not know about anything said of it'.[79] Some accept this report of a Messenian war, offering supporting evidence, though none of it strong.[80] Plato wrote this in the 350s, after Athens had been allied with Sparta against Thebes and the freed Messenians. He could be repeating anti-Messenian propaganda of the 360s. A major revolt in 490 could not have remained secret – the rebels would have sent abroad for help, if nothing else – and must have affected Sparta's ability to fight Persia, so Herodotus should have discussed it. But only the Aristagoras quote noted above even hints at it, and that is more easily explained as Herodotus' reference to Sparta's long-term strategic situation than to a revolt he otherwise failed to mention.

In any event, a contingent of two thousand Spartans finally marched after the full moon, to arrive in Attica on the third day out of Sparta, only a day longer than a trained runner had taken to cover the distance. It is an impressive achievement, especially for a force of heavy infantry. Either they had a remarkable level of fitness, or they were mounted for the journey. By the time they arrived, however, the Athenians had defeated the Persians at Marathon. The Spartans went there anyway, viewed the Persian corpses, praised the Athenian achievement, and went home.[81]

To sum up, from the 550s to the 490s Sparta's military strength was recognised by states in Greece and abroad, leading to requests for assistance. Cautious opportunism marked Sparta's approach to intervention, since its situation did not allow bold aggression. Its militia army, although powerful, could only take the field for short periods, and picked forces of other cities could match the best that Sparta could raise. The Spartans could be routed by surprise attacks. Spartan siegecraft was unimpressive. The Spartans could take to the sea, but relied largely on their allies for naval power and sea transport. Allied aid was also needed against the most powerful opponents, but Sparta's control of its allies was not firm. Spartan military power proved largely unsuccessful in interventions outside of the Peloponnese. Even so, Sparta did crush Argos and dominate the Peloponnese. That strength and dominance would prove decisive when Greece was invaded by the Persian Empire in 480.

~ Three ~

THE GREAT KING INVADES, 481–480

Herodotus' entire purpose in writing his history was to record the great deeds of the Persian invasion of Greece in 480–479, and he put much effort into it. He sought out Greek sources on both sides, and went over the ground of the battlefields. He was no military analyst, attributing the outcome of events as much to the gods as to men, and he passed on biased accounts of individuals' and states' actions, and in particular reflected aristocratic Athenian viewpoints. It is not difficult to allow for these, however, and the fundamental soundness of his work comes through in the analysis. The same cannot be said for fourth-century and later accounts, all too subject to the mythologising that already affected reporting of the invasion in Herodotus' time.[1]

Xerxes Marches, Greece Prepares, Summer 481–Spring 480[2]

In 481, news reached Greece that the Great King himself was heading for Europe. The Persians had spent most of the decade after Marathon preparing the expedition, their initial efforts being spoiled by an Egyptian revolt and Darius' death in 486. Finally, in spring 481 Xerxes, Darius' son and successor, left his capital. He reached Sardis with his army that autumn. However, storms demolished the bridges that engineers had constructed across the Hellespont (Dardanelles), preventing the army crossing into Europe; it wintered in Lydia. Meanwhile Xerxes sent heralds to the Greeks, demanding that they surrender and furnish provisions for his army. Most peoples of northern and central Greece submitted. The Persian army finally resumed its march in early spring 480, crossing a month later into the Thracian Chersonese (Gallipoli peninsula). The fleet also massed.[3]

Xerxes of course held supreme command, his officers being Persian princes and nobles, as well as subject kings and despots. Having them along prevented their rebelling in his absence, and allowed them to demonstrate to him their abilities and the quality of the forces they commanded. The Persian army was raised, Herodotus claims, from every province of an empire that stretched from the Danube and the

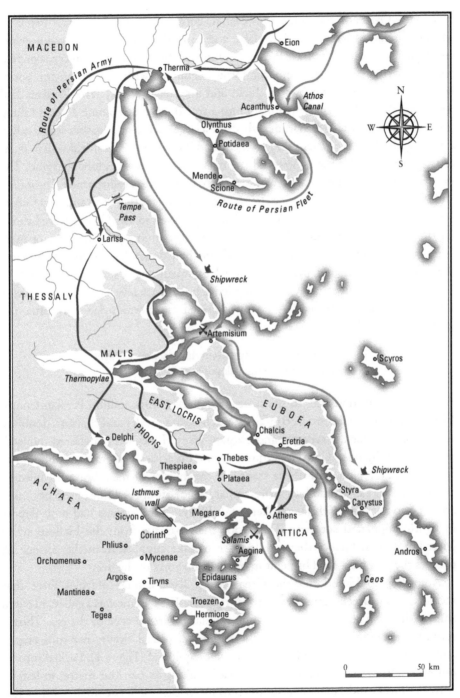

Map 3.1: Xerxes' invasion

Nile to the Oxus and the Indus. However, its core consisted of Iranians – Persians, Medes, Cissians, Hyrcanians, Bactrians, and so forth – along with Sacae nomads and Indians. In the Near East in recent centuries the dominant infantry type had been the archer–spearman team, the former equipped with a powerful composite bow, the latter with a single-grip shield and a spear (*Plate 15*). The Persians had developed the archer–spearman team into a squad, with up to nine archers taking shelter behind a spear-armed leader who bore a large wicker-and-leather shield called a *gerra* by the Greeks (*Plates 21, 22*).[4] The squad leaders created a shield wall in front of the bowmen, who then showered the enemy with arrows before charging. The cavalry consisted of bow- or javelin-armed Asians, with javelin-armed Thessalian and Boeotian Greeks later joining them. They rode horses that were small by today's standards, doing so without saddles and stirrups. Even so, the Greeks feared them, for they could ride around isolated units of infantry, shooting them down, or mass and charge into unformed infantrymen and ride them down. Against formed infantry that could not be isolated, they would attack by squadrons in succession (*Plate 23*).[5]

The Greeks thought the Great King led a huge mass levy of all his subjects – a belief Xerxes encouraged.[6] A poem inscribed at Thermopylae soon after the campaign claimed:

> Against three hundred myriads in this place once fought
> Four thousands from the Peloponnese.[7]

A 'myriad' is ten thousand, so the poet gives Xerxes three million Persian troops. Herodotus estimated 1,700,000 infantry and 100,000 cavalry and chariots, doubling that to account for the servants and baggage train.[8] Later writers offered reduced, but still vast, figures.[9] Considerations of route capacities and water supply in the Hellespontine region, and of the transport capabilities of men, beasts of burden, and carts, have caused modern writers to argue for an upper limit of 210,000 men and 75,000 animals, with far smaller totals likely.[10] The Persians had built depots in lightly populated southern Thrace for their passage from the Hellespont to Macedon, but in Greece they would have to take supplies from the conquered peoples there or have food brought in by the transports of the fleet.

According to Herodotus, the Great Kings' fleet, a huge polyglot force that included many Greeks, consisted of 1,327 triremes. The trireme was a galley, an oared ship, with a ram at the prow. It was the standard warship type of the era. Thirty-seven metres long, nearly six wide, the trireme displaced twenty-five tons empty, and almost twice that when fully manned and equipped (*Figure 4*). Packed into its hull were 170 rowers set on three levels, each pulling an oar four metres in length. Sixteen officers and sailors and fourteen to forty-four soldiers completed the crew (*Plates 18, 19*). There was scant room for stores, since the lowest level of oarsmen

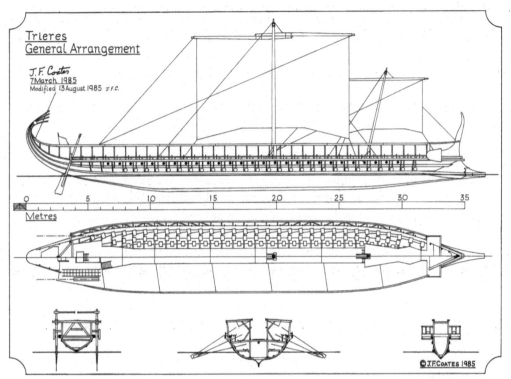

4. General arrangement of a trireme, according to the modern reconstruction. The trireme was fought from the front – note the ram in the prow – and steered from the stern. Rowed by three banks of oarsmen on each side, with the oarsmen in the lowest bank sitting in the hold, the trireme lacked storage, but enjoyed high speed under oars. (*Drawing by John F. Coates, used by permission of the Trireme Trust*)

essentially sat in the hold. Water was the most vital store, for an oarsman at work in hot weather could drink a litre of water every hour, losing most in perspiration. In a long day of rowing a full crew could consume two tons of water and food. Triremes could be sailed, reducing water consumption, but even so crews still had to go ashore to get water, forage, cook, and camp, there being no room in the cramped ships even to allow everyone to lie down. Therefore a trireme fleet needed to base itself daily at harbours or beaches, take supplies from transports or settlements, and access springs or rivers for water. Since triremes could readily approach any accessible shore, they served infantry as amphibious landing ships; cavalry needed special horse transports. Smaller oared ships and merchant sailing ships served as transports and auxiliaries (*Plate 20*).[11]

Herodotus' 1,327 triremes would put over a quarter of a million men at sea if the ships were fully manned, an incredible figure. Perhaps many of these triremes had only skeleton crews, serving as supply transports, reserves, and amphibious vessels for the army. However, since Herodotus reports the existence of a large support force,[12] his figures may have been based on 'paper' strengths, and a much smaller force was actually mobilised. In any case, the Persians faced considerable difficulties finding sufficient safe harbourage for their huge fleet.

Evidence in Herodotus,[13] and the actual course of the campaign, indicate that the Persians intended to advance south down mainland Greece with army and fleet acting in mutual support, exploiting Greek internal divisions, overawing most cities into surrender, and crushing all resistance. Destroying the enemy fleet was a priority, since it threatened Persian resupply by sea and prevented amphibious landings. Herodotus claims that Demaratus, who accompanied the expedition, advised Xerxes to send part of the fleet to occupy Cythera and raid Lacedaemonian territory, saying the Spartans would not come forth if they had a war at home. However, his advice was only sought and given after the fleet's losses made its division impossible.[14] Whether or not he actually gave such advice, Demaratus probably claimed to have done so. He and his descendants later ruled cities in north-western Asia Minor, and Herodotus probably had the story from his children or grandchildren.[15]

The Greeks who chose to resist formed what scholars call the 'Hellenic League', a coalition of Sparta and its allies, especially Corinth, along with Aegina, Athens, Plataea, Chalcis, Eretria, and the island of Ceos. Efforts to bring Argos or Greeks abroad into the league failed. Members of the league ended ongoing strife between their states, notably Athens' decades-long conflict with Aegina,[16] and swore to 'tithe' any state that voluntarily joined Xerxes — that is, destroy it and dedicate a tithe of the spoils to the gods. This kept pro-Persians from acting openly.[17]

Spartans commanded on both land and sea, even though Athens provided over half of the league fleet. Athens' leading strategist, Themistocles, had persuaded the Athenians in c.483 to use income from the silver mines of Attica's Laurium district to increase their fleet to two hundred warships. Earlier Themistocles had sought to create a fortified port at the Piraeus and evacuate Athens' non-combatants there in the event of a Persian invasion, planning to man the fleet with all the fittest citizens and leave the rest to hold the walls. The Piraeus remained incomplete, however, so the island of Salamis had to be the Athenian people's chief refuge from the Persian army.[18] Despite Athens' naval strength, Sparta's Peloponnesian allies had rejected Athenian naval command. The Athenians yielded the point, for now.[19]

The Greeks of the league thought themselves unable to face the Persian host and its powerful cavalry in the open field. Instead they attempted to hold mountain passes and sea straits, evidently in the hope that supply problems and lack of harbourage would erode the Persians' superiority or even force Xerxes' withdrawal.[20] Thus, in spring 480 the Hellenic League sent ten thousand hoplites to Thessaly to aid friendly Thessalians in holding the narrow pass of Tempe between Thessaly and Macedon. The Thessalians were divided between the pro-Persian Aleuads, the clan ruling the city of Larisa south of Tempe, and factions favouring resistance. The Spartans were led by Euaenetus, one of the polemarchs: the first mention of that type of Spartan officer. No doubt a king would have led the main levy north later.

The army and its Thessalian cavalry may have entered Macedon briefly, perhaps hoping to pressure its king, Alexander I, a Persian subject ruler, into joining them. However, after only a few days the league forces departed for home, and Thessaly submitted to Xerxes. Various reasons are reported: the hostility of mountain tribes and of the Aleuads; the discovery that Tempe could be circumvented by other passes; and warnings from Alexander about Xerxes' might. In any case, there was no point in remaining mobilised – the Persians took two months to cross southern Thrace, and built a road into Thessaly that avoided the Tempe Pass entirely.[21]

Leonidas at Thermopylae, Summer 480[22]

That summer the league decided to try to hold the pass of Thermopylae in central Greece, 'calculating that the barbarians would be unable to make use of their numbers or of their cavalry,' says Herodotus.[23] The fleet would take station at Artemisium (Pevki Bay) on the north coast of Euboea, to block the strait between it and Thessaly's Magnesian promontory, and prevent Persian landings behind Thermopylae or on Euboea. When the Great King began heading south, the Greeks went north.[24] Commanding the land army was Sparta's King Leonidas, the eldest surviving half-brother of Cleomenes. His forces consisted of small units, picked levies or *epilektoi*. Herodotus says that the nine-day Carnea festival at Sparta and the four-day festival of the Olympic Games were occurring at this time. Both festivals probably culminated on the night of the full moon on 19 August.[25] Once the gods had been honoured, complete mobilisation would occur. The king and his men were forerunners of the main army, meant to rally local allies and hold the position until relieved. As we shall see, delaying campaigns for religious reasons was in character for the Spartans. However, the delay must have pleased those Peloponnesians who preferred defending the Isthmus of Corinth to fighting at distant Thermopylae. Also, the expense of the expeditions already sent no doubt discouraged a more extensive mobilisation now. Characterised by Thucydides as small farmers lacking funds, the Peloponnesians likely wished to postpone levying a large army for as long as possible.[26]

Herodotus lists Leonidas' hoplites: 300 Spartiates, 2,120 Arcadians (including 500 from Tegea and as many from its northern neighbour and rival, Mantinea), 400

Corinthians, 200 Phliasians, and eighty Mycenaeans.[27] Herodotus calls the three hundred Spartiates 'both the established three hundred and those who already had sons.'[28] The phrase 'established three hundred' suggests the *Hippeis*, but Herodotus does not use this name, men with sons were enlisted instead of youths, and the king chose them instead of the three *Hippagretai* of Xenophon's era. The unit probably combined members of the *Hippeis* who were fathers with other Spartiates.

Later sources report some thousand Lacedaemonian hoplites in all, implying the presence of seven hundred Perioecs or armed Helots.[29] Herodotus mentions Helots, but not as hoplites,[30] and his detailed account and knowledge of Helot participation argues that he had good sources and was unlikely to have missed the existence of a Perioecic contingent. The line about 'four thousands from the Peloponnese' in the Thermopylae poem – perhaps a careless poetic reference to the total Greek losses, which included many Boeotians[31] – probably inspired later writers to add non-Spartiates to Herodotus' 3,100 to reach 4,000.

What actually raised the total to 4,200 hoplites were 400 Boeotians from Thebes and 700 from Thespiae, west of Thebes. The Thespiaeans were the full hoplite levy of their city, which was hostile to Thebes. The Theban unit matched the picked Peloponnesian forces, but was tiny compared to the resources of Thebes' Boeotian confederacy. This is because Thebes had submitted already to Xerxes, but now had to send a contingent or risk being 'tithed' by the resisting Greeks. It is also reported that the Thebans were ruled by a tight oligarchy, and that those who had opposed submission joined Leonidas.[32] The Phocians, who lived north-west of Boeotia and south of Thermopylae, undertook to guard their own region, and sent one thousand hoplites, while the Eastern Locrians, living east of the pass, sent their full levy, probably also a thousand hoplites, and even contributed ships.[33]

Named 'Hot Gates' for its warm springs, Thermopylae lay in Trachis, a district in southern Malis, the region of the valley of the Spercheius River south of Thessaly. The route was the main line of communication between northern and central Greece. It ran for several kilometres along the northern side of the mountain – then called Anopaea, today Kallidromos – and the southern shore of the Gulf of Malis, which came much closer to the mountainside than it does today.[34] Arriving at Thermopylae, Leonidas camped behind an old wall, now restored, that had been built by the Phocians during a war with Thessaly. It stood at the central pass, called by scholars the Middle Gate, where the route narrowed to about fifteen metres and the mountainside was precipitous. It narrowed even further, to a cart's width, at the East and West Gates, but there the mountainsides were easier to cross. The rugged cliffs on the northern face of Kallidromos showed no obvious path to the Persians except along the streambed of the Asopus, which runs around Kallidromos to its north and west through a narrow, difficult gorge. However, it was possible to ascend the mountain, and a wide, easy route led to the area behind the East Gate. Leonidas only learned of it on his arrival, a consequence of his uninvited arrival in (to Spartans) strange and distant territory. The Phocians volunteered to guard this route.[35]

Xerxes' army finally arrived. He waited four days before attacking. Herodotus says that he had marched south along one route, so his march columns probably extended so far back that it took that long for the entire force to gather. It was also good to rest his men after a long march before sending them into battle. Herodotus says that Xerxes expected the Greeks to be terrified by the might of his army and flee. At a council of war the Peloponnesian officers did argue for returning to defend the Isthmus of Corinth. They certainly had reason to fear that Xerxes would turn the pass. The Phocians and Locrians angrily denounced this attempt to abandon them. Leonidas refused to retreat, but he did send for help.[36]

On the fifth day, Xerxes sent the Median and Cissian infantry into the pass. They fought all day, suffered badly, and achieved nothing.[37] Next, the Great King ordered in his elite Persian infantry, nicknamed the 'Immortals' since their numbers were not allowed to fall below ten thousand.[38] He was sure they would carry the pass.

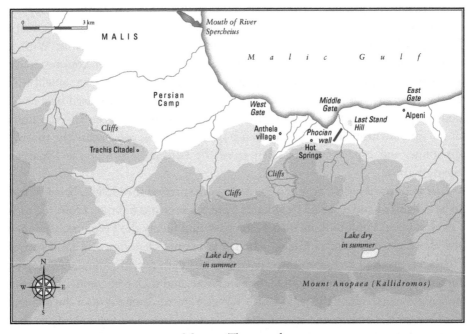

Map 3.2: Thermopylae

However, when these joined battle with the Greeks, they got no further than the Median unit, but fared the same, as they were fighting in a narrow place and using shorter spears than the Greeks, and were unable to profit from their numbers. The Lacedaemonians fought memorably, showing in various ways that they were men who knew how to fight facing men who did not, as they did whenever they would turn their backs, together feigning flight; on seeing this the barbarians would set off in pursuit of them with shouting and noise; however, on being overtaken, they would turn back to face the barbarians, so that having done so, they overthrew countless numbers of the Persians; and a few of the Spartiates fell at these moments. Since the Persians, making attempts unit by unit and attacking in every fashion, were unable to take any of the entry, they withdrew. In these onsets it is said the king, viewing the battle, thrice leaped up from his throne, fearing for his army.[39]

We must understand Herodotus' remarks on the Persians' incompetence to reflect their lack of training in concerted group hand-to-hand combat. Marathon had shown that hoplites could defeat Persian infantry in hand-to-hand combat. Rather than man the Phocian wall, which would have given the advantage to Persian strengths in missile weapons and siege warfare, Leonidas decided upon an active defence, seeking to punish the invaders, not just block them. At first glance, use of a feigned-flight tactic might appear unlikely for heavily armed hoplites. However, the Spartans had visited Marathon, and so knew about Persian shield walls. Facing the prospect of attacking shield walls in the close confines of a pass, Leonidas evidently trained his picked Spartiates to perform feigned retreats, hoping to lure the enemy into breaking the wall and pursuing rashly. With it down, unshielded archers would have been easy prey for a sudden counterattack. Plato, in fact, refers to just this tactic being used against the Persian shield wall by the Spartans at Plataea in 479.[40] It seems a tactic more likely used by a small body of picked men than by an entire army, but it may have been tried by units of the Spartan army in that battle. Its use speaks volumes concerning the control, discipline, and capacity for manoeuvre of the elite members of the Lycurgan Spartan army.

The Persians attacked again on the next day, expecting the Greeks, being so few, to be exhausted and disabled by wounds from the previous fighting. However, each Greek state and unit took its turn in the pass, and finally the Persians abandoned the effort. At this point a Greek, whom Herodotus identifies as a local named Ephialtes, revealed to Xerxes the existence of the path over the mountain, hoping for a reward. Xerxes had him guide the 'Immortals' and their commander Hydarnes on a night march along the path, which was also called Anopaea from the name of the mountain. The Persians set out after dark and marched all night. At dawn they reached the highest part, where they stumbled on the thousand Phocian hoplites.

Oak woods at first hid their approach, but the Phocians heard the sound of feet treading upon storm-fallen leaves and hurriedly armed. Hydarnes at first worried that he might be facing the Spartans, who evidently were not yet distinguished from other Greeks by distinctive gear. But Ephialtes identified these men as Phocians. Hydarnes deployed his troops, who fired arrows 'many and thick' into the Phocians. Instead of massing and charging, the Phocians fled to the summit to make a last stand, thinking that the Persians had come just to attack them. Their isolation from the other Greeks had cost them vital experience. The Persians coolly bypassed them and descended the mountain rapidly.[41]

Lookouts from the heights ran to warn Leonidas, who had learned of the flanking move already from deserters from the Persian camp. A council of war ended in divided views, some saying they must retreat, others that they must not abandon their post. In the end, all left except Leonidas, the Spartiates and their Helot servants, and the Thespians and Thebans. According to Herodotus, Xerxes, following the plan made with Ephialtes, sent his troops to attack the pass at mid-morning. Leonidas and the remaining Greeks left the Phocian wall and came into the wider section of the pass to meet them. This allowed them to inflict further damage on the Persian army while still fighting it in the controlled conditions of the pass. Fierce combat followed. Herodotus describes a mob scene among the Persians, who were driven forward by the whips of their officers. As the Greeks fought, their spears became broken, and they drew their swords. This gave the advantage of reach to Persian spears. Leonidas, fighting courageously, now perished. A battle was fought for his body, the Spartans recovering it and routing their enemies four times.

This phase ended when Hydarnes and his troops finally arrived, whereupon the Thebans surrendered. The surviving Spartans and Thespians then retreated to the Phocian wall, and after that to the hill behind it, where they defended themselves with their swords, or with fists and teeth, until the Persians surrounded the hill and shot them down with missiles. Hundreds of bronze arrowheads were found in the sandy soil of the hillock identified as the site of the last stand when it was excavated in the mid-twentieth century. The Helots and the other servants also perished, if Herodotus' figure of four thousand Greek dead is correct, and each Spartiate had seven Helots, as he reports for the campaign of Plataea in 479. The accuracy of Herodotus' account has been questioned, but nothing in it seems incredible, and Greeks in the Persian camp could have passed on details. Certainly it was a ferocious struggle, in which many Persian notables, including two of Xerxes' half-brothers, were slain.[42]

Herodotus presents Thermopylae as a moral victory for Leonidas and for Sparta and Thespiae, and provides some of antiquity's most famous anecdotes about Spartan courage and devotion to Lycurgus' laws.[43] Still, he admits Thermopylae was a strategic defeat for the Greeks. Later writers sought to 'spin' matters more positively. Their accounts of the battle even include a heroic night attack by Leonidas and the Spartiates on the Persian camp, with the aim of killing Xerxes. This story flatly contradicts Herodotus' rich and credible account, and it is extremely unlikely that Leonidas would have left the protection of the pass to lead a few hundred heavily armoured men into a strange camp at night in the faint hope of finding Xerxes before his guards spirited him off.[44]

Herodotus was uncertain why Leonidas and his followers stayed to fight. He says the Delphic Oracle informed the Spartans that either their city would be destroyed, or one of their kings would be slain.[45] Arguably this was a story created after the event,[46] but since Demaratus accompanied Xerxes, perhaps some thought Sparta could avoid war by restoring him as the Eurypontid king and executing his enemy Leotychidas. Herodotus, in any case, believed that the king stayed in order to fulfil the oracle and save Sparta, as well as to secure the glory of the last stand and avoid abandoning his post. The Thespians stayed to share the glory, while the Thebans were kept as hostages. Even in antiquity, however, the notion that the Thebans were hostages was derided. The Thebans themselves reportedly claimed they had been hostages when they surrendered to Xerxes,[47] but this explanation was required to excuse their presence on the battlefield despite Thebes' submission to Persia. That all of Thespiae's levies would have stayed to die for glory, rather than return to evacuate their families, is also dubious. Later writers stressed honour and the oracle.[48]

Modern scholars suggest Leonidas and his men performed a sacrificial rearguard. This would have been an unusual action for a Greek army in this era, but then the circumstances were atypical. It is difficult to understand why the Boeotians should have agreed to sacrifice themselves for Peloponnesians, however. Other explanations can be suggested. Leonidas and his followers clearly hoped to maul their enemies further. Moreover, the king had sent for reinforcements. Herodotus says that the Athenians expected the Spartans to be in Boeotia shortly after Thermopylae.[49] It explains the presence of the two Boeotian contingents and the Helots if Leonidas and his men hoped to give the Peloponnesians time to mobilise to save Boeotia and Athens. And, on learning of the fall of the pass, the Spartans and other Peloponnesians did mass at the Isthmus of Corinth, commanded by Leonidas' brother Cleombrotus. However, instead of heading east into Boeotia, they laboured day and night to build a wall across the isthmus.[50] If Leonidas and his men had sacrificed themselves to give their people time to beat Xerxes into Boeotia, they had done so in vain. But if Leonidas had known what his brother was likely to do, he may have tricked the Boeotians into staying in order to gain Sparta an extra day to fortify the isthmus. Either way, later Spartans would have had every reason to offer more glorious (and less embarrassing) explanations.

As for Xerxes, he rested his army for two days after the battle, then force-marched south. The Locrians and Boeotians surrendered, while the Phocians, Plataeans, and Thespians fled for refuge. Their abandoned cities were burned. Xerxes and his van forces reached Attica quickly. They found Athens abandoned, aside from the Acropolis, held by volunteers. The Great King's hardy mountaineers quickly stormed it. Xerxes seemed poised for final victory.[51]

Eurybiadas at Artemisium and Salamis, Summer 480[52]

It was not on land but at sea that the Persians were stopped. First, the Persian fleet was caught by a storm off the harbourless Thessalian coast while on its way south. It reportedly lost over four hundred triremes and large numbers of light galleys and transports. Then the Greeks of the league fleet fought it in the waters off Artemisium for three days, inflicting worse losses than they suffered. A detachment of two hundred Persian ships, sent to round Euboea and block the Greeks' retreat by seizing the Euripus Strait between Chalcis and the mainland, was shipwrecked off the south-eastern coast of Euboea by another storm, or so Herodotus reports.[53]

When news arrived of the fall of Thermopylae, the Greeks of the league fleet retreated to the island of Salamis off the west coast of Attica, where they repaired battle damage, received as reinforcements the final naval levies of the league, and brought over all those Athenian evacuees who had not transferred to Aegina or to Troezen on the Argolic Acte. The Persian fleet arrived the day after Xerxes did, anchoring at Phalerum. Fearing that the Greeks would escape to the Isthmus of Corinth, on the night of the day after its arrival Xerxes sent his fleet to block the eastern and western exits of the straits between the island and the mainland, and on the following morning ordered it to attack the Greeks in the eastern strait. The Greeks had the better of the battle, inflicting heavy losses.[54] Realising that his fleet was incapable of further combat, Xerxes bluffed the Greeks into inactivity by having his army begin building a mole towards Salamis while his fleet rested and refitted.[55] It then withdrew by night, sailing to the Hellespont to hold the bridges there. The Great King and his army soon headed north as well.

The Spartan role in this was in one sense minor, in another vital. It was minor in that Sparta contributed only ten ships of the 271 first stationed at Artemisium, and sixteen of the 380 reported at Salamis. The coastal Perioecic towns were too small to support a large fleet effort. The Athenians manned 180 ships in a mass levy. The contribution of Sparta was vital in that it provided the fleet commander: Eurybiadas, son of Euryclidas, the first attested navarch. He was not the genius behind the naval campaign; even the Spartans acknowledged that this was Themistocles' role.[56] Eurybiadas' task was to make the final decisions about the fleet's actions and maintain its unity – no small matter in a force drawn from diverse and often mutually hostile city-states.

In the campaign, Herodotus reports a tale that both Eurybiadas and the Corinthian commander, Adeimantus, were bribed by Themistocles to stay at Artemisium after the arrival of the Persian fleet.[57] Since the Artemisium battles were fought on the same days as Thermopylae, however, withdrawal would have exposed Leonidas to being outflanked by an amphibious landing, making it unlikely that Eurybiadas would have considered it. Before Thermopylae, the Greeks did withdraw to the Euripus, a move Herodotus attributes to cowardice.[58] However, they may have believed, mistakenly, that a Persian force was attempting to seize the Straits, for they left men to keep watch in northern Euboea, and returned to Artemisium after the storm damaged the Persian fleet off Thessaly. Certainly the Greeks fought resolutely at Artemisium. Herodotus accepted rather too readily Athenian aristocrats' tales hostile to Themistocles and non-Athenians.

Eurybiadas' most important moment came when the arrival of Xerxes in Attica and his capture of the Acropolis caused the Peloponnesian commanders to demand that the fleet withdraw to the Peloponnese, which was now threatened with attack. The Greek fleet risked being cut off by the Persians and blockaded on Salamis if it remained. Eurybiadas at first agreed, and a night move was planned, but before it happened Themistocles persuaded him to hold a second meeting. There he threatened to withdraw the entire Athenian fleet – indeed, the entire Athenian people – to southern Italy, if no attempt was made to hold Salamis. The Aeginetans and Megarians also wanted to fight at the island, in the hope of distracting Persian attention from their own cities. Eurybiadas chose to stay, and did not change his decision when the Persian fleet arrived and threatened battle. When the Peloponnesians that same evening again called for retreat, Eurybiadas held a council of war, and kept them at it all night, while Themistocles reportedly sent a servant to inform the Persians of the proposed move and urge them to cut off the Greeks' retreat, promising that sympathisers would revolt once the Persian attack began. Xerxes was readily persuaded and deployed his fleet accordingly, no doubt hoping to destroy the Greek navy and easily turn the Isthmian Wall thereafter. Eurybiadas had held the Peloponnesians until then, thus forcing a battle.[59]

How important Eurybiadas' leadership was can be seen by comparison of the Greek naval effort in 480 with that of the Ionian rebels in 494.[60] A headless coalition of cities, the rebels had given up practising for naval battle after only one week. Soon after, when they fought the Persians at Lade, entire squadrons deserted at the moment of battle. That this could occur again was doubtless hoped, indeed expected, by Xerxes, and helps explain his willingness to act on Themistocles' notice.

By contrast, at both Artemisium and Salamis the Greeks held together and fought in good order, doubtless the result of careful drill under their Spartan leader, and at neither battle did the Greeks suffer desertion. Rather, Greek men and ships of the Persian fleet deserted, bringing vital information to the league Greeks.

How had the Greeks defeated the Persians? The trireme was manoeuvrable and fast, capable in favourable conditions of nearly ten knots in short bursts and seven to eight knots over a long day's sail. It could engage in boarding actions, or ram and sink enemy vessels using the bronze-encased waterline ram at its bow. Fleets usually formed triremes in line abreast for battle, to protect their vulnerable sides and sterns by their formation. A faster, better-handled force would try to flank an enemy in a *periplous* ('sailing around'), or penetrate his line and then turn to attack in a *diekplous* ('sailing out through'). Combat in crowded conditions, or between less able fleets, could lead to a 'land battle at sea', dominated by boarding actions.[61]

The Persian fleet was numerous, so much so that even after Salamis the Greeks expected further action. Herodotus says it had lighter and faster triremes than the league fleet, especially the Phoenician squadrons from what is today Lebanon.[62] The Greeks therefore feared their opponents' ability to perform a *diekplous*. At Artemisium, the Greeks first made a late afternoon attack upon the Persian fleet, to test its ability to break through their circular or semicircular defensive formation. It may have been formed in two lines, so that ships breaking through those in the front would be set upon by those in the rear. If the Greek formation proved vulnerable, at least night would end the battle before too many losses occurred. In fact it held, despite being encircled. Even when they were attacked on the third day at Artemisium, the Greeks held off their enemies. By comparison, at both Artemisium and Salamis the ships of the polyglot Persian fleet fell into disorder during battle. The Athenian playwright Aeschylus, who was probably present, says that the Greek fleet in the narrow strait at Salamis formed a semicircular formation facing inward, which outflanked the Persian ships. Crowded in the narrows, these collided with each other. Also, at Salamis the kings, despots, and nobles of the rearward squadrons pushed ahead, Herodotus says, conscious that Xerxes was watching them from the shore. Their squadrons trapped the leading ships, which were then rammed and sunk. The Greeks thus avoided a massive boarding battle, which the Persians could have reinforced from the shore. Unlike the Greeks, many in the Persian fleet could not swim, and therefore drowned.[63] For these reasons Xerxes' fleet was defeated decisively. Without it, he could no longer maintain his offensive by land.

After Salamis the Greeks, astonished by the Persian withdrawal, sailed in pursuit of the Persian fleet. Halting at Andros, an island in the Cyclades chain south-east of Euboea, Eurybiadas and the Peloponnesians persuaded Themistocles to drop his proposal to cut off Xerxes' retreat by destroying the Hellespontine bridges, since this would trap the huge and still-dangerous Persian army in Europe. The Greek fleet spent time harassing cities in the islands subject to Persia, while the Spartans dispatched a herald to Xerxes in Thessaly, ostensibly to demand satisfaction for Leonidas' death. Their real aim may have been to learn Xerxes' intentions. He made it clear that he meant to leave behind an army in Greece under the command of his cousin Mardonius, a leading advocate of the invasion.

At the Isthmus of Corinth Cleombrotus sacrificed, Herodotus says, 'with a view to the Persian', only to get an evil omen: 'the sun became darkened in the heavens.'[64] A partial eclipse in fact took place on 2 October. Cleombrotus dismissed his army and went home, dying soon afterwards. Since the Spartans had avoided fighting Xerxes before, and wanted him to go home now, 'the Persian' in this passage must be Mardonius. The Greek fleet also disbanded for the winter, and the Athenians returned to their ravaged homeland. The Great King had departed, but the Persian threat remained.[65]

~ Four ~

The Fairest Victory, 480–479

Mardonius Takes Command, Autumn 480–Spring 479[1]

Left to complete the conquest of Greece, Mardonius wintered in Thessaly with his main army, which Herodotus sets at three hundred thousand Asians and Egyptians (i.e. a tithe of the thirty myriads of the Thermopylae poem), and fifty thousand Macedonians and Greeks.[2] His subordinate, Artabazus, fought Greek rebels in the Thracian Chalcidice, south-east of modern Thessaloniki. He destroyed the city of Olynthus, but lost heavily in an attack on the Corinthian colony of Potidaea on the neck of the isthmus of the Pallene peninsula.[3] Meanwhile, Mardonius consulted Greek oracles and sent Alexander of Macedon, a friend of the Athenians, to seek an alliance with them. Mardonius needed Athens' fleet if he was to attempt to invade the Peloponnese.[4] The Athenians waited until the alarmed Spartans also sent envoys before spurning the Persian effort. They hoped to pressure Sparta into fighting in Boeotia if Mardonius came south.[5] Although worried at the prospect of an Athenian defection, the Spartans preferred to delay action, offering instead to feed the Athenians' families if another evacuation occurred.6 Perhaps they expected the burden of supplying Mardonius' army to cause further revolts among his Greek subjects.

Mardonius marched on Attica in late spring 479, ten months after Xerxes' capture of Athens.[7] It was the season for campaigning, with grain ready to harvest and fodder plentiful. The Athenians evacuated ahead of his arrival; they refused to hear his renewed offers and sent envoys to Sparta to demand action. The story in Herodotus is that the ephors delayed, saying they had the Hyacinthia festival to celebrate, but were actually waiting for the Isthmus Wall to be completed. They acted only when a Tegean pointed out that no walls would save them if Athens and its fleet joined Mardonius.[8] This must be Athenian or Tegean mythmaking, because Herodotus elsewhere shows the Spartans worried that the Athenians might defect, and the Spartans had to mobilise to defend the isthmus now that Mardonius was in Attica. With everyone gathered for the festival, however, it must have made sense to the Spartans to celebrate it before marching north, whatever the Athenians preferred.⁹ When they did march, five thousand younger Spartiates left first, each accompanied by a reported seven Helots, followed later by five thousand picked hoplites and five thousand light-armed men of the Perioecs. The staggered departure would have helped reduce road congestion and allowed the Perioecs to sweep up Helot stragglers.

The Spartan commander was Pausanias, son of Cleombrotus, who was guardian of Pleistoanax, Leonidas' underage successor. He had his cousin Euryanax as colleague and second-in-command. They were both Agiads in their mid-twenties.¹⁰ Herodotus says that the Argives promised to Mardonius that they would block the Spartans' departure, but since little Tiryns and Mycenae, Argos' neighbours, sent contingents north, it is likely that Argos was still too weak to threaten Sparta. Overenthusiastic pro-Persians likely made the rash promise. The Argives did warn Mardonius of the Spartan march. He decided to withdraw from Attica, not wanting to fight in terrain difficult for his cavalry, with mountains blocking his line of retreat. He did briefly lunge at Megara on receiving word that an advance party of one thousand Spartans had arrived there. However, since the other Peloponnesians were also massing at the Isthmus of Corinth, he reconsidered and finally withdrew east, then went north into Boeotia and west to Thebes, encamping south of the city along the Asopus River. He would fight in plains suitable to his cavalry, with a friendly city at his back.¹¹

Pausanias at Plataea, Summer 479¹²

Obtaining favourable sacrifices, Pausanias led his army on, rendezvousing with the Athenians on the plain of Eleusis. The united army crossed Mount Cithaeron, which separates the north-eastern Megarid and north-western Attica from southern Boeotia, exiting from either the Dryoscephalae or Eleutherae passes, and reached Hysiae, just north of the two passes. The army then turned east, only to find the enemy already north of the Asopus. The Greeks posted themselves in the foothills around Erythrae, a town six kilometres east of Hysiae.¹³ The Persians initially camped along the Asopus from north of Erythrae to north of Plataea, six kilometres west of Hysiae, probably to ease gathering of water and foraging for their large force of cavalry.¹⁴

This cavalry Mardonius now sent against the Greeks. They attacked the Megarian contingent, deployed in open terrain, making attacks by squadrons in succession. To lure the Greeks into breaking formation and charging, they called them 'women', one of the few Greek words that all Persian soldiers would have learned. Hard-pressed, the Megarians asked for relief, and at a council of war Pausanias asked for volunteers. The Athenians had raised a specialist corps of

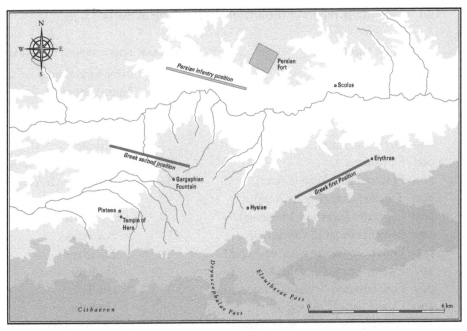

Map 4.1: The campaign of Plataea

archers, training a picked band of three hundred hoplites to support them in archer–spearman fashion (*Plate 23*). These now went, and successfully held off the Persians, killing their commander Masistius.[15]

Encouraged by this victory over the enemy's powerful cavalry, which otherwise threatened to make operations on the plain of the Asopus impossible, Pausanias and his officers decided to move to the low hills and level terrain in the area of the Gargaphian Fountain, in order to access its water supply. Their line of battle may have stretched from Pyrgos hill north of Plataea to Agios Demetrios hill north-west of Hysiae. Mardonius formed his infantry north of the river facing the Greeks, deploying his cavalry separately. The Spartans had the Greek right wing, the post of highest honour. The Athenians and the Tegeans quarrelled over who would have the left wing, the second most honourable post. The Athenians won it in a debate decided by the vote of the army's officers. Pausanias set the Tegeans next to the Spartans as consolation. Herodotus gives the Greeks 38,700 hoplites. His figures are neatly rounded, but not incredible.[16]

This is Herodotus' report of the infantry deployment of the two sides:

Greek hoplites	Persian foot opposite them
10,000 Lacedaemonians	Native Persians
1,500 Tegeans	Native Persians
5,000 Corinthians	Medes
300 Potidaeans	Medes
600 Orchomenians	Medes
3,000 Sicyonians	Medes
800 Epiduarians (Argolic Acte)	Bactrians (north-east Iranians)
1,000 Troezenians (Argolic Acte)	Bactrians
200 Lepreates (north of Messenia)	Bactrians
400 Mycenaeans and Tirynthians	Bactrians
1,000 Phliasians (north-west of Argos)	Bactrians
300 Hermioneans (Argolic Acte)	Indians
600 Eretrians and Styrians(Euboeans)	Indians
400 Chalcidians (Euboeans)	Indians
500 Ambraciots (north-west Greece)	Sacae (nomads)
800 Leucadians and Anactorians (north-west Greece)	Sacae
200 Paleans from Cephallenia (north-west Greece)	Sacae
500 Aeginetans	Sacae
3,000 Megarians	Subject Greeks
600 Plataeans	Subject Greeks
8,000 Athenians	Subject Greeks

If the hoplites were formed eight ranks deep – a normal depth for a Greek phalanx – with each man standing in enough space for his shield to cover him with a little more to either side, the hoplites would have stretched over 4,800 metres. Twelve ranks deep, another normal depth, would have made the formation over 3,200 metres in length. These figures fit the Greeks' reported movements and locations.

Herodotus also reports that the Greeks had one light-armed man for every hoplite, including the Perioecs. However, 35,000 light-armed Helots accompanied the Spartiates. The huge figure is suspect,[17] but fear of revolt gave the Spartans reason to remove most Helot men while the citizen forces were away, leaving the Helots' families as hostages. As at Thermopylae, the Helots and other light-armed men vanish from Herodotus' account, although he insists on the Helots' presence in the battle and reports a tomb for their losses.[18]

Mardonius' infantry probably roughly matched in number the hoplites deployed against them. His Asians were organised in ten-man squads, with a line of shield-bearers protecting a mass of archers. There were also Egyptians and other picked troops whose stations Herodotus does not give. Cavalry numbers are unknown. Confirming this rough estimate is the wooden-walled fort that Mardonius built north of the Asopus as a refuge in case of defeat. It was ten *stades* – six thousand Greek feet, or 1,760 to 1,998 metres – on a side. Meant to protect the entire army, the fortification's area sets an upper limit for the Persian force. Estimates range from 60,000 to 120,000 people, including noncombatants.[19] In short, each army was the size of a large Greek city-state – and would have needed supplies accordingly.

The two armies lay against one another for eight days after the Greek move, with the Persian cavalry always harassing the Greeks' lines, guided by the Thebans, who knew the terrain well. No general attack developed, however. Herodotus says that the seers on both sides, Sparta's Teisamenus and Mardonius' Hegesistratus, warned that the omens only favoured defence.[20] They were perceptive, for if the Greeks had tried to cross the Asopus and attack Mardonius, they risked rupturing their phalanx, and would have exposed its flanks and rear to attack by his cavalry, while if the Persian infantry advanced past the Asopus, it would face a strong army of hoplites, in formation and as well-positioned for defence as possible. However, on the eighth night Mardonius took the Thebans' advice to guard the Cithaeron passes, sending his cavalry against Dryoscephalae Pass. The cavalrymen caught a train of five hundred oxen pulling wagons carrying provisions from Corinth to the Greek army, and slaughtered men and beasts alike. Emboldened, for two days thereafter Mardonius deployed his army along the river, but did not cross it.[21]

At a council of war on the eleventh day Mardonius decided to ignore his seer and cross the river.[22] That night, Alexander of Macedon rode alone, Herodotus says, to warn the Athenians of the coming attack. He claimed that Mardonius was running short of supplies and aimed to defeat the Greeks before they received further reinforcements.[23] On learning this, Pausanias proposed that the Spartans and Athenians exchange positions. Herodotus says that his idea was to have the Athenians fight the Persians while the Spartans faced the Boeotians and Thessalians, because the Athenians had beaten the Persians at Marathon, while the Spartans had no experience of the Persians, but plenty of their fellow Greeks. Herodotus views this proposal as a result of Pausanias' fear, not a stratagem, but the idea makes sense as a tactic, especially in view of the Athenian corps of archers. At dawn the two shifted positions, probably unit by unit, not all at once, while Mardonius deployed his men. But the Boeotians spotted the exchange and reported it to Mardonius, who in turn shifted the Persians to face the Spartans again. Pausanias then returned the Spartans and Athenians to their original posts, and Mardonius switched his units as well.

Mardonius did not begin a general engagement, probably because shifting forces along lines five kilometres long would have taken much of the day and worn out his men. He did send a herald to accuse the Spartans of cowardice and challenge them to a mass duel with the Persians to determine the victory. Having experienced the futility and waste of the Battle of Champions two or three generations earlier, the Spartans did not reply. Encouraged, Mardonius dispatched his horsemen to make a major attack. They threw javelins or shot arrows for hours all along the Greek lines, and managed to foul and choke the Gargaphian Fountain, even though the Spartans themselves guarded it. Unfortunately Herodotus does not say how this happened. No doubt the Spartans were laconic about this setback. Perhaps the spring lay to the rear of the Spartan line of battle and was taken by a surprise cavalry attack.[24]

Deprived of food and water, the Greeks decided at a council of war to move that night to a feature called the 'Island', which lay, according to Herodotus' text, in front of Plataea and ten *stades* from the Gargaphian Fountain and the Asopus. This 'island on land' was formed by the splitting of the Oëroë stream, which ran from Mount Cithaeron. After the move, half the army would go over Cithaeron to get supplies, while the other half was protected from cavalry attack by the stream. However, that night all the units of the centre marched to the Sanctuary of Hera at Plataea and camped. Herodotus calls this move cowardice, but cowards would have fled over Cithaeron. The movement probably resulted from a last-minute change of plan that sent on ahead the units chosen to fetch supplies.[25]

Meanwhile the Athenians, supposed to hold the 'Island' with the Spartans, waited with growing suspicion for them to start. Finally they sent a herald to the Spartans. Herodotus says that he found Pausanias and Euryanax arguing with Amompharetus, 'lochagos of the Pitanate *lochos*'.[26] He had not participated in the council of war, and he refused to retreat and bring shame upon Sparta. He and his men, he declared, were staying. The argument lasted a long time and became heated. 'In fierce dispute, Amompharetus took a stone in both hands and, laying it at the feet of Pausanias, said that he cast his voting-pebble for not fleeing from the foreigners.'[27] It was likely a reference to the use of pebbles as secret ballots at the council of war. Pausanias told him he was out of his mind, and then asked the herald to explain the situation to the Athenians and have them follow the Spartan lead in the retreat.[28]

After he left, Pausanias argued with Amompharetus all night, unwilling either to stay or leave behind Amompharetus' men. Finally, as dawn came on, he gave the order to move out. He led the obedient contingents not to the 'Island', since the Persian cavalry would soon cross the river, but south through the hills and into the foothills of Cithaeron, using the terrain for shelter from cavalry attack. The Athenians also moved south, but across the plains. Realising, contrary to his expectation, that Pausanias had really gone, Amompharetus finally ordered his men to march. Moving slowly, he reached Pausanias, now about two kilometres from the start position, near Hysiae, at the shrine of Eleusinian Demeter, either north or east of the modern town of Kriekouki. Pausanias stopped there to see if Amompharetus would move, and if he did not, to be able to return to aid him. No sooner did Amompharetus arrive than the Persian cavalry caught up with Pausanias.[29]

Scholars, incredulous at such insubordination in a Spartan army, have denounced this report as an Athenian fantasy, or a wild distortion of a well-planned withdrawal, with Amompharetus and his unit acting as a rearguard, or as bait for the Persians. Adding to their doubts is Thucydides' denial that the Pitanate *lochos* ever existed.[30] Nevertheless, while it is possible that Herodotus was badly mistaken, much of his description covers events after the Athenian herald departed, for which the Spartans were his likeliest sources. We have seen that he spoke to Archias of Pitana, who perhaps told him about the Pitanate *lochos*. Aristotle is cited as reporting that Sparta had five lochoi, named *Edolos* or *Aidolios*, *Sinis*, *Arimas* or *Sarinas*, *Ploas*, and *Messoages* or *Mesoates*, the meanings of which are debated.[31] Scholars have suggested that the five lochoi comprised the army found in Herodotus, raised from the five villages constituting the city of Sparta.[32] If so, Amompharetus may have led as many as two thousand Spartiate and Perioecic hoplites, and their *psiloi*. Conversely, since the pentecostys was presumably once a 'fiftieth' of the Spartan army, as its name indicates, and Herodotus has the Spartans operate in units of 1,000 men, or in multiples thereof, then Amompharetus may have commanded a lochos of 1,000 hoplites, divided into five pentecostyes.

In short, there is no reason to think that Amompharetus led a small force. Since the army's centre had time to shift to Plataea, the Spartan wing had time to withdraw too, so no rearguard was needed. The stated plan of action did not call for 'bait', and it would have been uncharacteristically reckless for the Spartans to have sought to lure the enemy into battle without co-ordinating this first with the allies. Lycurgan law forbade retreat in battle, so it is no shock to find a Spartan opposed to retreating. Many may have considered Amompharetus' stand heroic. Certainly it was not cowardly. His men obeyed his commands, and the ephors, two of whom were on hand, did not act, perhaps because Pausanias was too proud to ask for help. The curse on those hindering a king on campaign did not apply, since Pausanias was a king's guardian, not a king. He was also a young man who had humiliated his troops by switching them to the less honourable left wing and refusing a challenge to champion combat. His drop in status allowed Amompharetus to refuse his orders and try to force a battle.

Elated by his enemy's apparent vulnerability, and unable to see the Athenians or the others due to the rolling terrain, Mardonius sent his Persian infantry against the

Spartans, the other Asian infantry following along behind. The Athenians and the Greeks of the centre marched towards the Spartans – probably at this time – but Mardonius' Greeks attacked the Athenians and held them. Herodotus has the centre forces leaving only after the Spartan–Persian battle. This is later Athenian 'spin', since the Theban cavalry caught the Phliasians and Megarians moving out of formation through the plain and rode them down, killing six hundred, while the Corinthians and other hoplites of the centre units marched through the foothills, and so proceeded slowly. Neither would have happened after the Persian rout.[33]

The Spartans and Tegeans therefore faced Mardonius by themselves:

> Left thus alone, the Lacedaemonians and Tegeans, being with their light-armed fifty thousands, the Tegeans three thousands (for in no way would they be separated from the Lacedaemonians), repeatedly sacrificed about joining battle with Mardonius and the army at hand. And as the sacrificial victims never proved favourable for them, many of them fell during this time, and more by far were wounded; for the Persians, making a barricade of wicker shields, lavishly loosed a multitude of arrows, so that, with the Spartiates hard-pressed and the victims still unfavourable, Pausanias lifted his eyes to the Heraeum of the Plataeans and called on the goddess, asking that their hopes might in no way be belied. While he was still invoking her concerning this, the Tegeans arose and went out against the barbarians ahead of everyone, and at once after the prayer of Pausanias the victims became favourable for the sacrificing Lacedaemonians. As the time had now come, they also advanced against the Persians, and the Persians stood against them, dropping their bows.[34]

Here we find Herodotus' Spartan sources stressing Pausanias' piety and their own discipline, and insisting that they had waited patiently under a hail of arrows while their commander and his seer Teisamenus desperately sought favourable omens from his animal sacrifices. We need not doubt it: Pausanias' invocation of Hera, rather than nearby Demeter, shows that he wanted to remain on the defensive until the contingents from the forces camped at the Heraeum came to his aid. Teisamenus picked up on his thinking and, consciously or otherwise, found the sacrifices unfavourable until the Tegeans forced his hand. The Persian infantry had formed a shield wall in front of the Spartan and Tegean hoplites and shot arrows at close range. Herodotus mentions a tale he had from a Plataean that Callicrates of Sparta, the handsomest of contemporary Greeks, was sitting in place when he was mortally wounded by an arrow striking him in the side.[35] This, and his saying that the Tegeans 'arose and went out [proexanastantes] against the barbarians ahead of everyone', shows that the Greeks were sitting. Plutarch states that Pausanias had ordered the Spartans to sit with their shields placed in front of their feet, making them smaller, better-sheltered targets. Shields and armour designed to resist strong spear thrusts also did well resisting tens of thousands of arrows.

The close combat ended as Thermopylae had shown it must:

Combat first took place around the wicker shields. When these had fallen, a fierce battle then developed around the Shrine of Demeter and lasted for a long time, in which things came to close quarters; for the barbarians would take hold of the [Greek] spears and break them. Now, the Persians were not inferior in spirit and bodily strength, but they were unprotected and besides lacked experience and were not equal to their opponents in skill. Darting out in front by ones and tens, and joining in greater and lesser numbers together, they fell upon the Spartiates and were destroyed. Wherever it happened that Mardonius himself was at hand, fighting from atop his white steed and with the picked men of the Persians, the best thousand, around him, there they pressed their enemies especially hard. Now while Mardonius survived, they held out and, defending themselves, threw down many of the Lacedaemonians; but when Mardonius perished and the corps stationed around him, being the mightiest one, fell, then indeed the rest turned about and gave way before the Lacedaemonians. For what most injured them was that their coverings lacked armour; against hoplites they struggled like men naked.[36]

These remarks are of the same kind as in Herodotus' account of Thermopylae, almost certainly reflecting Spartan judgements. The shield wall went down, leaving most of the Persians unshielded and vulnerable (*Plates 21, 22*). Knowing now of the Greek spears' longer reach, the Persians countered by the desperate expedient of seizing them. Their own attacks, performed singly and in small groups against the hoplite formation, show them still unable to imitate the Greeks in formed hand-to-hand combat. Herodotus notes that the Spartans present at Plataea denied the award of valour to Aristodemus, the persecuted survivor of Thermopylae, because he left his position in the formation and charged out in a rage, seeking death in order to clear his name. They considered that men who had gone to their deaths bravely without seeking to die were the ones who deserved to be honoured.[37]

Mardonius' ill-considered attack, which committed his Persians to battle before his non-Persian infantry could deploy, played to his enemies' strengths. No doubt he thought Thermopylae no fair field for the Persian infantry, and thought their time-tested tactics would work once given the chance. He and his men paid the price for his error. As for the subject Greeks, they fought the Athenians, but it was only the Boeotians, old foes of Athens, who did so long and stubbornly, in the end losing three hundred of their 'first and best men' (a picked band?). The surviving subject Greeks all fled to Thebes. The Asian infantry, of which only the Persians had been committed to battle, fled in disorder to the timber fort, their retreat covered by their cavalry. No prominent leader remained to rally them, for Mardonius and Masistius were dead, and Artabazus had fled with his men upon Mardonius' defeat.[38]

The Persians in the fort put archers in its towers just before the Spartans arrived, defeating their assaults: a setback that Herodotus attributes to the Spartans 'not having experience in wall fighting'. Perhaps so, but men in towers with composite bows would have had a terrific advantage over Helots throwing javelins and stones. The reliance of the Greeks upon hand-thrown weapons often hurled by untrained men was one of their main weaknesses in siege warfare (*Plate 16*). The Athenians now arrived, and fought for a long time, until 'by courage and persistence', says Herodotus,[39] they scaled the walls and then created a breach. Actually, the Athenian archers were probably the decisive factor, providing covering fire while their hoplites scaled the walls. The Greeks entered the fort through the Athenian breach, the Tegeans leading the way, presumably because they had not engaged in the assault and were massed and rested. A massacre followed, with only three thousand Persians left alive.[40]

Herodotus says that ninety-one 'Lacedaemonians from Sparta', seventeen Tegeans, and fifty-two Athenians perished, aside from the six hundred Megarians and Phliasians. These figures seem low, and they exclude Perioecs and Helots. Plutarch gives a total of 1,360 Greek dead, citing a source who said that all the Athenian dead were from one of their ten tribal regiments.[41] After collecting and dividing the spoils, with some set aside to be used for dedications to the gods, the Greeks set about burying the dead.[42]

Herodotus says that the Lacedaemonian fallen were interred in three vaults: one for Amompharetus, Callicrates, and others of note, called *ireës*; one for 'the rest of the Spartiates' (*hoi alloi Spartiētai*); and one for the Helots.[43] While all manuscripts use the term *ireës*, 'priests' or 'holy ones', scholars have argued on the basis of an ancient dictionary that *irenes* was the original reading, this being a Spartan word referring to men in their twenties. It has been argued further from this that Amompharetus commanded the *Hippeis*.[44] Since Herodotus knew of this unit, it is unlikely he would term it the 'Pitanate *lochos*' in his account of Plataea. Emending *ireës* is itself a questionable approach,[45] and it has been suggested that *ireës* indicates a special status accorded the most honoured dead.[46] The issue remains unresolved.

More important is the absence of a tomb for, or report of, Perioecic dead. Perhaps in the tomb passage Herodotus uses 'Spartiates' for 'Lacedaemonians', as elsewhere, but the subject demands accuracy, and he is very precise about the ninety-one dead being 'Lacedaemonians from Sparta'. If the Perioecs were stationed in units of their own along the front of the formation, it is impossible that they failed to suffer losses. If Perioecic hoplites were in the rear ranks of a formation in which the Spartiates fought in front, however, it is possible that they avoided serious casualties. We have seen in Chapter One how this could have been organised.

However, it has been argued that at Plataea the Helots stood behind their masters, present at the final battle just as Herodotus says, with a front rank of Spartiate *promachoi* and seven ranks of Helots.[47] If so, the Perioecs must have fought separately from the Spartiates. But in fact this theory fails under critical analysis. The eight-deep Spartiate–Helot formation would have stretched five kilometres by itself – too far to fit Herodotus' reports of Greek deployment. Herodotus always calls the Helots *psiloi*, but unshielded and unarmoured men sitting in tight ranks would have proven very vulnerable to the Persian arrow-storm on the final day's battle, with only a line of sitting hoplites providing cover. In 9.28.2 Herodotus says that '*psiloi* of the Helots were guarding' the Spartiates, 'seven being stationed around each man' (*psiloi tōn heilōtōn . . . peri andra hekaston hepta tetagmenoi*), phrasing that he repeats in 9.29.1. 'Around' is not 'behind', and if taken literally would mean Spartiates stood scattered among a mob of light-armed Helots. Herodotus is clear that the Greeks' usual response to Persian cavalry attack was to draw closely together.[48] The disaster suffered by the Phliasians and Megarians shows what would have befallen the Spartans during the days of cavalry attacks had they fought as skirmishers.

Given the vulnerability of unformed units to cavalry charges and of light-armed men packed into formations to missiles, one must suppose that the Helots took station well behind the Spartiates and Perioecs on the last day. Herodotus' use of *peri andra hekaston*, 'around each man', must mean only that seven Helots accompanied each Spartiate. Helots joined in combat on occasion, since a number of them were slain, but Greek *psiloi*, being militia, were typically untrained and ineffective. This is why the Athenian corps of archers, specialists hired for, or trained in, skill with the bow, played a notable role in this battle, while the rest of the *psiloi* did not.[49] Helots were less likely than most *psiloi* to be effective skirmishers, because the Spartans normally denied them weapons. So, as pleasant as it would be to accord the Helots a notable share in the honour of Plataea, neither the ancient sources nor military considerations permit it.

On the eleventh day after the battle the army marched against Thebes, demanding the surrender of the leading pro-Persian Thebans. For nineteen days the league army assaulted the city walls and ravaged farmlands, until the Theban leaders agreed under pressure to surrender themselves – in the hope, Herodotus says, of escaping condemnation through bribery. However, Pausanias dismissed his army, took the prisoners to the Isthmus of Corinth, and executed them.[50] Noteworthy here is the fact that Pausanias had been willing and able to remain in the field for a month after the battle. He was not forced to attain immediate results in his confrontation with Mardonius.

Mardonius, by contrast, felt such pressure due to lack of supply and continuing Greek reinforcement, and attacked rashly. Herodotus contradicts the report that he lacked supply, however. He twice notes with approval advice that Mardonius supposedly received from Artabazus and the leading Thebans, namely to take refuge behind the walls of Thebes and send bribes to Greek leaders, thereby creating divisions among the Greeks. Indeed, he may have used bribes: contingents from Elis and Mantinea arrived too late for the battle, and their commanders were banished. Presumably they were accused of taking Persian gold, whether that caused the delays or not.[51] Although this advice had some point when first made – before Mardonius' march south had caused the Spartans and their allies to mobilise – its being made again during the deadlock period in the Plataean campaign is almost certainly later mythmaking, meant to excuse Artabazus for his desertion and the Theban pro-Persians for involving the city in this defeat. The Thebans would not have wanted to leave their fields open to Pausanias' ravaging, or offered to cram the entire Persian army and its animals within their walls to consume their supplies, even assuming Thebes itself could have accommodated such numbers.[52]

Certainly the presence of two large armies must have greatly strained Boeotian resources. Transport by sea of grain to Mardonius, from Thessaly and Macedon or from Asia Minor, would have been open to Greek interception. Overland transport would have been costly and open to interception by those Phocians who had taken refuge on Mount Parnassus and were raiding Persian forces and pro-Persian Greeks.[53] In any case, Mardonius had spent the winter draining the resources of Thessaly and Macedon. Alexander was surely telling the truth when he claimed that Mardonius was running short of supplies and forced to fight.

Mardonius had also underestimated his foes and overestimated the capabilities of his troops. Pausanias, by contrast, proved cautious, god-fearing, and, most importantly, lucky. The strategic situation greatly favoured him, and Amompharetus' insubordination and Mardonius' recklessness combined to bring about a battle on Greek terms – Spartan, Tegean, and Athenian courage had done the rest. And so, as Herodotus says, Pausanias won 'the fairest victory of all those known to us'.[54]

Leotychidas at Mycale, Summer 479[55]

The Eurypontid king Leotychidas served as navarch in 479, and Themistocles received extravagant honours in Sparta after Salamis.[56] At first glance these facts suggest that the Spartans meant to campaign at sea in 479. However, the failure to employ Leotychidas in 480 and the fact that supreme command of the army went to two young men in their twenties suggest that the Spartans made Leotychidas navarch to keep him from army command. Many Spartans will have wanted no part of a leader who had offended Apollo by taking part in Cleomenes' bribing of the Delphic Oracle.

During spring 479, Leotychidas merely maintained a presence in the Aegean with 110 ships. However, in late spring Samian envoys came seeking his aid in overthrowing the despot whom the Persians had recently installed at Samos – where the remnants of the Persian fleet were based to help garrison Ionia and prevent a new revolt. The envoys claimed that the Persian ships were growing unseaworthy from neglect. Leotychidas was persuaded. His fleet reinforced perhaps to 250 ships, he sailed to Samos, only to find the enemy fleet had crossed to the southern coast of the Mycale peninsula, joining there the Persian army in Ionia. The Phoenicians were sent home, perhaps to preserve a cadre of skilled sailors.[57]

After some indecision, Leotychidas sailed around to Mycale, his ships prepared for a boarding action. On his arrival, he found the remaining Persian vessels drawn up on the beach and surrounded by a fence of fieldstones and tree trunks, with stakes set around it. The Persian army had made preparations for siege or open combat, disarmed the Samians in the camp, and sent the men of Miletus, whom they also mistrusted, inland to defend the passes of the heights above the site. Then they had formed a shield wall outside the camp and awaited their foes.

The league Greeks landed their forces east of the campsite and readied for battle. Encouraged by rumours of a victory at Plataea, reportedly fought that day, the Greeks advanced. Their left wing, consisting of the Athenians, Corinthians, Sicyonians, and Troezenians, was drawn up on the beach and advanced quickly to the attack, wanting the glory of the victory. Leotychidas and the Spartans, deployed further inland on the right, had to make a circuit through a ravine and hills before they could attack. As long as the shield wall stood, the Persians resisted, as at Plataea, but its fall signalled their defeat (*Plates 21, 22*). The surviving Persians fled into the fortifications, but the Greeks pressed in after them, with happier results than Archias and Lycopas had met with at Samos. Although disarmed, the Samians helped the league Greeks. The Spartans arrived, the native Persians fought to the death, and the remaining Asians fled, many being slain by the Milesians in the passes. Afterwards the Greeks buried their dead, the losses being heavy in the left-wing forces. They then collected their loot, burned the Persian ships and camp, and returned to Samos to make plans. The Persian threat to Greece was over.[58]

To Herodotus, the Persian defeat was due first and foremost to the gods, and most Greeks would have agreed. The gods favoured Greece due to Persian arrogance, recklessness, and destruction of cities and shrines, as well as Greek prayers, moderation, and superior understanding of, and obedience to, oracles and omens. The Greeks did enjoy good fortune, and being on the defensive they were not forced into reckless actions. Herodotus was also aware of the logistical and geographical difficulties faced by the Persians, as well as Greek superiority in close combat and fighting in formation. These the Greeks exploited as best they could, avoiding fighting on Persian terms. In its native environment, the Greek way of war was superior to the Persian.

As for Sparta's role, Herodotus argues that if the Athenians had submitted to Xerxes or fled abroad, the remaining Greeks would have been incapable of

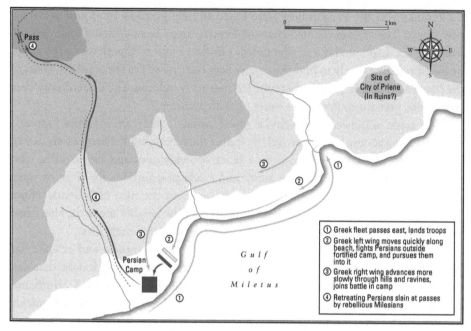

Map 4.2: The Battle of Mycale

resistance at sea. The Persian fleet would have bypassed the Isthmus Wall and subdued Sparta's allies. The Spartans, isolated, would have sought terms or gone down fighting.[59] This is surely true, but the historian then exaggerates by saying that Athens roused the free Greeks and held the decisive balance in the campaign. In fact, some cities rallied around Athens, but most clearly followed Sparta. Had Sparta yielded, most of the Peloponnesians probably would have done so also, leaving those who did fight with no leading power. It is only necessary to recall the fierce division between the Peloponnesians and Athenians in the fleet, and the role of Eurybiadas in holding them together, to realise what could have happened had Athens, Corinth, Aegina, and other cities tried to fight at sea without Sparta providing a commander. Even if they had won there, could they have destroyed a Persian occupying army alone, without the Spartans? In this war Athens and Sparta were 'yokefellows', as the Athenian general and politician Cimon later said, comparing them to two oxen pulling a load.[60] Neither could have pulled Greece through this great crisis without the other.

~ Five ~

MESSENIANS AND ATHENIANS, 479–431

Tensions with Athens, 479–464[1]

Sparta and Athens did not work together long. Indeed, after decades of sporadic hostilities the Spartans began full-scale war with Athens in 431. The Athenian historian Thucydides explains in detail the outbreak of that war, known to us as the Peloponnesian War, and provides detailed coverage of over two decades of its history. However, the period from 479 to 435 was not the main subject of his narrative, and his coverage is brief, meant to show that Athens' power and interference with Sparta's allies produced an irrational fear in the Spartans and caused the war.[2] Other sources provide information, but not much. Therefore, one cannot provide close analysis of Sparta at war during the *Pentēkontaëtia*, the 'fifty-year' span between the Persian and Peloponnesian Wars. However, a general outline of events is possible.

The Spartans and Athenians had united in defence against Persia, but this cooperation soon decayed. After Leotychidas returned home, the Athenians besieged Sestos on their own in winter 479/8,[3] and rebuilt their city walls in the same period despite Spartan urgings against it.[4] Pausanias led an allied fleet against Cyprus, conquering most of the island and establishing an eastern sea frontier, and then besieged and took Byzantium (modern Istanbul). Taking this and Sestos cut off the crossing-points into Europe.[5]

However, Pausanias made himself unpopular with the allies, Plutarch specifying that he treated the officers of the allied contingents 'with anger and harshness, and punished the masses with blows or forced them to stand all day holding an iron anchor. No one could get bedding or fodder or go down to a spring for water before the Spartiates, but servants bearing whips would drive away those who approached.'[6] He was also accused of treasonous communications with the enemy. Brought to trial in Sparta, he was acquitted on the major charges. When the Spartans sent another navarch, the Aegean Greeks rejected him and gave the naval command to the Athenians.[7] Thucydides says that the Spartans willingly let Athens take over the war with Persia,[8] a conflict Sparta had tried to avoid before 480. The first-century general historian Diodorus, however, claims that the Spartans considered war with Athens over the naval command, but were dissuaded by Hetoemaridas, a Heraclid and a member of the Gerousia.[9] Certainly they would have lacked a pretext to use to rally allied support against Athens.

Like his uncle Dorieus, Pausanias struck out on his own – going east in a private effort, ostensibly to continue fighting Persia – but was forced from Byzantium by Athens and recalled to Sparta, accused of intriguing with the Persians. Perhaps he hoped to unite Sparta and Persia against Athens. He escaped trial at first, but later was discovered conspiring with Persia and certain Helots against Sparta. He was starved to death in the temple where he had fled for sanctuary.[10] Meanwhile, Leotychidas had led an army into Thessaly against the Aleuads, the leading pro-Persian faction there. No doubt he was aided by their Thessalian enemies, since he would have needed their horsemen to help him campaign on Thessaly's plains in the face of the Aleuads' cavalry. However, Herodotus reports, 'even though it was possible to bring everything under his control, he took as a bribe a large amount of silver; caught in the act in camp, sitting on a sleeve filled with silver, he was brought before a court but fled from Sparta, and his house was razed. He fled to Tegea and ended his life there.'[11] He died in 469, to be succeeded by his grandson Archidamus, who ruled for forty-two years.[12] Leonidas' heir, Pleistarchus, was also still young, so Sparta now lacked royal leadership.

The Spartans could only watch while the Athenians won as allies most islands of the Aegean apart from Crete, along with the cities on its northern and western shores, as well as those on the Hellespont, Propontis, and Bosporus. Under Cimon, son of Miltiades, the Athenians and their allies captured enemy bases and cities and, in the early 460s, crushed a Persian army and fleet at the Eurymedon River in south-western Asia Minor. Assessed to provide ships or funds, most of Athens' allies preferred giving money and sparing their citizens constant military duty. The Athenians used the wealth to hire and train crews of their poorer citizens and foreign mercenaries, and sternly punished cities that failed to pay the tribute or tried to leave the alliance.[13]

Finally, in 465 the islanders of Thasos in the northern Aegean quarrelled with Athens over control of trading posts and a gold mine on the mainland. War broke out. Thucydides says that the Thasians, defeated and besieged, sent envoys to ask the Spartans to invade Attica. In secret, they agreed.[14] Reports of secret undertakings are suspect, but the Eurymedon victory would have made a Thasian appeal to Persia useless, leaving the Thasians nowhere to go but Sparta. Athenian oppression of fellow Greeks was a pretext the Spartans could advance to mobilise their allies – but they did not get the chance.

The Great Earthquake and the Helot Revolt, 464–455[15]

Thucydides says that before the Spartans could act, they 'were prevented by the earthquake that had happened, in which their Helots and, of the Perioecs, the Thuriatans and Aethaeans, seceded to Ithome'.[16] Thucydides calls it the 'Great Earthquake'. He says the Spartans viewed it as a punishment from Poseidon, god of earthquakes, for their forcibly removing and executing Helot suppliants at his sanctuary.[17] Diodorus and Plutarch provide lurid tales of over twenty thousand Lacedaemonians dying as house walls fell on them, of all but five homes in the city being destroyed, of numerous ephebes being killed by a collapsing portico, and of the Taÿgetus mountain range itself being rent asunder.[18] These late accounts may well exaggerate the extent of the losses and damage, but the earthquake was grave enough to seem a divine punishment to the Spartans themselves, and it ignited a major Helot revolt.

Diodorus, Plutarch, and Polyaenus, author of a second-century AD collection of stratagems, all say that Archidamus mustered the surviving Spartiates under arms at once. Diodorus and Plutarch have him doing so to fight Helot rebels, but Polyaenus says that he saw men trying to retrieve possessions from their ruined homes, so he had the trumpeter sound the call of an enemy attack to bring them out before further collapses occurred.[19] This account, less dramatic than the others, is for that reason more likely the truth. Archidamus did take command against the rebels, however.[20]

Thucydides says that 'most of the Helots were descendants of the old Messenians who had been enslaved; for which reason all were called Messenians'.[21] Since Thucydides is referring to the rebels, it seems Laconian Helots formed only a minority among them. Also taking part were the Perioecic towns of Thuria, overlooking the lower Pamisus valley, and Aethaea, the site of which is unknown. Their inhabitants would have wanted to take over Spartiate lands and lead liberated Messenia. The rebels won a striking victory, probably early in the revolt: Herodotus says Aeimnestus, who in his younger days had slain Mardonius at Plataea, 'commanding three hundred men joined in battle in Stenyclarus against all the Messenians, there being a war, and he and the three hundred perished'.[22]

Moreover, Corinth, Argos, and probably Elis used the distraction of the earthquake and revolt to attack pro-Spartan neighbours. Mycenae and Tiryns fell to Argos.[23] Sparta had to react. Herodotus notes that the seer Teisamenus won five 'great contests' for Sparta, 'one, and the first, that at Plataea, then the one coming about at Tegea against the Tegeans and Argives, after that the one in Dipaieis against all the Arcadians except the Mantineans, then in the one with the Messenians, that at the Isthmus [revised to 'before Ithome'], and finally the one occurring at Tanagra against the Athenians and the Argives'.[24] From the sequence one would think that the battles at Tegea and at the central Arcadian town of Dipaieis came before the Messenian revolt, and many scholars believe so. However, Isocrates speaks of 'those who contested at Dipaea against the Arcadians, of whom they say that, arrayed one shield deep, they raised a trophy over many myriads'.[25] That the entire Lacedaemonian army was only a line of *promachoi* is incredible, but the tale might have arisen because the Spartiates after their losses could form only the front rank of a Spartiate-Perioecic army. The Messenians had to refuse battle until they could acquire hoplite arms, which meant the Spartans could have tackled the Arcadians first. Even the battle at Tegea may have occurred after the earthquake. After all, any foe of Sparta must have hesitated to face the victors of Plataea before the Great Earthquake had weakened them.

Sparta was not friendless, however. Mantinea, always hostile to Tegea, stayed loyal to Sparta and aided it against the Messenians. So did Aegina, Plataea, and, ironically, Athens. Cimon reportedly led four thousand hoplites to Laconia soon after the earthquake.[26] Between this aid and their own efforts, the Spartans stabilised the situation in Messenia and defeated the Arcadians. Polyaenus reports how the Spartan commander Cleandridas conquered Tegea: 'Since the noblest Tegeans were suspected of being pro-Spartan, he rendered them more suspect by alone not ravaging their lands, while harming those of the others. Therefore the Tegeans, with great anger, put the men on trial for treason. Fearing the vote, they acted beforehand and betrayed the city, forced by fear to make the false charge true.'[27]

In 462, Cimon brought another army to help in the siege of the Helot rebels on Mount Ithome. The Spartans wanted the Athenians 'since they seemed able to fight at walls [*teichomachein*], the need for which was evident from the great length of the siege; for they should have captured the site by force', Thucydides says.[28] The Athenians had taken many fortified cities, including Sestos and Thasos, but by investment and blockade, not by storm, and a fortified mountain was a much harder target than a wooden fort in a Boeotian plain. The assaults failed, and the Spartans dismissed the Athenians, alone of the allies, saying only that they had no further need of them. Thucydides says that they suspected the Athenians might change sides, and no ancient author disagrees.[29] It is unlikely that anything other than massive suspicion would have caused the Spartans to single out the Athenians in such an insulting fashion, or shame Cimon, a friend of Sparta, in this way.[30]

Whatever the cause of their dismissal, the Athenians were enraged. They exiled Cimon and allied with Thessaly, Megara, and Argos. Sparta remained at war with Argos until 451, and the Messenian revolt continued until about 455. This dating is disputed, but Thucydides and Diodorus both report a ten-year struggle, and

Sparta's absence from most of the fighting with Athens in the 450s is explained by its preoccupation at home. Finally, obeying a Delphic Oracle, the Spartans allowed the surviving Messenians to leave the Peloponnese, on the terms that any who returned would be enslaved.[31]

The 'First Peloponnesian War', 460–445[32]

By about 460 Athens was engaged in war with Corinth, Aegina, and other cities in the northern Peloponnesian, this while still fighting Persia and aiding a revolt in Egypt. Argos and Athens are said to have defeated a Spartan army in a battle at Oenoa in the Argolid, perhaps in this era. Oenoa was a mountain village on the route between Argos and Mantinea, suggesting that the allies blocked an invading Spartan army on its march.[33] Herodotus mentions that the Spartiate Aneristus took the city of Halieis on the southernmost tip of the Argolic Acte 'by sailing into port with a merchant ship filled with men'.[34] Otherwise we know nothing of Spartan warfare in this theatre.

In about 457, the Spartans were drawn north when the Phocians invaded Doris. 'The Lacedaemonians brought aid to the Dorians with 1,500 hoplites of their own and 10,000 of their allies, led by Nicomedes son of Cleombrotus on behalf of King Pleistoanax, the son of Pausanias, who was still a youth, and compelling the Phocians to yield the city by agreement they began their return homeward,' Thucydides reports.[35] Pleistarchus had passed away in 458, leaving the Agiad kingship to Pausanias' son. Archidamus presumably stayed at home with the rest of the army to guard against the Argives and Messenians. Doris was the Dorians' legendary motherland, and gave Sparta its only voice in the religious league that controlled Delphi, so the Spartans' willingness to send forces into central Greece was understandable even in the current circumstances.

Since the Athenians were heavily engaged in Egypt and in the siege of Aegina, any effort by them to prevent Nicomedes' return home must have seemed unlikely. But word reached him in Boeotia that an Athenian fleet operating out of the Megarian port of Pegae in the Corinthian Gulf blocked the sea route home, while the land route was blocked by a force occupying the pass over Mount Geraneia between Corinth and Megara, held to prevent invasions from the Peloponnese. He halted to consider his next move. Thucydides also mentions a report from the period that a faction within Athens conspired with the Spartans to overthrow the democracy and prevent completion of the 'Long Walls'. These were walls six kilometres long, linking Athens to Phalerum and the Piraeus, the latter having been completed after the Persian invasion. Once finished, the Long Walls would prevent blockade by land of Athens and allow the countryside to be abandoned in event of invasion, a response dreaded by the land-owning Athenian aristocracy. Also, Diodorus states that the Thebans offered to take the Athenian war off Sparta's hands if their city was fortified and they were given control of Boeotia. He sets it after the battle, but it would explain why the fight occurred at Tanagra, twenty kilometres east of Thebes, if the Spartan army went there to bring the city over to the Theban side.

In any case, the Athenians gathered fourteen thousand men, including their entire citizen levy, contingents from their allies, a thousand Argives, and cavalry from Thessaly. They went against the Spartans at Tanagra. Diodorus reports that they fought two battles – the first ended by nightfall, the second by defection of the Thessalians to the Spartans. Although considered a Spartan victory – Teisamenus' last as seer – losses on both sides were heavy. An inscription shows that at least four hundred of the Argives perished. Thucydides says that the Spartans and their allies then entered the territory of Megara, devastated it by cutting down fruit trees, and retreated over Geraneia and the Isthmus of Corinth. The Athenians marched north on the sixty-second day following Tanagra, won a battle at Oenophyta, and conquered Boeotia, Phocis, and eastern Locris.[36] The Spartan army was saved, but the Athenians were stronger than ever before.

Soon after this, the Athenians sailed around the Peloponnese, Tolmides son of Tolmaeus being in command, and burned the dockyards of the Lacedaemonians, took Chalcis, a city of the Corinthians in south-western Aetolia, 'and defeated the Sicyonians in a battle during a landing on their territory', or so says Thucydides.[37] Diodorus and Pausanias make grander claims, having him take Boeae in south-eastern Laconia, Cythera, and Methone in south-western Messenia, as well as burning the dockyards at Gytheum on the coast south of Sparta, and then go on to win over the Ionian Sea islands of Zacynthus and Cephallenia and capture Naupactus, at the narrow entrance of the Gulf of Corinth. The Athenians certainly did take Naupactus – a fine base for a fleet seeking to control the entrance to the Corinthian Gulf – at some point before 455, when they settled the rebel Messenians there following their departure under truce from Ithome. Later Athenian operations in the Corinthian Gulf saw a fleet under Pericles, son of Xanthippus, raiding Sicyon and unsuccessfully besieging Oeniadae on the coast of Acarnania, the mainland region south of the Gulf of Arta. Pericles had the aid of the Achaeans, the people of the northern coastal region of the Peloponnese, whom Tolmides may have won over earlier.[38]

During the Egyptian revolt, Xerxes' successor Artaxerxes sent an envoy named Megabazus to induce the Spartans to invade Attica in the hope of causing the Athenians to depart Egypt, but Thucydides says that the money he had brought was spent in vain.[39] As long as Geraneia was occupied by Athens, invasion was unlikely. In 454 the Persians finally overcame the Athenian fleet in Egypt, raising concerns that they might again invade Greece. The Athenians and Peloponnesians reached a five-year truce, while Sparta and Argos made a 'Thirty Years' Peace' treaty in 451. Cimon, back from exile, led an expedition to Cyprus, where he died, and Athens and Persia made peace in 449.[40]

The Spartans did march into central Greece during the five-year truce, ejecting the Phocians from the sanctuary at Delphi, which they had seized, and returning it to the Delphians. After their departure, however, the Athenians took Delphi and restored it to the Phocians. Athens' era of power in central Greece ended in 447, when a revolt in Boeotia saw an Athenian army defeated at Coronea, with many men taken prisoner. The Athenians abandoned Boeotia in order to gain the return of their men.

Soon afterwards, in 446, Euboea rebelled. Just as Pericles crossed to the island with an army, the Megarians also rebelled, destroying the Athenian garrison with aid from Corinth, Sicyon, and Epidaurus, a Dorian city on the northern coast of the Argolic Acte. With Geraneia open, Attica now faced invasion, forcing Pericles' immediate return. Thucydides says that: 'After this, advancing into Attica as far as Eleusis and Thria the Peloponnesians ravaged the land, Pleistoanax son of Pausanias King of the Lacedaemonians being in command; but without going on further they left for home.'[41] He later reports that both Pleistoanax and his adviser Cleandridas fled into exile afterwards, Pleistoanax living at the Arcadian mountain sanctuary of Zeus Lycaeus from fear of the Spartans, who accused him of taking bribes to withdraw from Attica.

Pericles now returned to conquer Euboea. However, Attica remained vulnerable, and not long after these events, in 445, Athens agreed to its own 'Thirty Years' Peace' with Sparta and its allies. The Athenians withdrew from those Peloponnesian cities they held: the Megarian ports of Pegae and Nisaea, Troezen in the Argolic Acte, and the cities of Achaea. Archidamus, a guest-friend of Pericles, probably helped negotiate the peace. He had taken no part in the campaigns against Athens, and hostility to Athens had been an Agiad policy, not a Eurypontid one. Whatever hopes the king had for the agreement, however, proved to be in vain.[42]

The Thirty Years' Peace and the Outbreak of War, 445–431 [43]

The fragility of the peace showed itself as early as 440. Athens intervened in the government of Samos, only to cause a revolt that invited Persian involvement. The Samians appealed to Sparta. Historic ties between Spartan and Samian aristocrats, along with Samos' possession of a strong fleet, an expectation of Persian aid, and the concurrent revolt of Byzantium – which could interdict Athens' vital imports of grain from the Black Sea region – caused the Spartans to bring the question to a vote among the allies. The proposal failed, chiefly due to Corinth's opposition, and the matter was dropped. That it even came up for a vote

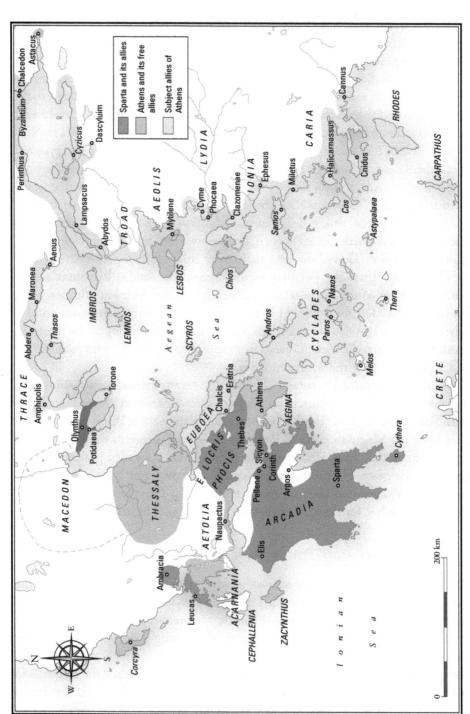

Map 5.1: The Peloponnesian League and Athenian Empire, 431

shows that the Spartans had considered breaking the peace. Athens subsequently defeated Samos and recovered Byzantium.[44]

In 433 Athens intervened to protect Corcyra (modern Corfu) from invasion by its mother city and old enemy, Corinth. With Corinth now hostile, the Athenians thought to prevent the possible revolt of Potidaea, the Corinthian colony on the isthmus of Pallene in the Thracian Chalcidice, by razing one of its walls. However, Potidaean and Corinthian envoys went to Sparta and received from the authorities there – presumably the ephors and Gerousia – a promise that the Spartans would invade Attica if Athens attacked Potidaea.[45] The outcome of the fighting in the 450s had shown that Corinth and its allies could not hope to defeat Athens by themselves, so they must have sought, and received, a promise of Spartan aid.

The Potidaeans therefore rebelled, allying with the Chalcidians and Bottiaeans, local Greek peoples, and with Perdiccas, King of Macedon. The Athenians overcame the rebels at Potidaea and laid siege to the city. Envoys from Corinth descended on Sparta to demand action. The Megarians and Aeginetans also sent envoys. The Megarians, engaged in a border dispute with Athens, had been denied access to ports and markets in its empire. The Aeginetans, Athenian subjects since the 450s, were distressed by their lack of autonomy. The Spartans heard them, deliberated, and voted that Athens was injuring their allies and had broken the peace. They sought a prophecy from Delphi, received Apollo's blessing, and summoned the allies to an assembly to secure a united war effort. At the assembly the Corinthians lobbied the allies heavily, and most delegates voted for war. Only at this point did the Spartans seek negotiations, but the Athenians refused to yield anything under pressure, although they did propose arbitration. The Spartans sent one last embassy late in 432 to tell the Athenians that 'the Lacedaemonians want there to be peace, which there shall be, if you leave the Hellenes autonomous,' Thucydides says.[46] Of course the Athenians refused to abandon their imperial rule, so it would be war.[47]

The Spartan and allied votes for war were not acts of desperation. The Spartan hoplite army remained the best in Greece, and every people in the Peloponnese except the Argives and Achaeans were Sparta's allies. In fact, Pellene in Achaea was an ally, and the rest of the Achaeans joined soon after the war began. Outside of the Peloponnese, Megara, all the Boeotians save Plataea, the Phocians, the Eastern Locrians, and Corinth's colonies of Ambracia, Leucas, and Anactorium were Spartan allies. Corinth, Megara, Sicyon, Pellene, Elis, Ambracia, and Leucas provided ships, and more were expected from the Dorian Greek cities of Sicily and Italy. The Boeotians, Phocians, and Locrians provided cavalry, and everyone provided hoplites. An ancient estimate placed their first invasion army at sixty thousand hoplites. This is an exaggeration, but perhaps near the total levy if one includes overage and underage reservists.[48]

This powerful army would invade and ravage Attica. Thucydides has Archidamus, who opposed the war, admit that 'perhaps one might be emboldened by the fact that we surpass them in arms and numbers, so that we may constantly come to ravage their land', and has Pericles admit that, 'in a single battle, the Peloponnesians and their allies are able to oppose all the Hellenes.'[49] Most Spartans, he adds, believed 'that they would eliminate the power of the Athenians within a few years, if they should ravage their land', and claims that in the Greek world in general, 'at the beginning of the war some thought [the Athenians] would hold out one year, some two years, some three years, but no one any longer, if the Peloponnesians should invade their country.'[50] Given the size of the massed levy of the Spartans and their allies, with its hoplites, free *psiloi*, and servants, it was reasonable to expect that a major invasion by the Spartans and their allies would inflict serious damage in Attica.

The use of ravaging is rarely attested before the Peloponnesian War, but it was known.[51] The Spartans destroyed crops or trees at Eleusis, Sepeia, Thebes, Tegea, and the Megarid, as we have seen. Most Greeks worked on the land and feared attacks on their farms, crops, and animals, so we cannot be surprised that they put great faith in the tactic. This was why Greeks and Persians had requested Spartan invasions of Attica.

Not everyone agreed, of course. In the speech that Thucydides gives him at Sparta in 432,[52] King Archidamus argued that ravaging would merely enrage the Athenians. They would exploit land in their empire and import by sea whatever they needed. Alternative strategies, he noted, were faulty as well. Sparta and its allies lacked funds, warships, and skilled crews, all necessary for supporting revolts among Athens' overseas allies, severing its lines of supply, and defeating its fleets. Archidamus urged them to develop their native resources and seek allies with ships and money – even the Persians. Hold Attica hostage by threatening ravaging, he urged, and negotiate while preparing for war. The strategic analyses and proposals attributed to him are quite credible for someone familiar with the events of the past fifty years and intent upon preventing or delaying military operations. With Pleistoanax in exile, Archidamus would command the massed levies of the Spartans and their allies in the invasions of Attica. The king did not want to fight a war he did not believe he could win. Overruled, he found himself doing just that, and being proven prescient.

~ Six ~

Defeat and Disgrace, 431–421

Archidamus' War, 431–428[1]

For the first twenty and a half years of the Peloponnesian War, the primary source for events – often the sole source – is the history of Thucydides. Fortunately, Thucydides, an Athenian commander in the war, was a careful, critical researcher whose analytical abilities command respect even today. His condensed and difficult Greek, as well as his biases, omissions, and obscuring of his sources, all offer problems for modern understanding of his work. Even so, his account seems in the main to be reliable, and it certainly provides remarkable insights.

In spring 431, a two-thirds levy of the forces of the Spartans and their allies from inside and outside of the Peloponnese mustered at the Isthmus of Corinth. Their supreme commander was King Archidamus of Sparta, whose mission was to invade Attica. The king, as we have seen, had expressed strong doubts that invasions would prove effective, but having been handed the task, he made the best of it. He started by sending an emissary to Athens while his army was mobilising at the Isthmus of Corinth. The Athenians, busily evacuating their countryside, sent his man away unheard. Nevertheless, on entering Attica the king halted at Oenoe, a fort on Attica's north-western frontier, and assaulted it unsuccessfully. It was said that he hoped the Athenians might still decide to negotiate, now that war was upon them. He may have had other motives, as we shall see. Whatever his motives, the Athenians sent no envoys, and Archidamus finally abandoned the siege and moved on.[2]

After ravaging the plains of Eleusis and Thria, the king then marched to the district of Acharnae, several kilometres north of Athens. Thucydides says 'he hoped the Athenians, at the peak of their youthful manpower and prepared for war as never before, might perhaps come out against him and not allow their land to be ravaged',[3] and that the numerous Acharnians, whose homes and farms he was ravaging, would force a battle, or if not, that they would oppose fighting to defend others' property when he neared Athens itself. We shall see that undertaking ravaging or other operations near a walled city was risky, since the garrison could surprise portions of the attacking army in sudden sorties. Scholars often write that Archidamus' invasion was expected to cause a battle, and that this was how the Spartans and their allies expected to win the war. But Greeks seldom sought battle against the odds. Indeed, the king is depicted before the invasion seeking to persuade his officers that the Athenians might fight despite being outnumbered.[4] The Acharnae stratagem was Archidamus' own, an attempt to exploit the Athenians' aggressiveness and anger. Had he brought a smaller army, he might have had his battle, but it is unlikely that a fight at narrow odds would have proven decisive.

In the event, Pericles maintained order and, with some difficulty, kept the angry Athenians from seeking battle. He had made his own estates public property, to prevent Archidamus using their ancestral guest-friendship as an excuse to spare them. It is clear Pericles knew of Cleandridas' stratagem at Tegea, and expected the king to use ravaging as a political weapon, to cause him to be resented and suspected by his fellow Athenians. Pericles also sent out Athenian and Thessalian cavalry to harass the invaders, but the Boeotians' cavalry protected the army, which ravaged some north-eastern districts before leaving Attica and heading home.[5]

In 430 Archidamus invaded again, and this time ravaged all of Attica, including the city plain. After expending his supplies he departed some forty days later, the longest invasion during this period of the war:[6] the armies' militia character and the problems of feeding so many men kept the invasions short. However, during the second invasion, a plague out of Africa reached the Aegean and Attica, killing or crippling thousands of the Athenians crowded inside the fortifications. With trade halted due to the war, the plague scarcely entered the Peloponnese. During winter 430/29 the Athenians, facing the combined pressure of war and plague, deposed Pericles and sent envoys to Sparta to seek terms. Receiving none they could accept, they reinstated Pericles, who died in 429. They also dispatched a squadron around to Naupactus to guard the Corinthian Gulf.[7]

In 429 Archidamus marched against Plataea, not Athens. Thucydides does not explain the king's motives. Both Plataea and Oenoe, attacked in 431, lay close to the main route between Megara and Boeotia. Their garrisons could not block an army's movement, but could ambush smaller groups, launch raids, and aid a major Athenian invasion – something the Boeotians feared.[8] With the aid of traitors, the Thebans had tried to seize Plataea in 431 before Archidamus even marched, but they lost over three hundred men, most killed after surrendering.[9] The Thebans wanted vengeance, and Sparta wanted to please these important allies.[10] Retaliation for the fall of Potidaea the previous winter perhaps was intended as well, and Archidamus may also have wanted to avoid entering Attica while the plague raged, or wished to let the Athenians rebuild before ravaging again. Since Pausanias and the Greeks swore after the 479 battle to protect Plataea, the king offered the Plataeans generous terms, perhaps hoping to split them from Athens. The Plataeans were tempted, but finally had to refuse, for the Athenians vetoed any agreement."

Plataea lay on a large sloping plateau projecting northwards from Mount Cithaeron. Protected on three sides by steep slopes or a depression, it could be approached from level ground only on the south-east and south, so its garrison of four hundred Plataeans and eighty Athenians could concentrate their efforts there. The king had the city surrounded with a palisade to prevent escapes, but did not make an immediate assault. In 431 he had tried to take Oenoe 'with machines and in every other way', Thucydides says,[12] experimenting unsuccessfully with storming tactics and siege engines. Here Archidamus ordered his men to raise a siege mound, as this seemed the best way to employ the labour of so great an army. Men cut timber on Cithaeron and laid it crosswise on either side of the mound to contain the earth, and then threw on wood, stones, dirt, and anything else that would add to its height. They worked in shifts, with some carrying earth while others slept or ate, and Spartan *xenagoi*, first mentioned here, kept the men at their tasks. The texts of Thucydides say that they worked continuously for seventy days and nights, but this figure is surprisingly large and probably became corrupt over the centuries of re-copying manuscripts.

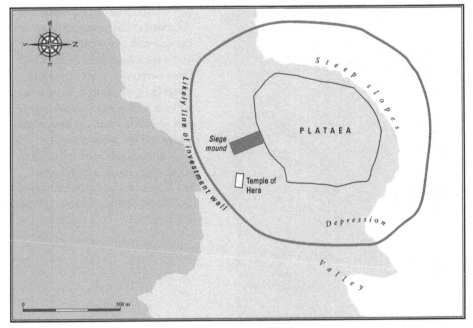

Map 6.1: The Siege of Plataea

The defenders reacted by increasing the height of the wall opposite the mound. They took bricks from nearby houses and placed them in a timber framework covered by skins and hides to shield it from fire arrows. Next, they dug through their own wall and began removing dirt from the mound. When the besiegers realised what was happening, they threw into the open space between the mound and the wall clay packed into reed mats, to keep it from scattering and being carried off easily. The besieged then tunnelled out from the city under the mound and again began to draw away earth. For a long time they escaped the notice of the besiegers, who made less progress than expected, since the mound, being sapped from below, continuously settled into the hollow space beneath.

The defenders also began constructing an inner, crescent-shaped wall behind the threatened part of the circuit wall, to force the enemy to build a second mound if the first succeeded. In response, the Spartans and their allies now brought up siege engines against the city, with one, which was taken up the mound itself, shaking down much of the raised wall structure. The machines clearly were battering rams, likely protected from missiles by 'tortoises', movable wooden sheds. But machines had failed at Oenoe, and did so here as well. The defenders threw nooses over

5. A bronze head of a battering ram dedicated at Olympia, and dated to the mid-fifth century by the style of the ram's head decorations. Only some twenty-five centimetres high, it was likely meant to be elevated to strike at a mudbrick (adobe) upper wall and battlements. Its long central wedge and five heavy triangular teeth on each side seem suited to cut through mudbrick. (*Olympia inv. B 2360, photograph by Herrmann, D-DAI-ATH-Olympia 2760. All rights reserved*)

the ramheads and pulled them up, a mode of defence found on an Assyrian relief (*Plate 15*), or broke them off by dropping upon them a great beam, to which chains were attached so that it could be drawn up for another attack. They were probably relatively small devices, meant to attack mudbrick (adobe) upper walls or wooden gates (*Figure 5*).

Seeing that the machines were ineffective and the counter-wall was keeping up with the mound, the besiegers began preparing to blockade the site. Before doing so, however, they threw brushwood into the space between the wall and the mound, and then threw more behind the now-shattered brick and wood structure atop the circuit wall, as far as they could reach. They then threw sulphur and pitch on the wood and set it aflame, hoping to incinerate the town. The fire grew so great that the defenders could not approach it. Had the wind begun blowing toward the city, as the attackers hoped, it would have been destroyed. Instead, a heavy thunder shower reportedly arose and quenched the flames.[13]

The besiegers abandoned direct attacks and surrounded the city with an elaborate double siege wall, facing both inwards and outwards, leaving behind a strong garrison – half Boeotian, half Peloponnesian, and likely manned by shifts of levies. Yet, during winter 428/7 over half of the Plataeans and Athenians escaped to Athens in a well-planned and daring surprise night action. In summer 427, renewed assaults caused the starving survivors to surrender. To appease the powerful Thebans, the Spartans executed all the captives after a *pro forma* trial.[14]

This effort was an unusual one for Greek city-state armies. As we have seen, they were willing to attempt simple assaults by storm or surprise. The Athenians had the funds and manpower to invest a site with a wall and starve it out by a passive blockade. Active siege warfare was rare, however, since it required resources, discipline, organisation, and engineering skills – things Greek militia armies usually lacked. Yet the basic technical skills did exist in Greece, for in peacetime *mēchanopoioi*, 'machine-builders', built cranes, stage machinery, and the like, and in wartime could turn their skills to creating siege engines. Archidamus presumably had some at Plataea. His use of a mound suggests Near Eastern influence, for there construction of siege mounds had been honed to a science in the Bronze Age, and used with great success by the Persians.

Archidamus had besieged Ithome, so he had reason for interest in these methods. However, his army lacked the suppressive missile fire which the Persians' archers furnished in their sieges, so his men could not hinder the defenders' counter-measures. His rams were easily caught or broken. Defending against Persian assaults may have given the Athenians insight into defeating siege mounds, and in any case the defenders demonstrated more energy and creativity than the attackers, whose inexperience is evident. If Archidamus had planned to use active siege methods to assault the Athens–Long Walls–Piraeus complex, or at least threaten to do so in the hope of bringing the war to a favourable close, the failure of his experiments at Oenoe and Plataea would have ended any such thoughts. No other Spartan leaders showed a similar interest in this form of warfare.[15]

In 428 Archidamus led one more invasion of Attica; he died the following year. Other invasions were performed or attempted in 427, 426, and 425, but increasingly as diversions for other operations.[16] Although the damage seemed bad at the time, Athenian agriculture survived. Wheat and barley, perennial crops, were planted anew if destroyed by fire or trampling. Vines could be cut or trampled, but were thickly planted and hard to destroy. Olive trees, the core of Athenian agriculture, were famously tough and resilient. Mansions aside, farm buildings were simple and easy to rebuild, while most gear, people, and herds were evacuated in the face of invasion. Except where fire could be used, all damage required difficult, labour-intensive effort. Anywhere the army itself went would suffer, but other areas could be ravaged only by sending out bands of *psiloi*, who risked being attacked by Athenian cavalry. Also, once the army left, the Athenians could return to their countryside, to make whatever use of it they could.[17] Invasion and ravaging therefore proved unable to achieve the results the Spartans and their supporters had expected before the war.

As the king had warned, moreover, the Athenians had much land in their empire. In 431 they expelled the Aeginetans for their role in causing the war, resettling the island themselves. In winter 430/29 the Potidaeans, starved into surrender, were expelled, a thousand Athenians resettling the city. The Athenians retaliated against Megara by twice-yearly invasions and ravaging. This did not bring the Megarians to heel, but certainly injured them. The invasions of Attica had proven worse than useless for these peoples.[18]

Failures at Sea and Abroad, 431–426[19]

In 431 and 430 Pericles sent large fleets against the Peloponnese, to retaliate for the invasions of Attica. They ravaged coastal districts and assaulted cities, failing to take Methone in south-western Messenia in 431, but sacking Prasiae on Laconia's eastern coast in 430.[20] Pericles claimed before the war that the raids would injure the Peloponnesians badly, but they proved relatively ineffective. This was not for lack of manpower – fleets of 150 triremes meant thirty thousand soldiers and sailors – but the crews and troops could not go far inland, and the fleets could only attack where they could anchor. Even so, the raids prompted counteroffensives against Athenian allies in north-western Greece, who provided bases and aided the raiders: Corcyra, the Ionian Sea isles of Zacynthus and Cephallenia, the mainland coastal regions of Acarnania and Amphilochian Argos, and Naupactus on the Gulf of Corinth.[21]

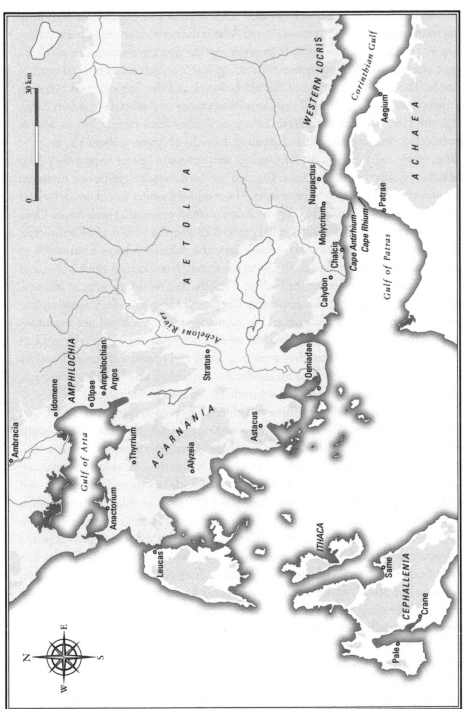

Map 6.2: North-western Greece

In winter 431/30 the Corinthians sailed to Acarnania and Cephallenia with forty ships, recovering a town in Acarnania lost to Athens the previous summer, but suffering defeat in a Cephallenian ambush. In summer 430 the Spartan navarch Cnemus led a fleet of one hundred Peloponnesian triremes against Zacynthus and ravaged most of its lands. The islanders would not submit, however, and the fleet returned home. In the same summer, the people of the Corinthian colony of Ambracia (modern Arta), across the Gulf of Arta from Acarnania, joined allies from nearby Epirus against Amphilochia, ravaging the land and assailing the walls of Argos, without success.[22]

In summer 429, however, the Ambraciots sent envoys to Sparta to propose a joint expedition against the Acarnanians. The plan was for Cnemus to bring one thousand Peloponnesian hoplites as reinforcements. The combined armies would invade by land while a fleet raided the coast, to keep the Acarnanians from uniting their forces. Once the Acarnanians yielded, the allies could proceed against Zacynthus and Cephallenia, and even perhaps Naupactus. This would deny the Athenians bases from which to operate against the Peloponnese. The Spartans agreed, sent Cnemus and his men, and had their allies ready a fleet in the Gulf of Corinth. At first things went as planned, with the fleet threatening the coast and Cnemus leading the allied army against Stratus, the largest city in Acarnania. He meant to storm it if it did not surrender. However, the Epirotes advanced while the others encamped, hoping to take and loot Stratus by themselves. Instead they were ambushed and routed with heavy losses by the Stratians, whose slingers then harassed the unsupported allied hoplites, for rough, backward Acarnania produced good skirmishers. Cnemus had to retreat.[23]

Meanwhile forty-seven Corinthian and allied ships passed Naupactus and Capes Rhium and Antirhium (Rio and Andirio), entering the Gulf of Patras. They thought the twenty triremes that Athens had sent to Naupactus the previous winter would not dare to attack so many warships. However, the daring Athenian commander, Phormio, did follow them, even at night. Loaded with troops and equipment and therefore unable to escape, the Peloponnesians formed a circular formation, with five triremes inside to attack any vessel that penetrated it. Tactics on these lines had worked well at Artemisium, but after fifty years of naval warfare the Athenians had the lightness and speed of the Phoenicians, the good order of the league Greeks, and a level of experience and confidence all their own. They circled around the formation in a single line ahead, daring the enemy to break ranks and attack, and gradually compressed the circle tighter. As they had expected, at dawn the usual strong breeze arose from the gulf, throwing the circular formation into confusion. The Athenians attacked, rammed and took twelve ships and their crews, and chased the rest to Patrae and Dyme in Achaea.[24]

Unable to fathom how their fleet could have been so badly defeated, the Spartans sent Cnemus, a group of counsellors, and additional allied ships to join the survivors. All went to Cyllene in Elis, which had a shipyard for repairs. Phormio sent for help. Athens dispatched a relief fleet, but sent it first to Crete, where bad weather delayed it. Phormio was unwilling to remain on the defensive and lose the moral advantage he had gained, so he anchored off Cape Antirhium, supported by the army of the Messenians of Naupactus. The Peloponnesian fleet of seventy-seven ships, also supported by a land army, deployed at Cape Rhium. After several days of practice, the Peloponnesians set forth, but against the unguarded city of Naupactus rather than Phormio, who was forced to put to sea and sail east along the coast, the Messenians following on land. Seeing his ships in single file near the shore, the Peloponnesians turned and attacked, as planned, forcing nine Athenian ships ashore. One was taken with all its crew, while the Messenian hoplites came to defend the other eight.

The rest of the Athenians fled for Naupactus, pursued by the fastest twenty enemy ships. The rearmost Athenian trireme, passing a merchantman anchored in the harbour, swung around it and surprising the lead pursuer, a Leucadian ship, rammed and sank it. On board the Leucadian was Timocrates, a Spartiate, who committed suicide, presumably to avoid the shame of capture. The startled Peloponnesian ships halted – a bad mistake in the circumstances – and some ran aground in the shallows. The Athenians cheered, charged, and routed the enemy, taking six ships and recovering all but one of their own triremes. After this fiasco, and with the relief fleet finally approaching, the Peloponnesians returned home.[25]

Cnemus and his men, returning from Rhium, were persuaded by the Megarians to attempt a raid on the Piraeus with vessels from Nisaea, Megara's Saronic Gulf port. Had it succeeded, it might have reversed the moral results of the defeats and injured Athenian naval power. But the raiders turned aside and attacked Salamis instead, causing a brief panic in Athens but having no significant impact upon the war.[26]

The battles off the capes set the tone for Peloponnesian naval efforts. In summer 428, the oligarchs ruling Mytilene, the leading city of the island of Lesbos, sought to get the entire island under their control and rebel against Athens. The Athenians responded by sending a fleet, which blockaded the city. The Mytileneans asked the Spartans and their allies to attack Attica by land and sea in the autumn, arguing that the Athenians were badly weakened by expenditures and the plague. The Spartans were enthusiastic, but the other allies had already participated in Archidamus' spring invasion and now were busy harvesting. In a show of strength the Athenians sent one hundred triremes against the Peloponnese. The invasion was cancelled, and the Athenians subsequently sent troops to blockade Mytilene by land. In spring 427 the Spartans did invade Attica, hoping to distract the Athenians while forty ships under the navarch Alcidas sailed east. He reached Ionia undetected by the Athenians, but on learning that Mytilene had just fallen, he rejected advice to surprise the enemy there or incite other revolts in Ionia, quickly returning to the Peloponnese instead. Thucydides considered this a glaring example of the Spartans' lack of enterprise, which he thought cost them many opportunities to injure Athens during the entire war.[27]

Once back, Alcidas was reinforced to fifty-three ships, and Spartan counsellors came to stiffen his spine. He then went against Corcyra, which had fallen into civil strife between pro-Athenian democrats and oligarchs suborned to the Peloponnesian side while in captivity in Corinth after the 433 fighting. Facing sixty Corcyraean and twelve Athenian ships, Alcidas won a tactical victory because the Corcyraeans fought among themselves, freeing him to concentrate on forcing back the Athenians. However, an Athenian fleet arrived soon after, and the Peloponnesians fled by night. Corcyra's democratic faction slaughtered any oligarchs who had not fled.[28]

Thucydides uses Mytilene and Corcyra as paradigms for revolts against Athens and for the civil strife that the war encouraged in Greece, because oligarchs could seek Spartan and allied aid, while democrats could appeal to Athens. Because most of Athens' subjects were located on islands or on coasts whose hinterlands were held by Thracian tribesmen or Persian satraps (regional governors), they were easily isolated by Athens' sea power and reduced by blockade, since the Athenians' wealth allowed them to maintain blockading forces as long as necessary. The Spartans and their allies proved unable in this decade to deploy fleets large enough or skilled enough to break these blockades or incite new revolts.

In 426 an Athenian blunder created great possibilities for Sparta in the north-west. An allied expedition led by the Athenian general Demosthenes had suffered a defeat in the highlands of Aetolia, the region neighbouring Naupactus. Living in scattered villages, the Aetolians were skilled skirmishers rather than hoplites, and on their home terrain they tore apart the largely hoplite invading army.[29] The Messenians suffered heavy losses, and the Aetolians sent envoys to Sparta to report this, and to propose a joint campaign against Naupactus. The Spartans agreed, and sent three thousand allied hoplites under the command of the Spartiate Eurylochus in autumn 426. They marched through western Locris towards Naupactus, Eurylochus using threats to win over most of these Locrians, Athenian allies, and taking by force three settlements that resisted. The Aetolians joined him, and together they ravaged Naupactus' lands and took its unfortified suburbs. However, rather than attempt to storm Naupactus' extensive and weakly garrisoned walls, he moved against Molycrium, a nearby Corinthian colony allied to Athens, and captured it. The delay, which Thucydides fails to explain, saved Naupactus. Demosthenes persuaded the Acarnanians to reinforce the city with a thousand hoplites. Seeing them on the battlements, Eurylochus withdrew.[30]

The Ambraciots then persuaded Eurylochus to assist in a campaign against the Amphilochians and Acarnanians. In winter 426/5 he slipped past the Acarnanians to join the main Ambraciot army at Olpae, a coastal stronghold in Amphilochian territory. The Acarnanians and Amphilochians massed against them, and were joined by Demosthenes with two hundred Messenian hoplites and sixty Athenian archers, while twenty Athenian warships arrived as well. The two armies encamped near one another, separated by a streambed, and sat quietly for five days, deploying for battle on the sixth. Both armies' western flanks were against the coast. In the east, since the defenders were outnumbered, Demosthenes set an ambush force of some four hundred Acarnanian hoplites and light troops in a sunken road overgrown with bushes. He had the right wing, with the Messenians and a few Athenians, and faced Eurylochus and his best soldiers, stationed on that army's left. When battle was joined, the ambushing force fell upon the enemy's rear and cut down Eurylochus and his followers, causing those deployed next to them to rout.

The Ambraciots on his right won their fight, but found themselves trapped. They barely escaped to Olpae. There they were blockaded by land and sea, along with many Peloponnesians. Eurylochus and his second-in-command, Macarius, had perished, so his third-in-command, Menedaïus, took over and sought a truce. The Acarnanian generals and Demosthenes persuaded him to escape with only the Peloponnesians, abandoning the Ambraciots. He agreed, but his attempt to slip away quietly became a general flight, in which pursuing Acarnanians killed Peloponnesians and Ambraciots alike.

Meanwhile Ambraciot reserve forces, summoned before the battle, came to Idomene in the hills north of Olpae. Ignorant of the battle, they encamped. Alerted to the Ambraciots' movements by a messenger, Demosthenes and his forces attacked their camp by surprise at dawn. Many Ambraciots perished immediately, and the Amphilochians hunted down most of the rest in the hills. Ambracia had suffered a disaster comparable to Argos' at Sepeia. Corinth had to send a garrison to help hold the city.[31]

During these years no strategy pursued by the Spartans and their allies succeeded. In 431 they had decided to amass a fleet of five hundred triremes to match the reserves possessed by Athens and its naval allies. They counted on getting funds and ships from the Dorian cities in southern Italy and Sicily, many with strong ties to Corinth. The small sizes of the Peloponnesian fleets deployed show that little aid actually came.[32] In 427 the Dorian cities in the west went to war with the Ionian Greek cities there. The Athenians sent squadrons to aid the Ionians, and the fighting continued into 424. No help came from Sicily.[33]

Peloponnesian envoys also went repeatedly to barbarian powers, especially the Persians, who at least could have financed Peloponnesian naval efforts. They accomplished nothing. The Persians would have wanted to regain control of the Greeks of Asia Minor in return for their aid. As the self-proclaimed liberators of Greece, the Spartans could not have agreed to this openly, and were in no position to offer it in any case.[34]

In 426, the Spartans responded to a request for aid from the people of Trachis and Doris by founding a pan-Hellenic colony at Heraclea, north of Thermopylae. It was a good base for a fleet to raid Athenian-held Euboea or for land expeditions to Thrace's coastal districts. However, harassment of the Spartan colony by the Thessalians, whose domination of the region it threatened, and the harsh and sometimes unjust administration of its Spartan governors, caused its eventual depopulation. Heraclea never achieved its potential.[35]

For five decades most Spartans, and most Greeks, had believed that Athens could be defeated by the classic Spartan way of war: mobilise the levies in the spring or in between the summer festivals, march into enemy territory and ravage it, and defeat in pitched battle the enemy if they dared come out of their fortifications to fight. This doctrine had worked well against other Peloponnesians, most of whom lived by agriculture and concentrated on hoplite warfare. The limits of this way of war, evident already in the Spartan expedition against Polycrates, showed themselves clearly when faced by Athenian resources and determination. In five years of war the Athenians had seen Attica ravaged repeatedly, had spent money and lost men, but still held most of their empire. Plague, not Spartan arms, had punished them most. Some of Sparta's allies, by contrast, had suffered severely, as had the coastal regions of Lacedaemon itself. Nevertheless, as 425 began, Sparta still had the initiative, and Athens remained on the strategic defensive. Shortly, and abruptly, that would change, and the Spartans would find themselves hard-pressed to escape the war they had sought.

Pylos and Sphacteria, 425[36]

In 426, five hundred oligarchic exiles from Corcyra seized forts on the mainland opposite the island. Their raids proved so effective that a famine arose among the islanders. They then crossed to the island and continued their depredations from Mount Istone north of the city.[37] In spring 425, sixty ships under the navarch Thrasymelidas sailed against the beleaguered island, while King Agis, Archidamus' eldest son, led a very early invasion of Attica in order to distract the Athenians.[38]

The Athenians meanwhile sent forty ships around the Peloponnese, with orders to aid the Corcyraeans before going on to Sicily to join the war there. While on the coast of Laconia, the Athenian generals learned of the Spartan expedition to Corcyra, and wished to sail there at once. Also present, however, was Demosthenes, who had persuaded the Athenians to let him use the fleet while it sailed around the Peloponnese, keeping his intentions secret – a necessity given the lack of security inherent in the open planning discussions in Athens' Assembly.[39] Only when the fleet anchored in the Bay of Navarino on the western coast of Messenia did he reveal that he wished to fortify the headland at the northern end of the bay, called Pylos by Athenians, Coryphasium by Spartans. The other commanders refused, stressing the need to relieve Corcyra and the fort's expense.

Up until this point in the war only exiles had used *epiteichismata*, owing to the expense of maintaining garrisons, the difficulty of defending exposed forts, and the wish to avoid retaliation in kind.[40] No doubt inspired by the example of the Corcyraean oligarchs, Demosthenes wanted one built here, saying that the Messenians of Naupactus would hold it, sparing Athens the expense. He believed that their raids would prove destructive, given their familiarity with the region and their Dorian dialect. The generals refused, but delays caused by adverse winds gave Demosthenes the chance to bypass them by winning over to his plan the ordinary Athenian sailors. They built the fort's rough stone walls in six days without tools, using mud for mortar. When the fleet headed north, Demosthenes stayed behind with a garrison of five triremes and their crews.[41]

Thucydides says that the Spartans at home were holding a festival (the Hyacinthia?). Surprised by the unexpected seizure of Pylos, they did not act at first, seeing the fort as likely to be abandoned or easily captured once they marched. However, when they reported the occupation of Pylos to their army and to the fleet at Corcyra, the army returned home, and the fleet headed south, slipping past the Athenians. The Spartiates and those Perioecs living nearest to Pylos went there at once, the others arriving more slowly, and the fleet also finally reached the bay.

The Spartans planned an assault by land and sea, thinking that a fort so ill-garrisoned and crudely built would fall quickly.[42] Demosthenes responded by sending two ships to bring back the Athenian fleet, and arming the crews of the rest with makeshift wickerwork shields. Two Messenian raiding galleys also arrived on the scene, providing additional arms and forty hoplites.[43] A steep hill dominated the headland, needing defences only at the northern and southern ends. The Athenians had built a high wall in the south-eastern sector to protect the ships beached there and prevent movement along the hill's edge. South of the headland and separated from it by a narrow strait was an island, Sphacteria (Sphagia). The island, lying across the mouth of the Bay of Navarino, was some four and a half kilometres in length, uninhabited, and covered with thick brush. A small rough fort lay atop Mount Elias at its northern end.[44]

Demosthenes stationed the majority of his troops on the landward fortifications of Pylos, but took sixty hoplites and a few archers down to the sea to those few places

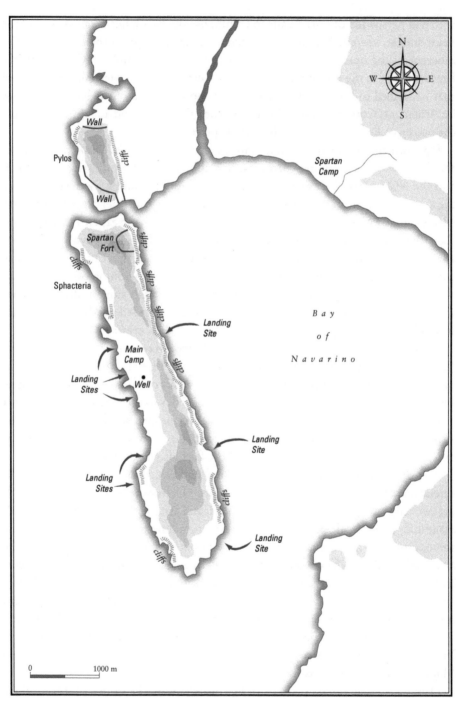

Map 6.3: Pylos and Sphacteria

where ships could land troops. There he and his men fought off determined assaults for a day and a half. On the third day the Spartans sent vessels to Asine to get wood for siege engines, hoping to take the south-eastern wall.[45] Before they returned, the Athenian fleet arrived, reinforced to forty triremes. On the morning after its arrival it entered the bay from both north and south, routing the Peloponnesians, capturing five ships and crippling the rest.[46]

The Athenians then began a patrol around the island. To prevent Sphacteria being used as a base by the Athenian fleet, the Spartans had garrisoned it by sending over in relays men chosen by lot. Now 420 Spartan hoplites and their Helot servants were cut off there.[47] Thucydides says that the Spartans had planned to block both entrances into the bay if Pylos had not fallen by the time the Athenian fleet arrived, in order to avoid a naval battle while maintaining the blockade of the fort. Given the kilometre-plus width of the southern entrance, and the lack of shipping and equipment for closing it, such a plan would not seem practical. Errors in Thucydides' text about the sizes of the island and the southern entrance suggest that he may have been deliberately misinformed by a Spartan source who sought to excuse the error of leaving the men there.[48] One thing is certain: the Spartans could have withdrawn their garrison on the night that the Athenian fleet arrived. Instead they chose to offer naval battle and leave their men on the island. This rash action was uncharacteristic of the cautious Spartans. It probably resulted from their apprehension of the strategic threat posed by the Pylos fort and their frustration after six fruitless years of warfare.

The magistrates came from Sparta to assess the situation. Considering a rescue too risky, and afraid the men on the island would be overwhelmed or starved out, they made a truce with the Athenians, handing over their own ships until it ended. During the truce the men on the island were to receive rations and Spartan envoys would be taken to and from Athens on Athenian ships. At Athens, the envoys offered peace in return for the trapped men, some of whom were prominent Spartiates. Thucydides, who stressed (if not exaggerated) the role of chance in these events, seems to have felt that the Athenians should have accepted the offer. However, guided by Cleon, an aggressive leader who had gained prominence after Pericles' death, the Athenians responded by demanding the return of cities lost as a result of the Thirty Years' Peace – something the Spartans could hardly have arranged. The envoys returned empty-handed, and the truce ended.[49]

Claiming truce violations, the Athenians refused to return the surrendered ships, and resumed their blockade. Now reinforced to seventy triremes, the Athenian fleet suffered from inadequate water sources and anchorage space, as well as difficulty in obtaining supplies. The Spartans offered rewards, including freedom for Helots, to those who would bring food to the island, and individuals did so at night, by boat or by swimming and towing food-filled skins. Fearing winter might force abandonment of the blockade, or that the Spartans might escape by boat, the Athenians voted to send a force to Sphacteria, led by Cleon, with Demosthenes as his colleague.[50] Demosthenes had already begun preparations for an attack, inspired by a massive brushfire ignited by the cooking fires of a crew that had landed on a promontory of the island to eat. Now movement over the island would be easier and safer for the Athenians, who had feared being surprised and cut apart by a small, hidden force familiar with the terrain. Deprived of cover, the Spartans' numbers and locations were visible.[51]

After demanding the garrison's surrender without success, the Athenians struck. Most of the Spartans were encamped in the level terrain in the centre of the island, near the water supply. Thirty men held a guard post a kilometre to the south, and in the north a section manned the Mount Elias fort. Shortly before dawn eight hundred Athenian hoplites landed on both sides of the island and advanced at a run against the guard post, surprising and slaying the men there. At dawn the Athenians landed a second wave, composed of Messenians and light-armed troops, including eight hundred archers and eight hundred peltasts – light-armed javelin-throwers who bore the Thracian *pelta* shield. This would be a common mercenary armament in times to come (*Plates* 12, 13). The largest body, some eight thousand men, comprised two-thirds of the crews of seventy triremes. Armed with stones and organised into ad hoc bands of two hundred *psiloi*, they and the other light-armed men surrounded the Spartan main body.

In response, the Spartans formed up and advanced against the Athenian hoplites, who outnumbered them two to one. However, the hoplites stood quietly while the light-armed men attacked the Spartans' flanks and rear with missiles. The Spartans would charge against the skirmishers and get them to turn and run. This tactic, called *ekdromē* ('running out'), was performed by the younger hoplites of a Spartan force.[52] But the rough, uncultivated terrain made it easy for the *psiloi* to avoid the hoplites, who had no cavalry or light troops to send off in pursuit. The Spartans presently became exhausted, and unable to rush out promptly when attacked. Seeing this, the skirmishers, dejected at first at having to face Spartans, grew confident and attacked in a body, hurling stones and javelins, and shooting arrows. Attacked from all sides, struck wherever their shields failed to give cover, poorly protected otherwise against missiles, blinded by clouds of dust rising from the burned brush, and unable to hear orders over the attackers' shouts, the Spartans were helpless.

At last, with many wounded, the Spartans massed and headed north to the Mount Elias fort, hotly pursued by the Athenian light-armed. The majority of the Spartans reached it, and held out for most of the day against the frontal assaults of the Athenians. The eastern side of Elias is a forbidding cliff facing the sea, while the northern and western sides are steep, the best approach being from the south. Finally Comon, general of the Messenians, persuaded Demosthenes and Cleon to give him some bowmen and light-armed men, so that he could try attacking the enemy from the rear. Starting out of sight of the Spartans, he and his men worked their way along the precipitous eastern coast of the island and climbed to the unguarded high ground to the rear of the enemy position. The Athenians attacking from the front saw it, and were greatly encouraged. The Spartans were stunned. Caught between two forces, the exhausted, waterless, and badly outnumbered Spartans now began giving way. They survived only because the Athenian generals wanted them as prisoners and halted the assault. When the Athenian herald proclaimed the generals' surrender offer, most of the soldiers lowered their shields and lifted up their hands in agreement. Cleon and Demosthenes spoke with Styphon, the third-in-command, for Epitadas, the commander, was dead, and the second-in-command had been left for dead. They arranged for heralds to communicate with the mainland. The officials there avoided any responsibility: 'The Lacedaemonians bid you yourselves deliberate about yourselves, but do nothing shameful.'[53] After further discussion among their ranks, the 292 survivors surrendered, and were taken by Cleon to Athens. The bronze facing of one of their shields, displayed in the Athenian marketplace as a trophy, has been found (*Figures 6, 7*).[54]

Nothing in the war, Thucydides says, surprised Greeks everywhere as much as the surrender on Sphacteria, 'for they did not expect the Lacedaemonians to hand over their arms due to hunger or any necessity, but to keep them and die fighting as best they were able.'[55] There had been evidence for more than a century to support that belief. Now, however, of the 420 hoplites that had crossed to the island, 'living there were carried away eight fewer than three hundred,' as Thucydides acidly notes, 'and the Spartiates among them were, of those living, about one hundred and twenty.'[56] The 'about' (*peri*) may reflect Athenian uncertainty about the status of some of the prisoners, who may have been 'inferiors' of various kinds. The majority of the prisoners will have been Perioecs, who were not reared in the Lycurgan system. Their willingness to surrender in these circumstances is quite understandable. Their desire to capitulate doubtless made it easier for the surviving Spartiates to agree.

Another factor in the surrender appears in an exchange Thucydides reports:

> And when later one of the Athenian allies by way of an insult asked one of the prisoners from the island if those who died were *kaloi k'agathoi*, he answered him 'the spindle [meaning the arrow] would be worth much if it could discern the *agathoi*', showing that it was those chancing to be hit who were destroyed by the stones and bow shots.[57]

The phrase *kaloi k'agathoi*, literally 'fine and good', referred to Greek elites like the Peers. *Agathoi* also had the meaning of 'brave men'. The questioner was asking if

6 and 7. The bronze face of a Spartan shield captured in the Pylos and Sphacteria fighting of 425 and displayed at the Stoa Poikile in Athens. Slightly oval in shape
(95 x 83 centimetres), it had elaborate guilloche ornamentation on the rim, and was inscribed 'Athenians from Lacedaemonians out of Pylos.' (*Photo [6] and sketch [7] of the 'Brasidas Shield' [B262]. American School of Classical Studies at Athens: Agora Excavations*)

the prisoners were cowards. The laconic reply denied the manliness of the means of attack, and implied that it made courageous resistance pointless.

Thucydides in one passage compares the situation on Sphacteria to that at Thermopylae,[58] but it is the differences that are illuminating. The men on Sphacteria were randomly chosen, not picked, and more than half were non-Spartiates. They were attacked in an unexpected manner, struck down from a distance seemingly at random, and unable to strike back at their tormentors. Helpless, despairing, suffering, and trapped, they were given the opportunity to surrender to Greeks who would spare their lives and, once peace came, free them. Small wonder the two battles differed so starkly in their outcomes.

After Pylos and Sphacteria Athens gained and Sparta lost in both initiative and morale. As Demosthenes had expected, the Messenians garrisoned Pylos and launched damaging raids into Spartan territory. Helots began deserting, and the Spartiates feared another revolt. The Athenians threatened to kill the prisoners from Sphacteria if Attica was again invaded, preventing Sparta from pressuring Athens by this means. The Spartans kept sending embassies to seek for peace and the return of Pylos and the prisoners, but the Athenians kept increasing their demands, so nothing resulted.[59] In the meantime the Athenians launched a major descent upon Corinth, built an *epiteichisma* at Methana in the Argolic Acte to harass Sparta's allies thereabouts, and helped the Corcyraeans destroy the oligarchs and their fort.[60]

Brasidas' Gamble, 424–422[61]

In summer 424, the Athenians increased their pressure on Sparta by sending a major expedition under the command of Nicias, one of their more successful generals. He quickly seized the port of Scandea on Cythera, defeated the Cytherans in battle, and obtained the surrender of the island with the aid of a subversive faction among its Perioecs. Knowing what was coming next, the Spartans scattered small garrisons throughout their coastal regions, raised a body of four hundred cavalry and archers, 'contrary to custom', as Thucydides says, and stood on the defensive. The shocking defeats, rapid enemy actions, and fear of a Helot revolt combined to paralyse the Spartans. Nicias struck at Asine, Helos, and most other coastal districts for seven days. Only once did a garrison attack his light-armed ravagers, with little effect. After devastating part of the district of Epidaurus Limera on the east coast, Nicias ended his operations by capturing the town of Thyrea after overrunning an unfinished coastal fort. The Spartiate governor of Thyrea was added to the captives of Sphacteria, but the town's inhabitants, Aeginetans who had settled there after being expelled from Aegina in 431, were executed.[62]

Although the raiding continued and Helots deserted to Pylos, the Helot revolt the Spartans feared did not take place.[63] One reason for this may have been that the Spartiates took effective countermeasures. Thucydides says that the Helots were once invited to choose from among themselves those who had most distinguished themselves in the wars, so that they might be freed. Some two thousand were chosen, and went round the temples as freed men, but soon afterwards the Spartans quietly executed them, so that none knew how they had perished. This eliminated the most high-spirited Helots. Scholars disagree on whether or not to believe the story.[64] It seems doubtful that so many men could have been disposed of in such secrecy at this time, given the decline in Spartiate numbers. It may have been an atrocity story developed by the Messenians of Naupactus to affect

Spartan recruitment of Helot soldiers, for in 424 the Spartans raised a force of seven hundred Helot hoplites, offering them freedom if they served abroad. As we shall see, they not only performed capably, but the survivors returned to Lacedaemon afterwards, and were not done away with mysteriously. Sparta thereafter raised thousands of *neodamodeis*, 'new populace', freed Helot hoplites. This took some Helots out of Lacedaemon, and held out the hope of freedom to others – which probably did more than massacres to reduce the chances of revolt.

However, the most important reason that no revolt occurred was the difference between the situation in the 460s and the 420s. The Spartans saw the Great Earthquake as Poseidon's punishment for violating his sanctuary, and no doubt the Helots of the era agreed, since they seized this apparently heaven-sent opportunity to revolt. By contrast, in the 420s the Spartans had suffered an embarrassing and disturbing defeat, but they had not been crushed. The Athenians and the Messenians at Pylos did not make themselves masters of the country, but raided it instead, attacking Helot-worked farms and flocks. This was unlikely to have endeared them to the Helots. We shall see that many Helots subsequently volunteered to aid Sparta when Laconia was invaded after Leuctra, probably to protect their homes and livelihoods. The raiding, therefore, proved counterproductive.

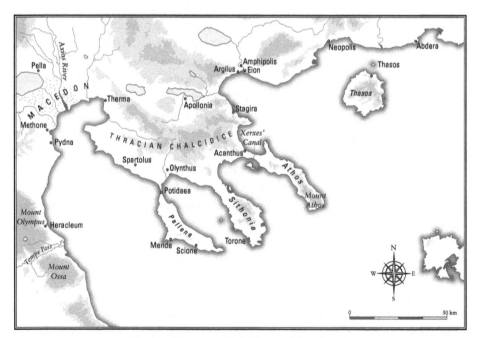

Map 6.4: Thracian Chalcidice and Amphipolis

Although no revolt occurred, the Spartans remained nervous. They needed to find a way to recover their men and end the war before 421, when the Thirty Years' Peace with Argos expired. When envoys from Perdiccas of Macedon and the Chalcidians of Olynthus, which Athens had failed to suppress after taking Potidaea, came to seek aid, the Spartans saw an opportunity to strike back.[65] They turned to their most gallant and daring officer, Brasidas. Son of the diplomat Tellis,[66] Brasidas became prominent in 431, when he rescued Perioecic Methone from an Athenian assault by charging with one hundred men directly through the surprised attackers to reinforce the hard-pressed defenders. This exploit won him the first official vote of thanks to a Spartan officer in this war, as well as election to the ephorate for the year 431/430. In 429 he was one of the counsellors sent to Cnemus before the second Rhium battle, and in 427 he counselled Alcidas in the Corcyra expedition. Commanding a trireme at Pylos in 425, he ran his warship aground attempting to force a landing against Demosthenes' shoreline defence. He suffered several wounds trying to get ashore, and lost consciousness. His shield fell into the sea and became part of the trophy that the Athenians erected at the site of their victory.[67]

The Spartans gave Brasidas no citizen troops, instead raising the seven hundred Helot hoplites just mentioned, and having him hire one thousand Peloponnesian mercenaries.[68] In the meantime, the Athenians were planning to restore their strong defensive position of the 450s by taking Megara and Boeotia. Brasidas was mobilising his army at the Isthmus of Corinth when the enemy moved against Megara. Aided by a democratic faction there, the Athenians took by surprise and treachery the long walls from Megara to its Saronic Gulf port of Nisaea, which fell in turn after a short blockade. However, opponents of the democrats prevented them from betraying Megara itself.

At this juncture Brasidas arrived with his own men as well as Corinthians and other Peloponnesians. Boeotian infantry and cavalry also joined him. It happened that his forces outnumbered those of the Athenians, who withdrew after an indecisive cavalry battle. Nisaea was lost but the city of Megara was secured. Brasidas presently went north with his 1,700 hoplites.[69] By speed, deceit, and the assistance of pro-Spartan locals, he crossed Athenian-aligned Thessaly in two days and reached Macedon in the autumn of 424.[70]

Avoiding an attempt by Perdiccas to use his army against foes in upper Macedon, Brasidas joined the Chalcidians and moved against Acanthus (modern Ierissos) on the south-eastern coast of the Chalcidice, as a pro-Spartan faction there had summoned him. He addressed the citizenry, falsely claiming to have the army that had faced down the Athenians at Megara. He vowed to respect the Acanthians' autonomy, urged them to help liberate themselves and Greece from Athens, and made veiled threats of what their grape harvest would suffer if they refused. The

Acanthians, moved by his eloquence, his supporters in the city, and their fears for their vines, voted to revolt. Soon after, Stagirus on the coast to the north joined.[71] The revolt of Acanthus first demonstrated the combination of internal subversion and armed suasion by a Spartan or allied general that became typical of most future revolts by Athens' subjects.

In winter 424/3 the Athenian effort to conquer Boeotia ended in a staggering defeat at Delium, with one thousand Athenian hoplites and many *psiloi* being slain. Plague and strategic dispersal had reduced the Athenian hoplite forces to parity with those of the Boeotians. The battle saw the Thebans fight in a column twenty-five men deep. Also, if Diodorus is correct, the front rank of the entire Boeotian army consisted of a picked body of three hundred hoplites called 'charioteers and sidemen'.[72] Deep columns and picked bands of 150 pairs of fighters were to play major roles in future Boeotian warfare. Stunned by this defeat, the Athenians responded feebly to Brasidas' operations.

Brasidas used the opportunity to target the Athenian colony of Amphipolis. Situated on a hill in a great bend of the Strymon River, Amphipolis provided ship timber and revenue to Athens, and controlled the lower crossings of the Strymon, preventing movement to eastern Thrace. At the river mouth to the south-east lay Eion, a commercial port, while to the south-west across the Strymon was the city of Argilus.[73] The founding of Amphipolis had injured the interests of the Argilians, many of whom now lived in the colony. Once Brasidas arrived, they lost no time plotting to revolt.[74] The plot went undetected by Eucles, Athens' governor at Amphipolis, or by the commander of the small patrol squadron based there, a prominent local magnate, none other than the historian Thucydides. Alas for them both, foreknowledge was the only real defence against betrayal.[75]

Waiting until Thucydides went on patrol, Brasidas led his men on a stormy winter night to Argilus, which promptly rebelled. Before dawn he arrived at the bridge across the Strymon north-west of Amphipolis, took it by betrayal and surprise, and crossed the river, seizing many of the citizens who lived outside the walls. Since he expected the conspirators to open the gates, he did not attack, and let his army plunder. However, Eucles and the Athenian loyalists secured the gates and sent for help to Thucydides, then at Thasos, half a day's sail away. Hoping to take Amphipolis before Thucydides could arrive to stiffen its resistance, Brasidas proclaimed that, if the city yielded, any inhabitant could depart with his property within five days, or remain there in safety, enjoying full rights, even if he was an Athenian. Few were Athenians, while many had relatives in Brasidas' hands and found his generous terms reassuring. The conspirators began to argue openly for surrender, and the city soon capitulated. Eucles evacuated with other Athenians. Thucydides reached Eion that same night, received the refugees, and held Eion against Brasidas' sudden assault by land and river. After losing Amphipolis, however, he went into exile for twenty years, probably after facing trial for treason and negligence.[76] The Athenians were notoriously hard on their defeated commanders.

Thereafter Brasidas won over Thracian tribes and Greek cities near Amphipolis and on the Chalcidice's Athos Peninsula, ravaging the lands of those cities on Athos which refused to submit.[77] He then captured Torone on the central peninsula, Sithonia, by a combination of surprise, betrayal, suasion, and assault.[78] Everywhere his personality, diplomacy, and record of success, combined with Athens' evident weakness, encouraged men to plot revolts.[79] Brasidas sent urgently to Sparta for reinforcements, but instead the Spartans arranged a one-year truce with Athens in spring 423. They wanted the prisoners back and the war ended, as we have seen, and their leading men were jealous of Brasidas, the *only* successful Spartan commander in the war.[80]

Nevertheless, on Pallene, the western peninsula, Scione rebelled before word of the truce reached the north, and Mende rebelled afterwards.[81] Brasidas received both as allies, accusing the Athenians of violating the truce. He could not aid the cities by land because Potidaea, occupying the neck of Pallene, had been resettled by Athenians, although even there a group reportedly conspired to betray the site to him.[82] Brasidas evacuated women and children from Mende and Scione and sent five hundred Peloponnesian hoplites and three hundred Chalcidian peltasts as a garrison under his subordinate Polydamidas. The Athenians prepared an expedition under Nicias to retake the cities.[83]

That summer, Brasidas campaigned with Perdiccas against Lyncestis, a district in upper Macedon. When Perdiccas' Illyrian allies turned on him, the king and his people fled, leaving Brasidas to make a fighting retreat with his three thousand Peloponnesian and allied hoplites and some Chalcidian cavalry. He deployed his hoplites in a large square formation, stationed the mob of *psiloi* inside it, and prepared to use the *ekdromē* tactic seen at Sphacteria, ordering the youngest hoplites to charge out against the light-armed enemy whenever they attacked. He himself led three hundred picked men in a rearguard. The initial attacks were repelled, so the enemy bypassed the Greeks to harass the fleeing Macedonians, and then sought to cut off Brasidas from the pass that led to Perdiccas' territory. But Brasidas sent his picked men in a charge, taking one of the hills covering the pass, and the enemy gave way. Enraged at having been abandoned, Brasidas' soldiers pillaged Macedonian property on the retreat. Infuriated by the plundering, Perdiccas went over to Athens.[84] He later used his influence in Thessaly to block some reinforcements that were finally being sent from Sparta. Only their commander and a number of younger Spartiates arrived; they were placed in command of garrisoned cities. Another reinforcement attempt in 422 was aborted by Thessalian opposition.[85]

On his return to the Chalcidice, Brasidas found that Mende's citizens had mutinied against Polydamidas when he used violence on a seditious inhabitant, and that the Athenians had recovered the city.[86] The surviving Peloponnesians managed to escape a blockade of the citadel and reach Scione, which was already coming under siege.[87] Hoping to relieve them, Brasidas attempted a surprise night assault on Potidaea, but a guard discovered his first ladder against the wall before anyone could climb it, foiling the attempt.[88]

At the end of the truce in spring 422, Cleon arrived in the north with twelve hundred Athenian hoplites, three hundred cavalry, many allies, and thirty ships. Adding men taken from the besiegers of Scione, Cleon sailed against Torone and took it by storm before Brasidas could intervene. The city's wall had been extended to include the suburbs, making it difficult for the Spartan governor, Pasitelidas, and his troops to hold it against Cleon's assault. Worse, they were unable to respond when an Athenian squadron entered the harbour and seized its defences.[89] Cleon then sailed to Eion and, after assaulting two local towns and taking one, he camped and made plans to storm Amphipolis with the aid of Perdiccas and friendly Thracians.[90]

Brasidas went to aid Amphipolis with two thousand hoplites, three hundred Greek cavalry, and fifteen hundred Greek and Thracian peltasts; he also summoned more Thracian allies. Cleon marched eventually to Amphipolis to reconnoitre the terrain, posting his army on a strong hill in front of the town. Seeing this, Brasidas led his army across the river into the city. Feeling unable to match Cleon's army in a pitched battle, he decided to attack it by surprise. He would lead 150 picked hoplites in a sudden charge against the enemy's centre, after which Clearidas, governor of Amphipolis, would bring out the rest of the army and fall upon the surprised and panicking Athenians. When Cleon learned that the enemy was massing at the city gates, he gave orders to sound the retreat. When his left wing proved too slow in moving off, he ordered those on the right wing to turn in place, exposing their unshielded sides to the city. No doubt he expected Brasidas to deploy for a normal phalanx battle, and expected to depart before he could do so.

His expectations were disappointed, fatally. Brasidas and his picked men suddenly charged out of the gates and up the hill against the Athenian centre, routing it; Clearidas followed with the rest. The Athenian left wing, most likely allied units, was already heading south – it simply fled. Attacked on both sides, the right wing held out against two or three onsets by Brasidas and Clearidas, but fled after being surrounded by the cavalry and peltasts. Cleon and some six hundred Athenians perished, but only seven attackers. Among them was Brasidas. Mortally wounded, he lived long enough to learn of his victory.[91]

The deaths of Brasidas and Cleon removed those leaders most opposed to making peace. Stimulated by a Spartan threat to build an *epiteichisma* in Attica, the Athenians, led by Nicias, reached the so-called 'Peace of Nicias' with Sparta in spring 421.[92] It ended the first period of the Peloponnesian War, a little more than ten years after Archidamus first invaded Attica.[93] Ironically, the Athenians would name this the 'Archidamian War' after his invasions, even though Archidamus had argued against the war.

Combined with the Boeotian victory at Delium, Brasidas' campaign had allowed Sparta to rid itself of the Archidamian War. It also showed the possibilities for raising revolts among Athens' subject allies, and for using freed Helots, mercenaries, and local allies under Spartiate command on extended expeditions abroad. However, Brasidas had shown too much independence of the home authorities, and too much concern for his own glory. He had succeeded in breaking the bonds of Lycurgan Sparta, and created a precedent that other Spartiates would follow. His campaign had also shown that it was difficult to aid an expedition by land even in the most accessible region of Athens' empire. As long as Athens preserved its naval power, its rule would remain strong. Athens had suffered in the Archidamian War, but it had survived, as had its might at sea. Sparta had not come close to cracking it, and now would have to fight merely to regain its position in the Peloponnese. And yet, less than nine years after swearing the oaths of the Peace of Nicias, the Spartans would be again at war with Athens and on the offensive both on land and sea.

~ Seven ~

TURN OF THE TIDE, 421–413

Trouble in the Peloponnese, 421–418[1]

The Peace of Nicias left Sparta facing several threats in the Peloponnese. The Thirty Years' Peace with Argos would soon expire. The Argives refused to make another treaty unless they received the Thyreatis. Yielding it would have been shameful and an admission of weakness. To avoid having both Argos and Athens as threats, the Spartans made a 'Fifty Years' Alliance' with Athens after concluding the Peace of Nicias. In it each agreed to treat as an enemy any state that invaded the other's territory, and the Athenians swore to aid Sparta in the event of a Helot revolt.[2] This secured the return of those taken on Sphacteria. The Spartiates among them were barred from office or from buying and selling anything, in effect being reduced to the status of young men in their twenties. Thucydides says this was done more as a security measure than as a punishment, apparently to satisfy the need to take some action, while limiting its effects and the potential for serious conspiracy. In time their rights were restored. Harassment of isolated 'tremblers' such as Aristodemus was one thing, punishing so many well-connected Spartiates quite another.[3]

In the summer of 421, King Pleistoanax led a Spartan army into south-western Arcadia, intervening in civil strife among the Parrhasians, who lived west of the Alpheius River. They had become subjects of the Mantineans during the waning years of the Archidamian War, when Mantinea had taken advantage of Spartan distraction to start building its own mini-empire. Mantinea was now aligned with Argos.[4] Pleistoanax, exiled in 446, had been restored in 427 with Delphi's help. He had spent his exile at the sanctuary of Zeus at Mount Lycaeus in Parrhasia, so he was familiar with people in the region, and could aid any pro-Spartan factions there. He used ravaging to help gain control of the Parrhasian cities, and dismantled a Mantinean fort meant to threaten the Sciritis. The Mantineans and Argives reacted too late to affect his operations.[5]

A year later, the Spartans settled at Lepreum the freed Helot hoplites, both the so-called 'Brasideans' who had served with Brasidas and the recently raised *neodamodeis.* Located just beyond the northern border of Messenia, Lepreum had been a tribute-paying ally of Elis, but recently it had won Spartan support, probably due to Spartan concerns for security along the border.[6] The Eleans tried to pressure Sparta into abandoning Lepreum by banning Spartans from Olympia and its festival games of 420. They claimed Sparta had attacked an Elean fort and sent 1,000 hoplites into Lepreum during the Olympic truce. The Spartans neither yielded Lepreum nor acted against Elis, observing the truce instead. Not even the Eleans' punishment of Lichas, a wealthy Spartiate who went to Olympia secretly and whose team, run as Boeotian, won a chariot race, caused the Spartans to take action, although they never forgot the affront.[7]

Meanwhile, the Peace of Nicias gradually disintegrated. Unhappy with the peace, the Corinthians attempted to form a third axis of alliances around Argos. Mantinea and Elis allied with the Argives, as did the Chalcidians of Thrace. However, oligarchic Megara and Boeotia disdained democratic Argos and rejected alliance. With their refusal, the Corinthians also lost their zeal and abated their efforts. A dizzying series of negotiations and conspiracies followed from late 421 into spring 420, in which ephors belonging to a pro-war faction at Sparta sought to subvert the policy of peace with Athens. Sparta regained the Boeotians as allies, and almost negotiated a peace treaty with Argos – one that provided either side with the right to demand a new champions' battle for the Thyreatis, an Argive proposal that the Spartans thought foolish but agreed to anyway.[8] However, Sparta had proven unable to return Amphipolis to Athens or to meet other conditions of the peace. The angry Athenians held on to Pylos. In 420 Alcibiades, a charismatic young Athenian politician, led the formation of a defensive alliance between Athens and Argos, Mantinea, and Elis, ending the Argives' tentative peace negotiations with Sparta. Corinth, hostile to Athens, backed away from Argos. Neither Athens nor Sparta openly abandoned the Peace of Nicias, but the new battle lines were now drawn.[9] In summer 419, Alcibiades led a small Athenian army through the northern Peloponnese, attempting to create an Athenian presence there.[10]

In the same summer the Argives went to war with Epidaurus, the Dorian city on the north coast of the Argolic Acte. They did so in part to awe Corinth into inaction, and in part to make it easier for Athenian troops to reach Argos, for if Epidaurus became available, they could cross the Saronic Gulf by sea and march overland, avoiding the need to sail around the Acte. The Spartans responded by going in full force to the border with western Arcadia, but King Agis' border-crossing sacrifices proved unfavourable, and he dismissed the army until after the Carnea, a festival that all Dorians celebrated. However, the Argives craftily delayed the start of the festival month by adjusting their calendar, and ravaged Epidaurian territory. Epidaurus' allies, Sparta included, kept the original timing of the festival and sent no aid. Hoping to win over Corinth, Argos and its allies halted their invasion, but when negotiations proved fruitless they invaded again. When the month had passed, the Spartans marched north to Caryae, but again the border sacrifices proved unfavourable, and Agis disbanded his expedition. The importance of religion in Greek warfare, and the potential for its manipulation, could not be clearer.[11]

In winter 419/18, the Spartans succeeded in sending a garrison of three hundred men by sea to Epidaurus, eluding Athenian vigilance in the Saronic Gulf. The Argives complained to the Athenians, who in turn announced that the Spartans had violated the Peace of Nicias. They returned the Messenians and Helots to Pylos; they had been withdrawn to prevent raiding after the Peace began. This will have forced Sparta to garrison the vicinity of Pylos and the coasts of Lacedaemon against raiders. The northern borders already had to be garrisoned, as we have seen. Meanwhile forays and ambushes occurred in Epidaurus' countryside, and the Argives made an unsuccessful attempt to storm the town itself.[12]

Deciding that matters had deteriorated too far, in mid-summer 418 the Spartans went against Argos in full force, evidently waiting until the grain harvest had been gathered. Thucydides says the Helots were also mobilised fully, but he must have meant the hoplite freedmen, since Agis' army moved freely, not hindered by a vast mob of slaves. Sparta's northern allies, including Corinth, Boeotia, Megara, Sicyon, Epidaurus, and Pallene in Achaea, also sent forces. These mustered at Phlius north-west of Argos. Phlius provided its total levy, while the rest sent picked men, notably two thousand Corinthian hoplites and five thousand Boeotian hoplites, five hundred cavalry and five hundred hamippoi ('with horses'), light troops trained to operate with cavalry. The Argives mobilised in full force, perhaps seven thousand hoplites, and were joined by three thousand Elean hoplites and, Diodorus reports, a little fewer than three thousand Mantinean hoplites. The Athenians and their cavalry had not yet arrived.[13]

Finding themselves in a difficult situation, the Argives and their allies sought to take advantage of the separation of the Spartans from their northern allies by advancing on Agis and the Spartan army, which they encountered at Methydrium in central Arcadia, west of Mantinea across Mount Maenalium. Agis had been proceeding through western Arcadia, presumably gathering Spartan allies there and seeking to avoid contact until he reached Phlius. Each army deployed on a hill, and the Argives prepared to fight on the following day. However, Agis led his army off by night, and soon reached Phlius.

The Argives and their allies returned to Argos and then headed north to Nemea, where they hoped to block the invasion route of an army now twice as large as theirs. However, Agis led his Spartans and Arcadians along a difficult alternate route through the mountains to the Argive plain, sent the Corinthians, Pellenians, and Phliasians in over another steep mountain route, and ordered the Boeotians, Megarians, and Sicyonians to advance on Nemea and send their cavalry against the rear of the Argive army if it left to intercept the king's other columns.[14]

Agis' division of his forces nearly proved fatal. The Argives and their allies did head south from Nemea, first pushing back the Corinthians, Pellenians, and Phliasians, and then catching Agis' column with its back to the city of Argos. Both sides formed for battle. The Spartans were outnumbered, threatened by the prospect of an attack on their rear from the city, and faced a body of one thousand picked hoplites that the Argives had been training in an effort to match the Spartans' quality. However, Sparta's northern allies were also in the Argives' rear, and had powerful forces, including cavalry that would ride down men dispersed in flight. A great murderous battle that could destroy Sparta, Argos, or both, seemed inevitable.

It did not occur. The Argive general Thrasyllus went with Alciphron, who was a *proxenos* (volunteer guest-friend and representative) for Sparta at Argos, to meet with Agis as the two armies advanced. They urged him not to start a battle, saying that the Argives were willing to accept arbitration of their differences with Sparta and make peace. They spoke only on their own initiative, but Agis believed them and, after consulting with only one ephor, halted his army and made a truce for four months, during which the Argives were to fulfil this agreement. He then led his army away without explanation. Although enraged, the Spartans and their allies obediently headed homewards.[15]

Agis must have believed his demonstration of the strength of Sparta and its allies had produced the desired effect, dissuading the Argives from a war that could easily last for years. He had also escaped from a dangerous situation. Thrasyllus and Alciphron had also saved their army. However, most Spartans and Argives thought of the victory they had 'lost', not of the danger they had escaped. In a rage the Argives began stoning Thrasyllus, who barely escaped being killed. At this moment the Athenians arrived with one thousand hoplites and three hundred cavalry. Alcibiades, present in a diplomatic capacity, persuaded the Mantineans and Eleans to ignore the truce. The Argives at first hesitated, and then joined their allies at Orchomenus in north-eastern Arcadia, located on the route from Methydrium to Phlius. The Spartans had left Arcadian hostages there for safekeeping during their earlier march. The allies now besieged the town, whose walls were weak. Afraid that they could not hold out, the Orchomenians yielded, joined the allies, and handed over the hostages. Debating their next move, most of the allies voted to move against Tegea, where a faction wished to surrender the city to them. In a demonstration of the perils of Greek coalition warfare, the Eleans, angry that their proposal to attack Lepreum had been rejected, marched off home.[16]

The Battle of Mantinea and its Consequences, Summer 418–Winter 418/417[17]

On the news of the fall of Orchomenus, the Spartans, already angry with Agis, at once resolved to raze his house and impose a crippling fine. He pleaded with them to do neither, but to let him absolve himself of the charges by his courage when he led forth the army again. The Spartans held off, but assigned him ten Spartiates as counsellors, an unprecedented action with a king, although it had been done with navarchs. Now word came from friends in Tegea that it would likely yield to the enemy unless Sparta acted quickly. The Spartans marched at once with their largest levy ever, Thucydides says. They must have ordered mobilisation when news of renewed enemy activity first arrived. Arriving at Oresthasium on the Arcadian side of the frontier, they sent back the oldest and youngest hoplites, one-sixth of the total, to keep guard at home. Perhaps they had learned that the enemy was not yet at Tegea, and that the Eleans had departed and now posed a potential separate threat. The army marched to Tegea, gathered Sparta's Arcadian allies, and invaded Mantinea, laying waste to the countryside. The Spartans also sent for their northern allies, now including the Phocians and Locrians, but these could not be expected to arrive immediately, since they had to pass through enemy-held territory, and so needed to mass first.[18]

Mantinea was located in the middle of the largest of three plains north of modern Tripolis in Arcadia. The southern end of this Plain of Mantinea runs into that of Tegea, with a bottleneck at their boundary formed by the spur of Mytika and Mount Kapnistra. Mildly undulating and composed of alluvial soil, the plain is a basin in which water either soaks into the soil or flows into underground channels within the limestone. To the south-east is the smaller Plain of Louka, to the north-east the Plain of Nestane, the ancient Argon Pedion, separated from the city by Mount Barberi. The Argives and their allies reacted to the Spartans by deploying for battle on a steep, difficult slope, most likely that of the south-western spur of Barberi. The Spartans themselves encamped at the sanctuary of Heracles, about a kilometre south of this spur.[19]

Agis at once advanced against the enemy, 'and they proceeded as far as the throw of a stone or javelin; then one of the older men called out to Agis, seeing they were going against a strong place, that he intended "to cure evil with evil", meaning his desire to make amends for his culpable retreat from Argos produced his current ill-timed zeal,' says Thucydides.[20] Moved by this cry, or perhaps another motive, such as trying to draw the Argives down into the plain, Agis led his army away without a fight.[21] Withdrawing in an orderly fashion after coming so close to the enemy is impressive, but note that here, as earlier at Argos, the Arcadian allies also stopped

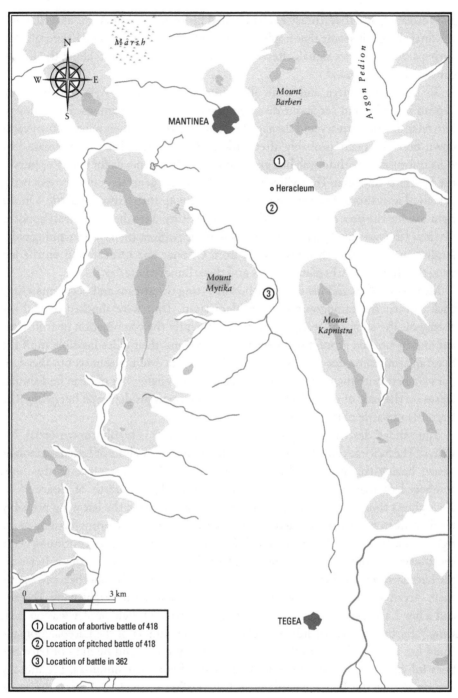

Map 7.1: Mantinea and Tegea

and retreated, and that Thrasyllus had halted his own forces at Argos as well. Until the final charge, it seems that hoplites advanced slowly and could be halted quickly, perhaps by a trumpet signal, after which orders could be passed along the line to command a withdrawal.

To lure the Argives and their allies into seeking battle, Agis retreated into Tegean territory and set about diverting the course of a stream, so that it flowed into Mantinean territory and damaged it. The Argives and their allies in turn came down onto the plain, probably after dark, and encamped. Their men, amazed by Agis' unexpected withdrawal, had grown angry at their generals for failing to pursue the Spartans, and after Thrasyllus' lynching the Argive generals could not risk being perceived as traitors. The next morning they drew up their army for battle. On the right, having the post of honour in their own territory, were the Mantinean hoplites. To their left were the thousand picked men of the Argives, then the remaining older Argives in five lochoi, then their allies from Cleonae and Orneae, and on the left wing the thousand Athenian hoplites and three hundred cavalry.

Meanwhile Agis and his men finished diverting the stream and began marching back to their old campground at the Heracleum. They were shocked to find the enemy off the spur and ready for battle. Apparently the combination of fruit trees and mildly uneven ground had kept the Argives and their allies invisible until the Spartan army came close. It says little for Agis that he had not sent scouts ahead, or put watchers onto the nearby heights to observe the enemy, but one can find similar lapses on the part of other Greek generals.[22] The Spartans deployed hurriedly. The largest land battle of the war was about to start.[23]

Thucydides' description of the Spartan deployment is highly controversial. He writes: 'The Sciritae took the left wing for themselves, they alone of Lacedaemonians always having this post for their own.' This is the first appearance of this unit, composed of men from the hilly Sciritis border district north of Sparta.[24] In Xenophon's time it led the army on the march, so its taking the left wing probably resulted from it starting the deployment, with the rest of the army forming to its right as units left the line of march. 'Next to them', Thucydides continues, 'were the Brasidean soldiers from Thrace, and neodamodeis with them; thereafter now the Lacedaemonians themselves stationed their lochoi one after another, and beside them Arcadian Heraeans, after these Maenalians, and on the right wing Tegeans and a few Lacedaemonians held the outermost part, and their cavalry was on each wing.'[25] Further on, Thucydides complains that 'the number of the Lacedaemonians could not be known, due to the secrecy of their system,'[26] and he did not trust the boastful claims the other states present made about their numbers. He did say elsewhere that the Lacedaemonians and their allies seemed, and were, the more numerous of the two armies.[27] He offered this for the Spartans:

Seven *lochoi* were fighting besides the Sciritae, these being six hundred, in each *lochos* there were four *pentēkostyes*, and in the *pentēkostyes* four *enōmotiai*. In the first rank of the *enōmotia* were fighting four [men]; in depth they were not all arrayed alike, but as each *lochagos* wished, but over all they were deployed eight deep. The first rank along the whole length, except for Sciritae, was four hundred and fifty (minus two) men.[28]

A depiction of this organisation appears in the Appendix. Each lochos had about 512 hoplites. The *Hippeis* were also present, although whether stationed in a lochos or fighting as a separate unit is unclear. Since this organisation omits a unit for the polemarchs, two of whom at Mantinea each have a lochos, and yields a relatively small Spartan army compared to the six thousand Spartans and seven thousand Argives that Xenophon has at the Nemea in 394,[29] many scholars have decided that 'the secrecy of their system' was too much for Thucydides. Only a few defend Thucydides' description of the army's organisation.[30]

It should be defended. In 394 Argives and Spartans alike sought decisive action from the start, and would have raised all available forces. In 418, as we have seen, the Spartans had to garrison their borders and coasts against attack, while the Argives had set forth in some indecision and had to leave guard units facing the Epidaurians, who in fact invaded and defeated them while the main army was at Mantinea.[31] Thucydides was well-informed about Spartan actions in this campaign – what he lacked were numbers. As a substitute he used his knowledge of Spartan military organisation, probably derived from the questioning of captives and deserters by Athenian generals, himself included. His denial of the existence of the Pitanate *lochos* shows his interest in Sparta's military organisation, and also his belief, arguably mistaken in that instance, that he had superior knowledge. Intriguingly, seven lochoi of *c.*512 men each and 600 Sciritae produce a total of some 4,200 men, exactly ten times the number of Spartans on Sphacteria in 425. Arguably the Spartans sent a tithe of their forces to the island, less the *Hippeis*, if they were not in a lochos. The Brasideans and *neodamodeis* cannot be one of the seven lochoi, since they did not exist in 425, and Thucydides' phrasing in the passages cited above separates them from the Lacedaemonians, the Sciritae, and the lochoi. Of course, it is possible Thucydides was wrong in assuming the same number of lochoi were present at Mantinea as at Pylos, or that the enomotia only had a front of four men, not more. All the Lacedaemonians probably outnumbered the Argives and Athenians present by at least a few hundred men, and the Tegeans and the other Arcadians outnumbered the Mantineans by a few hundred men as well, each side having over eight thousand hoplites at least.

With both armies deployed, the commanders of the various allied contingents exhorted their men, but the Spartans sang their war-songs and encouraged one another, trusting more in their long training than in last-minute speeches, according to Thucydides.[32] Then the two armies advanced, the allies eagerly and

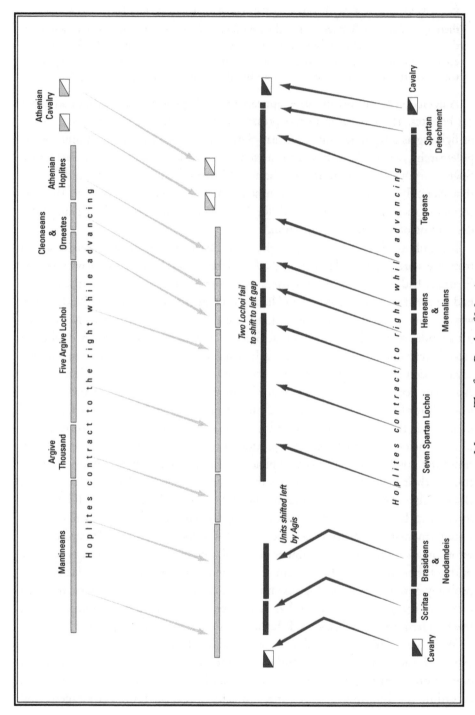

Map 7.2: The first Battle of Mantinea

passionately, the Spartans slowly and to the sound of their pipers, carefully keeping their phalanx unbroken. Thucydides also notes that advancing hoplite formations veered to the right, and that this took place now, with the Mantineans extending past the Sciritae, the Spartans and Tegeans well past the Athenians.[33] Seeking to prevent encirclement of his left wing, Agis ordered the Sciritae and freed Helots to shift left. They did so, opening a gap between themselves and the lochoi of the Lacedaemonians. At the same time Agis passed word to the polemarchs Hipponoïdas and Aristocles to lead two lochoi they had from the 'right wing' to fill the gap. Evidently each polemarch took temporary command of a lochos after bringing the king's deployment commands to its lochagos. Since Thucydides speaks only of the lochoi of the Lacedaemonians, he must have meant the 'right wing' of the Lacedaemonians, not of the entire army. This would have opened a second gap in the Spartan phalanx, but perhaps Agis thought that the Arcadians would move left to fill it, or felt that the enemy was so overmatched on this wing that a gap here did not matter, since it could not be exploited.[34]

However, on receiving this order only very shortly before contact, Aristocles and Hipponoïdas refused to shift their men, rejecting a command from the humiliated king just as Amompharetus had rejected an order from the humiliated Pausanias. Perhaps they saved their army from being doubly outflanked, but afterwards they were exiled from Sparta, albeit for cowardice rather than disobedience. Agis now ordered the Sciritae and freed Helots to move back, but it was too late. The Mantineans charged, defeated the isolated Sciritae and freed Helots, and then joined the Argive picked thousand in rushing into the unclosed gap. They surrounded and put to flight the lochoi of the Lacedaemonian left wing and then pushed on to the Spartans' wagons, killing some of the guards, older men who had been taken out of the lochoi to guard the baggage train.[35]

It went very differently in the centre, where Agis had taken station with the Hippeis. The Spartans attacked and routed the five lochoi of the Argives, the men from Cleonae and Orneae, and the Athenians who faced them. Most did not fight, but gave way at once when the Spartans came on, with some being trodden underfoot by those striving to get away before they were trapped. The fear of being flanked and encircled had produced defeat on each side's left wing. The rest of the Athenians, outflanked on both sides, faced annihilation, but they and the surviving Argives escaped, thanks to their cavalry's loyal assistance and to Agis' decision to order his entire army to rescue his left wing.

The Mantineans and picked Argives, seeing their left defeated and the enemy now bearing down upon them, turned and fled. Many of the Mantineans and quite a few of the picked Argives were slain, but the majority escaped, 'for the Lacedaemonians stay in their battles long and firmly until the enemy's flight, but once he has turned their pursuits are brief and short.'[36] As their controlled advance shows, they were more concerned to protect their formation than to inflict injury on their enemies. Diodorus claims, moreover, that Pharax, one of the advisers of Agis, directed the king to allow the picked Argives to escape, rather than trap them and force them to fight hard to survive.[37] Some have suggested that Agis for political reasons attempted to spare the Argive thousand by opening the gap in his lines,[38] but this seems both unnecessary and incredibly hazardous.

The battle over, the Spartans set up a trophy, stripped the enemy corpses, and then returned them under truce before withdrawing to Tegean territory to bury their own dead. Thucydides heard that they had lost about three hundred men, although Spartan secrecy made certainty impossible. Few Spartan allies perished. The Argives, Cleonaeans, and Orneates had lost some seven hundred men, the Mantineans two hundred, and the Athenians two hundred. Pleistoanax, who had been leading the oldest and youngest hoplites back north to aid Agis, returned home on news of the victory, and the northern allies were dismissed. The Carnean festival month had arrived, and the main army returned to celebrate it. Belatedly reinforced by another thousand Athenians and the three thousand Eleans, the Argives and their allies went against Epidaurus while Sparta's attention was diverted by the festival, and began to invest the city with a siege wall. Most soon left off, presumably returning home before the month ended and Sparta mobilised again. The Athenians finished their part, turning it into an *epiteichisma*, which all the allies helped garrison.[39]

Aside from avoiding a potentially disastrous defeat, it might seem that Sparta had no profit from the battle. In fact, it repaired the Spartans' damaged reputation. Thucydides notes, 'the charge of softness once brought by the Greeks, on account of the disaster on the island, and otherwise of bad judgement and slowness to act, they now dismissed for this one action, so they were considered as having been worsted earlier by chance, but in spirit were still the same.'[40] Exploiting this, at the beginning of winter 418/17, the Spartans mustered an army at Tegea, and then sent Lichas, who, as it happened, was the *proxenos* of Argos at Sparta, to offer terms for peace or, if they wished it, war. Faced by this threat, and urged on by a pro-Spartan faction hoping to overthrow the democracy at Argos, the humbled Argives chose to accept the peace offer, against the opposition of Alcibiades and others.

Soon the Argives renounced their alliance with Athens, Mantinea, and Elis, and allied with Sparta.[41] The fighting with Epidaurus ended, the Athenians being the last to leave the fort there. Mantinea, isolated in the interior, now surrendered its rule over other Arcadians, made a Thirty Years' Peace with Sparta, and renewed its allegiance.[42] The Eleans received more generous terms, probably because they had greater access to Athenian aid: they recovered Lepreum, most likely before the

Olympic Festival of 416. The Lepreates may have welcomed a deal after hosting so many freed Helots.[43] Finally, late that winter a thousand Spartans went to Sicyon to establish a more oligarchic government there, and then joined a thousand Argives – Diodorus says the elite thousand – in overthrowing the Argive democracy itself.[44]

By spring 417, Sparta's combination of diplomacy, armed suasion, ravaging, aid to subversives, and demonstration of strength in hoplite warfare had broken the Argive alliance in the Peloponnese, ending what had been a serious threat to Sparta's position. Similar efforts probably established Sparta in its dominant position in the sixth century, and restored it during the fighting in the 460s. This position may seem weak compared to Athens' empire, but the two states faced different strategic situations. Athens' subjects lived on islands or along coasts with hostile Persian or Thracian hinterlands, and so were isolated except by sea. Few had fleets, and Athens' powerful navy could cut off rebel cities and blockade them at leisure. Sparta had a fine army, but every Greek state had hoplites, and several sizable Peloponnesian states could combine forces by land with ease. Sparta needed loyal allies to help counter its enemies, and so had an alliance system, not an empire. It was not easy to control, since each Greek city-state had its own interests and goals, while the separate factions within each city had diverse goals as well. The same considerations, however, also affected any anti-Spartan coalition of cities, so if such a coalition met an outright defeat, as at Mantinea, it probably would shatter, lacking a tradition of unity under a powerful leader. Even if it held together, the Spartan army could operate offensively and assist in diplomatic efforts, while the beaten forces could act offensively only in the victor's absence. Long resistance was unlikely. As long as the Spartans and their allies could win victories in pitched battles, Sparta would dominate the Peloponnese.

Sparta Returns to Open War with Athens, 417–413[45]

Had the Argives and Athenians remained quiet, it is unlikely that Sparta would have returned to war with Athens, whose strategic situation remained strong. However, in 417 Argos' democrats waited until the Spartans were celebrating the Gymnopaedia and then attacked the oligarchs. The Spartans delayed responding to the oligarchs' pleas for help, but finally put off the festival and marched, showing that they could act at such times if they felt pressed. On reaching Tegea, however, they learned that the oligarchs had been overthrown, and returned home to hold the festival, ignoring the pleas of those who had escaped. Later, after hearing both sides, the Spartans decided to march against Argos, but then delayed, during which time the democrats sought an alliance with Athens, and began building 'long walls' to the sea to permit them to receive supplies in case of siege.[46]

The following winter, 417/16, the Spartans marched against Argos with all their allies, aside from the Corinthians. With Agis in command, they destroyed the Argive long walls, and also hoped to regain control of Argos with the aid of a group within the city, though this did not occur. In frustration, or as revenge for an ancient defeat there,[47] the Spartans took a border refuge, Hysiae, and killed all the free men taken. On their withdrawal, the Argives invaded and ravaged the territory of Phlius, where most Argive oligarchs lived in exile.[48] In summer 416, Alcibiades returned to Argos with some troops, arrested three hundred Argives suspected of favouring Sparta, and imprisoned them on nearby islands.[49] The Argives attacked Phlius again, but were ambushed and lost eighty men. The Pylos garrison made a profitable raid into Lacedaemonian territory, but the Spartans still did not renounce the Peace of Nicias.[50]

In winter 416/15, the Spartans began an expedition against Argos, but the border-crossing sacrifices proved unfavourable, causing its cancellation. It did incite yet another round of arrests in Argos, however.[51] That same winter the Spartans and their allies made another attempt. Only the Corinthians, who had returned to open war with Athens, were absent. The army collected grain from enemy territory and settled the Argive exiles at Orneae, in the hills north-west of Argos. They made a truce between the settlers and the Argive democrats, so they may not have been as interested in creating an *epiteichisma* in Argive territory as in removing the exiles from Phlius and elsewhere, refugees being as problematic in ancient Greece as today. However, the Athenians arrived with an army, and joined the Argives in full force in besieging Orneae for a day. The defenders fled that night. The Argives razed the town to prevent it being reoccupied, and then withdrew.[52]

Athenian support, therefore, allowed the Argives to remain at war with Sparta. Athens' concerns shifted from the Peloponnese, however. In winter 416/15 the Athenians decided to send a major expedition to Sicily, ostensibly to support allies there under pressure from the Dorian cities of Selinus and Syracuse, but in fact to conquer the island. Although strong in warships and infantry, the Athenian expedition lacked cavalry and money, and spent the summer of 415 seeking additional allies and funds. In winter 415/14 it landed outside of Syracuse, where it defeated Syracuse's hoplites but fared poorly against the Syracusans' powerful cavalry. The Athenians spent the winter at the allied city of Catana north of Syracuse, gathering horsemen in preparation for the next summer's campaign.[53]

The Syracusans used this respite to send envoys to Corinth, their mother-city, and to Sparta. They sought reinforcements, and also asked the Spartans to resume attacking Athens, in the hope that the Athenian expedition would be recalled from Sicily, or at least not be reinforced. Although inclined to agree, the Spartans first sent for Alcibiades, now in exile from Athens after being accused of sacrilege. One of the leading proponents of the Sicilian expedition, he had served as one of its generals before his recall and flight. The Spartans wanted to hear from someone who had been deep in the Athenians' counsels. Seeking the Spartans' favour, the angry renegade told them that the plan had been first to conquer Sicily, then the Greeks of southern Italy, then Carthage, and finally to use the wealth gained to hire barbarian mercenaries and amass a huge fleet before returning to the Peloponnese to storm or blockade its cities, and so conquer all of Greece. Thucydides says the Spartans believed him, but never says that such a plan was debated before the Athenian people. If not a fiction, it will have been a private scheme among some of the leading men.

Alcibiades urged them to send forces to bolster the raw Siceliotes against the experienced Athenian troops, and especially to send a Spartiate to take command, organise the fighting, and press into action the uninvolved. He also encouraged the Spartans to fortify the site of Decelea in north-central Attica as an *epiteichisma*. From there, raiders could threaten the Attic countryside and interfere with Athens' income from the silver mines of Laurium in southern Attica.[54]

The Spartans were sufficiently convinced to prepare to send an expedition and a commander to Sicily, but held off from attacking Athens for a year. Thucydides says that they rationalised their defeat in the Archidamian War as due to having been the first side to break the Thirty Years' Peace oaths, and now wanted there to be no doubt as to the guilty party.[55] In spring 414 they invaded the Argolid, and reached Cleonae before an earthquake made them turn back. The Argives retaliated by raiding the Thyreatis and carrying off much booty, likely a combination of herd animals and human captives. In the summer the Spartans and their allies again invaded Argive territory and ravaged most of it. It will have been a major operation, for Argos' territory was large. The Athenians responded by sending a fleet of thirty ships to raid Laconia, landing at Epidaurus Limera and Prasiae on the east coast as well as other locations, and ravaging some of the land. This broke the old Peace of Nicias oaths to the last degree, giving the Spartans every excuse to act against Athens. As a result, they prepared to build the Decelea Fort, and also to send a force to Sicily.[56]

For the Athenians, the part of the Peloponnesian War that they called the 'Decelean War' began in spring 413, when the Spartans and their allies invaded Attica and built the fort at Decelea, this being on the hill of Tatoï north of Athens and within sight of the city. Agis himself commanded the garrison, which consisted of Lacedaemonian and allied levies regularly rotated into and out of Attica. Agis and his men supported themselves by forays into the Attic countryside, joining in major invasions on occasion as well. The Athenians saw their farms and estates plundered and slaves deserting in large numbers, their silver mine revenues fall, and the cost of imported food rise. Athens' closeness to Decelea compelled the Athenians to stand watch day and night against the threat of surprise assault or betrayal. Constant patrols in Attica's stony countryside exhausted Athens' cavalrymen and maimed their horses. However, since the continuous warfare provided vital experience to Athens' cavalry and picked infantry, these proved able to win impressive victories, protect the city, and even regain some control over the countryside.[57]

It must have been about this time that Sparta reorganised its army into the one Xenophon describes (and attibutes to Lycurgus) as comprising 'six *morai* of cavalrymen and of hoplites. Each of the citizen [or, more likely, hoplite] *morai* has one *polemarchos*, four *lochagoi*, eight *pentēkostēres*, sixteen *enōmotarchoi*'.[58] This army organisation is also depicted in the Appendix. Each polemarch commanded one mora (*mora*, 'part', plural *morai*). Ancient sources report different strengths for the mora: 500, 576, 600, 700, 900, and 1,000, with the lower figures the most secure.[59] Numbers varied according to the level of mobilisation, and of course losses from battle, accident, or illness affected the unit sizes. The continuing decline in Spartiate numbers, the multiple theatres of combat in this war, the lack of available royal commanders thanks to Pleistoanax' age and Agis' stationing in Attica, and the desire to split the year-round burden of manning Decelea into equal shifts, will have joined to bring about this reorganisation. Polemarchs continued to command morai until the end of the Spartan empire in Greece.

Gylippus in Sicily, 414–413[60]

The commander the Spartans appointed to go to Sicily was Gylippus, son of the Cleandridas who had taken Tegea in the 460s. He had been accused of sharing in the bribes taken by Pleistoanax in 446, and fled into exile to the Athenian colony of Thurii in southern Italy. Growing up in Sparta under that shadow, Gylippus had been a *mothax*, an impoverished free boy raised in the Lycurgan uprbringing as a foster-brother of a boy from a rich family. This practice helped prevent social revolution by poorer Spartiates, provided clients for rich families, and slowed the decline of Spartiate manpower. Two other notable Spartiates, Lysander and Callicratidas, are also identified as *mothakes*.[61]

In spring 414, Gylippus headed west with four triremes, two manned by Helots and *neodamodeis*, two by Corinthians. Indeed, the ships themselves came from Corinth, for the Spartans had not rebuilt their fleet after handing it over at Sphacteria. At Alcibiades' urging, the sailors had been trained to fight as hoplites. At Leucas, Gylippus heard false rumours that the Athenians already had cut off Syracuse. He sailed for southern Italy to rally the Greeks there against the expected Athenian invasion. He won few converts, being received only at the old Spartan colony of Taras. Storm damage then forced him to halt for repairs. Luckily Nicias, the only surviving Athenian general at Syracuse, judged Gylippus by the number of his ships and dismissed him as a raider. By the time Nicias realised his mistake and sent a force to intercept, Gylippus had learned that Syracuse was not yet fully invested, and had reached Himera on the northern coast of Sicily. He won the city over and collected troops from it, from Syracuse's allies Selinus and Gela on the southern coast of the island, and from native tribes in the interior, also arming seven hundred of his sailors as hoplites. Having mustered a force of three thousand infantry and two hundred cavalry, he then proceeded overland to Syracuse.[62]

Syracuse, modern Siracusa, on the southern half of Sicily's east coast, was itself situated on the northern side of a large bay, the 'Great Harbour', and on the island of Ortygia, which closed in the bay from the north, while a promontory called Plemmyrium closed it in from the south, leaving an entrance over a kilometre wide. South-west of the city near the coast there were marshes, and further south-west and inland the settlement and shrine of the Olympieum, which the Syracusans had fortified. North of the city was Epipolae, a large triangular plateau ascending in the west to a hill, Euryelus.[63] The Athenians made a surprise landing north of Epipolae, climbed onto it, and routed its defenders. They built a fort at Labdalum on its northern edge, then the Circle Fort to its south, pushing two walls from there south towards the harbour.

The Athenian effort was slowed by the absence of the men of the fleet, still based north of Epipolae, as well as the need to build the walls to the Great Harbour through the marshes and against Syracusan opposition, which included two crosswalls built across the path of the walls to the harbour. However, the Athenians took both crosswalls in surprise assaults, and later brought their fleet around into the Great Harbour. Demoralised by their defeats, the Syracusans were discussing surrender when a Corinthian ship, the first of a squadron sent to Syracuse, arrived with news of Gylippus' coming and that of the other reinforcements. Heartened, the Syracusans marched out to meet Gylippus upon his arrival, his army ascending Euryelus. Luckily the Athenians had not completed their wall on Epipolae, concentrating instead upon finishing the walls to the sea in order to protect their fleet. Syracuse had come close to being fully blockaded, and to surrendering.[64]

After initial confusion, the Athenians deployed their army upon Epipolae. They made no reply when Gylippus, now commanding the Syracusans on land, sent a herald offering a five-day truce, to give the Athenians time to pack up and leave Sicily. This bit of bravado was no doubt meant to encourage his men. They needed encouragement: Syracusan hoplites were undisciplined and inexperienced, and even now Gylippus found them failing to form into line. He led his army away from the Athenian wall onto more open ground, where the Syracusan cavalry and light troops would be able to operate. Nicias, however, refused battle.[65]

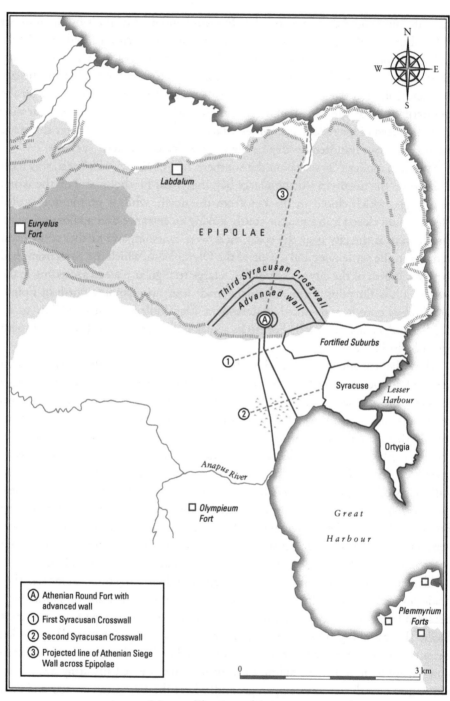

Map 7.3: The siege of Syracuse

On the following day Gylippus drew up his army again before the Athenian walls, distracting the foe while a strong body of infantry seized the Labdalum Fort. It had been built in the early days of the siege to contain the Athenian's gear and supplies. These had been moved long ago, leaving a large fortress likely held now by too small a garrison. It was surprised and taken. After its capture, Gylippus had his army begin building a crosswall through Epipolae to block further Athenian construction there. The Athenians advanced their wall. Gylippus led his men against a weak section of it at night, but Athenian units bivouacking in front of another section counterattacked and compelled him to make a hurried withdrawal. However, Nicias did not like his chances against the reinforced enemy, and instead seized Plemmyrium and built forts for naval bases from which to blockade the city by sea. It cost him manpower he could have used on Epipolae, but it guaranteed his access to the sea, across which his supplies came. He could not afford to let the Syracusans fortify it first.[66]

Meanwhile, Gylippus and the Athenians kept forming phalanxes in front of their walls on Epipolae. Finally Gylippus felt confident enough to launch an attack, only to be defeated by the Athenian hoplites. Gylippus called the troops together and took the blame for the defeat, saying that he had deprived them of the aid of their cavalry and light-armed by fighting between the walls, where these could not deploy. He urged them to take heart in their numbers and equipment, and 'played the race card' by reminding them they were Peloponnesians and Dorians facing a rabble of Ionians and islanders. As the two walls neared, the opportunity for battle came again, for Nicias felt that he had to fight or see his wall blocked by the Syracusans. This time Gylippus led his hoplites forward nearer the gap between the walls, and had his light-armed and cavalry deploy outside in the open space. His cavalry routed the Athenian left wing, and then the rest of his army finally drove the Athenians back into their fortifications. That night the crosswall passed the Athenian wall, ending the threat of blockade by land.[67]

In the autumn and winter, Gylippus travelled about Sicily raising new forces, while the Syracusans, reinforced from Corinth, began practising their fleet. Nicias himself was ill, and his fleet was deteriorating. The ships were poorly maintained, mercenary oarsmen were deserting, and crewmen were slain while foraging by enemy forces based at the Olympieum. In spring 413, Gylippus joined in urging the Syracusans and their allies to seek a major naval action. They did, and were defeated, but Gylippus used the distraction of the battle to lead his army around and take the Plemmyrium forts by surprise assault. This cost the Athenians heavily in men, supplies, and stores, and forced them to convoy in supplies against enemy attacks.[68]

Thereafter Gylippus had a less prominent role in the campaign, despite retaining command of the land forces and strengthening them with reinforcements from Greece and from elsewhere in Sicily. The Athenians clung to the Circle Fort and their seaward walls, and Gylippus never took these despite repeated attempts. Also, the Syracusans gained in confidence and increasingly took the lead in the war. But, instead of abandoning the siege and keeping enough strength in Sicily to guard their allies, the Athenians decided to send another fleet with just as many troops, hoping to win an outright victory. This action stripped Athens of its reserves of ships and men.[69] This fleet raided Epidaurus Limera in Laconia and built an *epiteichisma* on the coast of the Malea peninsula, presumably as retaliation for the Decelean Fort, built in 413.[70] These and other delays, mostly to recruit more men, gave the Syracusans time to defeat Nicias' ships in battle. They did this by strengthening the ends of the outriggers of their ships, a Corinthian development that would have been disadvantageous on the open sea, but which worked well in the close waters of the Great Harbour.[71]

The reinforcing fleet arrived, and Demosthenes, one of its commanders, led an effort to take the Epipolae crosswall. He caught Gylippus and the Syracusans off-guard in a surprise attack that got him behind the crosswall, but his army was crushed in the confused night battle that followed.[72] Demosthenes now called for withdrawal. However, Nicias resisted, fearing exile if he returned to Athens in defeat. His contacts in Syracuse told him that the city was becoming impoverished, and he argued for trusting in the reinforced Athenian fleet. A lunar eclipse on the night of 27/28 August 413 also helped convince the Athenians to remain, despite Gylippus' bringing in further Sicilian reinforcements.[73] In time the Syracusans defeated the Athenians in a great naval battle, and trapped them by creating a chain of boats across the mouth of the Great Harbour – yet another benefit of Gylippus' capture of the Plemmyrium forts. A last desperate attempt by the Athenians to break out by sea was defeated in another great battle.[74] The Athenians finally abandoned their ships and tried to retreat by land, but were trapped, with more than forty thousand men killed or taken.[75]

Gylippus asked to take back to Sparta as personal prizes Nicias and Demosthenes, now captives, but the Syracusans voted to execute them instead. Thucydides says that the Syracusans with whom Nicias had been in contact wanted him dead in order to keep their treason secret, while the Corinthians and others feared that Nicias, a rich man, would bribe his way to safety. Plutarch claims that the Syracusans had found Gylippus' harshness grating, and were contemptuous of his penuriousness and greed, so they took delight in confounding him. It could be true.[76] Even so, Gylippus had played an important role in the defeat of Athens' Sicilian expeditions, helping to cause a disaster comparable to that met by the Persians in their invasion of Greece. Sparta and its allies could now wage war against Athens with every hope of success.

The remarkable change in Sparta's fortunes from 424 to 413 was due primarily to the Athenians' failures in battle and on campaign, and to their folly in reinforcing their defeat in Sicily despite increasing perils at home. Athens had failed in the Peloponnese because it lacked the hoplite forces needed to invade the interior of Spartan territory or to face Sparta and its northern allies. Even if the Athenians had heavily reinforced Argos in 418, the overall balance of land forces would still have favoured Sparta and its allies, and the Spartans would have avoided battle until their northern allies appeared on the scene. Despite the decline in Spartiate numbers, the Spartan army retained its qualitative edge. Its victory at Mantinea restored Spartan dominance of the Peloponnese and allowed renewal of the war against Athens. Gylippus' generalship then rescued the Syracusans, whose triumph over the Athenians gave Sparta and its allies hope for victory at last. Nonetheless, that victory would prove difficult to achieve.

~ Eight ~

THE NAVARCHS' WAR, 413–404

Revolts, Athenian Civil Strife, and Indecision at Sea, 413–411[1]

The disaster in Sicily raised hopes among Athens' foes for the speedy downfall of its democracy and rule. The Spartans and their allies started building a hundred triremes, while anti-Athenian factions on Chios, Lesbos, and Euboea sent embassies to Agis or to Sparta seeking aid for revolts. Agis led an expedition north in winter 413/12 to levy funds from the allies for the fleet and to plunder the Oetaeans, enemies of the struggling colony at Heraclea. He may have been investigating the possibilities of sending forces overland to the Thracian Chalcidice; but no forces went that way.[2] The Persian ruler, Darius II, ordered his satraps to regain control of the Greeks of Asia. Soon Tissaphernes, based in Sardis, and Pharnabazus, based in Dascylium in Hellespontine Phrygia, were vying to get Spartan aid. After some indecision, in spring 412 the Spartans decided to send their available ships to Chios, a large island north of Samos. By causing its revolt they could add its sizable fleet to theirs, then unite with Tissaphernes to cause further revolts in Ionia and Lesbos before moving into Pharnabazus' region. Additional forces from Greece and from Sparta's allies in Sicily and Italy were to join the effort.[3]

The campaign almost proved abortive. Relieved that the Spartans and Siceliotes had not attacked immediately in autumn 413, the Athenians had used the winter to build ships and make various economies, including abandoning the new *epiteichisma* in Laconia.[4] In spring 412 the Corinthians held up the departure of the first squadron in order to celebrate the Isthmian Games. Athenians attending the festival under sacred truce learned of the campaign. The Athenians seized Chian ships operating with their fleet and sent forces to intercept the squadron when it sailed. The Athenians finally chased the squadron to the shores near Corinth's border with Epidaurus, damaging all its ships and killing its commander, the Spartan Alcamenes. An army came to guard the ships, and the Athenians imposed a blockade.[5] Already unnerved by an earthquake in Laconia, which led them to reduce their initial contingent from ten to five triremes and change its commander, the Spartans began to reconsider the entire plan. However, Thucydides says that Alcibiades persuaded the ephor Endius, a family guest-friend and rival of Agis, to send the five to Chios anyway. Alcibiades accompanied the expedition as adviser to its commander, Chalcideus.[6] Alcibiades had backed the Chian request for aid, and also had to leave – Plutarch says that he had seduced Agis' wife and fathered the heir-presumptive, Leotychidas. Whatever the truth of it, Agis certainly became Alcibiades' enemy.[7] The squadron sailed, and reached Chios. Aided by conspirators, and the fact that news of the recent defeat had not arrived, Alcibiades and Chalcideus persuaded the Chians to rebel. Brasidas' approach to causing revolts from Athens through armed suasion and subversion had been adopted again, and quickly became commonplace.

The Chians, now committed to revolt, joined the Spartans and Tissaphernes in a scramble to bring about more rebellions. The Greeks brought over cities on Lesbos and on the Erythraean peninsula opposite Chios, and also engineered Miletus' revolt. Tissaphernes won over other mainland cities, notably Ephesus and Cnidus. However, the Athenians tapped their last financial reserves and responded strongly, aided by a Persian rebel, Amorges. Their fleets recovered some mainland sites, blockaded a Chian squadron at Miletus, and overwhelmed another at Lesbos and regained the island. Raids on Chian and Milesian territory proved successful, and Chalcideus was killed. Gathering an army, the Athenians then defeated the Milesians and their allies in pitched battle and began building a siege wall. However, the squadron blockaded on the Corinthian coast surprised and defeated the reduced Athenian forces there, and vessels coming from Sicily evaded Athenian attempts at interception and reached Corinth. Fifty-five triremes sailed east and reached Milesian territory, where twenty-five Chian ships were blockaded in the city. The Athenians had only sixty-eight triremes, some of them troop transports. Their commanders made the controversial decision to withdraw to Samos. Although unfortified, the city offered the support of a population loyal to Athens after a democratic revolution. The Spartans and their allies exploited this unexpected turn of events to surprise Iasos, an island off the Carian coast that Amorges used as his base. He was taken captive.[8]

In the winter of 412/11 naval operations continued, despite storms that sent both sides scurrying into sheltered waters. The Athenians received reinforcements, and sought battle once the odds were even. Astyochus, the Spartan navarch for 412/11, refused battle until he had superior numbers. When he did, the Athenians refused it. Both sides sheltered in defended positions, and lacked the land forces to threaten the enemy refuges. Each sought to intercept the other side's detachments, with little success.[9]

Heavy Athenian raids on Chios, in which the Chians suffered three defeats on land, turned some on Chios against the revolt. Astyochus took hostages

Map 8.1: Ionia and Caria

in response. Later Pedaritus, the Spartan harmost at Chios, executed some suspected conspirators. Later the same winter, the Athenians began building an *epiteichisma* at Delphinium on Chios' north-east coast. The island's large chattel slave population began deserting to the Athenians there, increasing the effectiveness of their raids. Pedaritus and the Chians sought help from Astyochus, and complained to Sparta when he did not send it.[10]

The Spartans sent a board of eleven Spartiates to advise the navarch. Its leader, the same Lichas who took part in the Olympic Games of 420,[11] demanded that Tissaphernes change the terms of the provisional treaties already negotiated, since these could be taken as restoring to the Great King all the lands his ancestors had held, even in Greece. In a show of anger Tissaphernes refused to pay the fleet. In fact, he had already cut its pay by almost half after the rebel Amorges was captured, and was being advised by Alcibiades to play Sparta off against Athens, so that neither could win and turn on him. Alcibiades had joined Tissaphernes during the siege of Miletus, anticipating that the ephors of 412/11 would be hostile to him, and in fact they did order his execution.[12] However, the *Hellenica Oxyrhynchia* – a continuation of Thucydides' work by an unidentified historian of, probably, the mid-fourth century, found at Oxyrhynchus in Egypt – noted that the Great King habitually sent down only enough funds to start a campaign, leaving the rest to be paid by his satraps, and had done so in this case. Evidently he considered recovering the Greeks of Asia an opportunistic venture, not a high priority.[13] Alcibiades' advice aside, Tissaphernes had insufficient funds, or motivation, to pay some nineteen thousand sailors month after month on top of his normal expenditures.

Left unsupported, Astyochus and his fleet secured the revolt of the island of Rhodes off the coast of south-western Asia Minor, and wintered there. The Athenian main fleet deployed against them and harassed the island. In the end, both returned to their posts at Samos and Miletus. In desperation, Pedaritus and the Chians assaulted Delphinium, but were routed by an Athenian sortie, and Pedaritus was killed. Blockaded by the Athenian flotilla at Delphinium, and their agriculture disrupted, the Chians began to starve, as the Corcyraeans had done in 426–425 under similar circumstances.[14]

Seeking recall by Athens, Alcibiades convinced leading men in the Athenian fleet that he could persuade Tissaphernes to aid Athens if the city abandoned its democratic government and became an oligarchy. This ignited a conspiracy by members of the Athenian upper classes against the democracy, disgraced by its disaster in Sicily. Phrynichus, an Athenian commander at Samos and a foe of Alcibiades, informed Astyochus of this, even offering to betray the Athenian fleet in order to prevent Alcibiades' return. Instead of grasping this opportunity to win the war at a single blow, Astyochus went to Tissaphernes and reported everything. Rumour had it that he had been bought off by the Persian, but he may simply have distrusted Phrynichus' offer and sought to use the evidence of Alcibiades' dealings with the Athenians to pressure Tissaphernes into supporting his fleet. After a show of negotiating with the Athenians, Tissaphernes made a formal alliance between Darius II and Sparta. The Spartans agreed to Persian rule of the Greeks of Asia in return for pay for the fleet. Tissaphernes could not allow the defeat of Astyochus' fleet by the Athenians, or let it dissolve or turn against him due to lack of pay, as his own military position was weak. The Spartans and their allies returned to Miletus, and Tissaphernes undertook to gather a Phoenician fleet.[15]

In early spring 411, the Spartiate Dercylidas led a small force north by land and caused the revolt of Abydos and Lampsacus on the Hellespont, while at the same time the Chians, reinforced by an allied squadron led by the new harmost, Leon, fought a battle with the Athenian squadron at Delphinium. It was a draw, but the Athenians had to send ships to the Hellespont, which ended their blockade of Chios. They managed to recover Lampsacus and contain Dercylidas.[16]

In Athens, the oligarchs continued their conspiracy despite Alcibiades' failure to deliver on his promises. By bluff and terror they succeeded in establishing an oligarchic government led by a council of four hundred, who were supposed to choose a larger body of five thousand hoplites to govern the state. The 'Four Hundred' put that off, however, and tried to negotiate an end to the war with Agis. Some had already set about changing governments among the subject allies, believing that oligarchies would prove more loyal. This proved untrue, Thasos revolting after its change of government. As for Agis, he knew that the oligarchs wanted to retain their fleet and empire, which Sparta would not accept, and thought the democracy would be restored quickly in any case. He therefore mobilised the Peloponnesian and Boeotian levies and marched against the Long Walls, expecting the Athenians to fall into open civil war on his approach, and either yield or let him seize the walls without opposition. However, the Athenians manned their battlements, sallied, and killed some soldiers that approached too close to the walls. Agis abandoned the effort.[17]

A democratic counterrevolution soon occurred in the Athenian fleet at Samos. Astyochus again sought battle, but the Athenians were cautious and refused, until they had been reinforced to match his numbers – at which point he refused battle. His situation was bad. Tissaphernes had failed to provide regular and adequate pay despite the treaty, and for this Astyochus was blamed. His fleet was deteriorating from desertions and lack of practice, and his crews were becoming mutinous. He tried to send ships north to Pharnabazus' territory, but bad weather caused most to return to Miletus. Eight did reach Byzantium and caused it to revolt. By holding

Byzantium and Abydos, the Spartans could threaten to block the transport of grain to Athens from the Greek cities on the northern coast of the Black Sea.[18]

The Athenian democrats at Samos recalled Alcibiades and made him a general. He promised to win the support of Tissaphernes and the Phoenician fleet, which now had reached Aspendus in south-western Asia Minor. He urged them to remain at Samos, and rejected sailing to Athens to restore the democracy. This prevented civil war and checked Astyochus. Alcibiades did have an ulterior motive: if the fleet left, Astyochus would have begun to make progress, forcing Tissaphernes to aid him. This would have revealed Alcibiades' lack of influence over Tissaphernes.

Alcibiades' recall also crystallised disgust with the satrap among Astyochus' crews. They protested, and mobbed Astyochus when he raised his staff as if to strike one of the complaining officers, Dorieus of Rhodes. The Milesians rebelled against Tissaphernes, seizing a fort that he had built in their city. Things quietened when Mindarus, navarch for 411–410, arrived in late summer, and Astyochus left for home. Tissaphernes went to the Phoenician fleet, and Alcibiades also sailed south to meet with him, promising either to win him over or keep the Phoenicians from action. In fact, the fleet never came north. Either Darius changed his mind and recalled it, or it was underfunded and incapable of combat, being used only to bolster Tissaphernes against the hostility of his erstwhile allies.[19]

Alcibiades' return caused a split at Athens between extremist oligarchs and more moderate ones, who called for the creation of the 'Five Thousand'. Matters came to a head when a fleet of forty-two Peloponnesian, Italian, and Sicilian triremes left Las in Laconia. Commanded by the Spartiate Agesandridas, it entered the Saronic Gulf, raided Athenian-held Aegina, and then sailed around to Salamis. Theramenes, a leader of the moderate oligarchs, incited troops to demolish a fort that the extremists were building in the Piraeus, claiming its purpose was to allow the enemy fleet to be admitted to the harbour.

Whether disappointed of this expectation, or because no civil war erupted in Athens, Agesandridas sailed on to Euboea, his initial goal. He and his fleet staged out of Oropus in north-east Attica, a border town betrayed to the Boeotians the previous winter. Its fall had re-ignited Euboean plots for revolt from Athens. Although lacking trained seamen – such men had either perished in Sicily or were in the east – the Athenians manned a fleet and massed thirty-six ships at Eretria. They had sailed into a trap. Eretrian conspirators arranged for food to be sold only in distant parts of the town. Athenian crews seeking meals scattered accordingly. The Eretrians then signalled Agesandridas, who struck suddenly with his fully prepared fleet against the poorly manned and haphazardly responding Athenian vessels. After a brief struggle, the Athenians were routed, losing twenty-two ships and their crews.

Most of the rest of Euboea rose in revolt. It was a terrible blow to the Athenians. Besides the losses in ships and crews, Euboea had become their main source of supply after the occupation of Decelea. They now expected Agesandridas to return and blockade the Piraeus. He did not, and Thucydides uses this occasion to condemn the Spartans for their slowness and want of energy, which made them convenient foes for the quick, aggressive Athenians. However, Athenian speed and activity had been supported by a plentiful supply of money, want of which slowed Athenian operations throughout this war. As for Agesandridas, he had orders to secure Euboea. Had he begun a naval blockade of the Piraeus, he would have needed support on land from a major call-up of Spartan and allied forces, if only to support and protect his fleet. Agis had mobilised the levies already in 411; it would not have been easy to make a second major call-up in the same year, as events in 428 show. The relieved Athenians ended the government of the Four Hundred and organised the Five Thousand, which proved able to reconcile the moderate oligarchs at Athens with the democrats at Samos. Athenian unity was restored.[20]

In autumn 411 Mindarus decided to move north. Tissaphernes had provided no pay, Spartan officers at Aspendus told Mindarus that the Phoenician fleet would never move, and Pharnabazus was begging him to come and help raise the northern cities in revolt. When he put to sea, however, bad weather halted his progress, and he proceeded to Chios. The Athenians under Thrasyllus and Thrasybulus, two of the leading democratic commanders, moved ahead to Lesbos, where they laid siege to the rebel city of Eresus, landing their seamen to do so. This made their fleet vulnerable to a sudden attack, but they expected scouts on Lesbos and the mainland to spot enemy movements.

However, Mindarus had his fleet take on two days' rations, and then set out along the mainland coast. After dining in Phocaean territory and at the Arginusae islands south-east of Mytilene, the fleet passed Lesbos at night and proceeded along the coast of the Troad, arriving at Rhoeteum about midnight – a voyage of some 189 nautical miles in thirty-six hours. An Athenian squadron at Sestos, stationed to watch an enemy flotilla at Abydos, fled to the open sea, but lost four ships to Mindarus' fleet. The main Athenian fleet quickly departed Eresus and massed at Elaeus, a city on the tip of the Thracian Chersonese. There the Athenians spent five days preparing for battle. With Euboea lost, Athens' food supply depended upon grain from the Greek trading cities of the northern Black Sea littoral. Mindarus now threatened to block its importation. Although outnumbered seventy-six to eighty-six, the Athenians had to fight.[21]

On the sixth day the Athenians headed up the Hellespont, making for Sestos but staying close to shore. Seeing this, Mindarus put to sea from Abydos. Both sides now deployed on their respective sides of the Hellespont. On Mindarus' right,

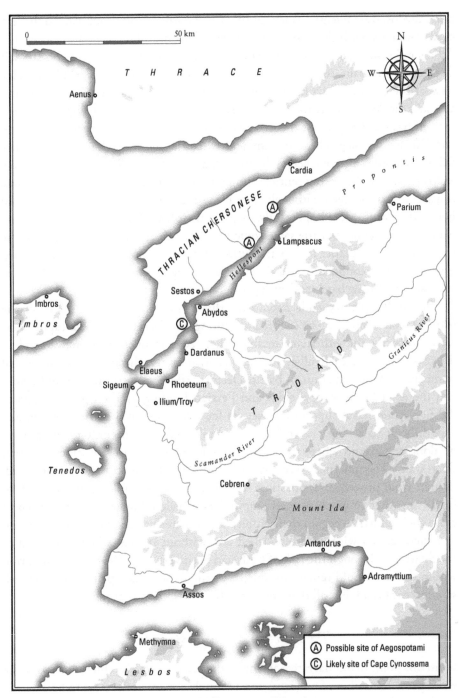

Map 8.2 Hellespont and Troad

near Abydos, were twenty Syracusan ships. Mindarus himself commanded the left, near Dardanus, with the best sailing vessels of his fleet. He hurried to engage the Athenians' centre and right, commanded by Thrasybulus. Thrasyllus on the left faced the Syracusans, the Cynossema promontory (modern Kilibakir) blocking his view of the rest of the battle. He did not react, therefore, when Mindarus' centre attacked the Athenian centre, driving it ashore and disembarking troops. Mindarus himself hastened to prevent the Athenian right's withdrawal down the Hellespont, but Thrasybulus kept ahead of him, and when he saw the Peloponnesian centre fall into disorder after its victory, he turned, attacked, routed Mindarus' squadron, and then struck the enemy centre, routing it also. The Athenians took twenty-one ships and lost eighteen, although they likely recovered most of the waterlogged hulks afterwards. More importantly, they lost their fear of their enemies. Mindarus' plan had been good, but the same could be said of the Peloponnesian plans at the two Cape Rhium battles in 429. Execution of battle plans requires skill, discipline, experience, and confidence, and these were lacking in the Spartan fleet after two years spent refusing battle and sitting ashore.[22]

Thucydides' history ends soon after this point, but one finds in it all the features that explain Sparta's fortunes during the Decelean War. Despite their losses in Sicily, the Athenians retained their edge in open-water naval combat. The Spartans and their allies needed surprise or treachery to overcome equal numbers of Athenian ships in battle. Despite Athenian losses to war and revolt, and the acquisition of new allies and Persian funding by the Spartans, Sparta did not attain naval superiority over its foe. Decisive naval battles were in any case difficult to arrange, since fleets could take refuge in friendly fortified ports or along any strand where their armies could offer support. Relations between Sparta and Tissaphernes were strained, and Persian military and financial aid, though vital, proved disappointing. The Athenians also suffered from a lack of funds now that so much of their empire had rebelled. However, they refused to cease their efforts to regain their empire. For this reason an oligarchic revolution in Athens ended with little bloodshed and without the city's being betrayed to the Spartans, although the risk of both had been very real. The political situation within the city would remain troubled, but the Athenians repelled Agis and still sent forces abroad. For all these reasons, therefore, the war ground on.

The Athenian Revival, 411–408[23]

From this point in our narrative and on to the last chapter, the chief sources are the writings of Xenophon, Diodorus, and Plutarch. These works tend to be careless, overly condensed, biased, prone to moralising, and unreliable in chronology.

Yet Xenophon was a contemporary and actor in the events of 411–362, and knew Sparta well. Diodorus and Plutarch were late authors, but they used fourth-century sources, including, in Diodorus' case, the *Hellenica Oxyrhynchia*. The different accounts often contradict each other, but often complement one another as well. Although the situation is not ideal, we can reconstruct Spartan military history in this half-century in detail.

After Cynossema, the Athenians entered the Propontis, captured a small squadron operating there, and recovered the rebel island city of Cyzicus in the south. Mindarus in turn recovered some lost ships and sent two officers, Hippocrates and Epicles, to bring Agesandridas' fleet from Euboea. Epicles led off over fifty triremes. Hippocrates may have stayed to prepare other ships, and perhaps also helped Agesandridas stop a renewed Athenian attack. However, while Epicles was sailing along the Thracian coast, a storm drove his fleet onto the Athos peninsula, where a Persian fleet had wrecked in 492. All the ships and ten thousand men were lost. This horrific catastrophe prevented a speedy revival of Mindarus' fleet.[24]

Mindarus also sent for Dorieus, who had been suppressing dissent on Rhodes and keeping an eye on Alcibiades, now busy with minor operations in the south. Dorieus and his squadron headed north and at the beginning of winter 411/10 entered the Hellespont. The resulting actions do not receive entirely satisfactory accounts from either Xenophon or Diodorus. A possible reconstruction is that Dorieus entered the Hellespont at dawn, to be intercepted by an Athenian squadron near Rhoeteum on the Asian side. He resisted from the shore successfully, but on the following morning was intercepted by the entire Athenian fleet as he neared Dardanus, halfway up the coast from Rhoeteum to Abydos. Mindarus responded with his entire fleet. A long struggle ensued, ending in an Athenian victory when Alcibiades, sailing on the track of Dorieus, arrived. Mindarus' fleet fled to shore, taking refuge with the satrap Pharnabazus and his army. The Athenians captured some of Mindarus' ships during this second Battle of Cynossema, or, as moderns call it, the Battle of Abydos, but failed to destroy his fleet.[25]

During the rest of the winter the Athenians split up, some ships remaining in the Hellespont to monitor Mindarus, while Thrasybulus went to Thrace to campaign and levy funds there, and Thrasyllus went to Athens to raise a new army and fleet for the east. In fact, thirty ships had already set forth from Attica under the command of Theramenes. He attacked without success a bridge being built across the Euripus to connect Boeotia and Euboea, and then plundered enemy territory and fined enemy sympathisers in the islands. The money he raised probably went to purchase timber in Macedon, for the new king there, Archelaus, favoured Athens and aided its shipbuilding, and Theramenes went there next to aid the king's siege of Pydna. Meanwhile Alcibiades sought to meet with Tissaphernes, only to be arrested; with the Spartans and their allies now openly hostile to him, the satrap could not afford to be seen consorting with the Athenians. Nevertheless, Alcibiades escaped and reached the coast after only a month in captivity.[26]

During the winter Mindarus and Pharnabazus made preparations to lay siege to those cities in Asia still allied to Athens. As winter ended, they went against Cyzicus, now in Athens' camp. Persian siegecraft made short work of the defences. Soon after, an Athenian squadron sailing in from the north-west approached the captured city, which lay on the southern tip of the island of Arctonnesus. Probably believing this to be the Athenian force from the Hellespont, come to relieve the city and ignorant of its fall, Mindarus put to sea with all his ships. On passing the peninsula and island at the south-western tip of Arctonnesus, however, the trap was sprung: the rest of the Athenian fleet, under Theramenes and Thrasybulus, sallied forth from hiding and blocked Mindarus' line of escape to Cyzicus, while the bait force under Alcibiades turned and attacked.

The Athenians in the Hellespont had retreated when Mindarus left Abydos, and sent for the other squadrons. Once massed, the Athenians had rowed up the Hellespont, passing Abydos at night so that their numbers would not be

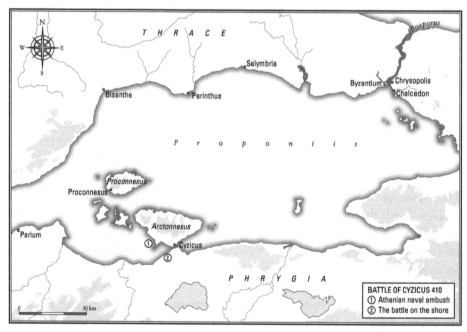

Map 8.3: Propontis and the Bosporus

known, and, after another brief stop, rested at the Proconnesus islands north-west of Arctonnesus the next night, seizing all boats in order to keep word of their numbers from reaching Mindarus. The next morning they advanced to the coast of Arctonnesus under cover of rainstorms. Having used up the money they had collected over the winter, they were determined 'to fight on sea, on land, and at walls', Xenophon says,[27] seeking a decisive action; Diodorus says they landed troops under Chaereas on the island with orders to attack Cyzicus, most likely during the confusion that would occur if Mindarus managed to escape to the city. To be sure, Xenophon simply has Alcibiades lead in the fleet under cover of a storm and catch the entire enemy force practising at sea. This must oversimplify the action. The Athenians had no reason to expect Mindarus to be at sea during a storm, and no hope of taking Cyzicus by assault or of luring him out of port if they found him within. They needed a stratagem.

Outflanked and outnumbered, Mindarus and his fleet fled to Cleri on the main-land south-west of the city. Pharnabazus' army was encamped there. The satrap was not at hand, but his troops came to aid the Spartans and their allies. Alcibiades, having taken or sunk some ships, pursued the rest to shore and tried to drag them off with grapples, but the Greek and Persian infantry fought him off. Thrasybulus landed with his marines and attacked, but Mindarus sent part of his infantry under Clearchus, harmost of Byzantium, to fight off Thrasybulus' flanking attack. Thrasybulus was soon hard-pressed. However, before his attack Thrasybulus had passed word to Theramenes to join with Chaereas, who may already have crossed to the mainland on troop transports, and return as quickly as possible. Theramenes and Chaereas did so, and the reinforced Athenians routed Pharnabazus' and Clearchus' men. Mindarus fought on desperately, but was slain. The entire Spartan and allied fleet was captured or destroyed, although the majority of the crews escaped. The Persians and Peloponnesians in Cyzicus abandoned the town and fled to the mainland. The Athenians had won their decisive victory, and deserved it.[28]

The situation of the surviving Peloponnesians was revealed in a message sent to Sparta by Hippocrates, Mindarus' secretary and second-in-command, and intercepted by the Athenians: 'Timbers lost, Mindarus gone, men starving, we know not what to do.'[29] Pharnabazus came to the rescue, providing funds and clothing to the men, arming them for guard duty, and offering the forests of Mount Ida in the southern Troad for shipbuilding. Even so, the defeat brought a peace embassy headed by Endius to Athens. He proposed that each side retain what it held and withdraw its garrisons from the other's lands. The Athenians rejected the proposal. Diodorus attributes this to evil counsellors, but with so many major subject states in revolt, such a peace offered Athens little. To be sure, it might have severed the ties between Sparta and Persia, but their cooperation had not proved overwhelming to date.

Perhaps to pressure the Athenians, Agis raided toward Athens from Decelea. Still there preparing his expedition, Thrasyllus led the Athenians into the open space of the Lyceum gymnasium east of the city to form for battle. Caught in order of march, Agis withdrew hastily, losing some of his rearmost men to the Athenian light troops. Later, seeing merchant ships bringing grain into the Piraeus from the Black Sea region, Agis manned fifteen triremes with Megarians, Boeotians, and other allies and sent them under the command of Clearchus to Byzantium. The Athenians took three in the Hellespont, but the rest made it to the city, which needed the help. The Athenians after Cyzicus had fortified Chrysopolis on the Bosporus opposite Byzantium, and based Theramenes there. He raided the territories of Byzantium and of Chalcedon on the Asian mainland, and levied a toll on merchant ships passing through the straits.[30]

In the mid-spring of, probably, 410,[31] Thrasyllus finally led his expedition east. He raided Pygela, won over Colophon, and made an incursion into Lydia before trying to take Ephesus by assault. However, Tissaphernes had learned of Thrasyllus' intentions to attack the city and rallied significant forces there, defeating the Athenians in detail as they divided their forces to perform, as the Oxyrhynchus Historian shows, a series of diversionary assaults. It was a rare defeat on land for the Athenians in the east. Thrasyllus did capture four Syracusan ships, from a squadron hastily rebuilt at Mount Ida after Cyzicus, and sent their crews as prisoners to Athens. He and Alcibiades spent the winter of 410/9 raiding Pharnabazus' Hellespontine territory, defeating him in battle, and also making Lampsacus a fortified base. Meanwhile Thrasybulus carried out operations on the Aegean coast of Thrace.[32]

The Spartans took advantage of Athenian concentration abroad by attacking Pylos that winter. They cut it off by sea with a small squadron of five Sicilian ships and six of their own, and assailed its walls. The Messenians and Helots of the garrison fought off the attacks, but they lacked supplies and had many wounded. A fleet sent to their relief from Athens failed to round Cape Malea due to storms. Finally they evacuated the fort under truce. Somewhat offsetting this victory for Sparta was the defeat of the Heracleans by the Oetaeans. They lost seven hundred men along with Labotas, the Spartan harmost.[33]

In spring or early summer 409, the Megarians recaptured their port of Nisaea, which Athens had held since 424. The Athenians retaliated by invading the Megarid with one thousand infantry and four hundred cavalry under Leotrophides and Timarchus. They were met south of Mount Cerata on the Megarian side of the border by an army that included Megarians, Lacedaemonians, and Syracusans. The Lacedaemonians were most likely a mora under a polemarch, detained while transiting to or from Decelea. The Syracusans would have been Thrasyllus' captives, who had escaped during the previous winter. Although outnumbered, the Athenians won, killing many Megarians but only twenty Lacedaemonians, who withdrew in good order into the hills. The mora likely had the left wing, the Megarians the right wing towards the coast. Perhaps the Athenian cavalry skirmished the Lacedaemonians and Syracusans to a standstill while the Athenian infantry routed the Megarians. The Oxyrhynchus Historian notes that, even though happy with this victory – their first over Spartan citizen forces since Pylos – the Athenians were angry with their generals for risking their men in battle. With so many now abroad, Athens' safety depended on the small number of experienced troops still in Attica.[34]

In a further setback for Sparta, in summer 409 Carthage attacked the Greeks of Sicily. The Carthaginians showed what could be accomplished in siege warfare by those who possessed the necessary skills, organisation, resources, and outlook: they assaulted and sacked two major Greek cities, Selinus and Himera. The Syracusan flotilla was summoned home, and never returned to Greece.[35]

Meanwhile, in spring 409 Alcibiades, Thrasyllus, and Theramenes laid siege to Chalcedon (modern Kadikoy), cutting off with a wooden wall the peninsula on which the city was situated. Hippocrates, the harmost, led the Chalcedonians and his own troops against the Athenians, while Pharnabazus tried without success to pass between the wall and the Chalcedon River. Hippocrates and Thrasyllus fought a lengthy hoplite battle until Alcibiades arrived with the cavalry and a few more hoplites. Hippocrates was slain and his army routed. Frustrated by two years of defeat, Pharnabazus agreed to take Athenian envoys to the Great King in return for a truce. Chalcedon would pay Athens tribute, but escape further punishment.

The Athenians now turned to the European side of the Bosporus. Alcibiades levied forces from the Thracian Chersonese, took Selymbria by treachery and trickery, and then joined the other Athenians at Byzantium. That city, on the eastern end of the same peninsula occupied by Roman Constantinople, was held by Clearchus and the troops that Agis had sent – some Perioecs and a few neodamodeis along with Megarians and Boeotians, aided by the Byzantines. The Athenians tried to storm the city, and skirmished against the walls. They achieved nothing, and at length dismissed the levies, relying on blockade. Because their lands had been raided by Theramenes and their trade blocked since spring 410, the Byzantines soon experienced starvation. Clearchus reportedly seized provisions for the use of his troops.

In winter 409/8, he left the city in the hands of his Megarian and Boeotian commanders and sailed off to meet with Pharnabazus, who was waiting for spring before he could leave with the envoys. Clearchus hoped to get money, build or gather ships, and raid Athenian-held territory, with the goal of drawing the enemy away from Byzantium. While he was gone, however, certain Byzantines were moved by their people's starvation to betray the city to the Athenians. To lure the foreign garrison away from the landward gates, the Athenians staged a fake withdrawal and then launched a night attack on the harbour. It worked, and the traitors admitted Alcibiades, Theramenes, and their men. They defeated Clearchus' troops in a hard battle in the marketplace, but only after proclaiming that no harm would befall the Byzantines, who promptly changed sides and turned on the garrison, which then surrendered.[36]

In spring 408, the Athenians sailed down the Hellespont, taking every city except Abydos. Most of the ships then returned to Athens for the summer. Alcibiades, who had played a prominent role in most of Athens' victories from Abydos onwards, saw his fortunes reach a peak: he was chosen as supreme commander to end the war. He returned east that autumn with a large fleet.[37] However, the course of the war soon turned strongly in Sparta's favour.

Lysander and Callicratidas, 408–405[38]

On leading the Athenian envoys inland in spring 408, Pharnabazus met Spartan envoys returning from the court of the Great King in the company of a teenaged Persian prince, Cyrus. The prince had been given supreme command in Asia Minor, with orders to aid the Spartan war effort. This does not mean that his father, Darius II, prioritised the Greek war any more than in 412–411. He sent Cyrus with only enough money to support a fleet for a year, and he never raised another Persian fleet. Cyrus' departure removed the troublesome prince from court, while his presence in Asia Minor brought unity to the Persian war effort there.

Cyrus ordered the Athenian envoys held to preserve secrecy, probably because he first had to secure his position and overcome restless tribes. When Cyrus finally came to Sardis he was met by the Spartan navarch, Lysander, who had sailed east in late summer 408. A *mothax* like Gylippus, but of Heraclid descent, Lysander persuaded the Persian prince to pay his fleet more than the amount promised, in the hope that the higher wages would cause mercenary oarsmen to desert the Athenian fleet and join his, improving his triremes' performance and injuring that of the Athenian ships. Cyrus had his own motives for aiding Sparta, as we shall discover. Freed from concerns about pay, Lysander concentrated his forces at Ephesus, increased them to ninety ships, and trained his crews. He could afford to adopt Astyochus' fleet-in-being strategy, avoiding battle but denying the Athenians operational freedom as well.[39]

Since some of Attica remained cultivated despite his raids, Agis levied a major army for an invasion of Attica: fourteen thousand hoplites, fourteen thousand light infantry, and twelve hundred cavalry. This probably occurred in spring 407. Having learned from deserters that the best Athenian troops were abroad with

Alcibiades, he made a night march to the plain north and east of Athens, drove in the outposts, and deployed his army in a line four deep surrounding two-thirds of its walls. This was an assault formation, with light-armed men operating under the cover of the hoplites (*Plate 16*). The idea was to approach the walls and attack with missiles everywhere, looking for weak spots where ladders could be put up, or gates fired or smashed.

However, old men and teenagers reinforced the guards on the walls while the cavalry sallied and fought a roughly equal number of Agis' Boeotian horsemen, defeating them. Agis advanced his infantry and the Athenian cavalry withdrew, but he decided against an assault. Armies already dispersed in assaults could be attacked and routed by strong sallies by the defenders, and Agis had seen his cavalry fail to stop their Athenian counterparts. Nevertheless, he did offer battle the next day, after the Athenians had set up a trophy for their victory. Since their cavalry had withdrawn before the advance of his infantry, they had not controlled the battlefield, so he claimed that they had no right to raise a trophy. Although badly outnumbered, the Athenian army came out and formed in front of the walls. Agis led his troops forward, only to come under heavy missile fire from the wall-tops. Forced to retreat, he led his men out of range, and finally consoled himself by going on to ravage Attica.[40]

In the east, Alcibiades could do little except raid and collect money, since his fleet could not risk engaging in sieges when Lysander had such a strong force. By now, most rebel cities accessible to the Athenian fleet would have developed strategies to hinder raiding, and been fortified against assault. Cyrus would have helped to defend them as well. At length Alcibiades led his fleet of one hundred ships to Notium on the coast north-west of Ephesus. He challenged Lysander to battle, without success. Finally, probably in winter 407/6, Alcibiades left with a small force to deal with threats to Athenian-allied Clazomenae and to meet with Thrasybulus, who had been free to conquer Thasos and regain Abdera, the largest city on the Aegean coast of Thrace. He had now come south to Phocaea.[41]

Alcibiades left his fleet under the command of Antiochus, the steersman of his flagship, an old crony of his and no potential rival. Although ordered not to seek battle, we learn from the Oxyrhynchus Historian that Antiochus did attempt to lure into a naval ambush a small number of Lysander's ships, probably those regularly sent to sea to train or serve as a guard. However, Lysander had learned of Alcibiades' absence, and struck Antiochus with a picked force, sinking Antiochus' vessel and routing the ambushing unit. He then put to sea with his entire fleet and fell on the rest of the Athenians as they sailed out in disorder to meet the unexpected attack. Twenty-two Athenian ships were destroyed or captured, the rest escaping to Notium's harbour defences. Lysander then withdrew to Ephesus, the Athenians to

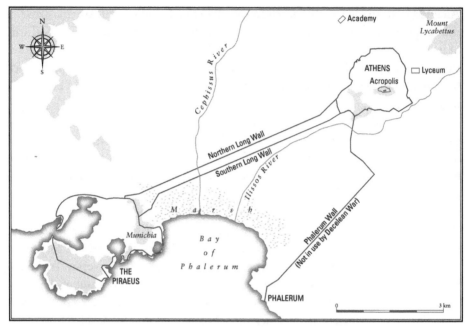

Map 8.4: Athens, the Long Walls, and the Piraeus

Samos. Alcibiades rejoined his fleet and again offered battle, but Lysander refused. Disgraced by this defeat, and by another that he suffered while raiding Cyme, a city on the mainland south-east of Lesbos, Alcibiades was deposed by the Athenians. He fled into exile in Thrace. His replacement, Conon, could do little other than return to raiding and collecting funds. He reduced his fleet to seventy fast, well-manned ships as an economy measure.[42]

In spring 406, Lysander's successor Callicratidas finally arrived. Whether he was delayed by naval preparations or because politicking in Sparta affected his appointment we do not know, but the sources are clear that Lysander was displeased at losing his post, although he had held it well past the end of his term. Lysander had begun forming cabals in the allied cities, offering their members power if they aided him. This secured him strong support at a time when war-weariness must have been high throughout the Aegean world, and gave him a personal power base. He had ambitions, and it would not be surprising if Callicratidas had been sent by factions hostile to him and desiring a rapid conclusion to the war.

On assuming his command, Callicratidas met resistance from within the fleet and among the allies. Cyrus refused to see him, and he lacked funds, for Lysander had returned everything to Cyrus before he departed. However, Callicratidas had brought significant reinforcements. His fleet totalled 140 ships, twice those of Conon. Facing down his Greek opponents, Callicratidas turned his back on Cyrus, secured funds from Miletus and Chios, both independent of Cyrus, and put to sea.[43] He repaid Chios by assaulting and taking Delphinium, whose five hundred defenders evacuated under truce, fearing the size of his forces. He then surprised and plundered Teos on the mainland, a city that had been neutral since 412, before going on to north-western Lesbos to assault Methymna. Taking it by betrayal, he released its free inhabitants, but plundered the town and sold as slaves the Athenians in the garrison. With 28,000 men to pay, he had to make war support war.[44]

Conon, meanwhile, had come north from Samos, probably hoping to attack when Callicratidas had large numbers of seamen ashore aiding in the siege of Methymna. Its sudden fall found him bivouacking on one of the numerous small islands off the north-east coast of Lesbos. Callicratidas presently headed east, making for Mytilene, and each fleet sighted the other. Callicratidas chased the Athenians, who made south for Mytilene, but Conon kept his fleet under control, for he meant to fight when near the safety of the city. As he probably expected, the best enemy ships pushed well ahead of the others in the pursuit. Nearing Mytilene, Conon raised a banner, a prearranged signal, and his entire force turned at once and attacked. However, he did not succeed in imitating Phormio's second victory. The enemy ships facing Conon's right wing bore up under its onset and backed water, awaiting the rest of their fleet, while his left, victorious over its foes, hared off in pursuit, splitting his forces. The rest of the Spartan and allied fleet now arrived and cut off the Athenian left, forcing it ashore. Thirty ships were abandoned as crews fled overland to Mytilene; Conon sailed there with forty. After gathering the wrecks and abandoned ships, Callicratidas headed to Mytilene. The city consisted of a small offshore island and a larger mainland section, with a sizable northern harbour connected by the strait to a small harbour in the south, probably fully enclosed at this time. Conon blocked the entrance to the northern harbour, but Callicratidas fought his way in on the following day, forcing Conon to withdraw his ships to the southern harbour. Conon was trapped, and the city besieged.[45]

Conon sent for help, but Callicratidas destroyed the squadron that came from the Hellespont to Mytilene's aid, and repaired and manned the damaged and captured ships, raising his fleet to 170 triremes. Athens responded by a mass levy of its citizens, resident aliens, and slaves freed for service, and added others from Athenian and allied squadrons in the empire, amassing over 150 ships. The relief fleet arrived at the Arginusae Islands south-east of Mytilene. Callicratidas was now receiving funding

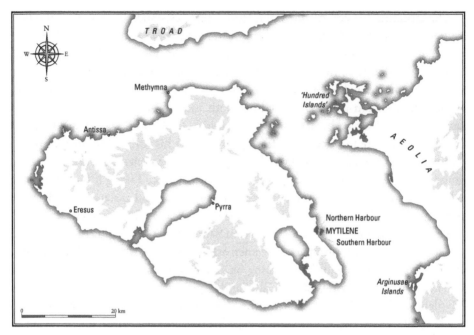

Map 8.5: Lesbos

from Cyrus, and could have withdrawn to a safe mainland base to resume pressuring the Athenians. Instead, he chose to fight. After a storm prevented him from making a night attack on the relief fleet, he sailed at dawn for the Arginusae Islands with 120 ships. The rest had been left to continue the blockade under Eteonicus, who had been active in the east since Astyochus' navarchy.[46] Possessing the faster fleet and steeled, we are told, by seers' predictions that he would die but his men would win, Callicratidas formed his fleet in a single line abreast for either *diekplous* or *periplous*. The Athenians lacked an army or base for support, so if he crushed them, he could win the war in a morning.[47]

The Athenians, with many poorly trained oarsmen and, perhaps, decks filled with extra soldiers to compensate for lack of mobility by focusing on boarding actions, formed in two lines to prevent a breakthrough. To prevent being outflanked they extended their lines by incorporating the islands within them. In the battle, Callicratidas attacked with his right wing. He was lost overboard when his ship rammed another too violently, and his outnumbered left wing was defeated by the Athenian right. Seventy-seven of his ships were sunk, as were twenty-five Athenian vessels. Callicratidas' surviving ships fled to Cyme and Phocaea on the mainland, or on to Chios. Reorganising to go against Eteonicus, the Athenian generals left lesser officers to carry out rescues of shipwrecked men, but a storm arose that prevented the attack and drowned most of the survivors. More than fifteen thousand of the Spartans and allies, and five thousand of the Athenians perished.[48]

Eteonicus learned of the defeat before the storm, and falsely proclaimed victory. This kept Conon inactive until Eteonicus could stage a withdrawal. He took command of the remnants of the fleet on Chios.[49] The Athenians were unable to follow up the victory in a meaningful way. Once back in Athens, anger at the generals for failing to rescue the shipwrecked men combined with political scheming to produce an unlawful mass trial and execution of the six accused commanders present.[50]

The Spartans again responded to a great naval defeat by offering peace, with each side to keep what it held. The Athenians had cause to accept the offer. They had regained much of their empire, and peace would have given them time to recover, while driving a wedge between Sparta and Persia. Nevertheless, the Athenian people voted to reject the offer.[51] Meanwhile, Cyrus stopped funding the fleet, whose crews survived the rest of the summer of 406 by working in Chios' fields. During winter 406/5, members of the crews, distressed now that farm work was no longer available, schemed to attack and loot the Chians. Eteonicus broke up the conspiracy by trickery and cold-blooded murder, and obtained temporary support for the fleet. Its continued survival remained in doubt.[52]

Aegospotami, 405–404[53]

At this juncture, the allies in the east decided to ask Sparta for Lysander's return as commander. Cyrus did so, too. Lysander's cabals no doubt played a leading role here, but they had a point. Xenophon notes protests following Callicratidas' arrival against the Spartan practice of replacing an experienced naval commander annually with a new and inexperienced one. The record of the navarchy had been atrocious: Astyochus left under a cloud; Mindarus lost three naval battles and died; his (probable) successor Pasippidas (410/9) achieved little and was exiled, accused of having assisted Tissaphernes in engineering a revolt in a Spartan-held city; his successor Cratesippidas (409/8) is recorded only as aiding a coup d'état on Chios;[54] and Callicratidas had gone to death and defeat after early successes. The Spartans could only agree, but since the law prevented any man holding the navarchy twice, they chose a man named Aracus as navarch, made Lysander his secretary and second-in-command, and ordered Aracus to obey him in all things. It would prove a fateful decision.[55]

In spring 405, Lysander arrived at Ephesus and concentrated all Spartan and allied triremes there. He approached Cyrus for funds and spent some time restoring his forces to fighting condition. The Athenians meanwhile formed a grand fleet of 180 triremes and supported themselves by raiding Spartan-allied territory. Probably taking advantage of the Athenians' absence on such a raid, Lysander sailed south with part of his fleet and surprised Iasos, which had returned to Athenian control. He executed as rebels all the adult men, sold as slaves the women and children, and razed the city. He also supported his cabal in Miletus in an oligarchic coup against the democracy there, even though the city was a loyal Spartan ally.

Having renewed the enthusiasm of his sailors and his followers for his leadership, Lysander could consider larger measures. Presently Cyrus was recalled to the sick bed of his father. Before departing, he turned over to Lysander the income from his province, along with sufficient control of its administration to guarantee funding. Cyrus secretly hoped to gain the throne instead of his older brother Artaxerxes, and now urged Lysander to remain quiet until he returned, promising him ample money and enough ships to crush the Athenians without risk. He probably also hoped for aid from Lysander if he had to rebel openly. However, Plutarch says that Lysander could not remain quiet with so great a fleet, perhaps because Ephesus' resources were strained by the expanded force. He sailed, and it was well for Sparta that he did: Artaxerxes assumed the throne and arrested Cyrus.[56]

Lysander took the entire fleet south, taking by assault the island city of Cedreae in Caria, and landed at Rhodes. The Athenian fleet continued raiding Ephesus and Chios from Samos, evidently hoping to compel Lysander to seek battle. Xenophon now has Lysander head north along the coast of Ionia right past the Athenians at Chios and sail to the Hellespont, while the Athenians follow from Chios but keep to the open sea, since the mainland was hostile. While the described actions parallel Mindarus' movement north in 411, the risk that Lysander might be intercepted or beaten to the Hellespont was very great, casting doubt upon Xenophon's account. Plutarch and Diodorus far more credibly have Lysander head west to raid Aegina, Salamis, and the coast of Attica, and greet Agis, thereby drawing the Athenian fleet out of position to chase him. On learning of its approach, Lysander first returned east and then sailed to the Hellespont, where he assaulted and captured Lampsacus. In this action he was aided by Thorax, an experienced Spartan commander and his friend, who had the command at Abydos and led its levies in the assault.[57]

With Lysander threatening other Athenian positions in the region and cutting off merchant traffic through the Hellespont, the Athenians entered the strait and took position on the Thracian Chersonese near Lampsacus, at a place where two streams, the 'Goat's Rivers' (*Aigospotamoi*), offered water for the thirsty crews. Unfortunately, the precise location is uncertain.[58] Every morning the Athenian fleet sailed over and offered battle; Lysander manned his ships but stayed quiet. When the Athenians returned to their camp, he sent scouts to follow and observe their actions. He did not bring his crews ashore until his scouts had returned. As the days passed, the Athenian crews went further and further from camp in search of food – triremes carried few stores, the Aegospotami area had few inhabitants, and the merchants who normally created markets for armies and fleets were probably still arriving, thanks to the unexpected movement of the fleet.

At this point Alcibiades arrived in the Athenian camp. He had spent his exile operating a small army out of the forts he held to the north, raiding independent Thracian tribes for loot and slaves.[59] Xenophon just has him give advice, but Diodorus says that he offered to persuade the Thracian kings Medocus and Seuthes to provide forces with which to attack the foe at Lampsacus. He wanted a share of the command in return. While he gathered his allies, the Athenians should shift their base to Sestos, where they would be supplied and secure. The generals sent him off, seeing no personal advantage in letting Alcibiades get the glory of a victory, and surely reflecting that he had promised more than he could deliver before.[60] They also may have been worried about what Lysander might attempt while they were absent.

They should have been more worried about what Lysander would do while they were present. Late on the fifth day, Xenophon reports, after the Athenians had scattered in search of supplies, Lysander's scouts signalled to him while still in mid-channel, indicating the Athenians were in disorder. The navarch promptly led his fleet across the Hellespont, catching most Athenian triremes only partially manned. In contrast, Diodorus omits the challenges, and reports that with famine gripping the fleet, the Athenian general Philocles put to sea with thirty ships, ordering the rest to follow when ready. Lysander had learned of the plan from deserters, however, and attacked with his entire fleet. Philocles and his ships fled to their camp. Lysander put ashore Eteonicus and his land forces, which captured part of the camp, while Lysander's ships tried to tow off Athenian vessels with grapples.

Xenophon omits these details, and since some of Diodorus' account parallels his report of Notium, it has been considered suspect. Nevertheless it is possible the two accounts complement one another. The Athenians may have planned to attack Lysander's position by night, with the operation to commence when they saw his scouts depart. Philocles' initial movement was meant to transport land forces across the strait, leaving them to march in and attack once the fleet reunited and sailed against Lampsacus. Since the decision would have been made the night before, however, deserters were able to take word of it to Lysander, who pre-empted the Athenian action.

In any event, Conon, one of the Athenian commanders, fled with his squadron, and other vessels escaped, but Philocles' squadron and the rest were crushed. Most of the fleet was taken, along with thousands of sailors, including three to four thousand Athenian crewmen, as well as Philocles and others of the generals. Invited by Lysander to decide their fate, the allies present voted to put all the Athenians to death, as punishment for recent atrocities.[61]

Lysander's victory did not result from his seizing a sudden, chance opportunity. Experience had shown that Athenian fleets could be defeated only by overwhelming numbers or surprise attack. It was also clear that no defeat could be decisive if the defeated had a refuge nearby. By taking Lampsacus, Lysander won a refuge and base, located on the crucial supply route from the Black Sea to Athens. This forced an Athenian response. Opposite Lampsacus was a defenceless beach with water but no food, promising supply problems, which acted to prevent full manning of the Athenian fleet in a way similar to that seen at Eretria in 411. Lysander had practised his forces in assaults at Iasos and Cedreae, and either put his friend Thorax in command at Abydos, or exploited the good fortune of having him there already. Aided by these preparations and his unexpected arrival, he seized Lampsacus. Even his meeting with Agis in Attica may have been arranged in advance, so the king could bring a land army to serve as a refuge if the necessity arose.

Lysander had out-thought the Athenians from start to finish, winning the Peloponnesian War in an afternoon by out-generalling a collection of admittedly second-rate Athenian commanders. Superior generalship had been necessary, for the Lycurgan land army could only guarantee Sparta's power in the Peloponnese. Victory abroad and at sea, with mostly allied forces, required good generalship and good luck. Brasidas, Gylippus, and Lysander had these; many others had not. Lysander's triumph was not inevitable: the Athenians could have intercepted him before he reached the Hellespont, or Lampsacus could have repelled his assaults, or the generals could have accepted Alcibiades' proposal and gone to Sestos, or pre-empted Lysander by attacking him first, as suggested above. A triumph would have allowed the Athenians once again to seek to negotiate with the Great King, split Persia and Sparta, and win the Decelean War. Lysander instead exploited their generals' errors and crushed their fleet. It helped his cause that, unlike the Athenians, he kept his plans to himself. This, and the Athenian orientation of the sources, explains why his planning is neither stated clearly nor better understood.

The rest may be summarised quickly enough. Lysander swept up city after city, sending all Athenians home under truce, to add to the number of mouths to feed. Only Samos and Athens continued to resist, and both came under blockade. Presently Lysander arrived in Attica, as did the massed levies of the Spartans and their allies, commanded by Pausanias, Pleistoanax' heir. The latter eventually departed, no doubt after doing as much damage as possible. Starvation would achieve the victory. Agis remained at Decelea to pressure Athens by land, while at

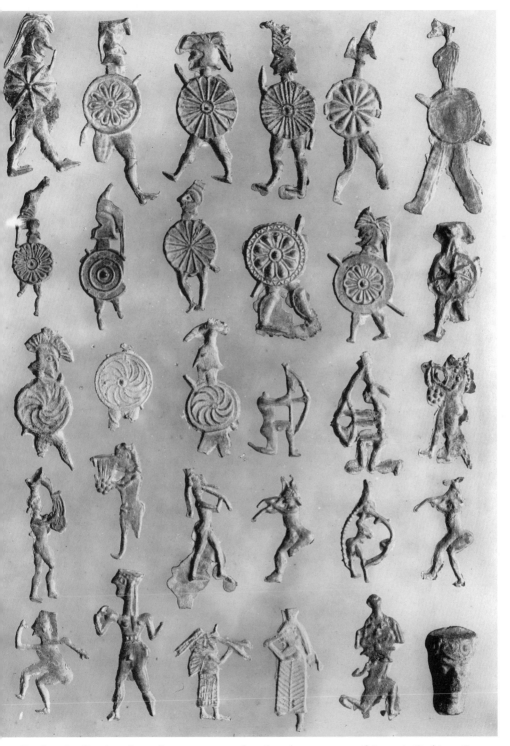

4. Lead votive figurines from the era 650–620 found at the sanctuary of Artemis Orthia at Sparta. Besides the hoplites, note two kneeling nude archer figures, one helmeted. Below them are musicians and dancers. (*Dawkins 1929: plate CLXXXIII [HS 7742]. Reproduced with permission of the British School at Athens*)

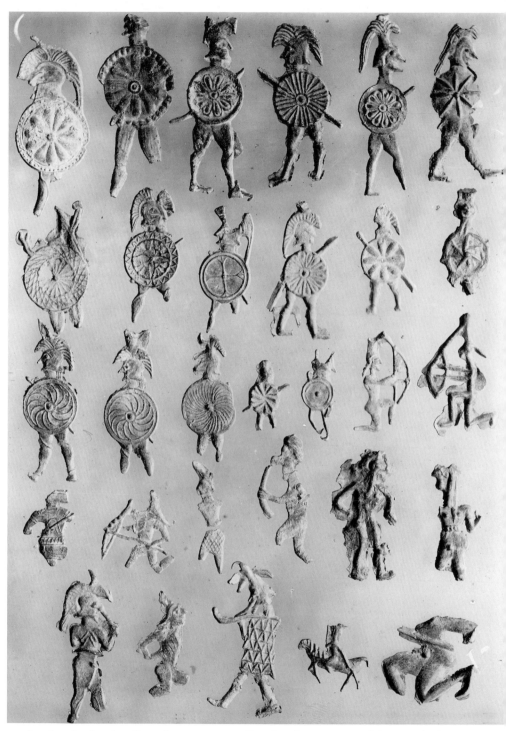

2. Lead votive figurines from the era 620–580 found at the sanctuary of Artemis Orthia at Sparta. Hoplites and kneeling archer figures continue, and what may be standing or running bowmen also appear. The geometric patterns on the shields appear on other Spartan depictions of the period. (*Dawkins 1929: plate CXCI [HS 7747]. Reproduced with permission of the British School at Athens*)

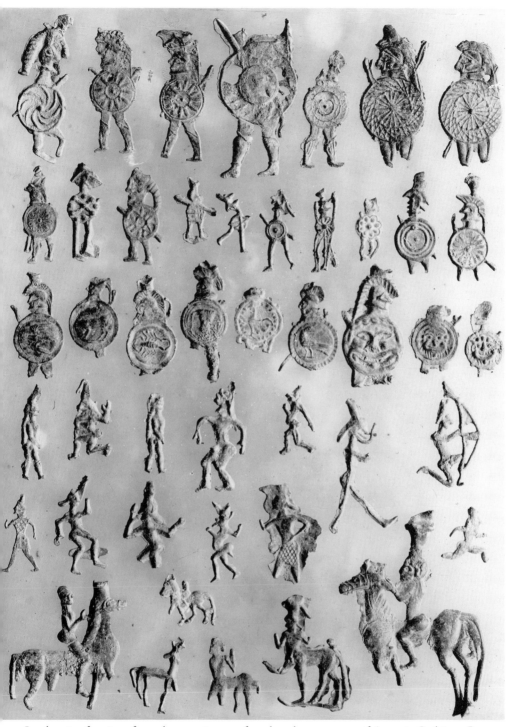

3.   Lead votive figurines from the era 580–500 found at the sanctuary of Artemis Orthia at Sparta.
The kneeling archer figure continues into this period, but not beyond it, while the shield devices change
from geometric patterns to the images of fierce animals and legendary beings. (*Dawkins 1929: plate
CXCVII [HS 7734]. Reproduced with permission of the British School at Athens*)

4.   (Left) This bronze figurine from the shrine of Apollo Korynthos in Messenia (540–525) depicts a heavily armed hoplite with a crested Corinthian-style helmet (with exaggerated eye openings), richly engraved cuirass, decorated tunic, upper and lower arm and thigh pieces, and greaves. His shield and weapon are lost. Arm and thigh pieces went out of fashion after this century. (*National Museum, Athens 14789, photograph by Emil Kunze, D-DAI-ATH-NM 2367. All rights reserved*)

5.   (Right) This bronze figurine, dated 535–525, was found at the sanctuary of Zeus at Dodona, an oracular site often visited by Spartans. It is similar in style to the figurine of Plate 4. The figure has a Corinthian-style helmet (with exaggerated eye openings), engraved cuirass, tunic, and greaves, and long, carefully dressed hair. The crest, shield, and weapon are lost. (*Ioannina Museum 4914, photograph by Hermann Wagner, D-DAI-ATH-NM 3760. All rights reserved*)

6.   A bronze statuette of the late sixth century, whose origin is uncertain. It is usually but not certainly identified as a Spartiate, due to its long cloak, bare feet, and carefully dressed locks. The unusual transverse crest on the helmet may indicate officer status. The figure once held a spear or staff, now lost. (*Wadsworth Atheneum Museum of Art, Hartford, CT. Gift of J. Pierpont Morgan, Jr. Accession number 1917.815*)

7.   This Attic red-figure cup from Caere (Duris painter *c.*500) shows hoplites arming. Note the bowl-shaped *aspis* shields, crested Corinthian helmets, spears, swords, padded undergarments, scale-reinforced linen corselets, and greaves. (*Kunsthistorisches Museum, Vienna, inv. 3694, Castellani Collection*)

8.   This frieze from the Nereid Monument of Xanthus in Lycia (Günük, southwestern Turkey, 390–380) shows two hoplites, one backed by an archer, fighting at close quarters, their left sides turned forward and shields in *Medium Ward*, resting on the shoulder and held close. This ward shielded the body below the head and permitted forceful shoving, but a weapon piercing the shield could cause a wound. The weapons have not survived. (*Frieze slab # 859. © Copyright the Trustees of The British Museum*)

9. This detail of an Attic volute krater attributed to the Berlin Painter (500–480) shows Achilles, left, battling Memnon, who holds his shield in *High Ward*, resting its top on his shoulder and holding it at an angle. This makes it harder for a spear thrust through the shield to reach his body, and covers his underarm sword swing. Achilles holds his shield in *Outside Ward*, with its edge pointed at Memnon's left shoulder. This makes it harder for Memnon to reach him with the sword, covers his underarm spear strike, and allows him to use his shield to knock aside or hook Memnon's shield. (*GR 1848.0801.1.* © *Copyright the Trustees of The British Museum*)

10. A detail of a fragmentary Middle Corinthian black-figure column-krater attributed to the Cavalcade Painter (590–570), showing in cross-section two hoplite formations in battle. Only the legs of the men actually engaged in combat can still be seen. Men move forward to join the action, or rise from where they have been kneeling. Bodies have been pulled back on both sides. It is uncertain whether this vase depicts a phase of a typical hoplite battle of this era, or recounts a tale in which two duelling champions have killed each other and the watching armies have begun to fight. (*The Metropolitan Museum of Art, Rogers Fund, 1912 [12.229.9]. Image © The Metropolitan Museum of Art*)

11 and 12. This Attic red-figure skyphos of *c*.450 shows on one side (*Plate* 11) a light-armed *psilos* protected by a rough cap and animal skin, bearing a sword, and about to throw a stone, and on the other side (*Plate* 12) a peltast with *pelta* shield ready to throw a javelin. (*Kunsthistorisches Museum, Vienna, inv.* IV 1922)

13. This detail of a fifth-century Attic red-figure amphora shows a peltast with a pair of javelins, a wicker-and-leather *pelta* decorated with good-luck symbols, and a helmet and thick cloak. Thracian peltasts more often wore fox-skin caps. (*Ashmolean Museum, Oxford, AN1971.867*)

14. This Attic black-figure vase by the Mastos Painter (*c.510*) shows two horsemen over a fallen hoplite. Both riders are lightly equipped, wield large javelins that double as spears, and ride stallions bareback. (*Vas 1500. Staatliche Antikensammlungen und Glyptothek, Munich*)

15. This detail from the Assyrian siege scene from Nimrud (865–860), shows a siege assault. Teams of archers and shield-bearers, including the king himself, provide covering fire for men operating a combined battering ram and siege tower (right), and undermining (centre) or digging through (left) the walls. The defenders shoot back, throw torches and inflammables at the engine, and try to draw up the ram using a chain. (*NW Palace, Room B, Panel 4 bottom.* © *Copyright the Trustees of The British Museum*)

6. This frieze from the Nereid Monument (390–380) shows a storming attempt by hoplites and archers. It is met by hoplites sallying forth from the beleaguered city and throwing stones, supported by fellow hoplites on the walls who are also throwing stones. (*Frieze slab # 869.* © Copyright the Trustees of The British Museum)

7. These friezes from the Nereid Monument (390–380) show an escalade, probably during a betrayal, to judge from the watchful inactivity of the two lone figures in the fort. Hoplites have set a ladder against the wall and are ascending it. The two figures beneath the ladder are either armoured archers or hoplites without shields, holding ropes (once painted on) to steady the ladder. (*Frieze slabs # 872 and # 877.* © Copyright the Trustees of The British Museum)

18. The modern reconstruction of trireme *Olympias* under oar. Note the top deck running the length of the ship, typical of triremes of the late fifth and fourth centuries. The mainmast and its sail could be left in camp to lighten the ship for action. (*Photo by John F. Coates, by permission of The Trireme Trust*)

19. The modern reconstruction of trireme *Olympias* under sail. Given the crowded conditions on board, crews usually camped ashore every night, anchoring their ships offshore. (*Photo by Paul Lipke, by permission of The Trireme Trust*)

10. This detail of a black-figure Attic kylix (520–500) depicts on the left a merchant 'round ship', economically powered by sail alone, and on the right a small oared warship with two banks of oars. (*GR 1867,0508.963.*© *Copyright the Trustees of The British Museum*)

11. This detail from the Attic red-figure Brygos Cup (*c.*490) shows a young Athenian hoplite, with his *aspis* held in *Outside Ward*, knocking aside the *spara* shield of his Persian opponent and about to make an underarm spear thrust. Made of wicker and leather, a *spara* could be propped up alongside others to form a shield-wall, or held by a central handhold, as here. (*Ashmolean Museum, Oxford, AN1911.615*)

22. Persian archers fighting behind *spara* shield-walls became vulnerable once these came down, as seen on the Nolan neck-amphora (Attic red-figure, 480–470). Note the depiction of the hoplite's shield in *Outside Ward* at its true angle, rather than out flat as in *Plate 9*. (*The Metropolitan Museum of Art, Rogers Fund, 1906 [06.1021.117]. Image © The Metropolitan Museum of Art*)

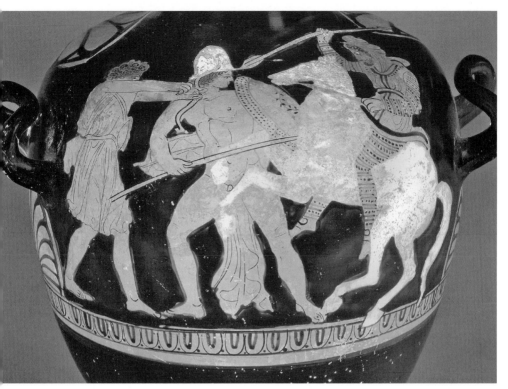

23. This Attic-style red-figure hydria of the Cyrenaic type, dating to 400–350, depicts a Persian horseman attacking a hoplite and an archer. This pottery imitated earlier Attic types, so the original may have depicted men of the picked body of three hundred Athenian hoplites and the archers they protected at Plataea in 479. (GR 372, E233.)

24. This fragment of a late-fifth-century Athenian victory monument from the Acropolis shows a hoplite in an Attic-style helmet gazing on a trophy, to which are attached a conical helmet, shield, and single-shoulder tunic, typical of Spartan warriors of the period. (Athens, Acropolis Museum, 3173, photograph by Eva-Maria Czakó, D-DAI-ATH-Akropolis 2062.)

25. This fragment of an Athenian funeral monument (c.390) depicts a hoplite standing triumphantly over a fallen man who wears a conical helmet and wields a short stabbing sword, characteristic of Spartan soldiers of the era. Judging from his short hair, he may be a Perioec or freed Helot. Absence of body armour is common in period depictions. (*The Metropolitan Museum of Art, Fletcher Fund 1940* [40.11.23]. *Image © The Metropolitan Museum of Art*)

least part of Lysander's fleet kept food from being brought in by sea. The suffering Athenians eventually capitulated in spring 404, the Samians later that summer, after Lysander threatened an assault.[62] The Athenians agreed, according to Xenophon, to 'tear down the Long Walls and the Piraeus walls, hand over all but twelve ships, receive back their exiles, and, holding the same peoples as friend and foe as the Lacedaemonians, follow them whithersoever they lead by land and by sea.'[63] At the cost of twenty-seven years of war, immense human suffering, tens of thousands of deaths, civil strife in most Greek cities, and the restoration of Persian rule over the Greeks of Asia, the Spartans had now become the sole leaders of Greece and the Aegean Greek world.

~ Nine ~

IMPERIAL ADVENTURES, 404–395

The Strategic Situation and Affairs in Greece, 404–399[1]

In 404 Sparta had triumphed over Athens and dominated Greece and the Aegean. It now ruled over Athens' naval empire. If there was opposition to this at Sparta, it is not attested. After all, the loss of the naval leadership to Athens in the 470s had led to a long, horrible conflict, and withdrawal would leave a power vacuum in the Aegean. The honour and profits of being leaders of all Greece no doubt appealed to the majority of Spartiates. In any case, Lysander had handed them a naval empire, establishing in many of Athens' former subjects ruling boards of ten men, decarchies, consisting of his followers. He also backed the creation of less narrow oligarchies. They needed Spartan support to survive. To provide it, Lysander aided in massacres of democrats.[2] He commanded a large fleet, left harmosts and garrisons in strategic locations, and sent great quantities of silver to Sparta as a financial reserve. An 'Allied Fund' (*To Symmachikon*) for the naval effort had already existed for some time. States submitting after Aegospotami had to contribute to it, while current allies remained responsible for payments still owed and for contributions to new Spartan-commanded operations.[3] Therefore Sparta had warships, manpower, and money – necessities for a naval empire in the Aegean.

However, Spartan naval rule was inherently fragile. Athens' seapower had been supported by its large and growing population, strong walls, fine port city, income from the empire and Attica, and ability to compel service and funding. The Spartiates were a population in decline. Helots rowed triremes, and freed Helots could serve as hoplite marines or in garrisons, but only a fraction of them could be employed in this way, given the need for Helot agricultural labour. No Perioecic coastal town could match the Piraeus, and if the Peloponnese held enemies, the Spartans could not leave the defence of unwalled Sparta to old men and teenagers and perform a mass naval levy in Athenian fashion. The general lack of naval experience in Lacedaemon would have made this impractical in any case. In finance, Aristotle claimed that wealthy Spartans easily avoided taxation.[4]

Income from loot and allied tribute evidently failed to meet expenditures. The Spartans probably found it politically infeasible to levy tribute in peacetime – the resemblance to the hated Athenian imperial tribute would have been too strong. As Thucydides noted, collecting funds only in wartime could not meet crises or properly develop naval forces.[5]

Sparta's naval strength, therefore, depended on allied support, but this support would prove fragile. The Sparta that had started a war with Athens by promising to bring freedom to the Greeks now supported massacres, installed decarchies and oligarchies, imposed harmosts and garrisons, and abandoned the East Greeks to Persian rule. The misdeeds of Spartan officials abroad proved damaging as well. A notable case arose in 403/2. The Byzantines, hard-pressed by war with Thracian tribes and civil strife, sought Spartan aid. Clearchus was sent. He hired mercenaries, now readily available in Greece after the war, and seized power. After envoys failed to persuade him to depart, Sparta sent an army under Panthoedas against him. Clearchus shifted base to Selymbria, thinking it more secure, and fought it out at a site called Porus. Defeated, he stood a siege, but finally left under truce. By 401, still unpunished, he was leading an army against the Thracians on Cyrus' behalf.[6] Cyrus had been released by his brother Artaxerxes on the pleadings of their mother. Returning to his provinces, Cyrus fell into conflict with Tissaphernes and in secret began to amass Greek mercenary armies.

In the west, the Spartans allied with the tyrant Dionysius I, who had seized power in Syracuse during the disastrous war with Carthage that began in 409. A Spartan agent even aided Dionysius in securing his rule. This move, supported by Lysander, kept the Corinthians from using their influence in the west to Sparta's detriment, but it cost Sparta even more of its legitimacy and reputation, and increased fears among Sparta's allies of its intervention in their affairs.[7]

In Greece, the coalition of 418 – the Argives, Mantineans, Eleans, and Athenians – had been neutralised, but could reappear. The Corinthians and Thebans could be added to their number, as both had been angered by Sparta's refusal to destroy Athens or to share the loot from the great victory. The Corinthians no doubt also resented their decline in power and prestige relative to Sparta, while the Thebans had the glory of their victory at Delium, greater population and territory thanks to the Archidamian War, and wealth from the looting of Attica during the Decelean War. Already heading the mighty Boeotian Confederation, the Thebans felt capable of much more.[8] Any state seeking to expand its power, however, faced the prospect of Spartan intervention.

In Sparta, the influx of coined money into a society used to only modest amounts of cash caused turmoil.[9] The Spartiates also refused to extend full citizenship, despite their declining numbers. Men who had served Sparta ably found themselves still lacking in status. In 399 this led to a conspiracy by Cinadon, an 'inferior'. He and his comrades planned to attack the ephors and Gerousia in the marketplace and encourage a general uprising by all classes of non-Spartiates. An informer revealed the plot to the ephors. In response, they ordered Cinadon, who had done police work for them before, to proceed to Aulon in north-western Messenia to arrest certain people, giving him an escort of *Hippeis*. Instead, the *Hippeis* arrested Cinadon. On questioning he gave up his accomplices, who were arrested in turn.[10] This threat had passed, but the potential for revolt remained. In any event, Spartiates continued to monopolise most commands, which meant that Sparta's pool of potential leadership talent was dwindling.

The most immediate political problem, however, was that there were three leading Heraclids instead of two: the Eurypontid King Agis, the young Agiad Pausanias, son of Pleistoanax, and the upstart Lysander. Each had his faction of followers, which in Agis' case included guest-friends from the leading families of the Peloponnese, and in Lysander's case men of the governments that he had created. Pausanias no doubt had some Spartan and foreign supporters, but decades of Agiad obscurity left him weakly positioned compared to his competitors. Spartan policy would be tugged in diverging directions as each faction sought to get the better of the other two.

This was certainly the case in Sparta's intervention in the civil war of 404–403 at Athens. After Athens' surrender, Lysander had backed the creation there of an oligarchic government led by a ruling council, the 'Thirty'. It sought, and received, a garrison of seven hundred Laconian hoplites under the harmost Callibius.[11] Athenian democrats rebelled against the Thirty's oppressive rule in winter 404/3. Thrasybulus, general and democratic leader in the Decelean War, seized the stronghold of Phyle north-west of Athens in the southern foothills of Mount Parnes, holding it against an assault by the Thirty and their men. Later, Callibius encamped with his men and some Athenian cavalry over two kilometres away from Phyle, in an effort to prevent the plundering of local farms – only to be routed in a dawn surprise attack by Thrasybulus, losing over 120 hoplites and a few horsemen. Thrasybulus soon grew strong enough to march to the unfortified Piraeus and raise it in revolt. He defeated the Thirty in a defensive battle on Munichia Hill, killing Critias, the leading spirit of the group. The Thirty were deposed and sought refuge at Eleusis, but an oligarchic government retained control of Athens.[12]

The democrats plundered the Attic countryside in search of food, and assaulted the city's walls. Both the Thirty and the oligarchs at Athens appealed to Sparta for aid. Lysander responded by arranging a loan to the oligarchs, and by having himself made harmost and his brother Libys navarch for 403/2. Lysander went to

Eleusis to raise an army and hire mercenaries, and had Libys blockade the Piraeus. His repetition of the tactics of the siege of 405–404 soon brought the democrats into difficulties.[13]

In Lysander's absence, however, the potential for factional conflict among the Spartan elite causing radical policy shifts became apparent. King Pausanias persuaded the ephors to give him command of an army levied from all the allies. The Corinthians and Thebans refused to serve, fearing Spartan control of Athens. When the king arrived, Lysander and his mercenaries necessarily joined his invasion. The democrats refused Pausanias' orders to disperse, so he assaulted their defences – likely a combination of ditches, palisades, house walls, and other expedients. However, he did not push the attack, and soon returned to camp. The next day, the king advanced with two Spartan morai and some Athenian oligarchic cavalry to examine the ground north-west of the Piraeus and judge where best to build a siege wall. That was the logical next step once assault was found to be unpromising, and would have protected the Attic countryside from raiding as well as cut the democrats off from supply.

However, on his return his men were attacked by light-armed troops. Instead of leading his men off carefully, as Agis had done in similar circumstances, the king angrily ordered the cavalry to charge, along with the hoplites up to ten years from manhood (i.e. twenty to twenty-nine years old). He followed with the rest, pursuing the retreating democrats to the Theatre of Dionysus on the north-western slopes of Munichia, where their comrades were arming. Reinforced, and supported by hoplites, the democrats' light-armed now swarmed forward, sending a hail of shot, stones, javelins, and arrows at the Spartans, who fell back in good order, but hard-pressed and with many wounded. Both polemarchs, Chaeron and Thibrachus, were slain, as well as Lacrates, who as an Olympic victor enjoyed the honour of fighting as a king's bodyguard. Thrasybulus led up his hoplites, and Pausanias withdrew to a hill several hundred metres back, ordering his army to his aid. On its arrival, he formed a very deep phalanx and led it forward. The Athenian hoplites fought back, but some were pushed into the marsh of Halae and the others gave way, falling back into their defences. Some 150 Athenians perished, and thirteen Lacedaemonians. The latter were buried later outside the Kerameikos Gate of Athens. Their tomb has been excavated (*Figure 8*), and several bodies found. One had a spear point between its ribs, another had two bronze arrowheads in its leg (*Figure 9*).[14]

We are told that Pausanias showed no resentment over the battle, but instead staged appeals to Sparta by the democrats, and finally reconciled them with the oligarchs in the city, restoring the democracy.[15] It is said that he was jealous of Lysander and afraid he would gain firm control of Athens, and also sought to rid Sparta of the accusation of aiding a brutal tyranny. Certainly Pausanias needed to

8. Spartan dead from the Battle of the Piraeus in 403, including two polemarchs and a bodyguard of King Pausanias, were buried with full honours in the outer Kerameikos Cemetery, on the road from Athens to the Academy north-west of the ancient city. These are the remains of the tomb, excavated in 1930. (*David Conwell*)

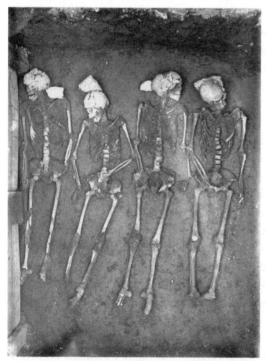

9. Four of the thirteen Spartan bodies buried in the collective tomb in the Kerameikos were found intact. The body on the far left has a spearhead between its ribs. Another had two arrowheads in its leg. The stones shown were placed under the heads. (*No photographer listed, D-DAI-ATH-KER 1992. All rights reserved*)

lead expeditions if he wished to gain prestige and reward his supporters. He probably also hoped to make the democratic leaders of Athens his clients. He aligned with democratic leaders at Mantinea later.[16]

And so the Spartans restored the democracy at Athens, a little over a century after Cleomenes had striven to overthrow it, and scarcely a year after they had brought Athens to surrender. Many at Sparta must have thought it madness. Pausanias was brought to trial before the Gerousia for his actions in Attica, barely escaping conviction.[17] His move may have seemed justified when Athens loyally aided Sparta against Elis in 402–400. Conscious of the Eleans' past slights and their potential threat to Messenia, and recently annoyed by their refusal to allow Agis to sacrifice at Olympia for victory in war, Spartan envoys instructed the Eleans to liberate their outlying subject towns. The Eleans refused, supposedly telling the Spartans to liberate their own Perioecs first. The ephors mobilised the Spartan and allied levies and gave them to Agis to lead. He had just invaded Elis by way of Achaea and begun ravaging the land when an earthquake occurred. Considering it a prodigy, he disbanded his army. Encouraged, the Eleans sent envoys to every state hostile to Sparta, but gained no allies. Without allies, they had no hope.[18]

In spring 401 the ephors held a new levy. Athens sent men; Corinth and Boeotia did not. Agis invaded Elis from the south, via Aulon and the Neda River valley, and won over Lepreum and various peoples of the southern districts. After sacrificing at Olympia, Agis entered the Eleans' home territory and ravaged it. The plunder of herds and slaves proved so extensive that more Achaeans and Arcadians came seeking loot. The city of Elis lacked walls, but it did have a strong acropolis and hurriedly built defences. Agis accordingly damaged the suburbs but made no assault. He relied on ravaging instead, and probably expected an uprising against the Elean democracy by Xenias, a wealthy pro-Spartan friend. The uprising occurred, but failed, and before departing Agis built a fort at Epitalium near the Alpheius River, garrisoning it with troops under the harmost Lysippus and the exiled Elean rebels. According to Xenophon, raiding from this fort caused the Eleans to surrender the following summer.[19]

However, Diodorus reports an invasion by Pausanias and omits any mention of Agis' operations.[20] Since the two kings' reported campaigns mesh well, it seems each writer focused on one Heraclid's actions and wrote out the other. In autumn 401, given four thousand Lacedaemonians and a large allied army (Corinth and Thebes again refusing service), Pausanias entered Elean territory from Arcadia. He campaigned in eastern and northern districts where Agis had not gone, winning over or capturing forts and towns before proceeding to Elis. There he made a careless attack on a fortified gymnasium north of the city, only to have a sudden sally by the citizens and a thousand Aetolians, now come to Elis' aid, put his men to flight,

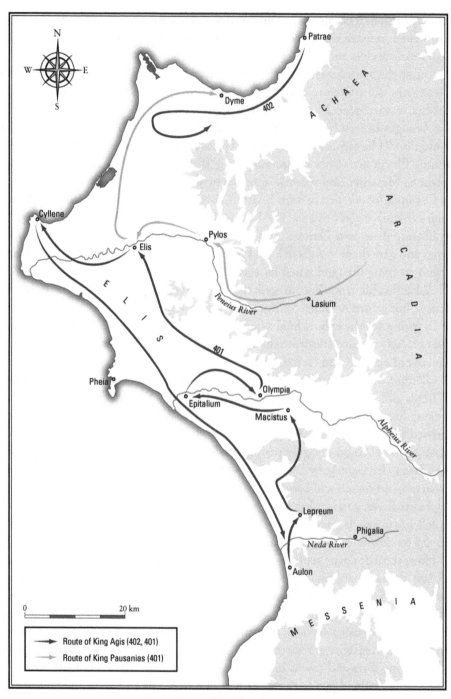

Map 9.1 The Elean War

killing thirty. Pausanias withdrew, resumed ravaging, built *epiteichismata*, and finally dismissed his levies before wintering at Dyme in Achaea with his remaining army, probably a body of picked men, *neodamodeis*, and mercenaries.

No doubt hoping to end the war before the next Olympic festival, the Spartans had Agis prepare a spring 400 invasion. The same reasoning would have been the cause of the autumn campaign by Pausanias, who of course had political need of it as well. The Eleans, though, pressured on all sides and facing a two-fold invasion, surrendered on Sparta's terms and liberated all their subjects. Ravaging by massed invasions and raiding from *epiteichismata*, standard tactics of the Peloponnesian War, had proven very effective in a situation of overwhelming Spartan strength and lack of outside support for the defence. As a result, one long-standing Spartan opponent had been crippled, and its forces would serve loyally in Spartan armies. After Elis' surrender, Pausanias and his forces expelled the Messenians from Naupactus and Cephallenia,[21] and the harmost Herippidas secured Heraclea, racked by civil strife, using massacre and extensive banishments.[22]

In 400 Agis passed away. The succession was contested, but the putative son of Agis was judged illegitimate, and Agis' younger half-brother Agesilaus became the Eurypontid king. He had been born with a club foot, allowing his enemies to use against him an oracle warning Sparta against a lame kingship. However, as a youth Agesilaus had been the beloved and protégé of Lysander, who now helped him win the kingship.[23] Agesilaus would become the most influential Spartan king since Cleomenes, and Sparta's best royal commander. However, his decisions would play no small role in bringing about Sparta's downfall.[24]

A Lukewarm War in Asia, 400–397 [25]

In 401 Cyrus gathered his Persian forces and over ten thousand Greek mercenaries and marched east, ostensibly to punish hostile tribes and rulers. Xenophon, who was present in Cyrus' army, claims that the prince sent to Sparta to request aid in return for what he had given Sparta. The response was modest: seven hundred mercenaries led by Cheirisophus, a Spartan officer, and assistance in coastal Cilicia and Syria from a fleet under the Spartan navarch Samius. This was appropriate given Cyrus' stated intentions, which would have been all that most Spartans knew.[26] Cyrus' actual intention, to overthrow his brother and become Great King, was known to only a few. Cyrus fell at the Battle of Cunaxa, but his Greeks twice routed the Persians, who were no more able to face a phalanx in pitched battle in 401 than in 479. Tissaphernes, who had warned Artaxerxes of Cyrus' intentions and fought in the battle, was handed the task of overcoming the Greeks. However, despite his treacherous arrest of Clearchus and other Greek officers during a parley, the majority of the Cyreans, as they were called, survived a trek through Asia Minor and reached the Black Sea in 400.[27] This made them a Spartan concern.

Anaxibius, navarch for 401/400, lured the Cyreans from Asia to Europe, and tried to force them to serve against Thracians threatening the Thracian Chersonese. This stopped their raiding Pharnabazus' satrapy and kept the peace.[28] However, Tissaphernes had been given Cyrus' provinces of Lydia, Greater Phrygia, and Cappadocia along with his own Caria, and he attempted also to rule the Ionian Greeks, previously Cyrus' subjects. They sought Spartan protection. The Spartans chose to send ambassadors to warn the satrap not to attack the cities. He did so anyway, undertaking a siege of Cyme, but withdrew as winter 400/399 came on. The Spartans in turn sent an army to Asia.[29] This violated their treaty with the Great King, but after their aid to Cyrus, Artaxerxes' hostility must have seemed a given. Tissaphernes had made himself vastly unpopular during the Decelean War, and Sparta's abandonment of the Greeks of Asia was an embarrassment. Prospects of victory no doubt seemed good: Athens had kept the cities on the coast free from Persia, the Cyreans had beaten the Great King in pitched battle and lived to tell about it, and Artaxerxes faced an Egyptian revolt as well as other distractions. The Spartans probably thought that they only had to hold off Tissaphernes and Pharnabazus until they came to terms.

This is apparent from the relative inaction of the Spartan commanders in the first two years of the Persian War. In winter 400/399 the Spartiate Thibron arrived in Ephesus with an army of one thousand *neodamodeis*, four thousand Peloponnesians, and three hundred Athenian cavalry. Adding two thousand Ionians, he took the city of Magnesia in the Maeander River valley, failed to take Tralles to the east, and then raided into Lydia, only to find that Tissaphernes' strong cavalry force compelled him to stay in rough terrain. He wintered in allied territory, preventing a major Persian invasion, though not Persian raiding.

In spring 399 Thibron shifted north to the Caicus River valley, adding to his army the remaining five thousand Cyreans, along with Xenophon, now their commander. Taking advantage of broken terrain and the friendliness of local dynasts, including the descendants of Demaratus, Thibron won over some cities and took others by storm. However, his attempt to cut off the water supply of Larisa, a city in the Hermus River valley, failed due to the defenders' vigorous sorties. Finally the ephors ordered him to invade Caria, Tissaphernes' home territory. However, before Thibron passed Ephesus he was replaced by Dercylidas, probably by command of the new board of ephors in mid-summer 399. Put on trial at Sparta for allowing his soldiers to plunder the allies, Thibron went into exile. He was later restored, however, as were other Spartiate officers who had merely offended allies or neutrals.[30]

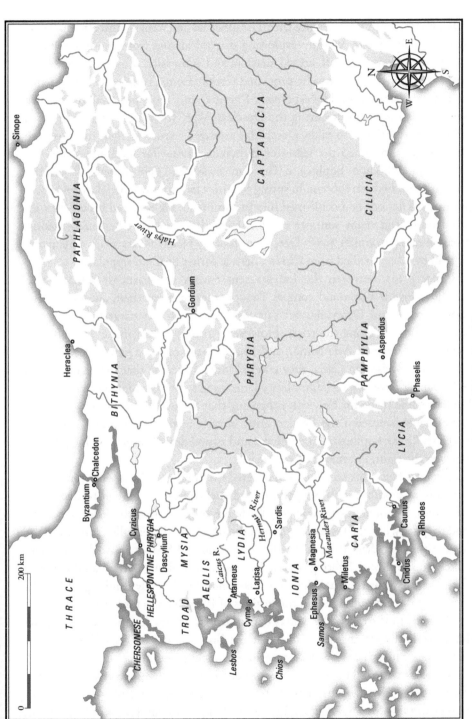

Map 9.2: War in Asia Minor

Dercylidas swiftly made a truce with Tissaphernes and went against Pharnabazus'
holdings in the Troad, cleverly exploiting discord arising from the murder of a
local dynast to take by bluff, armed suasion, and subversion a total of eight cities
in nine days. By these actions he protected Greeks from Tissaphernes, threatened
Pharnabazus' satrapy of Hellespontine Phrygia, and took personal revenge on
Pharnabazus for an insult during the Decelean War. To avoid wintering in allied
territory or exposing it to raids, Dercylidas arranged a truce of eight months with
Pharnabazus and raided the tribes of Bithynian Thrace for food and slaves. He
lost an isolated body of hoplites to Thracian cavalry and light-armed infantry, but
otherwise kept his men content. In spring 398 three fact-finding officials from Sparta
approved his actions and confirmed him in command. He renewed his truces with
both satraps, and spent summer 398 fortifying the Thracian Chersonese against
barbarian raids. In winter 398/7 Dercylidas took by blockade Atarneus, a mainland
fort held by Chians exiled from Chios a decade earlier by Cratesippidas.[31]

In spring 397, however, the Ionians sent envoys to Sparta to demand that
Dercylidas invade Caria and compel Tissaphernes to grant them autonomy. The
ephors agreed, and Dercylidas set out for Caria, with the navarch Pharax and
his fleet following along the coast. However, Artaxerxes had made Tissaphernes
overall commander in Asia Minor, and Pharnabazus came to join forces. Leaving
an adequate garrison in Caria, they entered Ionia. Learning that they had crossed
the Maeander River, Dercylidas followed, meaning to protect Ionian territory from
plundering. He made for Ephesus, supposing that the two had gone ahead already.
Instead, he encountered the Persian army already formed for battle: Carian and
mercenary Greek hoplites, Asian infantry, and a good deal of cavalry – Tissaphernes'
troops on the right, Pharnabazus' on the left.

Dercylidas began his sacrifices and ordered his hoplites to form eight ranks deep
as quickly as possible, with his peltasts and such cavalry as he had to deploy on
both wings. Xenophon, who was very likely present, says that the Peloponnesians
stood to quietly, but the Greek levies from the Maeander River valley, Ionia, and the
islands either left their arms in the standing grain and fled, or showed themselves
unlikely to stand once fighting began. Two years of avoiding battle had done little
to prepare them for combat. However, Tissaphernes, allegedly thinking all Greeks
as tough as the Cyreans, ignored the urgings of Pharnabazus for battle and sought
a conference. In the talks, Dercylidas demanded autonomy for the Greeks of Asia
Minor, while the satraps demanded that the Spartans depart Asia. They made a
truce, to last while their respective governments deliberated.[32]

Perhaps a peace could have been worked out, but Artaxerxes' anger was too great.
At some point Pharnabazus arrived at court to denounce Tissaphernes' inactivity
and seek funding for a naval effort. He received money to build ships in Cyprus and

Phoenicia. As his admiral he chose the Athenian commander Conon, who after Aegospotami had taken refuge at the court of Evagoras, a Greek ruler in Cyprus.[33] In late summer 397, news of the naval preparations in Phoenicia arrived in Sparta. Conon presently advanced with his fleet, basing it on a large lake in Caria near Caunus, connected to the sea by a river. Pharax blockaded the river mouth, but withdrew to Rhodes when Pharnabazus led an army against him.[34]

Agesilaus in Asia, 397–394 [35]

When the Spartans and their allies met to discuss the Persian threat, Agesilaus offered to lead to Asia an army of thirty Spartiate counsellors, two thousand *neodamodeis*, and six thousand allies, to win a peace or at least keep the enemy too busy to attack Sparta and its allies. In this he was encouraged by Lysander, who thought that the enemy could be beaten easily, and hoped to revive his decarchies in Asia, which the ephors had ordered suppressed. Receiving the command, Agesilaus raised his forces in winter 397/6. The Corinthians, Boeotians, and now the Athenians refused to participate. Indeed, many Athenians were heading east to join Conon. Moreover, when Agesilaus went to Aulis in Boeotia to sacrifice to Artemis, as Agamemnon had done before departing for Troy, Boeotian officials interrupted his sacrifices, refusing to let him use their site for his religious and propaganda purposes. This insult made Agesilaus hostile to Thebes and the Boeotian Confederation ever after.[36]

According to Xenophon, on his arrival at Ephesus in spring 396, Agesilaus agreed to a truce offered by Tissaphernes, who swore to send to Artaxerxes to negotiate a peace granting autonomy for the Greeks of Asia. Xenophon declares that Tissaphernes broke his oath and sent to the Great King for an army. The satrap's sudden combativeness goes unexplained. Once reinforced, Tissaphernes then sent an ultimatum demanding that the Spartans leave Asia. Reportedly never deceived, Agesilaus rejoiced that the satrap had offended the gods by breaking his oath. The king then notified the cities on the route from Ephesus to Caria to ready markets for his army, and ordered the Greeks of Asia to send their forces to join him at Ephesus.

Tissaphernes accordingly deployed his infantry in hilly Caria and took his cavalry onto the plain of the Maeander to attack Agesilaus as he came south. Since Xenophon in the *Anabasis* says that Persian cavalry was vulnerable to night attacks on its camps,[37] the absence of Persian infantry in the Maeander valley is surprising. Unexpectedly, the king marched north to ravage and pillage Pharnabazus' Phrygian lands, later returning to winter at Ephesus. Xenophon says nothing about Tissaphernes' actions during all this, and nothing about the fleets.[38] Other sources reveal that Conon secured the revolt of Rhodes and seized a large convoy of grain and ships' stores from the rebel ruler of Egypt, an ally of Sparta. The Spartan fleet thereafter used Cnidus in south-western Caria as its base, while Conon's fleet used Caunus and Rhodes. A long stalemate then developed, in the same fashion as in the early years of the naval campaigning of the Decelean War.[39]

During the winter Agesilaus assigned the richest men in Ionia the duty to raise cavalry, announcing that whoever supplied horse, arms, and a competent man would not have to serve himself – a proviso that resulted in zealous efforts, Xenophon notes, by men eagerly searching for others to die in their stead. The rout of the king's cavalry in a battle with an equal number of Pharnabazus' horsemen had caused Agesilaus to realise that he needed to improve his cavalry if he was to confront the enemy directly. Xenophon consistently mentions Spartan cavalry successes and failures, both for their own sake and because he himself wrote essays on cavalry command and horsemanship.[40]

Towards spring 395 Agesilaus brought his army together at Ephesus and trained it, offering prizes: to the hoplites for the unit whose men were the fittest, to the cavalry for the unit whose men were most skilled in horsemanship, and to the archers and peltasts for those most skilled in their specialties. Agesilaus then announced that he would lead the army by the shortest route into the enemy's country, and had cities north of Ephesus prepare markets. Thinking, Xenophon says, that Agesilaus meant to deceive him, Tissaphernes again deployed his infantry in Caria and cavalry in the Maeander valley, only to find that the king headed straight for the Plain of Sardis, where his troops pillaged and ravaged for three days, supposedly without opposition even from local forces.

Tissaphernes, Xenophon says, came north with his cavalry. The satrap went to Sardis, but his cavalry commander ordered the baggage train to encamp on the far side of the Pactolus River, which runs north past the site of Sardis into the Hermus, and led the cavalry to attack Greek camp followers looting the countryside. Seeing this, Agesilaus sent his cavalry to their aid, and the Persian horsemen formed for battle. Realising that the enemy had no infantry support, while all his army was at hand, Agesilaus sacrificed and led his phalanx forth, ordering his cavalry to charge, the peltasts to run after them, and the hoplites of the ten youngest age classes to close with the enemy, while he followed on with the rest. The Persians met the attack of the cavalry, but gave way before the infantry. Pinned against the river, some of the Persians were killed crossing it, and the rest fled. Agesilaus moved on to take the camp and its contents, including the camels of the baggage train.

Later, learning that Tissaphernes was accused of betraying the army and that the Persians were in confusion, Agesilaus entered the suburbs of Sardis to pillage and burn, challenging the enemy to fight and calling on those wanting freedom to revolt. Artaxerxes sent his vizier Tithraustes to behead Tissaphernes and to offer Agesilaus autonomy for the Greeks of Asia in return for their tribute.[41]

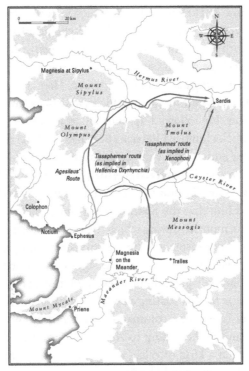

Map 9.3: The Sardis campaign

Although scholars argue for Xenophon's essential accuracy here, one must keep in mind that Agesilaus became Xenophon's patron, while Tissaphernes had brought about the death of Xenophon's friend Proxenus, one of the Cyreans' generals. Xenophon had strong cause to depict the king as pious, crafty, and competent, and the satrap as false, self-deceiving, and incompetent. Moreover, a writer as didactic as Xenophon had reason to offer an account that demonstrated the correct use of cavalry, the need to trap elusive foes against obstructions, and the value of co-ordinating heavy- and light-armed infantry and cavalry in combat, all matters he knew from experience.[42]

Xenophon's account of the Battle of Sardis, then, may reflect his personal interests. The actual events may have been quite different. A surviving section of the Oxyrhynchus Historian, also used by Diodorus, depicts Agesilaus meeting opposition from archers shooting from the hills, perhaps those of the Karabel Pass between Mount Tmolus and Lydia's Mount Olympus. Tissaphernes followed with his cavalry, light infantry, and camp guards, avoiding pitched battles and harassing Agesilaus, who operated in the foothills of Mount Sipylus or, when in open terrain, marched with his hoplites in a large square formation and his baggage train inside it. Xenophon's account of Persian and Greek tactics in the *Anabasis* yields precise parallels.[43] A poorly preserved section of the Oxyrhynchus Historian's text describes fighting, perhaps with the word for 'river' (*pot[amon]*); possibly Xenophon's cavalry battle. The decisive action consists of an ambush of the Persians by 1,400 Peloponnesians that the king had hidden in a grove. They charged out against those harassing the Greek army, putting them to flight, and Agesilaus sent his cavalry and light-armed in pursuit. He followed up with an attack on the camp, whose guard was poorly organised. Six hundred Persians perished, and the rich camp was looted, denying Tissaphernes' entire army vital logistical support.[44]

However it was won, the victory freed Agesilaus to ravage and plunder in Lydia and the Maeander valley. When Tithraustes arrived, executed Tissaphernes, and offered terms, Agesilaus told him that the Spartan government had the final decision, and agreed to a truce of six months, during which the king would leave Tissaphernes' old provinces, for which Tithraustes was now responsible, and plunder Pharnabazus' territory to support his army.[45] It is said that Agesilaus wished to pursue the war, which had brought him only glory and success, and it seems that the Spartans now felt the same way, for as he was passing north of Cyme, he received orders from the authorities at Sparta to exercise command over the fleet and appoint whomever he wished to command it. According to Xenophon, 'the Lacedaemonians did this in accordance with such a kind of calculation, that, if the same person could have command of both, the army would be far more the stronger, the strength of both being made into one, and the fleet [also], the army appearing where it was needed.'[46] Certainly king and fleet had been engaged in separate campaigns hitherto. The Spartans at home may have planned to crush the Persian fleet in Caria, which now suffered from a lack of funding that stalled Conon's efforts and forced him to face down a mutiny in the summer of 395.[47]

The logical person for Agesilaus to have appointed was Lysander, but the two had fallen out during 396. Xenophon says that Lysander had received so much attention from the Greeks of Asia that Agesilaus began refusing anything that Lysander asked, and Plutarch reports other insults. Xenophon also says that the king settled affairs in the cities, which were confused after the suppression of the decarchies. This means he took from Lysander the role of patron of the Greeks of Asia.[48] Lysander won the defection of one of Pharnabazus' nobles, Spithridates, but even so left Asia in 395 still unreconciled with the king.[49] Agesilaus instead gave the command to his brother-in-law, Peisander, despite his lack of naval experience, and ordered coastal and island cities to provide 120 new triremes. He may have had the current navarch, Cheiricrates, continue in his post until Peisander was ready.[50]

In the autumn Agesilaus fought in Mysia, pressuring its tribes to join his expedition, and pushed eastwards as far as Gordium in Phrygia and the borders of Paphlagonia. With the aid of Spithridates, Agesilaus won to his side the ruler of Paphlagonia. The Spartan king failed in his assaults upon three cities, however. In the winter of 395/4, Agesilaus based his forces at Dascylium, Pharnabazus' capital, and plundered the satrap's domains. A body of the king's troops suffered heavily from an attack by Persian cavalry and scythed chariots.[51] However, Spithridates learned the location of Pharnabazus' camp. Herippidas, now one of Agesilaus' counsellors, led a combined Greek and Asian force in a successful raid, taking the camp and its contents, although Pharnabazus and many of his men escaped.

Unfortunately for Agesilaus, Herippidas chose to strip the Asian troops of their loot, giving it to the booty sellers along with the rest, following Spartan custom. Greatly offended, Spithridates and the Paphlagonians deserted to Ariaeus, the new satrap at Sardis. He had been one of Cyrus' followers, and so was a living example of Artaxerxes' forgiveness for rebels.[52] This was a blow to Agesilaus personally – he loved Spithridates' son – and to his goal of winning over satraps and lesser dynasts and adding their forces to his army. The king met with Pharnabazus near spring, but gained little.[53] That same winter, Conon went to Artaxerxes' court and persuaded him to meet the fleet's needs, with Pharnabazus placed firmly in overall charge. The Persian fleet soon revived.[54]

Despite these setbacks, in spring 394 Agesilaus proceeded to the plain of Thebe south-east of Mount Ida and began amassing a large allied army. His plan, we are told, was to go east, conquering or winning over one nation after another.[55] Xenophon grandly claims that envoys from every people in the Persian Empire had come seeking his friendship. But while the king had managed to develop a Spartan army that could operate in the open field against Persian light-armed and cavalry forces, its siegecraft remained unimpressive, and the reality of the summer, autumn, and winter campaigns – in which Agesilaus did a great deal of ravaging and plundering and built up a solid war chest, but lost local allies and captured no cities, while Conon's fleet revived – does not support belief in the truth of the reports of grandiose plans. It would have been in character for Agesilaus to have put out a cover story to help him surprise the foe in Caria. In any case, whatever his plans may have been, circumstances rendered them irrelevant. Agesilaus did not march east, but west.

Haliartus, 395[56]

In summer 395, border strife broke out between the Phocians and the Eastern and Western Locrians – the ancient sources all give different accounts, no doubt the result of imperfect information and over-editing.[57] The Boeotians mobilised to aid the Locrians, and the Phocians asked the Spartans to intervene. They did so, ordering the Boeotians to avoid hostilities and appeal to the assembled allies for judgement. The Boeotians rejected this infringement on their sovereignty and invaded Phocis anyway, ravaging the land and making unsuccessful assaults on cities. None of this need have caused a larger war, had the Spartans not seized upon the Boeotians' disobedience as a pretext to punish them for their independence and acts of insolence, as they had the Eleans. The moment seemed opportune: Agesilaus' campaign was prospering, and no other wars distracted them. The citizen forces of Sparta and its allies were available for operations. Lysander, home after his humiliation in Asia, encouraged the decision, and Pausanias probably agreed. They both had to respond to Agesilaus' successes and gain new martial glory.

What the Spartans did not realise, however, was that hostile politicians among the Boeotians, Corinthians, Argives, and Athenians had been conspiring to lead their peoples into war against Sparta. Gifts of gold from a Persian agent, Timocrates of Rhodes, and promises of financial aid in case of war, stimulated the movement. All four peoples were regional powers fretting under Sparta's domination and dreading her intervention, so only fear of war with Sparta prevented formation of a coalition among them. In Boeotia this was overcome by the conspirators arranging to cause the Locrian and Phocian strife and then refusing the Spartans' orders to seek arbitration.[58]

Lysander took command of the Phocians and other northern Spartan allies, people of no great might and in some cases mutually hostile, while Pausanias obtained favourable sacrifices and led the Spartiates to Tegea, ordering the Perioecs and Peloponnesian allies to muster there. Xenophon says that Pausanias and Lysander were to meet at Haliartus, a town in western Boeotia, on an appointed day. Pausanias, coming from the Isthmus of Corinth, had to round or cross Mount Cithaeron, which could be held against him by the enemy. He could go through Attica to invade Boeotia from the south-east, but since the Athenians were hostile it made sense to stay clear of their territory – although he probably thought that fear of Sparta, gratitude for his aid to the democrats, and the Athenians' old hostility to Thebes would keep Athens neutral.

Lysander faced Lake Copaïs. Drained for farmland both in the Bronze Age and today, the lake in this era was wide enough even at the height of summer to come near the foothills of Mount Helicon, leaving only a narrow strip of level ground for an army marching from Phocis to cross before reaching Thebes. Going further south, or around Copaïs from the north-east, meant crossing mountainous territory on narrow routes. Whatever way was taken, a defender could block an invading army. A simultaneous double invasion, however, could divide the Boeotians' forces, although at the risk of defeat in detail of the separate Spartan armies by the massed Boeotians.

In the event, Lysander hurried his campaign after causing Orchomenus, a rival of Thebes located in north-western Boeotia, to revolt from the confederation.

Map 9.4: Boeotia

Reinforced by the Orchomenians – who in theory could raise two thousand hoplites and two hundred cavalry – Lysander stormed and sacked the town of Lebadeia, bypassed or won the surrender of Coronea, and came to Haliartus while Pausanias was still passing Cithaeron. What happened next is, as usual, variously reported. Xenophon says that Lysander opened negotiations with the Haliartians.

> And at first he attempted to persuade them to revolt and become independent; but when some of the Thebans, who were within the [city's] wall, prevented this, he assaulted the wall. On hearing of this, the Thebans came to the rescue on the run, both hoplites and horsemen. Whether they escaped Lysander's notice, falling on him unawares, or he saw them approaching but stood his ground, thinking he would win, is not clear; but this, however, is clear, that the battle took place alongside the wall; and a trophy was placed at the gates of the Haliartians.[59]

The victor of Aegospotami and creator of the Spartan empire perished near those gates, as did his staff. The Thebans pursued Lysander's fleeing soldiers into Helicon's foothills, but were driven back by a fierce counterattack, losing over two hundred dead. While the accounts in Plutarch and Pausanias contain many questionable elements, both report a sortie by the defenders of Haliartus, which fits the trophy's location. Perhaps the defenders saw the Thebans approaching and responded by making an unexpected attack of their own while Lysander was distracted.

What Lysander had not known was that, when the Boeotians learned of the planned invasions, they sent an embassy to Athens and secured an alliance. The Athenians reached Thebes the same day Lysander arrived at Haliartus, and stayed there to rest and ward off Pausanias while the Thebans moved en masse against Lysander. When Pausanias arrived at Haliartus the following day, he found Boeotians and Athenians in the field against him, Lysander's army dispersed, and his body and those of his comrades lying beneath the town walls. Pausanias took counsel with his polemarchs and pentecosters, omitting the allies and evidently leaving the lochagoi and enomotarchs to command the Spartan units. The council agreed that their own allies were dispirited and their cavalry greatly outnumbered by that of the enemy. Most importantly, the corpses lay near the city, so that even in victory their removal would have to take place under missile fire from the wall. Consequently the council members decided to ask for a burial truce – a humiliating admission of defeat. The Thebans added to the humiliation by insisting that Pausanias withdraw from the country as a condition of the truce. He agreed, and disbanded the army after retreating to Phocis and leaving a mora in Orchomenus. Once back in Sparta he was put on trial, and this time condemned. He went into exile in Tegea. His underage son, Agesipolis, now became the Agiad king.[60]

Lysander's death and Pausanias' exile cost Sparta two major leaders. Worse, an anti-Spartan coalition was forming among Thebes, Athens, Corinth, and Argos, so Sparta faced wars at home and abroad. None of this was inevitable. Peace with Persia, perhaps possible in 395, would have undercut the conspiracy in Greece. A more diplomatic approach to the Phocian crisis might have left the conspirators unable to act. More caution on Lysander's part might have found two Spartan armies fighting the Boeotians and Athenians. Instead the Spartans now had to fight on two fronts.

~ Ten ~

END OF EMPIRE, 395–386

One Decisive and Two Indecisive Battles, 395–394 [1]

Facing wars on two fronts, the Spartans proved wiser than the Athenians. They recalled Agesilaus in spring 394. It was not entirely certain he would comply – remember Dorieus and Pausanias – but, although terribly disappointed, Agesilaus obeyed. He put the best possible face on it, and persuaded the Greeks of Asia to provide volunteers for his army, using contests to encourage their officers to produce the fittest, best-equipped units possible, as he had done at Ephesus in winter 396/5. He started back in mid-July with perhaps fifteen thousand men and a vast amount of spoils, and left behind his brother-in-law Peisander as navarch to contain Conon and Pharnabazus, and the Spartiate Euxenus with four thousand troops to defend the allies by land.[2]

Meanwhile, both sides had been making preparations during the winter of 395/4. The coalition could not win adherents in the Peloponnese beyond Corinth and Argos, but in spring 394 Ismenias of Thebes captured Spartan-held Pharsalus in Thessaly, resettled Heraclea with the Trachinians exiled by Herippidas, and won over the Aenianians and Athamanians in the Pindus Mountains. Massing his allies, Ismenias then defeated the Phocians in battle at Naryx in Locris, albeit with heavy losses on both sides. However, the Spartans retained Orchomenus in Boeotia, Phocis, and other northern states.[3]

Around the time that Agesilaus started for Greece, the coalition massed its forces at Corinth and debated its next move. Timolaus, a leading Corinthian politician and an experienced general, proposed that they invade Lacedaemon, arguing that Sparta would be weakest when isolated from its allies. His motion carried, though disagreements about command and unit depth continued. The allies finally agreed to rotate command between the four major powers – a practice seen in other Greek coalition armies – and to form the phalanx sixteen ranks deep, making it wide enough to keep its flanks from being turned.[4]

While the allies debated, the Spartans acted. Under command of Aristodemus, guardian of Agesipolis, they marched north via Tegea and Mantinea to Sicyon, gathering their allies on the way. They then headed east over the coastal plain between Sicyon and Corinth, crossing the Nemea River (modern Koutsomadiotikos) on the border between the two states. There they came under fire from enemy light-armed troops on the cliffs south of the plain. These were the vanguard of the coalition army, which was returning to protect Corinth after an abortive march south to Nemea, either to invade Laconia as planned or to try to intercept Sparta's allies from the Argolic Acte. The Spartan army turned north onto the plain and began ravaging. The coalition army moved east and took a defensive position behind a stream, the modern Longopotamos. The Spartans then camped about 1,700 metres west of the enemy position.

The coalition had more light-armed troops and cavalry than the Spartans, but neither side had more than a few thousand of either. The hoplite levies predomi-nated. The coalition army had some six thousand Athenians, seven thousand Argives, five thousand Boeotians, three thousand Corinthians, and three thousand Euboeans, for a total of twenty-four thousand hoplites, or so reports Xenophon. He has six thousand Lacedaemonian hoplites, almost three thousand from Elis and its former subjects, at least three thousand from the Argolic Acte cities of Epidaurus, Troezen, Hermione, and Halieis, and fifteen hundred from Sicyon. He says nothing of the Arcadians or Achaeans, both also on Sparta's side. Diodorus gives the Spartans twenty-three thousand infantry and five hundred cavalry, the coalition over fifteen thousand infantry and five hundred cavalry. That Sparta could field six thousand hoplites, with a mora absent in Orchomenus and at least three thousand *neodamodeis* abroad, is explained by the absence of a naval threat to Spartan territory, allowing the coastal Perioecs to turn out in force.

For some days the two armies faced one another, while the Spartans devastated the farms in the area. They could afford to await Agesilaus' arrival, and had no desire to try to attack across the bushy banks and steep-sided streambed of the Longopotamos, as this would disorder their phalanx. With Corinthian land under attack and Agesilaus on the march, the coalition was under more pressure to act. When formed for battle, the Spartans had the right wing of their army, while in the coalition forces the state with the overall command on any day had the right wing of its army. 'The Boeotians in no way hastened to join battle, so long as they held the left wing', opposite the Spartans, claims Xenophon, 'but when the Athenians came to be against the Lacedaemonians, and they themselves had the right wing and were stationed against the Achaeans, straightway they declared the sacrifices favourable and passed along the word to make ready, as there would be a battle.'[5] They also ignored the agreed-on depth of sixteen ranks and formed wholly deep, as at Delium in 424, when the Thebans fought twenty-five ranks deep against Athenians eight ranks deep. The Boeotians even led the advancing army towards the right, so they could get on the flank of the Achaeans. This forced the rest of the coalition phalanx to shift right also, although this threatened to allow the Spartans to outflank the Athenians.

The Spartans did not at first see the enemy advance, due to the extensive brush along the stream. However, when they heard the soldiers chanting the paean, a battle hymn, they formed their phalanx, the *xenagoi* ordering the allied units to their planned places, and advanced. They also veered to their right, and so each side's right outflanked the opposing left – in the Spartans' case by so much that, despite equalling the Athenian numbers, two-fifths of the Athenians wound up facing the Tegeans on the left of the Spartan contingent. Except for the men of Achaean Pellene, who fought it out against the Thespians of Boeotia, the entire body of Spartan allies was defeated and put to flight, the coalition units pursuing eagerly. Since the Pellenians held out against the Thespians, it seems that only the Thebans, not all the Boeotians, formed deep. The Spartans controlled their allies' deployment and planned their rightward veer, so they may have formed the allies with fewer ranks than the coalition did in order to widen their phalanx, only to find it outflanked anyway, with the allies losing heart in the face of the stronger coalition units.

But if the Thebans sought to re-enact Delium, the Spartans did re-enact Mantinea. They outflanked and routed the Athenians opposite them with heavy losses, but instead of pursuing they turned, reformed at a ninety-degree angle to the initial line of battle, and then advanced. Bypassing those Athenians returning from their pursuit of the Tegeans, 'the Lacedaemonians encountered the returning Argives, and when the first polemarch was about to engage them from the front, it is said that someone shouted out to let the first of them pass by,' states Xenophon.[6] 'When this had been done, they struck those running by on their unprotected sides, killing many of them. They also attacked the Corinthians as they were returning. Then the Lacedaemonians also encountered some of the Thebans returning from the pursuit, and killed very many of them.'

The bypassed Athenians did not try to attack the Spartans from behind, and no coalition units rallied. Their levies, exhausted from battle and pursuit, and now just armed mobs beyond the control of their officers, fled across the stream to Corinth. They found the gates closed, either from panic or as an initial blow in the civil strife that would soon rock the city. The Spartans did not risk pursuit in the absence of their own allies, contenting themselves with raising a trophy. The Spartan allies lost 1,100 men, the coalition 2,800, according to Diodorus. Only six Lacedaemonians perished.[7]

By this victory, the Spartans again confirmed their dominance in hoplite battle. If nothing else, they had the only major contingent left on the field. The coalition made no further attempts to invade Lacedaemon. However, the flight of Sparta's

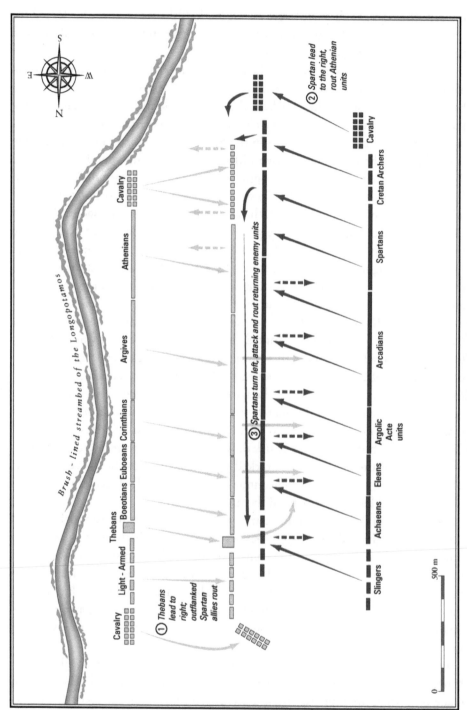

Map 10.1: The Battle of the Nemea

allies prevented further action by the army, while the coalition forces finally took refuge within Corinth's city fortifications and long walls, which ran north to the Corinthian Gulf and the port of Lechaeum. The two armies now sat, watched one another, and awaited Agesilaus.

They did not wait long. Agesilaus arrived in Phocis within a month after leaving Sestos, this despite having to fight Thracians, win over cities such as Amphipolis – where he learned of Nemea from Dercylidas, whom he then dispatched to the Hellespont – and bluff his way through Macedon. On his march through Thessaly, local coalition allies harassed his army with their cavalry. He drove them off with a charge of his hoplites and cavalry. Xenophon, in his account, notes that the king himself had to send orders to his horsemen to pursue the enemy vigorously, after seeing them failing to do so once their initial charge forced an enemy retreat. Evidently they lacked a discerning commander, and had no set doctrine for such situations.[8]

Once through, Agesilaus received orders to invade Boeotia, and was reinforced by a mora sent from Sicyon, half of the mora at Orchomenus, fifty volunteer bodyguards sent from Sparta, and levies from Orchomenus and Phocis. The coalition also sent forces north from Corinth, however, deploying the rest in strong points around the city. It is likely that the entire Boeotian contingent went north, except perhaps for a token force, while units chosen by lot from the other allies also went. Levies from Boeotia and its local allies joined them. The stage was set for another great battle.[9]

On 14 August 394, Agesilaus was entering Boeotia when a partial solar eclipse occurred, and a messenger reported the defeat of the Spartan fleet in a great battle near Cnidus. Xenophon says that Pharnabazus as admiral was with the Phoenician ships, while Conon with the Greek ones was stationed in front. Although outnumbered by Conon's Greeks, let alone by the entire Persian fleet, Peisander deployed for battle. It all sounds like Arginusae, only with worse odds for the Spartans. Peisander's allies on the left wing fled at once, while his other triremes were driven ashore. He died fighting on board his ship, while his men fled by land for the safety of Cnidus. Xenophon does not explain why Peisander accepted battle. Diodorus has a report, which seems poorly edited, of the two sides manoeuvring around the Rhodian Chersonese, and finally meeting at sea in an encounter in which Peisander at first had the advantage, only to be overcome by over ninety triremes (Conon's Greeks?), losing fifty of his eighty-five ships along with his life. Philochorus, a third-century author, mentions the Rhodian Chersonese, and the loss of fifty ships and the death of Peisander as the result of Conon's unexpected attack.[10]

Cnidus shattered Sparta's naval empire. Pharnabazus and Conon followed their victory first by winning over Cos and other nearby islands, and then also Erythrae, Chios, Mytilene, and even Ephesus, long a Spartan base. Further cities came over and expelled their Spartan garrisons. Conon persuaded Pharnabazus to announce that he would not create garrisons or fortify citadels in the cities, leaving them independent. This proved popular and undermined resistance. Some cities remained loyal to Sparta, but the only ones mentioned in our sources are Sestos and Abydos, held by Dercylidas and various Spartan harmosts expelled from other cities.[11] Sparta's naval strength depended upon its allies, as already noted. Now many of these allies were lost to the Spartans, while others, such as Corinth, were in arms against them. Sparta would contest the Aegean thereafter, but would only dominate it briefly in the 380s, with Persian assistance, and never again thereafter.

Agesilaus' army contained many Greeks of Asia and the islands whose cities would soon go over to the Persians, or be threatened by them. Morale was already a problem, since his troops were used to an easy war in Asia Minor, but now faced the prospect of a major hoplite battle. No doubt the partial eclipse unnerved them as well. The king had to order Orchomenus' gates closed to his men, who wanted to deposit their property there – or hide there. Therefore, on hearing the news of Cnidus, Agesilaus announced that it had been a great Spartan victory, and sacrificed as if giving thanks for good news. No ancient source condemns this deceitful rite as sacrilegious. His men were so encouraged that they won a skirmish with the enemy soon afterwards. However, Agesilaus had to exploit this boost to morale before the true outcome of Cnidus became known.[12]

Marching south from Orchomenus, Agesilaus found the enemy encamped on the northern foothills of Helicon west of Haliartus, near Coronea. As he advanced, they came down onto the plain and deployed. The two armies probably engaged south of the stream of the Kuraios, deploying parallel to it from south-west to north-east, with the Argives on the coalition left closest to Helicon's foothills, the Thebans on the right closest to the shore of Lake Copaïs.[13] Xenophon says that both armies seemed the same size, but offers no figures.[14] Here in their home territory the Boeotian hoplites should have been as numerous as at Nemea, while the Argives, Athenians, Euboeans, Locrians, and Corinthians sent up to half their units here – we can assume roughly fifteen thousand hoplites. Agesilaus would have had about one thousand Lacedaemonian citizen forces and perhaps two thousand *neodamodeis* on his right wing, the Phocians, mercenaries, and the Greeks of Asia in his centre, and the Orchomenians on his left. Each side had light infantry and cavalry, but, as at the Battle of the Nemea, it would be the hoplites that decided the action.

Xenophon, who had returned from Asia Minor with Agesilaus and should have been present now,[15] says that the two armies advanced in deep silence (no chanting or pipers for the Spartans?), but when they came within about 170 metres, the Thebans raised the war-cry and charged their Orchomenian rivals. When the armies were about a hundred metres apart, Agesilaus' mercenaries and the Greeks

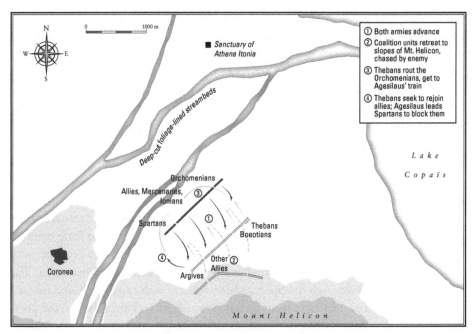

Map 10.2: The Battle of Coronea

of Asia ran forth against their opponents, whom they put to flight as soon as they came within spear-thrust distance, while the Argives turned and fled back to the foothills before their Spartan opponents reached them. Some of the mercenaries were already crowning Agesilaus with a garland as victor when word came that the Thebans had cut through the Orchomenians and were in the baggage train. Agesilaus could not let the spoils from Asia be looted – Sparta needed his war chest. He redeployed his phalanx, bringing his Spartan units, as well as perhaps any other centre units that he could reform, and led it against the Thebans. These formed in close order and came on stoutly, aiming to break through to Helicon's foothills and join their allies there.[16]

'Now here', says Xenophon, 'one may unquestionably call Agesilaus courageous; certainly he did not take the safest course. For it was in his power to let pass those trying to break through, then follow and overcome those in the rear, yet he did not do this, but smashed into the Thebans front to front; and with shields together they shoved, fought, killed, and died.'[17] In his *Agesilaus*, Xenophon adds that 'there was no shouting, nor indeed silence, but there was a sound of a kind such as wrath and battle might produce. Finally those of the Thebans who broke through reached Helicon, but many perished during the retreat.[18] The king himself was wounded, and many of his bodyguards killed. Plutarch and the stratagem writers Polyaenus and Frontinus claim that the Spartans wearied of this desperate combat, opened their ranks deliberately, and allowed the Thebans to go through, only to attack them from the rear, killing many.[19] Xenophon is silent on how the Thebans got through; if the Spartans did deliberately open their ranks, he clearly did not regard it as a stratagem of the king. Afterwards, Xenophon says, one saw 'the earth wet with blood, bodies of friends and enemies lying besides one another, shields broken into pieces, spears shivered, naked daggers, out of their sheaths, some on the ground, some embedded in bodies, some yet in hands.'[20]

Xenophon's accounts of Coronea provide a detailed description of actual hoplite combat, something rare in Greek historians. Its first phase featured little combat, but the second clearly saw ōthismos, massed shoving, take place. The great press of this action is shown by the report that many hoplite shields were shattered. The Thebans had to get through the Spartan formation in order to escape, and massed closely to do so. The Spartans seem to have responded in kind. The terrific press did not stop men from killing one another, using daggers or spears held overhand. Mass shoving was not just a Theban tactic. As we have seen, at the Piraeus in 403 Pausanias' troops formed in depth and pushed some of the enemy hoplites into a swamp. Note also that Spartans of the era used small swords, suitable for very close combat in such circumstances (*Plate 25*): Xenophon's 'daggers'. Still, from Delium in 424 onwards the Thebans fought hoplite battles in a deep formation. Evidently they specialised in massed shoving. Theirs was a tactic to which the Spartans lacked an adequate response, as this battle and others show.

Despite his wounds, Agesilaus piously ordered some eighty enemy soldiers who had taken refuge in the sanctuary of Athena north of the battlefield escorted safely back to their army. He had lost around 350 men, most probably Spartans or Orchomenians. More than six hundred of the enemy had died. On the following day he ordered the polemarch Gylis to draw up the army for battle, men garlanded and pipers playing. Forced to admit defeat, the coalition sought a burial truce. Plutarch says that the Thebans were proud of being the only men in the coalition army not defeated. If so, their pride was insufficient to induce them to face a Spartan army in pitched hoplite combat again until the accidental Battle of Tegyra in 375.

Plutarch sees Agesilaus' decision to fight the Thebans head-on as resulting from anger with Thebes and an irrational desire for victory. Even Xenophon seems critical.[21] It was a quick decision, perhaps driven by passion instead of reason. However, after Cnidus, the one chance that the king had of gaining a decisive result in the war would have been to do to the Thebans what Cleomenes had done to the

Argives, or Lysander to the Athenians – destroy them utterly. To do this, he had to stop, surround, and crush them. With the Thebans destroyed, he could hope the Boeotian Confederation would collapse, leaving only the twice-defeated coalition army between his forces and Attica, where the Piraeus was still unwalled.

But he had failed. Now wounded, and with the coalition army holding a strong defensive position in Helicon's foothills, Agesilaus had to withdraw. Coronea had been a victory, but a fruitless one, even more indecisive than Nemea.

Leaving the army in Phocis, Agesilaus went to Delphi to dedicate a tithe of the spoils of Asia to Apollo before returning home. The Spartiate Gylis led the army into Eastern Locris to raid, but he and seventeen other Spartiates were killed in a rearguard action in which Locrian light-armed troops struck from the hills above the column. Gylis had begun his withdrawal late, and kept none of his own light-armed men. The Spartan hoplites counterattacked the Locrian light-armed, but became disordered and vulnerable in the growing darkness and unfamiliar terrain. It would not be the Spartans' only failure in fighting light-armed troops during this war.[22]

The War Around Corinth, 394–390[23]

Unable to maintain his army indefinitely in central Greece, Agesilaus dismissed its levied contingents to their cities. Pitched battle had not yielded a decision, so the combatants turned to attrition. Operations centred on Corinth, which dominated the isthmus and so kept Spartan armies from easily reaching Attica or Boeotia. The Spartans garrisoned Sicyon and attacked Corinthian territory. A siege of Corinth itself was impossible unless coalition military strength was first broken. The coalition allies sent forces to Corinth to hold it and counter these attacks. Pharnabazus and Conon aided the coalition in 393 by sailing across the Aegean and raiding Pherae in Messenia and other sites on the coast. Finding themselves unable to sustain operations due to lack of supply and safe harbours, and fearing counterattacks, they seized Cythera and made it a base for further raiding. Then they proceeded to Corinth and Attica, where Pharnabazus encouraged the allies, provided funds, and aided the rebuilding of the Long Walls and Piraeus walls.[24]

Pharnabazus' funding allowed Corinth to raise a fleet to fight for control of the Corinthian Gulf. After initial success, it gave way to a Spartan fleet under Herippidas. His successor, Agesilaus' half-brother Teleutias, controlled the gulf. In Corinth itself, the constant raiding and ravaging turned many citizens against the war. However, before they could act, the anti-Spartan faction staged a massacre of its opponents, with support from the coalition allies. To secure control of the city, the anti-Spartan faction formed a shared-citizenship arrangement with Argos, which the Argives undertook to turn into a union of two cities.[25] The survivors of

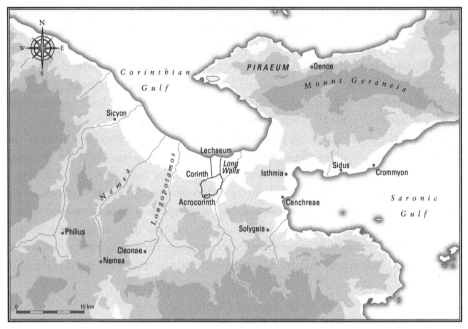

Map 10.3: The Corinthia

the peace faction went in turn to Praxitas, the Spartan polemarch at Sicyon, to offer to betray Corinth's long walls, either in winter 393/2 or spring 392. Despite having only limited forces available, Praxitas decided to make the effort. Arriving at night, he and his men were admitted inside the long walls. He had a Spartan mora (six hundred?), a small unit of cavalry, the levies of Sicyon (fifteen hundred?), and one hundred and fifty Corinthians who had been exiled following the massacre. He deployed the cavalrymen against the Boeotian garrison of the port of Lechaeum, and raised a stockade between the eastern and western long walls, which were about 1,300 metres apart.

The next day passed quietly as the Argives and their allies mobilised. They attacked the following day. The Argives, in full force, routed the Sicyonians in the centre of the line and chased them north to the sea – it seems that the port had few, if any, landward fortifications. Pasimachus, the Spartan cavalry commander, was unable to hinder the Argives with his horsemen. He dismounted with his followers, took shields from the fleeing Sicyonians, and counterattacked. He perhaps hoped to ignite a panic, but he and his men were killed. However, the Athenians on the Argive right, mercenary peltasts commanded by a young general named Iphicrates, were defeated in face-to-face combat by the exiles, who chased them back south towards Corinth.

The Corinthians on the Argive left fared no better against Praxitas and his mora. When the Argives realised that the Spartans stood between themselves and the city, they turned about and tried to flee past them, only to be blocked by the exiles, who were returning from their own pursuit. Many of the Argives died, with perhaps a thousand coalition dead overall. Praxitas then stormed Lechaeum, killed the Boeotians there, had large gaps torn in both long walls, took Sidus and Crommyon on the Saronic Gulf coast and garrisoned them, and built a fort to protect allied territory.[26]

The route by land to Attica and Boeotia was now open to Sparta, but instead of a major land campaign the Spartans sent an envoy, Antalcidas, to Tissaphernes' successor, Tiribazus. He persuaded Tiribazus that Conon sought to revive the Athenian empire, and offered to recognise Persian rule over the Greeks of Asia, so long as the independence of all other Greek cities was supported by the king. Tiribazus favoured these proposals, had Conon arrested, and went to plead his case with Artaxerxes. The Great King still refused to cease hostilities with the Spartans.

Also unsuccessful were negotiations between the coalition and Sparta in winter 392/1. The Boeotians offered to recognise Orchomenus' independence from their confederacy, but, despite regaining their walls, fleet, and the islands of Lemnos, Scyros, and Imbros, the Athenians wanted their empire restored, and the Argives wished to retain control of Corinth. Sparta could agree to neither goal.[27]

In the meantime garrisons on both sides held cities and made raids. Iphicrates and his peltasts proved extremely effective. First assembled by Conon, Iphicrates' mercenary peltasts were maintained year-round with Persian and, later, Athenian financial support.[28] Iphicrates understood as well as Agesilaus how to motivate, train, exercise, and discipline troops, and judging from his stratagems, as recorded by Polyaenus, he had a better grasp of how to create and inculcate a tactical doctrine to guide them in action, even when out of range of his voice – a necessity in light-armed skirmishing actions.[29] Iphicrates staged destructive raids and ambushes against Sicyon, Phlius, Epidaurus, and the Arcadians. When Corinthian exiles, based in a now-fortified Lechaeum, attempted to take Corinth by betrayal, Iphicrates trapped and killed three hundred of them. This apparently led to the coalition's recovery of the port, since the Athenians soon after rebuilt the long walls of Corinth, blocking Spartan access. The allies feared Iphicrates' peltasts, but the Spartans were dismissive, for they had caught and killed some by using 'running out' tactics.[30]

In spring 391, the Spartans sent Agesilaus to ravage the Argolid, perhaps ending an understanding between Argos and Sparta to avoid attacking each other's territories. The invasion would have drawn coalition forces into Argos, so when Agesilaus suddenly moved against Corinth, he evidently found its defences undermanned. With the help of Teleutias and the fleet, he took back the long walls and Lechaeum.[31]

In spring 390, Agesilaus mobilised another large allied army to invade Corinthian territory. He seized Isthmia at the time of the biannual festival in honour of Poseidon, and the Corinthian exiles with him held the games, a propaganda coup. He then invaded the mountainous Peiraeum district northeast of Corinth, capturing many people and herds, and cutting Corinth's last land route to Boeotia and Athens. Envoys arrived from several states, including the Boeotians, and for a moment it seemed that the war would be ended on Spartan terms. However, in the meantime the men from Amyclae in the Spartan army were returning home in order to celebrate the Hyacinthia. They were escorted to Sicyon by the hoplite mora and cavalry mora that helped garrison Lechaeum. Eventually the polemarch in command sent on the Amyclaeans and the cavalry, and started back to Lechaeum with his six hundred hoplites, crossing the same plain where the Battle of the Nemea had occurred four years before. Seeing them isolated, without cavalry or peltasts, Iphicrates and the Athenian general Callias decided to intercept them.

Iphicrates attacked with his peltasts several kilometres west of Lechaeum, Callias forming his hoplites near Corinth, ready to offer support. The initial casts of javelins killed or wounded several hoplites, and the polemarch, left unnamed by our sources, had those hoplites up to ten years from adulthood charge out. Whatever had allowed the 'running out' tactic to succeed in the previous encounter did not feature here on this open plain; Iphicrates had ordered his men to fall back when the enemy charge reached javelin range. They successfully avoided the hoplites, and when these turned back, they hurled missiles at their rear and unshielded right sides, killing some ten Lacedaemonians, and then pressed their attacks more vigorously.

A second 'running out' by those up to fifteen years from adulthood did no better, and more Lacedaemonians died. Presently the horsemen returned from their escort duty, and another 'running out' was performed. Had the cavalry ridden hard into the fleeing peltasts, they probably would have killed many and ended the attack. However, Agesilaus' lesson in Thessaly had not been absorbed by the Spartan cavalrymen, who timidly stayed with their charging hoplites, and then returned with them. With the best men killed or wounded and casualties mounting, the men of the mora, losing heart and becoming exhausted, took refuge on a hill a little less than three kilometres from Lechaeum and a few hundred metres from the sea. Small boats came out from Lechaeum just as Callias advanced with the Athenian hoplites. The now-desperate Lacedaemonians broke and fled to the boats, although a few joined the cavalry in making for Lechaeum. The peltasts pursued freely. Some 250 Lacedaemonians in all were slain.

This disaster ended any movement towards peace. Agesilaus ravaged the lands around Corinth, to show that the coalition still did not dare fight him directly, but finally had to withdraw. Iphicrates now retook the strongholds that the Spartans held east of Corinth, although Lechaeum remained in the hands of the Spartans and the Corinthian exiles.[32]

Another War in Greece Ends in the East, 391–386[33]

Spartan fortunes in Asia Minor proved as mixed as in Greece. After the failure of the negotiations of 392–391, the Spartans had sent east Thibron, now back in their good graces, with an army of mercenaries. He retook Ephesus and raided the Maeander River valley, only to be surprised in camp by a sudden Persian cavalry attack. He was killed along with many of his men. He was replaced by Diphridas, a former ephor, who managed to keep the Persians occupied and protect Spartan allies in the area.[34]

Ecdicus, apparently navarch in 391/90, sailed east also, to aid exiles banished by the democratic factions on Rhodes. He hoped to regain control of the Athenian-held isle, but finding that the Rhodians had twice his number of ships, he waited quietly in Cnidus, and was later replaced by Teleutias, probably in 390. For his part, Teleutias captured ten Athenian ships on their way to assist Evagoras, Conon's host in Cyprus, in his revolt against the Great King – Athens' ally. In retrospect, this act of Athenian folly marks the beginning of the end for the coalition: Corinth was crippled, Argos open to invasion, the Boeotians willing to lose cities to gain peace, and the Spartans too strong on land to fight in pitched battle, so a coalition victory depended on Athens. This meant keeping Artaxerxes' good will and funds for Athens, not Sparta – aiding Evagoras was no way to do this. Seeking to recreate Athens' empire in Asia was hardly advisable, either, but this Thrasybulus tried to do, probably in 390. He allied with the Thracian kings Amadocus and Seuthes, won over Byzantium, Chalcedon, and cities along the Hellespont, and re-established the 10 per cent tax on ships coming out of the Black Sea, and the 5 per cent tax on all imports and exports in the harbours of allied cities. He also defeated and killed Therimachus, the Spartan harmost on Lesbos, but lost twenty-three ships there to a storm. Later he died at Aspendus, killed by the locals whose territory his men were plundering. Meanwhile the pro-Spartan exiles retook Rhodes.[35]

The Athenians had better luck in, probably, 389, when Iphicrates attacked the mercenary army led by the ex-navarch Anaxibius, who was conducting land and naval operations in the Troad and Hellespont in support of Abydos. Staging an ambush deep in enemy-held territory, far from his fleet, Iphicrates caught the enemy army strung out on the march and routed its terrified troops. All Anaxibius could do was die like a Spartan, standing and fighting, along with his young lover and a dozen Spartan harmosts, now in the Hellespont after having been expelled from the cities they once had held. Iphicrates' peltasts pursued the rest almost sixteen kilometres to the city of Abydos itself, killing more than 250 men.[36]

Back in Greece, Agesilaus invaded Acarnania in 389, a sideshow forced upon the Spartans by their Achaean allies, who wanted their possession Calydon in south-western Aetolia protected from Acarnanian attacks. They threatened to make a separate peace with the coalition if nothing was done. A large army was duly levied and sent across the Corinthian Gulf, and Agesilaus threatened to ravage all of Acarnania unless its people left the coalition and joined Sparta. They refused, and for more than two weeks he advanced through south-eastern Acarnania at a rate of some two kilometres a day, devastating the land. He then suddenly marched north rapidly to a mountain-enclosed lake district where the Acarnanians had evacuated their herds, and seized them all. Acarnanian slingers and stonethrowers arrived and harassed his army from the mountainsides. Finding his way south blocked by the enemy forces, the king staged a 'running out' attack by his younger Lacedaemonian hoplites, with vigorous cavalry support, followed up by the king himself with the rest of the army. His forces advanced up the most accessible of the surrounding slopes, caught and killed many Acarnanian light-armed, and also routed their hoplites, who had taken position on the ridge above.

The king then resumed ravaging, and, at the insistence of the Achaeans, assaulted some Acarnanian cities, without success. He refused to remain long enough to keep the Acarnanians from sowing seed for next year's grain crop. The Achaeans were frustrated, thinking nothing had been achieved, but in spring 388, when word of a new mobilisation against them reached the Acarnanians, they sent to make peace with the Achaeans and an alliance with Sparta, 'judging that, because their cities were in the interior, they would be just as much besieged by those destroying their grain as if they were besieged by forces encamped around them', says Xenophon.[37] Importing grain was a normal response to a food crisis, whether natural or man-made, but carrying it overland into the interior was expensive compared to ship transport, and in any event, Spartan naval dominance in the Corinthian Gulf would have made importation uncertain.

With no campaign in Acarnania required, King Agesipolis in 388 took the massed army of the Spartans and their allies into the Argolid. The Argives had avoided invasion after 391 by altering their calendar to move the sacred month of the Carnea to whenever the Spartans were mobilising. Agesipolis, however, visited the oracles first at Olympia, then at Delphi, as his army massed, gaining permission from the gods to ignore the trick. Determined to surpass Agesilaus, Agesipolis did not end his invasion when an earthquake occurred on his first day in the region, arguing that Poseidon was urging him on. Instead he pushed his army into every part of the Argolid. It plundered and ravaged farms everywhere, doing all the more damage because the failure of the 'sacred month' tactic meant that the invasion was unexpected. The Argives and their allies could do little to stop Agesipolis. Only a thunderbolt striking the camp, killing some men, started him on his withdrawal, with clearly unfavourable sacrifices preventing his fortifying an *epiteichisma* in Argive territory. Realising that there would be no further hope of keeping the Spartans out of the Argolid, the Argives began to incline towards peace.[38]

That left Athens. After sitting out the war until about 390, the Aeginetans had resumed their ancient raiding of the Attic coast at the urging of the harmost Eteonicus. In response, the Athenians sent hoplites and ten triremes to build a fort on Aegina and harass its populace, but Teleutias and his fleet drove off the Athenian ships. Eventually the fort was abandoned and the raiding resumed. The Athenians based a guard squadron at Cape Zoster, on the Attic coast opposite Aegina. In 388 this squadron pursued the dozen ships of the new harmost, Gorgopas, on their return from escorting Antalcidas, the navarch for 388/7, to his command in the east. However, Gorgopas followed the Athenians unseen as they sailed back at night, catching them as their ships were anchoring at the cape and men going ashore. He took four triremes, the other eight fleeing to the Piraeus.

The Athenians regained the upper hand when Chabrias, who had taken over Iphicrates' post at Corinth, was sent to aid Evagoras with ten ships and eight hundred mercenaries. Getting more ships and hoplites from Athens, he sailed first to Aegina, landed with his peltasts at night, and took up position for an ambush. When the Athenian hoplites landed to raid the next day, Gorgopas, his men, and the Aeginetans went out against them, and fell into Chabrias' ambush, losing 350 men, including Gorgopas and every Laconian present. The victory left the Athenians feeling safe. However, the Spartans sent Teleutias to rally the survivors. Before the Athenians learned of his arrival, Teleutias led his squadron on a daring raid on the Grand Harbour of the Piraeus itself, seizing ships and merchants and thoroughly shocking the Athenians. He then sailed down the coast, taking merchantmen, ferries, and fishing boats. Athens' commerce was again threatened.[39]

As for Antalcidas, no sooner had he arrived in Ephesus than he turned the fleet over to his secretary and second-in-command Nicolochus and went to meet Tiribazus, whose return to the scene shows that Artaxerxes finally realised the Athenians posed a greater threat to Persian rule in the region than the Spartans. The two men went up to the Great King, and returned with an agreement that Artaxerxes would offer the coalition allies peace proposals. If they were rejected, the Great King would join the Spartans in the war. Pharnabazus, the only satrap likely to object, was summoned to Susa to marry Artaxerxes' daughter. Tiribazus and the Spartans manned ships. Antalcidas found Nicolochus blockaded at Abydos with twenty-five ships. Antalcidas took command, broke the blockade, lured the enemy into chasing him up the Hellespont, and then doubled back to capture eight Athenian triremes just as they arrived from the Aegean. Soon he was reinforced by Persian warships and by twenty triremes sent by Dionysius of Syracuse. Facing a Spartan–Persian fleet over eighty strong blocking the grain supply route from the Black Sea region, as well as ongoing raiding from Aegina, the Athenians folded.[40] To judge from the fleet sizes seen during the war, they never had the resources to match their great efforts of the Decelean War, sending out at most a few dozen ships at any time. Neither did they enjoy the superiority in naval operations seen in the fifth century. The Spartans and their allies had enough experience now to deploy squadrons and naval commanders as capable as those of weakened Athens.

The allies sent envoys to hear from Tiribazus the terms on which the peace oaths would be based:

> Artaxerxes the King considers it just that the cities in Asia are to be his, and of the islands Clazomenae and Cyprus, but that the other Greek cities, both small and great, should be left autonomous, except Lemnos and Imbros and Scyros; these, as of old, are to be Athenian. Whichever parties do not accept this peace, against them shall I make war along with those willing to help in this, both by land and on sea and with ships and money.[41]

The terms were accepted. Plutarch claims that Antalcidas was Agesilaus' political enemy, and that the king had opposed the peace, but now Agesilaus came forth to demand on pain of war that Thebes make the Boeotian cities autonomous and the Argives depart Corinth, allowing its exiles to return. He began mobilising, showing this to be a decision of the Spartan state, not just his alone. He performed the border-crossing sacrifices and summoned the Perioecs and allies to Tegea. The Argives swiftly left Corinth and the Boeotians dissolved their confederation.[42] Sparta lost the Persian War and its naval empire, but by gaining Persian support and remaining dominant on the battlefield had won back its hegemony in mainland Greece – for now.

~ Eleven ~

NEMESIS, 385–371

Sparta Tries to Dominate Greece by Land, 385–379[1]

The 'King's Peace' had given Sparta a commanding position in mainland Greece. To sustain it, the Spartans replaced hostile governments with friendly ones, and suppressed the expansionist efforts of regional powers. In the Peloponnese this led to campaigns against Mantinea in 385 and against Phlius in 381–380. The Mantineans were accused of disloyal behaviour during the Corinthian War and ordered to tear down their walls. On their refusal, Agesipolis led the Spartan and allied levies to ravage their lands and invest the city with a trench and siege wall. The Mantineans held out, however, as their last harvest had been good, and sympathisers in Agesipolis' army smuggled needed items in, at least until the king brought in guard dogs. Agesipolis hit on a solution: he had the sizable stream that flowed through the city dammed off, flooding the city site and dissolving the mudbrick of the city walls. Mantinea surrendered, and its ruling democrats went into exile. The Spartans then resettled the remaining Mantineans in the five villages which their ancestors had left to form the unified city-state. This put local government firmly in the hands of the major landowners, men who were likely to be pro-Spartan.[2]

In 385/4 Sparta intervened to protect Epirus against an invasion by the Illyrians, non-Greek tribes living north of Greece and Macedonia along the Adriatic. In 383 the Spartans reportedly concluded an alliance with Glos, a rebel Persian admiral, and supposedly contemplated war with Artaxerxes in order to regain their reputation after betraying the Greeks of Asia. Whether the alliance was fact or rumour, Glos' rebellion came to an end with his assassination, and Sparta remained at peace with Persia.[3]

At Phlius, an important crossroads town north-west of Argos, Sparta acted on behalf of exiled oligarchs with ties to Agesilaus against the city's democratic government, which was also accused of disloyal behaviour during the Corinthian War. Agesilaus quickly enclosed the city in a siege wall, but the Phliasians held out for twice as long as expected, as they had voted to consume half as much food as usual, and kept to this decision. The leader of the defence was Delphion, an energetic and effective commander. He formed a picked band of three hundred men and used it to block peace efforts, arrest and guard dissidents, watch the populace, maintain discipline among the defenders, and harass the besiegers by making surprise attacks from time to time on different parts of the siege wall. By these means he stretched out the siege to a year and eight months. In the end, however, the food ran out and the Phliasians were forced to surrender, although Delphion escaped. Agesilaus put in charge fifty of the defenders and fifty of the exiled oligarchs, provided them with a garrison, and ordered them to create a new constitution and punish those deserving punishment.[4]

The major Spartan campaigns of the late 380s took place against Olynthus in the Thracian Chalcidice. A former coalition ally, Olynthus was now creating, by persuasion and coercion, a federation of cities. It sought control of the rich resources of wealth, timber, horses, and men in the Chalcidice, southern Thrace, and Macedon. In summer 382, after embassies came from Acanthus and Apollonia seeking aid against Olynthus, a joint assembly of the Spartans and of (reportedly compliant) allied representatives voted for war. Each state had to supply a contingent for a total of ten thousand men, but could substitute money for men if it wished. Since the army would take time to mobilise, the Acanthians asked that a smaller force be sent north immediately. Agreeing, the Spartans sent two thousand *neodamodeis*, Perioecs, and Sciritae under Eudamidas, who reached the Thracian coast, won over Potidaea, garrisoned other cities, and carried on a war of raids and skirmishes.[5]

In August 382 the Spartan commander Phoebidas was on his way north with the rest of the army, but he stopped at Thebes, perhaps for supplies, and stayed. The story in Xenophon is that the anti-Spartan faction under Ismenias and the pro-Spartan one under Leontiades were in strife, and Leontiades met with Phoebidas and persuaded him to seize the Cadmea, the city's citadel, left unguarded during a women-only festival. Xenophon says that it was not an action planned by the Spartan state, but according to Plutarch Agesilaus arranged it, which is possible. The king strongly supported the action, and Phoebidas' arrival at the precise moment of the festival suggests advance planning. Phoebidas was fined, but later returned to favour. The Spartans were persuaded to accept his actions, garrison the Cadmea, and support Leontiades' rule. The Spartans even put Ismenias on trial and executed him for accepting Persian gold to start the Corinthian War. Other Theban notables fled into exile, and the Spartans established friendly oligarchies in the other cities of Boeotia.[6]

Teleutias replaced Phoebidas in command of the army, raised new forces, and in spring 381 headed north, adding cavalry from King Amyntas of Macedon and from Derdas, dynast of the southern Macedonian district of Elymia. Teleutias approached the city cautiously. Olynthus lay eleven kilometres north-east of Potidaea, extending from a long, plateau-like hill in the south to the slopes of another hill in the north. It dominated a broad valley, with a plain to the south and a stream, the modern Retsinikia, flowing past it in the west. Crossing the Retsinikia and approaching the city from the plain, Teleutias deployed his army about a kilometre and a half from it, taking the left wing, the one nearest the main city gates, for himself and the Lacedaemonian foot, and putting the allies on the right. He soon experienced a battle similar to the ones at Athens in 407. The Olynthians' hoplites deployed in front of the city walls while their cavalry attacked the Theban, Macedonian, and Spartan horsemen on Teleutias' right flank, putting them and some of the allied infantry there to flight. Seeing the gates left unprotected, however, Derdas and his cavalry, on Teleutias' left, rode straight for them, and Teleutias led his hoplites forward. Afraid that they might be cut off from the city, the Olynthians rode back quickly, and Derdas and his men killed many. Unlike the Athenians in 407, the Olynthian hoplites did not fight in front of their walls, but hurriedly withdrew into the city also.

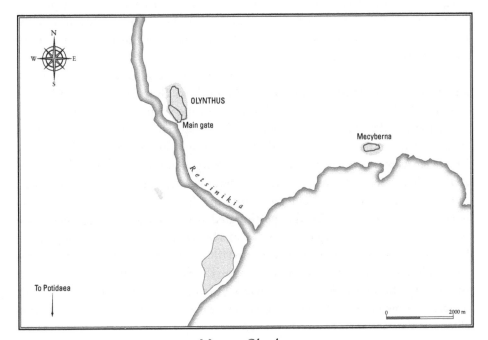

Map 11.1: Olynthus

This ambiguous victory allowed Teleutias to ravage the land on his withdrawal. At the end of the campaigning season, he sent the Macedonians home and entered winter quarters. The Olynthian cavalry staged raids that winter against Spartan-allied towns. However, in spring 380 six hundred Olynthians raiding Apollonia were surprised and routed by Derdas and his cavalry, losing eighty men to his sudden onset and strong pursuit. Cowed, the Olynthians stayed behind their walls. Teleutias presently set about ravaging near the city, but, on approaching it west of the stream, found the Olynthian cavalry in his path. He ordered his peltasts to charge. The Olynthians fell back, but the peltasts rashly pushed the pursuit across the stream, easily crossed in summer. The Olynthians counterattacked, killing over a hundred peltasts and their commander.

Enraged, Teleutias led the hoplites forward quickly and ordered his cavalry and remaining peltasts to pursue and not cease pursuing. Obediently they advanced up to the city walls, but were pelted with missiles from the towers and forced to fall back. The Olynthians regrouped and sallied – first their cavalry, then their peltasts, and lastly their hoplites. In his anger, Teleutias had not held back the older men of his phalanx, but charged ahead with them all. Due to their rapid advance and crossing the Retsinikia they had fallen into disorder, so they were vulnerable to the charge of the Olynthian hoplites. Teleutias was killed, and after that no one stood his ground – not even Perioecs, Sciritae, or *neodamodeis*. Men fled to every point of the compass – to Spartolus in the west, Apollonia in the north, and Acanthus in the east, but most fled to Potidaea in the south, pursued by the Olynthians. Diodorus says that over 1,200 died.

The Spartans could not afford to leave matters there, of course. They sent out a large force with Agesipolis in command and thirty Spartiates to advise him, as Agesilaus had in Asia. Many upper-class Perioecs also volunteered to serve the king, as did the so-called *trophimoi* foreigners and the *nothoi* of the Spartiates, 'very fine-looking men and not unfamiliar with the good things in the city', says Xenophon.[7] *Trophimoi* were non-Spartans raised in the Lycurgan upbringing, *nothoi* the bastard sons of Spartiates and Helots. This underlines just how few Spartiates took part in this Spartan expedition. Volunteers also came from the allies, as did Thessalian horsemen. Amyntas and Derdas participated with even greater eagerness than before. All those hoping to gain the notice of a Spartan king would be disappointed, however, for after ravaging Olynthian territory and taking Torone by storm, Agesipolis died of a fever in midsummer 380. The Spartans sent Polybiades to take command as harmost. He had the Olynthians suffering a famine by summer 379, unable to grow crops or to import them by sea. They agreed to become Spartan allies and abandon their empire building.[8]

The Boeotian War, 379–375[9]

By the autumn of 379, Sparta seemed in control of Greece. This control began to fragment in winter 379/8, when the Theban exiles staged a coup d'état during a festival. The 'Liberators', as scholars call them, killed Leontiades and his fellow leaders, and with the aid of Athenian forces expelled the Spartan garrison from the Cadmea. Later sources make it a grand siege, but Xenophon is probably correct in saying that the garrison was too small to defend the large citadel and evacuated on terms. The harmost was put to death at Sparta afterwards. It is said that the Liberators offered to remain Spartan allies on the same terms as before, and it is likely that they hoped Sparta would accept the coup, especially since the season precluded campaigning. However, pro-Spartan exiles from Thebes came to Sparta with sad tales of slaughter, and the ephors did not hesitate to mobilise.[10]

Agesilaus avoided taking the command, pleading old age: he was by now over sixty. Actually, Xenophon says, he feared incurring blame from his fellow citizens if he campaigned on behalf of the exiled tyrants. The ephors gave the army to Cleombrotus, Agesipolis' successor and younger brother. He crossed Cithaeron by destroying a small force of Thebans guarding the pass near Plataea, but then camped for sixteen days at the Cynoscephalae hills south-west of Thebes, taking no known action before departing, and leaving a garrison of allied troops at Thespiae under the harmost Sphodrias, one of his friends. The deep, gluey mud of the Boeotians plains in wintertime may have made any sort of movement difficult. His campaign did panic the Athenians, who put on trial the two generals who had aided the Liberators, executing one and exiling the other.[11]

Despite this, Sphodrias made a night march into Attica, claiming that he intended to seize the Piraeus by surprise before daybreak. In fact, it was two days' march from Thespiae to the Piraeus, and dawn found him still on the Thria plain east of Eleusis; he withdrew after plundering some farms. Although enraged, the Athenians held off from joining Thebes on the understanding that Sphodrias had acted without orders – bribed by Thebes, reportedly – and would be punished by the Spartans. Instead, Agesilaus' son Archidamus persuaded his father to join Cleombrotus in seeking Sphodrias' acquittal, since the prince was in love with Sphodrias' son. This was done, and so, when Agesilaus took command of the army in spring 378, he found himself facing the Athenians as well as the Thebans and their Boeotian supporters.[12]

Agesilaus used mercenaries to secure the passes over Cithaeron in advance of his army. On his arrival he found that the enemy had created extensive field fortifications of ditches and stockades around the most valuable parts of Thebes' territory, presumably the Teneric and Aonian plains north of the escarpment connecting Thebes and Thespiae, and the larger plain of the Asopus in the south. Other field fortifications may have protected the main route into Attica at this time. However, shaking off a raid by enemy cavalry, Agesilaus passed the defences, either by hurrying before daybreak to an unguarded spot before the enemy army appeared, or by using a feint to mislead the enemy commanders. He ravaged the farmlands inside the stockade. Nearing Thebes, he found the Thebans and Athenians deployed atop an oblong crest three and a half kilometres west of the city. Diodorus reports that he led eighteen thousand infantry, including five morai and the Sciritae, and fifteen hundred cavalry. No doubt he greatly outnumbered the Athenians and Thebans. Confident in his army's size and his Lacedaemonian troops, Agesilaus sent his light-armed ahead to harass the enemy, and led on his massed phalanx.

Awaiting them on the hill were armies whose front ranks consisted of well-drilled and fit hoplites, just as in the Spartan phalanx. The Athenians were fronted by mercenaries trained in the Iphicratean fashion by their commander, Chabrias. They most likely served under him in Egypt in the 380s.[13] The Thebans were fronted by the 'Sacred Band' (Hieros Lochos), so called because it normally guarded the Cadmea and its shrines. Led by Gorgidas, the Sacred Band was a unit of picked men, reportedly consisting of 150 pairs of homosexual lovers. Each man was expected to be afraid to play the coward in front of his beloved. The unit served as the front rank of the Theban phalanx in major battles, but it could also operate independently.[14]

Seeing Agesilaus' advance, Chabrias ordered his mercenaries to assume a rest stance, putting their shields on the ground and propping them against their knees while holding their spears upright; Gorgidas followed suit with the Sacred Band. The two units received their orders, and executed them smartly. Agesilaus now realised that he faced a large body of quality troops. He ordered a halt, and challenged the enemy to come and fight on the plain. They refused, so he led off his men and ravaged further before leading the levies home. He had done considerable damage, but he also had given the enemy a major moral victory – one that Xenophon, a friend and client of Agesilaus, delicately omits.[15]

Thereafter there occurred the defeat and death of Phoebidas, left in command of the Spartan garrison at Thespiae, while pursuing a Theban raiding force. It encouraged large numbers of Boeotians in the Spartan-allied cities to desert to Thebes, where the Liberators were re-establishing the Boeotian Confederacy on a new, democratic basis.[16]

Meanwhile the Athenians were organising a naval league, which scholars call the 'Second Athenian Confederacy'. In it the allies would have their own assembly and set the rates for their 'contributions' (the term 'tribute' was avoided). The Athenians abandoned all public and private claims to land, houses, or other possessions in allied territory, and established the allied assembly as sovereign to punish any Athenian who attempted to purchase property in allied cities. By avoiding imperial exploitation the Athenians were able to create a sizable confederation, including Chios, Mytilene, Methymna, Rhodes, Byzantium, most Euboean cities, and Thebes.[17]

The Spartans also reorganised, seeking to regain the loyalty of disaffected allies. This included changing the method of contributing troops, as Diodorus reports:

> For they divided the cities and the soldiers enlisted for the war into ten parts: of these the Lacedaemonians had the first part, the second and third the Arcadians, the fourth the Eleans, the fifth the Achaeans; and the sixth the Corinthians and Megarians filled, the seventh the Sicyonians and Phliasians and those living in what is called the Acte, the eight the Acarnanians, the ninth the Phocians and Locrians, the last of all the Olynthians and the allies settled in Thrace. A hoplite was set by them as worth two *psiloi*; a horseman was held equal to four hoplites.[18]

Each unit could provide three to four thousand hoplites or their equivalent in cavalry or light infantry. This gives a good picture of the military potential of the Spartans and their allies around 378.[19]

Since a Spartan mora had been sent to garrison Thespiae after Phoebidas' death, Agesilaus had it occupy the passes over Cithaeron before he even left Sparta in spring 377, and so had no trouble entering Boeotia. He used the trick of ordering a market to be prepared at Thespiae to draw the Thebans' attention there, allowing him to cross without hindrance their field fortifications south-east of Thebes. When the enemy took position on a hill, he forced them to race to Thebes by feinting at the city, and then devastated their crops for a second year.[20]

Elsewhere such deprivations had led to capitulations, as we have seen, but the Liberators were determined to do anything to avoid a second exile. They sent two triremes bearing men with money for purchasing grain to Pagasae in Thessaly. A Spartan harmost, Alcetas, held Hestiaea in Euboea, but because only one trireme could be seen exercising off its shore, the Thebans did not fear interception. Alcetas in fact had three triremes, but he exercised their crews in the same warship. When the convoy set sail, he struck, seizing the transports, both Theban triremes, and three hundred men. He imprisoned the men in Hestiaea's citadel. However, when Alcetas reportedly left the citadel to visit a boyfriend in the city, the Thebans broke loose, seized the citadel, and caused the city to revolt, most likely with the aid of an anti-Spartan faction. They recovered everything lost.[21]

Thebes therefore received its grain, frustrating Sparta's strategy of ravaging. In late 377 a vein in Agesilaus' leg ruptured, confining him to his bed, so Cleombrotus led the spring 376 invasion. This was blocked at Cithaeron, the allies defeating the peltasts sent ahead to the pass. Spartan commanders at Plataea and Tanagra may have undergone crushing defeats before this expedition, which would explain why no efforts to open the passes from the north took place. Cleombrotus withdrew and disbanded his army.[22]

Protesting the exhausting and futile war effort, Sparta's allies now demanded a naval blockade of Athens and transportation of armies by sea to Phocis for invasions of Boeotia. Sparta accordingly raised a fleet of sixty triremes, with Pollis as navarch. He operated out of Aegina, Ceos, and Andros, and won over islands in the Cyclades. The Athenians soon faced a food crisis, but they enlarged their fleet by making a mass levy and convoyed to the Piraeus grain ships that had gathered in south-eastern Euboea. In September 376, Pollis with sixty-five ships attempted to raise the siege of Naxos by Chabrias, who had eighty-three triremes. Pollis defeated the Athenian left and killed its commander, Cedon, but Chabrias sent reserves to rescue that flank, and overcame the Spartans' left, sinking twenty-four vessels and taking eight with their crews while losing eighteen.[23] Afterwards Chabrias may have captured other Spartan ships and made a raid on Laconia, probably in winter, surprising the Spartans. He likely landed in the Thyreatis, since he is supposed to have reached Sellasia, north-east of Sparta, and driven captured herds across the border to be sold. Argos was the only city near Sparta that might have allowed this.[24]

In 375 the Spartans and their allies attempted to use their fleet to convey an army across the Corinthian Gulf into Boeotia, where the military situation was deteriorating. The Thebans had taken advantage of the absence of Spartan armies to defeat garrisons in small actions and recover cities previously held by Spartan-supported narrow oligarchies. By spring 375 even Thespiae had yielded, leaving only Plataea and Orchomenus outside the Boeotian Confederacy.[25] The Thebans asked the Athenians to block the movement. They sent sixty ships under Timotheus, son of Conon. He raided Laconia, brought over Corcyra, Cephallenia, and Acarnania, and defeated the Spartan navarch Nicolochus in a battle at Alyzeia, near Leucas, in late June or early July. However, his effort suffered from a shortage of funds: despite the new confederacy, Athens still lacked sufficient income to support large naval operations.[26]

That same spring the Theban commander Pelopidas, a Liberator and ardent spirit, learned that the two morai garrisoning Orchomenus were to go campaigning in Eastern Locris. When they did, he set out with the Sacred Band and two hundred cavalry, circling around Lake Copaïs to approach the city unexpectedly from the east. However, on his arrival he found that a garrison force had arrived in the city, preventing whatever betrayal or uprising he had hoped to support. Heading back the way he came, he unexpectedly encountered the two morai returning by way of Tegyra, where the narrow route between the marshy coast of Lake Copaïs and hills to the north opened into a small plain suitable for battle. The two polemarchs,

Gorgoleon and Theopompus, hurriedly deployed their thousand hoplites and advanced on the Thebans. Plutarch, who has the only detailed account, says:

> When they first were seen coming out through the narrows, someone running up said to Pelopidas, 'We have stumbled into our foes,' he said, 'Why that, than they into us?' And he straightaway ordered all the horse to ride past from the rear in order to charge first, while he himself would gather together the hoplites, who were three hundred, into close formation, expecting that wherever they should attack they would certainly cut through their foes, who were superior in number.[27]

Pelopidas must have expected his cavalrymen to harass the front and flanks of the Spartans, as their ancestors had done at Plataea, and thus stop the enemy from using his superior numbers to surround the Sacred Band.

Plutarch continues:

> The onslaught being performed with passion and violence on both sides in the area where the leaders themselves stood, first the polemarchs of the Lacedaemonians, fighting together against Pelopidas, fell together; then, with those about them being struck and wounded, the entire army became fearful and it divided on both sides of the Thebans, as for those wishing to break through to the other side and slip out through; but when this was done, Pelopidas led his men against those still united and killed them as he went through, so that they all fled headlong.[28]

Remembering Nemea and Coronea, the Spartans had acted accordingly, but Pelopidas had chosen to attack, not escape. The Thebans did not pursue very far, fearing that the garrison at Orchomenus might intervene, but they did set up a trophy and went home in good spirits, having defeated twice their number of Spartan hoplites in pitched battle.[29]

An Unsuccessful Peace, 375–371[30]

In 375 the Athenians sought peace. They were distressed by their wartime expenses and by enemy raids from Aegina, and also concerned at the growth of Theban power. Artaxerxes reportedly also wanted peace in Greece, so mercenaries would become available for his projected campaign in Egypt. The Spartans agreed. Their war had not gone well, and now Jason of Pherae in Thessaly was expanding his power. He had used Sparta's distraction with the Boeotians to win over many cities and peoples of Thessaly, and had mobilised, trained, and exercised an elite army of six thousand mercenaries along Iphicratean lines. Xenophon claims that the Thessalians alone could field six thousand cavalry and over ten thousand hoplites when fully mobilised, and the mountaineers bordering Thessaly could add

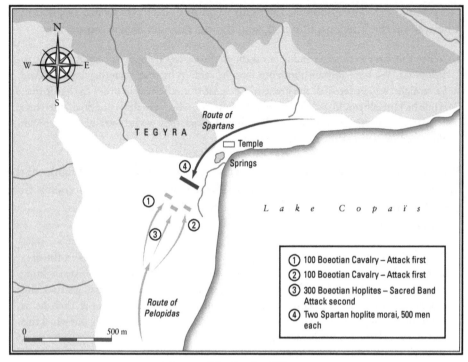

Map 11.2: The Battle of Tegyra

numerous light troops. Jason hoped to extend his rule into strife-torn Macedon, and beyond.[31] In 379, such news would have led to a Spartan mobilisation, but now the Spartans could not see how to stretch their already-strained resources any further. Peace with Thebes and Athens would free them to act, forcing Jason to be cautious. A broad peace resulted, with the same autonomy clause as in the King's Peace. The sources are split on whether or not the members of the Boeotian Confederacy swore separately to it or did not swear at all, but Thebes remained an Athenian ally.[32]

The peace did not hold. The removal of garrisons encouraged uprisings by exiles and democrats at Phigalia, Corinth, Megara, and Phlius. These were crushed, but both Athens and Sparta wound up backing factions in cities, and clashed over control of Ionian Sea islands and Corcyra.[33] Finally the Spartans sent the navarch for 373/2, Mnasippus, to seize Corcyra and the Ionian Sea region. He had Lacedaemonian troops, perhaps only Perioecs and *neodamodeis*, some fifteen hundred mercenaries, and sixty Spartan and allied ships. He landed on Corcyra, seized control of the countryside, and blockaded the Corcyraeans within their walls. They sent for aid to

Athens, which responded at once by sending six hundred peltasts under Ctesicles through Epirus, and voting Timotheus sixty ships. He failed to man them properly, however, and was replaced by Iphicrates, who took the manning and training of the crews in hand. The Corcyraeans in the meantime endured starvation.

Since the end seemed near, Mnasippus began cutting the pay of his mercenaries, dismissing some. Morale dropped, the watch grew slack, and men scattered into the now-looted countryside seeking food. Realising the opportunity, Ctesicles and the defenders made a successful sortie. Mnasippus armed himself, gathered his hoplites, and told the commanders of the mercenaries to lead them forth. When some of them replied that the men would not be obedient unless given provisions, Mnasippus struck one with his staff, and another with the butt-spike of his spear. This got them into line, and Mnasippus and those with him put the attackers to flight. When the fleeing men reached the funeral monuments outside the city walls, however, they climbed atop and hurled javelins and stones at their pursuers. Meanwhile, from other gates hoplites sallied, massed, and went against the far end of Mnasippus'

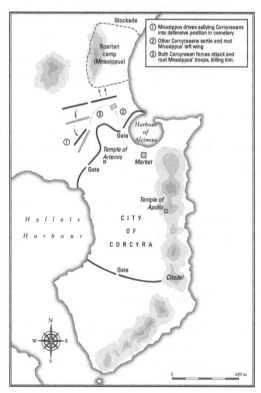

Map 11.3: The Battle of Corcyra

phalanx. Only formed eight deep, its men attempted to face about, march back their files, and turn to reform behind the neighbouring hoplites, with the intention of doubling the depth of their phalanx.

Evidently they were Lacedaemonians, given their organisation, and feared a massed Theban-style attack, not being outflanked. However, the attackers mistook the about-face for turning to flight, and charged. Those moving back were caught and began to run. Adjacent units soon fled also. Already engaged to his front, Mnasippus could do nothing but watch his phalanx crumble, until the enemy, now joined by the Corcyraean citizen levy, made the final charge. He was slain, and a pursuit began that stopped short of the Spartan camp only because the victors mistook the mob of camp followers, servants, and slaves inside for combatants. Learning that Iphicrates was on his way, Mnasippus' second-in-command, Hypermenes, abandoned the camp and sailed off with as much loot as his ships could bear. Iphicrates was too late to intercept him, but carried out several successful operations nevertheless.[34]

Meanwhile the Thebans had taken advantage of the renewal of hostilities to seize Plataea in a surprise attack, expelling its inhabitants and again destroying the city; they also razed the walls of Thespiae. Moreover, they and Jason threatened Phocis, forcing Sparta to send Cleombrotus there with an army in spring 371. Upset at Plataea's fate, the Athenians saw no point in continuing fighting that only profited Thebes, and sent envoys to Sparta to arrange for a new peace. The Thebans participated in this as well.[35]

Sparta agreed to peace, and everyone swore to remove governors and garrisons, disband armaments, and give cities autonomy. However, the next day, Xenophon says, the Thebans came back and asked to amend the treaty, so that they could swear also on behalf of the members of the Boeotian Confederacy. Agesilaus refused to allow any changes, except to strike out Thebes' name from the treaty. Ignoring advice from an elder Spartan to demobilise and wait for their enemies to provide a *casus belli* that left gods and men unquestionably on their side, the Spartans ordered Cleombrotus to invade if Thebes did not leave the cities autonomous. This time the Thebans refused.[36]

The Battle of Leuctra, 371 [37]

Cleombrotus dutifully marched from Phocis, only to find the main enemy army holding the narrows near Coronea against him. Other enemy units occupied passes on Mounts Cithaeron and Helicon. Cleombrotus withdrew, but went to Ambrossus, modern Dhistomo, in Phocian territory, and ascended Helicon from the west. Like Kallidromos, Helicon has a highland valley running across it, providing an easy route to the east after the initial ascent. He reached the Koukoura Plain, where he surprised and destroyed a Boeotian unit defending Helicon. From there he could have headed straight for Thebes, or gone against the rear of the main enemy army, but the risk of encountering a massed enemy with his own forces still in order of march probably seemed too great. Instead he headed south and surprised the port of Creusis, capturing some triremes and reopening his sea communications with the Peloponnese. He then made for Leuctra in the territory of Thespiae and camped on a ridge overlooking a small valley. If the Boeotians sought battle, he was well-positioned to accept it, and could look forward to ravaging Boeotian territory and winning over some of Thebes' more reluctant allies.[38]

The Boeotians did seek battle, and marched to Leuctra, where they encamped on the hills across the valley, about a kilometre and a half north of the ridge where the king was encamped. Xenophon claims that their leaders felt they had to fight, since otherwise they would be besieged, the cities would revolt, and the people of Thebes would turn on them. They preferred death to a new exile. However, later sources report strong debate among the Boeotarchs, the chief officials of the confederacy. Three of them preferred to stand siege, or offer battle only in a strong place, and send their families for safekeeping to Athens. Since by now many Athenians looked forward to Sparta finally 'tithing' Thebes, this may have been wishful thinking.[39] However, the most reasonable figures reported set six thousand Boeotians against four Spartan morai and allies – a total of ten thousand infantry and one thousand cavalry – so it is likely many sought an alternative to pitched battle.[40] All sources report prodigies and oracles, signs of nerves. But one of the leading minds of the Liberators, the Boeotarch Epaminondas, along with two other Boeotarchs and Pelopidas, leader of the Sacred Band, wanted to fight here and now. It is even said that Epaminondas and his fellows faked favourable omens to encourage their people to face the Spartans.[41]

As for Cleombrotus, he had to fight. After two failed invasions of Boeotia, his enemies were already saying that he was partial to Thebes, and his friends were warning that he had to fight now, or risk trial and exile. Xenophon mentions that he and his staff had eaten breakfast, and were said to have drunk a bit heavily. Thus, when large numbers of people were seen leaving the Boeotian camp, Cleombrotus sent the cavalry from Phlius and Heraclea along with Phocian and mercenary peltasts to attack them. The king probably thought that a withdrawal was underway, but in fact they were either non-combatants or men unwilling to fight. Late sources claim Epaminondas was aware of disaffection in his army, especially among the Thespians, and announced that any who wished could depart. He did not want men deserting during battle and disrupting the army. The Spartan attack, however, drove many back to the army and compelled them to fight.[42]

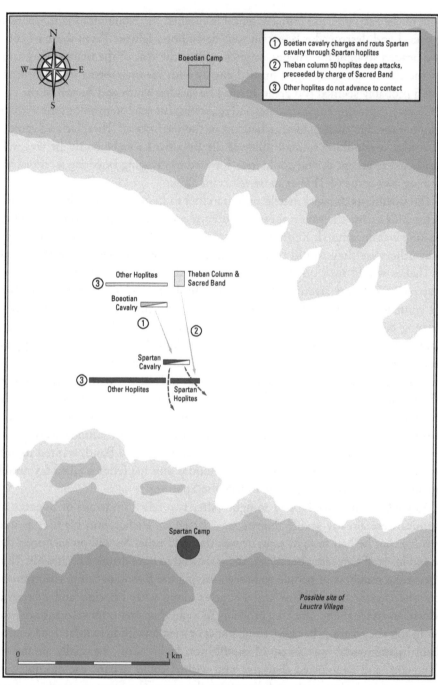

Map 11.4: The Battle of Leuctra

For the battle we have three different main accounts.[43] Xenophon gives the most detail, and writes from the Spartan viewpoint, probably from Spartan sources. The king brought his army onto the plain and deployed it twelve ranks deep, with the four morai on the right wing. However, 'since the space in-between was a plain, the Lacedaemonians deployed their horsemen in front of their phalanx, and the Thebans stationed their own opposite them', Xenophon notes.[44] This deployment was probably intended to prevent Boeotian cavalry from harassing the phalanx during its deployment or skirmishing to assist a massed infantry attack, as at Tegyra.

Since the Spartan and allied cavalrymen should have outnumbered their Boeotian counterparts, Cleombrotus had reason for confidence in his cavalry. However, the riders of Boeotia were experienced and capable, while their Spartan opponents were neither. Xenophon explains that 'the richest men reared the horses; but when mobilisation occurred, only then came the appointed rider; he would take his horse and whatever arms were given him and at once go on campaign. Moreover, those of the soldiers who were placed on horseback were the least physically fit and least ambitious.'[45] Peers fought together as hoplites, not as cavalrymen. Although the Spartans had possessed cavalry for over fifty years, the higher status of hoplite service had denied them an effective cavalry arm.

Events now moved quickly. 'When Cleombrotus began to lead against the foe', Xenophon writes, 'first, before it was even perceived by his army that he was leading on, the horsemen in fact had joined battle, and those of the Lacedaemonians were speedily defeated; fleeing, they burst in among their own hoplites; moreover, the lochoi of the Thebans were now charging in.'[46] Formed fifty ranks deep, they headed for the king's location, thinking that if they could defeat the Spartans there, the remainder would be easily overcome. Xenophon states:

> Nevertheless, that those with Cleombrotus were at first victors in the battle one may know from this clear sign: they could not have taken him up and carried him off, still alive, unless those fighting in front of him had been winning at that time. But when Deinon the polemarch perished, and Sphodrias, one of those sharing the king's tent, and Cleonymus, son of Sphodrias, then the *Hippeis*,[47] the so-called assistants of the polemarch, and the rest fell back, being pushed by the mob, while those on the left wing of the Lacedaemonians, when they saw that the right being pushed, gave way. Nevertheless, although many had perished and they were beaten, after they crossed the trench that happened to be in front of their camp, they grounded their arms at the position from which they had set forth.[48]

Xenophon says that almost a thousand Lacedaemonians were slain, including some four hundred of the seven hundred Spartiates present. He maintains that cowardice was not involved in their defeat, except as far as the Spartan cavalrymen were concerned, and this he explains. However, he does not explain the terrible casualties, perhaps a third of the Lacedaemonians present.

Of the other two principle ancient accounts, Diodorus gives a badly exaggerated version, bringing in additional forces that only appeared afterwards. He says that only part of the Boeotian army attacked the Spartans, while the rest faced the Spartan allies and had orders to avoid battle and fall back gradually if attacked. No doubt Epaminondas and the Boeotarchs ordered the Theban allies to stay on the defensive. However, it is not likely that they expected them to have the discipline to make a gradual withdrawal during combat. The vital factor was the speed of the attack. Once the Spartans had been halted by the Thebans' onset, the Spartans' allies, advancing in the usual slow way before their charge, would have halted also in shock, allowing the Theban allies to stay out of combat.

As for Plutarch, his account says nothing about the cavalry. His focus is entirely upon Pelopidas, subject of his *Life*. He describes Epaminondas leading his phalanx to the left, to draw the Spartan right wing as far away from its allies as possible before attacking and crushing Cleombrotus. The Spartan units in turn changed formation, so as to extend themselves further to their right and encircle the Boeotians – but Pelopidas led forth the Sacred Band at a run and caught the Spartans while they were still in the confusion of the change, before they had time to return to any set formation.

Distilling these reports into a single account, it seems that the Boeotians formed a line of battle with the Thebans on the left wing in a column fifty deep and perhaps as many wide. The Sacred Band will have formed the column's first five or six ranks, with the lochoi of the levies formed side-by-side behind it, forty-four or forty-five men deep. The Boeotian cavalry was deployed in front of the phalanx. Cleombrotus formed his hoplites into a twelve-deep phalanx, with the Lacedaemonians on the right, and his cavalry also in front, for the reasons stated above. Leaving the other Boeotian contingents to stand on the defensive, Epaminondas led his Thebans to the left to draw the Spartans right, and sent the Boeotian cavalry charging into its Spartan counterparts.

The Theban column would have advanced faster than a phalanx, since it did not have to stop to align ranks. Seeing its movement, the king ordered his forces to change formation and extend to the right to encircle it, doing so during the early part of the cavalry battle, before the Spartan cavalry routed. His mora and the *Hippeis* (who may or may not have been in the mora) extended beyond the area of the cavalry battle. When Pelopidas saw the opportunity offered by the process of extension, he led the Sacred Band in a charge. Only the Sacred Band attacked initially, so the Spartans held it off, but its attack halted the Spartans' rightward move, disrupted them, and mortally wounded Cleombrotus, making him the first Spartan king killed in battle since Leonidas.

The Theban column then struck the already-disorganised mora, perhaps coming up on its open flank. The mora and *Hippeis* were crushed – most Spartiate casualties would have occurred here, where many Spartiates were located. Most of the Perioecs and 'inferiors' would have stood in the three other morai, along with some four hundred Spartiate file leaders and officers. Caught in extension by their own routing cavalrymen and then by the Boeotian cavalry, as well as realising that the Theban infantry was coming their way, these morai broke. The three polemarchs survived and units reformed once past the trench and in camp, so it appears that the Spartiates in the three units kept their heads and defended themselves in the retreat, while the Boeotian cavalry cut down fleeing Perioecs. The Spartan allies also fell back, and the armies ceased fighting. After debate, with some hotheads wanting to renew the fight, the Spartans sought and received a burial truce. The two armies then watched each other for several days.

Thebes had developed a combined-arms force able to tackle the Spartan army in the field, with a standing unit of *epilektoi*, an efficient cavalry, and a combat tactic that enabled its hoplite levy to overpower any section of a normal phalanx. With cavalry protecting its flanks, the massed column of hoplites, spearheaded by the Sacred Band, could move more quickly than the phalanx and strike its flank or push through its front. The Boeotians had all the same elements available at Nemea and Coronea as at Leuctra, however, and far stronger allied armies in addition. What they lacked were commanders able to see the possibilities, and willing to attack head-on an army that had been feared for generations. Pelopidas and Epaminondas had the daring to face the Spartan army in pitched battle, and the insight to realise its growing weaknesses and how to exploit them. As a result, they won one of the most famous battles of Classical Antiquity and ended the era of Spartan dominance in Greece.

~ Twelve ~

Decline and Fall, 371–362 and Beyond

From 371 to 369[1]

One defeat, and that not total, could not have ended Spartan dominance by itself. However, now the Spartans were weaker in numbers, legitimacy, and reputation than at any earlier crisis. Argives, Arcadians, and Eleans would be as prepared to act against Sparta as back in the 460s or 410s, and Perioecs and Helots readier to revolt. And, unlike either decade, a power beyond the Peloponnese that was capable of defeating the Spartans in battle now existed, and would intervene to aid Sparta's foes. In this chapter, we shall see how these factors ended Spartan dominance in the Peloponnese, and why it never revived.

The news of the disaster at Leuctra arrived at Sparta on the last day of the festival of the Gymnopaedia. The ephors ordered the choral performance to continue, and told the women of the slain to bear their losses without lamentation. On the following day, Xenophon says, you could see the relatives of the slain going about looking cheerful, while the relatives of the survivors hid or looked gloomy.[2] The ephors called up the two remaining morai, along with every able-bodied man up to sixty, including those in public office – an extraordinarily thorough mobilisation. Prince Archidamus stood in for his still-disabled father, Agesilaus, and led the army north, gathering allied units on the way.

The prince might have been able to rescue the army and resume the offensive if the Thebans had not received aid. They sent first to Athens, but received a cold reception there. They did obtain aid from Jason, however, who headed south with his mercenaries and household cavalry. His speed was such that he was in Phocis before his foes realised that he was marching. On his arrival, the Thebans proposed a joint attack upon the Spartan army, still camped on Leuctra ridge. Jason dissuaded them, stressing the risk of attacking desperate men. He instead persuaded the Spartan commanders to withdraw under a truce, hinting that their allies were already negotiating with Thebes. Crossing Cithaeron, the army met Archidamus in the Megarid.

The truce in effect ended campaigning, and the prince disbanded the army and returned home with the survivors.[3] Jason, however, on his return home seized and destroyed Heraclea, and won neighbouring peoples as allies. Thebes secured Boeotia for itself and gained as allies the Phocians, Locrians, Acarnanians, Aetolians, and Euboeans. Two great powers were arising. However, in 370 Jason was assassinated, leaving a power vacuum in Thessaly that repeatedly drew in the Boeotians. The Athenians sought to become the leaders of a new 'Common Peace', but they failed to accomplish anything.[4]

In Sparta soul-searching and blame-casting began, with Agesilaus its chief target. However, handed the sensitive problem of what to do about the 'tremblers' defeated at Leuctra, the king humanely decided 'to let the laws sleep for a day, but from that day to be in power thereafter'.[5] Too many had survived for punishment to be practical, and an amnesty avoided shaming men who might have turned to conspiracy in response. This politic decision preserved Agesilaus' prominent position at Sparta.[6]

Inside the Peloponnese, the Eleans again laid claim to the peoples and lands lost in 400, the Mantineans began rebuilding their city and walls, Argos experienced brutal, class-based civil strife in which over twelve hundred of its richer (and more likely pro-Spartan) citizens were clubbed to death, and Tegea saw its pro-Spartan government overthrown in a coup.[7] In late autumn 370 the Spartans marched, ostensibly to aid the exiled pro-Spartan Tegeans and punish Mantinea for violating the peace by aiding the coup. In fact, they faced a growing Arcadian federation allied to Elis and Argos, which threatened their position in the Peloponnese.

Sparta still had as allies the cities of the Argolic Acte, Corinth, Sicyon, Phlius, the Heraeans of western Arcadia, the Orchomenians of northern Arcadia, and the people of Lepreum, all threatened by the ambitions of the anti-Spartan states. A Spartan commander, Polytropus, gathered mercenary peltasts at Corinth, and defended Orchomenus against the Mantineans. Agesilaus, now healthy enough to return to command, led the main army to Eugaea in Arcadia and fortified it, probably planning to use it as an *epiteichisma*. The Tegeans and their Arcadian supporters deployed at Asea, a central location in Arcadia several kilometres north of Eugaea.

An outright victory in this campaign might have restored the situation for Sparta, at least temporarily. However, after driving off a Mantinean attack on Orchomenus, Polytropus pushed his pursuit too far, and fell fighting against a counterattack. Agesilaus advanced into the territory of Mantinea and began ravaging, but the defenders, who included the Eleans and Argives, avoided pitched battle, sticking to the mountain slopes for their movements. At one point Agesilaus had to withdraw carefully from a narrow valley to prevent his rear units being attacked by the enemy on the slopes. He formed his army in a phalanx facing the enemy, and then gradually withdrew the endangered units behind the others, doubling the depth of his army. He led the army out into the plain in this formation, then extended it again, forming his phalanx to the depth of nine or ten ranks.

The king stayed three more days before heading home. Xenophon says that the king found operating in winter difficult, but gives the impression that he lacked confidence in his army.[8] Moreover, after an appeal to Athens failed,[9] the Arcadians, Argives, and Eleans had gone to the Boeotians and won an alliance. The Eleans even lent the Boeotians funds to pay for an expeditionary force. The king may have hoped that the season and his withdrawal would abort this relief effort, giving him time to prepare and seek aid.[10]

If so, he failed to allow for the aggressiveness of the new coalition, and especially for Pelopidas and Epaminondas, both now Boeotarchs, who arrived on the scene with a powerful army of the Boeotians and their allies. The Arcadians, Eleans, and Argives all urged the Boeotians not to miss this opportunity to join them in invading Laconia. Some of the Boeotarchs hesitated, reluctant due to the season, the end of their terms of office after the winter solstice, and the reported difficulty of invading Laconia, where garrisons held the northern passes. Nonetheless, Epaminondas and Pelopidas strongly supported invasion, and men of Caryae in the Sciritis offered to act as guides, while Perioecs came to say that many refused to serve in Sparta's army any longer. The opportunity was too great to ignore.[11]

The figures in the sources, likely exaggerated, give the invaders forty thousand hoplites and thirty thousand light-armed and cavalry. To complicate defence efforts and ease congestion, the Argives invaded along the borders of the Thyreatis, the Boeotians by way of Caryae, the Arcadians through Oeum in the Sciritis, and the Eleans by a western route starting in the vicinity of Asea. The Argives defeated the Spartan garrison defending the Parnon route and killed its commander, Alexander, and two hundred of his men, who included Boeotian exiles. At Oeum the Arcadians destroyed the defending *neodamodeis* and Tegean exiles as well as Ischolaus, their commander, whom Xenophon criticises for defending the town instead of the pass itself, because he wished to add its inhabitants to his effectives (perhaps the Oeans had refused to go to the pass). With the borders now opened and their positions flanked, the other garrisons no doubt retreated to Sparta. The Arcadians and Boeotians united forces at Caryae, which had come over to them, and the entire army joined at Sellasia, a town north-east of Sparta. Laconia lay open to the invaders.[12]

The allies pillaged and burned Sellasia, which reappeared later as a fortified post, probably held by rebellious Perioecs and an Arcadian garrison. Then the army marched down the east bank of the Eurotas, ravaging and plundering the rich country estates of the Spartiates. The allies arrived in the vicinity of Sparta, but

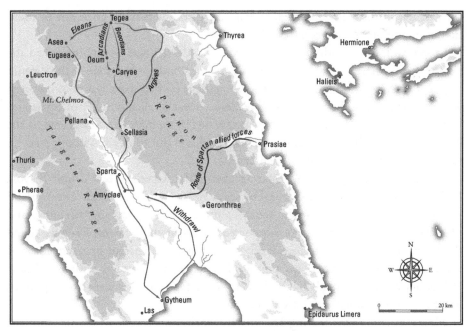

Map 12.1: The invasion of Laconia

Xenophon says that they did not try to cross the river, which was swollen with winter rain and snow, until they reached Amyclae. Late sources do report opposed crossings that resulted in battles with heavy losses, as well as an assault on the city. Whether Xenophon downplayed the fighting – his silences about events at this time are striking – or the later sources exaggerated it, is uncertain. After they crossed, Agesilaus took advantage of the river, the range of hills running north-west from the shrine of Artemis Orthia, and the lower elevations south of it, keeping his forces in the defiles and heights, and probably also ordered trenches dug and stockades raised. South of the city he staged an ambush at the race-course, driving off an enemy approach. Despite the city being unwalled, therefore, the allies did not push home their attacks on it, but destroyed what they could easily reach.

The invasion caused panic among Spartiate women, utterly unprepared by their upbringing to seeing an enemy destroying their property. Facing Perioecic desertions and having only several hundred Spartiates available, the authorities had proclaimed that any Helot who took up arms on Sparta's behalf would be freed. It is reported that over six thousand volunteered, frightening the authorities by their numbers. The fact that the lands they worked were being ravaged likely motivated them. In the event, it seems many deserted, perhaps after finding that the government could do nothing to protect the countryside.

Worse still, two hundred frightened and disaffected non-Spartiates seized the northern hill where the shrine of Artemis Issoria stood – a keystone of the defence – and planned to hand it over to the foe. Agesilaus bluffed them out of it, however, and later arrested and executed their leaders. Worst of all, a number of Spartiates conspired against the state. The plot was revealed by an informer. Supported by the ephors, Agesilaus had the conspirators arrested and put to death without trial, an event unprecedented in Spartan memory.

Meanwhile, contingents from Sparta's allies in the Argolic Acte, Corinth, Sicyon, Pellene in Achaea, and Phlius arrived by sea at Prasiae, and made their way overland to Sparta. The invaders turned south, continuing their burning, ravaging, and plundering, in which they were supported by dissident Perioecs. They assaulted Gytheum for three days and evidently took it, since a Theban garrison is found there later. Finally, after perhaps a month in Laconia, the invaders withdrew. Many Peloponnesians had already left with their booty, food supplies were running short, and the winter weather was miserable.[13]

However, soon after leaving Laconia the coalition invaded Messenia. Inspired by Epaminondas, and meeting no resistance, its forces began constructing a city at Mount Ithome, building great walls that remain visible today. They proclaimed it the new Messene, revived after 230 years of Spartan occupation (*Figure 10*). The coalition summoned all abroad who claimed Messenian ancestry to join the new city-state. Perioecs and Helots who had fled Laconia were added to those within Messenia who wished to rebel (the coastal Perioecs stayed loyal to Sparta for now), and other Greeks volunteered to settle in the new city. The allies may have fortified Thuria and other sites in the south-east as well, to hinder Spartan incursions.[14] Only when this was accomplished did the Boeotians go home, after just eighty-five days.[15] They easily marched through the Isthmus of Corinth, despite an attempt to block them made by the Athenians, who had been persuaded to join Sparta and its remaining allies.[16] The invaders left behind a liberated Messenia and ravaged Laconia, its northern border districts now in enemy hands, as were Sellasia and Gytheum. Centuries of Spartan rule had been overturned in less than three months.

From 369 to 362 [17]

The next several years found the Spartans struggling to recover their territory; the recovery of their dominion in the Peloponnese was beyond them. In 369 the Arcadians raided, captured Pellana, a town upriver of Sparta, and executed its garrison.[18] Later they attacked Asine on the coast of the Messenian Gulf, defeated

10. The remains of the northern walls of Messene, showing the Arcadian Gate, and beyond it the circuit wall ascending the slopes of Mount Ithome. The walls are built entirely of stone. In most Greek walls of the era only the lower two metres were stone, the upper levels being mudbrick (adobe). (*David Conwell*)

its garrison, and killed the polemarch in command, Geranor.[19] A defeat of the Spartan army during an invasion of Tegea may have occurred as well.[20] Laconia's vulnerability meant that Sparta could spare few forces to assist its northern allies, who depended on Athens.

Epaminondas led two major invasions. On the first he cracked the defences of the isthmus by surprising the Spartan polemarch and citizen forces at a position near Cenchreae east of Corinth.[21] On the second he punched through by having the Argives surprise mercenaries under Spartan and Athenian command.[22] Fortunately for Sparta, Epaminondas' attention was focused on the northern Peloponnese, divisions grew between the ambitious Arcadians and their allies, and problems in Thessaly distracted Thebes. Dionysius I sent expeditions to aid Sparta, while Philiscus, a diplomat in Persian service, provided mercenaries for Sparta after failing to negotiate a comprehensive peace.[23]

In (probably) 368, with Thebes distracted in Thessaly, Prince Archidamus led an offensive, aided by forces from Dionysius, including Celtic mercenaries. Marching on a waterless route, perhaps from Sparta to modern Barbosthenes, he bypassed Arcadian-held Sellasia and took Caryae by surprise, killing all those captured.

Entering south-western Arcadia, he ravaged Parrhasia. When the Arcadians and
Argives arrived, he withdrew to the hills above Malea (modern Boutsaras), north-
west of Mount Chelmos. At that point, the leader of Dionysius' forces announced
that the time had come for him to return to Sicily. He headed southwards, only to
find his route blocked by the Messenians, who had crossed Taÿgetus. Archidamus
came to the rescue, and the Messenians withdrew. However, the Arcadians and
Argives now moved to intercept him. Archidamus responded by deploying for
battle at a road junction south-east of Malea.

Xenophon notes of Archidamus:

> They say also that he, going along in front of the lochoi, exhorted them with suchlike
> words: 'Fellow citizens, now let us look up, eyes level, as becomes brave men. Let us give
> to those coming after us our country as it was when we received it from our fathers.
> Let us cease feeling shame before our wives and children and elders and strangers,
> among whom we were previously the most admired of all the Greeks.' After these words
> were spoken, they say that out of a clear sky lightnings and thunderings boding well
> for him appeared; and it also happened that on the right wing was a shrine and statue
> of Heracles, wherefore indeed they say that from all these causes so much ardour and
> courage filled the soldiers that it was a task for their leaders to restrain the soldiers as
> they pushed to the front. But when Archidamus led on, few of the enemy received them
> at spear point, and these perished; the others, fleeing, were slain, many by the horsemen,
> many by the Celts.[24]

Diodorus claims that ten thousand Arcadians fell. One would prefer a less
supernatural explanation for the Spartan victory, and a less suspiciously high casualty
figure, as such losses should have crippled the Arcadians, but did not. Perhaps
Archidamus struck the Arcadians and Argives while they were still deploying, and
the allies' ancient fear of the Spartans combined with the excitement of his men to
produce the outcome. The Spartans dubbed it the 'Tearless Battle', since not one of
their men was slain, although Xenophon says that many tears of relief and joy were
shed in Sparta at the news. Plutarch disapproved of the reaction, considering it a
decline from the restraint the Spartans had shown at previous victories. The real
decline from the old standards is shown by the delivery of a speech before the battle
– something the Spartans had scorned in earlier times.[25]

Plutarch might also have noted how Archidamus is said to have walked in front
of the lochoi, not the morai. After Leuctra, Xenophon never mentions the mora, but
twice speaks of the Spartan army as being organised into twelve lochoi.[26] These must
have consisted of Spartiates, Perioecs, and freed Helots, with Spartiates in front,
and were at least the size of the old lochoi of 418, since one can hardly picture an
army of fewer than six thousand men facing the Arcadians and their allies with any
hope of success. It is not surprising that the Spartans simplified their organisation

after 371 by dropping the mora, since they were no longer rotating citizen units abroad for long periods of garrison duty.

The Tearless Battle did not profit Sparta. The Arcadians responded to the defeat by undertaking a project already urged by Epaminondas: the construction of Megalopolis, a large walled city in south-western Arcadia. The inhabitants of over forty communities, including some in the Aegytis and Belminatis, were compelled to settle there. Thereafter Megalopolis joined Messene as a permanent hindrance to Spartan ambitions.[27] Probably it was also now that the Arcadians organised the *Eparitoi*, five thousand picked hoplites kept constantly under arms.[28] Even so, after Dionysius I died, his son Dionysius II sent Sparta more aid, through which Sellasia was regained.[29]

Finally, more than five years after Leuctra, Sparta's allies had had enough, and made peace with Spartan permission, ending the war and the alliance system that the Spartans had created in the mid-sixth century. The Spartans refused to swear to a peace that did not return Messenia, so their war continued.[30] It may have been during or shortly after this peacemaking that a young Spartiate, Isidas, son of Phoebidas, recovered Gytheum. He went with a hundred young men to the town's vicinity, where they stripped, put on olive garlands, and anointed themselves with oil, as though participants in celebratory games. Under their arms they hid short Spartan swords. Unarmed and naked, Isidas ran ahead to greet the Thebans garrisoning the town. Deceived, they let the Spartans enter, only to be surprised and cut down or chased out. Later stories of Isidas fighting naked in a hoplite battle at Sparta were probably inspired by this daring attack.[31]

In 364 the Arcadians and Eleans went to war over Triphylia, which both claimed as their own. The Eleans, getting the worst of it, allied with Sparta. The Spartans sent Archidamus and their citizen army into the Aegytis, where they seized Cromnus, which lay on the route between Megalopolis and Messene, on a hill over two kilometres north-east of the modern village of Paradhisia. The site was perfect for securing Elean–Spartan communications, and cutting those of Arcadia and Messenia. Archidamus left three of the twelve citizen *lochoi* there as a garrison and returned home. The Arcadians massed at Cromnus, however, and enclosed it in a double stockade. Finding their fellow citizens blockaded, the Spartans mobilised. Archidamus led the army into Sciritis and southern Arcadia, but his ravaging did not draw the Arcadians from Cromnus. He proceeded there, and decided that if he could take a hill – over which part of the outer stockade ran – the Arcadians would not be able to hold their position. He accordingly led his army against it by a roundabout route, probably intending a dawn surprise attack.

However, outside the stockade were stationed units of the *Eparitoi*. The cavalry and peltasts in Archidamus' van twice attacked them and were twice repulsed. Going to their aid, Archidamus led his hoplites forward straight from line of march, only to find the *Eparitoi* massed and attacking. They crushed the head of his column, wounding the prince himself and killing some thirty of the noblest Spartiates, who fought to protect his life. The rest of the Spartan army retired along the road and formed a phalanx once on open ground. The Arcadians came on, but clearly were outnumbered, while the Spartans were dispirited by their losses.

Before a renewed clash occurred, however, Xenophon says that one of the older men cried: 'Why must we fight, gentlemen, and not rather make a truce and be reconciled?'[32] The Arcadians halted and accepted the offer. The Spartans took their dead and retired. Later, after the Arcadians' allies sent forces to support the siege, the Spartans made a night attack where the Argives were located, seized part of the stockade, and called on their men in Cromnus to escape. Many did, but over one hundred Spartiates and Perioecs were cut off and taken captive. They were distributed among the Arcadians and their allies, the Argives, Messenians, and Boeotians, who had returned to the Peloponnese.[33]

Presently the Arcadians fell into civil strife, arising from a growing controversy over the seizure of treasure from Olympia to pay the *Eparitoi*. The Arcadians simply did not have the resources to keep five thousand men constantly mobilised. Once war booty ran out, sacred treasures were 'borrowed', but the Arcadians had no right to them, and a faction of Arcadians, centred at Mantinea, opposed those who had seized the treasures. These in turn tried to carry out mass arrests with Boeotian support. The confederacy broke apart. In summer 362, a Boeotian army entered the Peloponnese to aid pro-Boeotian Arcadians. Pelopidas had perished in Thessaly in 364, so the task fell to Epaminondas. He led the Boeotians and their allies, the Tegeans, Megalopolitans, and other southern Arcadians, as well as the Messenians and Argives. On the other side a coalition of Mantineans and northern Arcadians formed, joined by the Eleans, Achaeans, Athenians, and, of course, the Spartans. The coalition army massed outside of Mantinea, Epaminondas' army at Tegea. He believed his arrival would create diplomatic openings, but it quickly became clear that he had to fight.[34]

Learning that Agesilaus had come to Pellana on his way north with nine of the twelve lochoi, the other three already being at Mantinea with Sparta's mercenaries and cavalry, Epaminondas decided to take Sparta, now without defenders and still unwalled. He marched south at night with his entire army. However, Agesilaus was warned of the march by a Cretan, perhaps a deserting mercenary. He rushed back to Sparta from Pellana, twelve kilometres distant. Epaminondas' van crossed the Eurotas north of the city while it was still dark. He led it straight on in a dawn attack, seizing a hill there. His plan was to attack down into the city, to avoid having missiles thrown from the housetops on his troops. However, Archidamus made a surprise counterattack and drove the enemy off the hill, although his pursuit soon met fierce resistance and came to a quick end.

Other attacks penetrated the city, most likely from the river side, but were stalled short of the marketplace by men fighting behind field fortifications, namely baskets filled with material from houses that the Spartans tore down, placed to block every point of access or open area. Seeing how things were going, and knowing that the allied army was certainly on its way south by now, Epaminondas pulled back, rested his troops, and then headed back north. He had attacked with only fifteen thousand men, if we may believe one late report. Since he had a far larger army, he may have left the rest holding the passes along the route (through Oeum?) that he had taken on his way south. Sparta had escaped disaster by mere hours.[35]

While Epaminondas remained in the field, however, the danger remained. On his return to Tegea he sent his weary cavalry to attack Mantinea, hoping to catch its people harvesting their grain and tending their herds. He almost did – only the chance arrival of the Athenian cavalry contingent foiled it. In the ensuing combat many fell, including Gryllus, one of Xenophon's two sons.

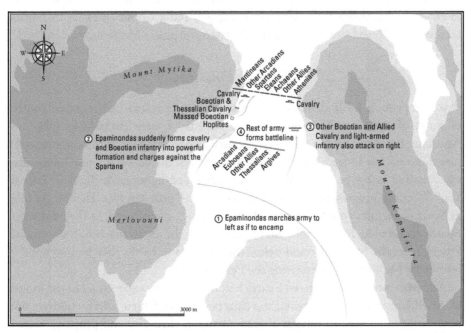

Map 12.2: The second Battle of Mantinea

Facing another failure, Epaminondas decided to risk a major set-piece battle. The enemy had returned, and deployed at the narrowest part of the Tripolis Plain, between Mytika and Kapnistra. This was a strong position, with each flank protected by a mountain. To crack it, Epaminondas led his army over towards the western hills, and had those in the van ground their arms. Thinking he intended to encamp, the enemy relaxed. But in fact he formed the leading forces, which were Boeotian, into a powerful mass, and formed his cavalry likewise, having the rest of his army stand on the defensive to the east as each unit came out of column of march. He then made a sudden charge, sending the massed cavalry into the enemy's right-wing horsemen while he led the Boeotians into the three Spartan lochoi. Once victorious, Epaminondas' cavalry and infantry could then have surrounded and annihilated the northern Arcadians. This would have allowed the southern Arcadians, Epaminondas' allies, to dominate a reformed Arcadian confederacy.

The attack succeeded brilliantly. Epaminondas' highly experienced cavalrymen could hardly have failed to rout Peloponnesian horsemen caught by surprise, while fifteen hundred Lacedaemonians had little hope of stopping several thousand Boeotian hoplites. Yet Epaminondas failed even so, for he received a mortal wound from a Spartiate, named either Machaerion or Anticrates. A late source claims that the Spartans deliberately targeted Epaminondas. Two other Theban generals, his successors, perished as well. Now directionless, the victors allowed their foes to escape to Mantinea. The campaign collapsed, and a 'Common Peace' of mutual exhaustion followed – one Sparta still refused to join unless Messenia was returned.[36]

From 360 Onwards

It would prove a futile demand, even though the Spartans had regained control of most of their northern borders, the Arcadians were irrevocably split, and Agesilaus and Archidamus sold their services as generals abroad to raise money to hire mercenaries. Indeed, Agesilaus died of old age in 360 on his way home after campaigning in Egypt,[37] and Archidamus was killed fighting for Taras in Italy in 338.[38] Nothing progressed as hoped, however. The problem was Thebes. As long as Sparta's enemies could summon Theban aid in times of need, as they did when Sparta threatened Megalopolis in 352 and 351,[39] the Spartans could accomplish little. Unless the Spartans could defeat the Thebans in battle, they had no hope of recovering Messenia or dominating the Peloponnese.

Athenian intellectuals offered Sparta helpful advice. In a speech set in the mouth of Archidamus, Isocrates advised the Spartans to send their wives, children, and other noncombatants to refuges abroad, abandon their city and property, seize a stronghold, and plunder their foes until Messenia was abandoned. Of course, this would not have solved the problem of Theban might.[40] It has been suggested that Xenophon meant his *Cyropaedia*, a historical novel set in Persia, to provide model military reforms for Sparta.[41] If so, he advised that the Helots be liberated and all Helots and Perioecs armed as hoplites, while all the Spartiates should become cavalrymen. The tactical problem of massed Theban attack would be addressed by having scythed chariots charge into the closed-massed infantry, and by having a skirmish line of heavy infantry backed by light-armed men and a final line of mobile towers engage the foremost ranks of the Theban column until the cavalry and other infantry could outflank and destroy it.[42]

The Spartans undertook no such radical measures, however. It was just as well. Attaining the throne of Macedon the year after Agesilaus' death was Philip, son of the Amyntas who had aided Teleutias and Agesipolis against Olynthus. As a youth, Philip lived as a hostage in Thebes, at the home of Pammenes, the leading general there after Epaminondas; he learned much. Tough, capable, innovative in military matters, and a fine statesman, Philip combined the already-excellent cavalry of Macedon and Thessaly with heavy and light infantry trained on lines that would have been familiar to Iphicrates and Chabrias. He armed his heavy infantry with small shields and long pikes, perhaps imitating Iphicrates' actions in Persian service. Following the lead of Dionysius I, who had taken the fortified island city of Motya in 397 in a spectacular siege assault, Philip developed an advanced siege train complete with towers, mining, and artillery. It was a major addition to the surprises, betrayals, blockades, and armed suasions typical of Greek warfare, at which Philip was also adept.

Philip subdued Thessaly, the Thracian Chalcidice, and southern Thrace, and used their manpower and resources to support his ambitions. In 338 he defeated the Boeotians and Athenians at Chaeronea, destroying the Sacred Band and making Macedon the leading power in the Greek world. Philip later invaded Laconia, stripping Sparta of its northern borderlands and other territories, but he did not attack Sparta itself. He wished Sparta to survive and threaten its neighbours, thus ensuring their continued loyalty to himself.[43] In 336, with all Greece suppressed or obedient and with Persia as his next target, Philip was assassinated. Unlike Jason, however, he had a capable successor, Alexander III, who 'tithed' a rebellious Thebes before conquering the Persian Empire. Although Alexander's realm fragmented on his death, Macedon remained more powerful than any Greek coalition.

Even so, the Spartans kept trying to recover their territory and dominance. In 331 Agis III led a coalition and mercenary army against Antipater, Alexander's governor in Macedon. Outnumbered by Antipater's army of Macedonians and allied Greeks, Agis was slain and his army crushed in another great battle at Mantinea.[44] The Successor kings Demetrius Poliorcetes in 294 and Pyrrhus of Epirus in 272 nearly captured Sparta itself, but were held off, and distracted by other opportunities. King Areus of Sparta managed to form coalitions that he twice led against the Macedonians and their allies, but he failed in a campaign against the Aetolians in 281, and died attacking Corinth in 265.[45]

In the 240s top-down social revolution finally began at Sparta, now reduced to seven hundred full citizens, of whom only one hundred were wealthy landowners. After an initial effort by Agis IV, who was murdered, Cleomenes III redivided the land, rescinded debts, gave citizenship to chosen foreigners and Perioecs, and revived the long-moribund Lycurgan social system, or at least what he and his followers identified as such. Arming his now-strengthened army with long Macedonian pikes, and aided by the attractiveness of social revolution in an era when the inhabitants of most Greek cities were sharply divided into rich and poor, Cleomenes threatened to restore Spartan domination of the Peloponnese.

This forced its dominant power – a federal league based in Achaea – to summon King Antigonus Doson of Macedon. He crushed Cleomenes' army at Sellasia in 222. Cleomenes fled into exile, and Doson became the first foreign conqueror to enter Sparta.[46] After further internal chaos, and defeat at the hands of the Achaean general Philopoemen at Mantinea in 207, Sparta fell under the rule of Nabis, who claimed descent from Demaratus. The tyrant executed all the Agiad and Eurypontid heirs, acted ever more unscrupulously and harshly, and attacked Messenia and Megalopolis. The Achaeans responded by bringing in their new allies, the Romans. In 195 T. Quinctius Flamininus invaded Laconia and threatened Sparta, now equipped with a full city wall. He forced Nabis to give up his conquests, his fleet, and most of the remaining Perioecs. A few years later Nabis himself was murdered by his allies, and the Achaean League gained control of Sparta.[47]

This was the end of Sparta as a power, if not as a city or an idea. Sparta had risen and fallen in the world of the Greek city-state. Led by its chieftains, it had conquered its Messenian neighbours, but failed against the Argives and Arcadians. The triple threat of Messenian revolt, war with Argives and Arcadians, and internal strife brought about the creation of the political and social system attributed to Lycurgus. This system maintained concord among the Spartiates and turned them into a fit, fierce, and disciplined hoplite militia army. Fighting similar militias, or Persian soldiers unsuited to fighting hand-to-hand with hoplites, the Spartans could win victories in pitched battles even when – as at Plataea in 479 and Mantinea in 418 – their generals proved inept.

This allowed Sparta to form the first major Greek alliance system, the Peloponnesian League, which secured Spartan power at a strategic level. Against Athens, Sparta could not attain victory, but stayed in contention due to its army.

This allowed the Spartans to send men to operate abroad with armies and fleets composed chiefly of allied forces. Some of these commanders failed spectacularly, but others succeeded spectacularly. In the end Athens fell, not Sparta. The Spartan empire proved fragile, its naval might collapsing at its first defeat, but its army's victories sufficed to keep Sparta powerful in Greece itself. However, the steady decline in Spartan strength due to oliganthropy, and the rise of military skill in Greece after many decades of large-scale wars and mercenary service, meant that Sparta's ability to dominate the battlefield would end once the right men took the right steps. This happened at Leuctra in 371. The rise of Macedon thereafter ended any real hope of a Spartan revival.

However, for two centuries the Spartans had been the best of the Greeks in hoplite battle, and thus wrote themselves indelibly into the history of Greece and the West. Of the Spartan soldier at war it truly can be said, with Tyrtaeus:

> Neither does his noble fame perish, nor his name,
> But although he is beneath the earth he is deathless.[48]

APPENDIX: SPARTAN ARMY ORGANISATIONS

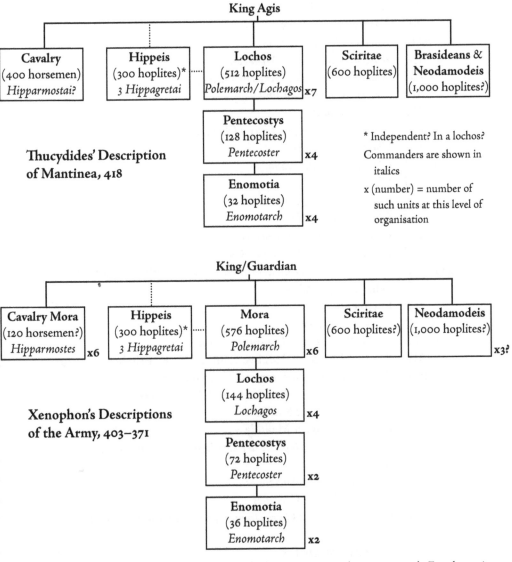

Thucydides' Description of Mantinea, 418

King Agis

| Cavalry (400 horsemen) *Hipparmostai?* | Hippeis (300 hoplites)* *3 Hippagretai* | Lochos (512 hoplites) *Polemarch/Lochagos* x7 | Sciritae (600 hoplites) | Brasideans & Neodamodeis (1,000 hoplites?) |

Pentecostys (128 hoplites) *Pentecoster* x4

Enomotia (32 hoplites) *Enomotarch* x4

* Independent? In a lochos?

Commanders are shown in italics

x (number) = number of such units at this level of organisation

Xenophon's Descriptions of the Army, 403–371

King/Guardian

| Cavalry Mora (120 horsemen?) *Hipparmostes* x6 | Hippeis (300 hoplites)* *3 Hippagretai* | Mora (576 hoplites) *Polemarch* x6 | Sciritae (600 hoplites?) | Neodamodeis (1,000 hoplites?) x3? |

Lochos (144 hoplites) *Lochagos* x4

Pentecostys (72 hoplites) *Pentecoster* x2

Enomotia (36 hoplites) *Enomotarch* x2

Note: The strengths of units will have varied with the circumstances (pp. 111, 118, 168). For alternative interpretations of Spartan military organisation, see the works cited in p. 20 n. 91 and p. 111 n. 30.

ABBREVIATIONS

ABSA   *Annual of the British School at Athens*

AC   *L'Antiquité Classique*

AHB   *Ancient History Bulletin*

AJA   *American Journal of Archaeology*

AJAH   *American Journal of Ancient History*

AJP   *American Journal of Philology*

AW   *Ancient World*

BCH   *Bulletin de Correspondance Hellénique*

CA   *Classical Antiquity*

C&M   *Classica et Mediaevalia*

CJ   *Classical Journal*

CP   *Classical Philology*

CQ   *Classical Quarterly*

CSCA   *California Studies in Classical Antiquity*

EMC/CV   *Echos du Monde Classique/Classical Views*

FGrHist.   *Die Fragmente der Griechischen Historiker*, fifteen volumes, Felix Jacoby, 1923–58

F   *Fragments*

G&R   *Greece and Rome*

GRBS   *Greek, Roman, and Byzantine Studies*

GSAW   *The Greek State at War*, five volumes, W. K. Pritchett, 1971–91

HCT   *A Historical Commentary on Thucydides*, five volumes, A. W. Gomme, A. Andrewes, K. J. Dover, 1945–81

JHS   *Journal of Hellenic Studies*

LCM   *Liverpool Classical Monthly*

RE   *Paulys Real-Encyclopädie der classischen Altertumswissenschaft*, Stuttgart

REA   *Revue des Etudes Anciennes*

REG   *Revue des Etudes Grecques*

SAGT   *Studies in Ancient Greek Topography*, eight volumes, W. K. Pritchett, 1965–92

YCS   *Yale Classical Studies*

ZPE   *Zeitschrift für Papyrologie und Epigraphik*

NOTES

All the translations from the ancient sources in this work are mine alone.

Chapter One

1 **The Rise of Sparta, c.950–c.550** references for this section: Fitzhardinge 1980; Hooker 1980: 1–114; Lazenby 1985: 63–80; Malkin 1994: 33–45; Daniel Ogden, *JHS* 114, 1994, 85–102; Graham Shipley in Cavanagh et al. 1996: 263–313, ills. 23.3, 23.4, 23.5; Hodkinson 1997a; Hans van Wees in Hodkinson/Powell 1999: 1–41; Matthew Trundle, *War & Society* 19, 2001, 1–17; R. W. V. Catling, in Cavanagh et al. 2002: 151–246; Cartledge 2002: 65–123, 293–8; Kôiv 2003: 62–6, 69–238; *Historia* 54, 2005, 233–64; Massimo Nafissi in Raaflaub/van Wees 2009: 117–37; Elena Zavvou and Athanasios Themos in Cavanagh/Gallou/Georgiadis 2009: 105–22; Kennell 2010: 20–53.

2 E.g. L. Pearson, *Historia* 11, 1962, 397–426; C. G. Starr, *Historia* 14, 1965, 257–72; Cartledge 2002: 43–51; Ogden 2004.

3 Hall 1997: 56–65.

4 Pausanias 3.7.2; Plutarch *Lycurgus* 2.4; Strabo 8.5.5.

5 Hall 1997: 61–2.

6 Strabo 8.4.8; Müller 1987: 779–81; N. Luraghi in Luraghi/Alcock 2003: 111–13; Luraghi 2008: 70–2, 112–13.

7 Morgan 1990: 65–79, 99–103; N. Luraghi, *JHS* 122, 2002, 45–69; 2008: 107–32.

8 Luraghi 2008: 70–3.

9 Tyrtaeus Fragment 5 West.

10 Tyrtaeus Fragments 2, 4 West; Plutarch *Lycurgus* 6.1–4.

11 Tyrtaeus Fragment 19.8 West.

12 E.g. T. Kelly, *Historia* 16, 1967, 422–31; *AJP* 91, 1970, 31–42; *American Historical Review* 75, 1970, 971–1003; Robertson 1992: 208–16; 233–49; J. M. Hall, *AJA* 99, 1995, 577–613; and Isabelle Ratinaud-Lachkar, *Opuscula Atheniensia* 29, 2004, 75–88. But see Christien 1992; Pritchett, *SAGT* III, 54–77; 1995: 205–28, 262–8; and Kôiv 2003: 46–7, 51–2, 120–4.

13 Tyrtaeus Fragment 23 West.

14 Tyrtaeus Fragments 6, 7 West; Pausanias 4.14.5.

15 Tyrtaeus Fragment 23a West.

16 Aristotle *Politics* 1306b36–07a2.

17 Tyrtaeus Fragment 2 West.

18 Tyrtaeus Fragment 10 West.

19 E.g. Thucydides 2.13.7; 4.44.4; 5.64.3, 72.3.

20 Tyrtaeus Fragment 11 West.

21 Homer *Iliad* 4.105–15; 8.266–72; 15.436–44.

22 Tyrtaeus Fragment 12 West.

23 Eustratius *Commentary* 20.165.1 on Aristotle, *Ethica Nicomachea* 3.8.5, 1116a36.

24 Tyrtaeus Fragment 23a West; M. W. Haslam in R. A. Coles and M. W. Haslam, *The Oxyrhynchus Papyri* vol. 47 (London, 1980), 1–6; compare Homer *Iliad* 12.71–4. But see Klaus Tausend, *Tyche* 8, 1993, 197–201; Pritchett, *SAGT* V, 52–8.

25 Herodotus 1.66–8, but see Pausanias 3.7.3, 8.5.9, 47.2–4; Polyaenus 1.8; D. M. Leahy, *Phoenix* 12, 1958, 141–65 for other 'Battles of Fetters'.

26 Herodotus 1.68.6.

27 E.g. Herodotus 1.65–66.1, 7.104; Thucydides 1.18.1, 84, 2.39.1; Xenophon *Lakedaimoniōn Politeia* 1–13, *Hellenica* 7.1.8–10; Isocrates 6.81, 11.17–19, 12.217; Plato *Laws* 2:666d–67a, 3:683e–85a, 690d–93e, 4:712d–13a; Aristotle *Politics* 1324b5–9, 1333b17–29, 1338b9–29.

28 Plato *Laws* 1.634d–e.

29 **Harmony and Army, c.530–362** references for this section: Lazenby 1985: 3–62; MacDowell 1986; Stephen Hodkinson *Chiron* 13, 1983, 239–81; 1997b; 2000; in Hodkinson/Powell 2006: 111–62; Cartledge 1987: 20–33; 2001: 79–90; Kennell 1995; J. Ducat in Hodkinson/Powell 1999: 43–66; 2006; Powell 2001: 222–51; Lipka 2002 on passages cited.

30 Thucydides 1.18.1, 19.

31 Andrewes 1966; de Ste Croix 1972: 124–38, 346–54; D. H. Kelly, *Antichthon* 15, 1981, 47–61; Cartledge 1987: 116–38.

32 Russell 1999: 115–21, 202–3; Thomas Figueira, *CQ* n.s. 53, 2003, 44–74.

33 Herodotus 6.56–8; Xenophon *Lakedaimoniōn Politeia* 13, 15; de Ste Croix 1972: 138–48; C. G. Thomas, *Historia* 23, 1974, 257–70; Carlier 1984: 249–301; Cartledge 1987: 99–110; 2001: 55–67; Scott 2005: 233–52.

34 K. J. Beloch, *Griechische Geschichte* vol. II.2 (Leipzig, 1931), 269–89; R. Sealey, *Klio* 58, 1976, 335–58.

35 E.g. Cnemus, navarch summer 430 to winter 429/8 (Thucydides 2.66, 80.1–2, 85.1–3, 93.1).

36 H. W. Parke, *JHS* 50, 1930, 37–79.

37 Thucydides 2.75.3; Xenophon *Hellenica* 3.5.7; 4.2.19; 4.5.7–8; 5.1.33; 5.2.7; 7.2.2–3.

38 Peloponnesian League with 'constitution': J. A. O. Larsen, *CP* 27, 1932, 136–50, *CP* 28, 1933, 257–76, and *CP* 29, 1934, 1–19; Kagan 1969: 9–30; de Ste Croix 1972: 89–166, 333–42. No 'constitution': J. E. Lendon, *GRBS* 35, 1994, 159–77. Defensive only early: G. L. Cawkwell, *CQ* n.s. 43, 1993, 164–78. No 'follow' oath early: D. C. Yates, *CQ* n.s. 55, 2005, 65–76. Only some had 'follow' oath: Sarah Bolmarcich, *GRBS* 45, 2005, 5–34; *Historia* 73, 2008, 65–79.

39 Shipley 1997a; J. M. Hall in P. Flensted-Jensen, ed., *Further Studies in the Ancient Greek Polis* (Copenhagen, 2000), 73–89; Powell 2001: 251–2; N. Mertens in Powell/Hodkinson 2002: 285–303; Cartledge 2002: 153–66.

40 E.g. Thomas J. Figueira in Hodkinson/Powell 1999: 211–44; Nino Luraghi, *JHS* 122, 2002, 45–69; *CQ* n.s. 52, 2002, 588–92; and in Luraghi/Alcock 2003: 109–41; Jonathan M. Hall in Luraghi/Alcock 2003: 142–68; but see also Hans van Wees (33–80) and Orlando Patterson (289–307) in Luraghi/Alcock 2003.

41 Critias Fragment 37 (Diels/Kranz 88); Xenophon *Hellenica* 3.3.7, *Lakedaimoniōn Politeia* 12.2.

42 E.g. R. J. A. Talbert, *Historia* 38, 1989, 22–40; Paul Cartledge, *Historia* 40, 1991, 379–81; 2001: 127–52; 2002: 138–53; and in Luraghi/Alcock 2003: 12–30; Michael Whitby in Powell/Hodkinson 1994: 87–126.

43 Compare Xenophon *Cyropaedia* 2.3.10.

44 D. Ogden in Alan B. Lloyd, *Battle in Antiquity* (Duckworth, London, 1996), 107–68; Cartledge 2001: 91–105; Davidson 2007: 388–425.

45 Herodotus 1.65.5.

46 Xenophon *Hellenica* 5.4.13; Plutarch *Agesilaus* 24.3.

47 Xenophon *Hellenica* 6.1.5.

48 Xenophon *Lakedaimoniōn Politeia* 12.5; Herodotus 7.208.3.

49 Aristotle *Politics* 1338b25–9.

50 Herodotus 7.104.5.

51 Herodotus 1.82; 7.205.2, 223–8; 9.64.2.

52 Thucydides 5.73.4; 4.40.1 (quote).

53 Lycurgus *Against Leocrates* 106–7; Athenaeus 14.630e–f; Plutarch *Cleomenes* 2.3, *Moralia* 235f.

54 Jean Ducat in Hodkinson/Powell 2006: 1–55.

55 J. E. Lendon in Hamilton/Krentz 1997: 105–26.

56 Herodotus 7.229–31; 9.71.2–4.

57 E.g. Herodotus 1.82.8, 7.232; Thucydides 2.92.3; Xenophon *Hellenica* 4.4.11, 8.38–9.

58 Xenophon *Lakedaimoniōn Politeia* 9; Lipka 2002: 174–80.

59   Xenophon *Hellenica* 4.5.10; 6.4.16.
60   Anderson 1970: 18–20; E. David, *Eranos* 90, 1992, 11–21; Sekunda 1998: 20–2, 24–5, 26–8; Hodkinson 2000: 221–6; Lipka 2002: 191–4.
61   Xenophon *Lakedaimoniōn Politeia* 11.1–2; Lipka 2002: 188–91.
62   Xenophon *Lakedaimoniōn Politeia* 13.1–5; quote: 13.5; Lipka 2002: 209–17.
63   Xenophon *Lakedaimoniōn Politeia* 12; Lipka 2002: 202–9.
64   Snodgrass 1999: 48–77, 89–98; Hanson 1989: 55–88; J. K. Anderson 1970: 13–42, and in Hanson 1991: 15–37; Sekunda 1998: 25–31; van Wees 2004: 47–54; Connolly 2006: 51–63; Lee 2007: 111–17; Schwartz 2009: 25–101. For linen corselets, see <http://www.uwgb.edu/aldreteg/Linothorax.html>.
65   Hand/Wagner 2002; Hand 2005.
66   A. J. Holladay, *JHS* 102, 1982, 94–103; Peter Krentz, *CA* 16, 1985, 50–61; *AHB* 8, 1994, 45–8; Hanson 1989; G. L. Cawkwell, *CQ* n.s. 39, 1989, 375–89; Robert D. Luginbill, *Phoenix* 48, 1994, 51–61; A. K. Goldsworthy, *War in History* 4, 1997, 1–26; van Wees in van Wees 2000: 125–66; 2004: 166–97; Adam Schwarz, *C&M* 53, 2002, 31–63; 2009: 102–200; Christopher A. Matthew, *Historia* 58, 2009, 395–415.
67   Amyx 1988: I, 197–8, for bibliography. Discussions by Hans van Wees in van Wees 2000: 132–3, and Adam Schwarz, *C&M* 53, 2002, 50–1, 2009: 123–5. My own interpretation is offered here.
68   Paul Bardunias, *Ancient Warfare* 3.1, October/November 2007, 11–14; <www.hollow-lakedaimon.blogspot.com>.
69   Thucydides 5.71.1.
70   Anderson 1970: 84–93; van Wees 2004: 90–2.
71   Louis Rawlings in van Wees 2000: 233–59.
72   Thucydides 5.70; Lipka 2002: 220–1 on pipers.
73   Thucydides 5.73.4.
74   Thucydides 5.66.3.
75   Thucydides 5.66.3, 5.68.3.
76   Xenophon *Lakedaimoniōn Politeia* 11.4, 13.4 (Lipka 2002: 194–5), *Hellenica* 3.5.22, 4.5.7 (the Oxford text has *pentēkontēras*, Dindorf's 'correction' for *pentēkostēras*, found in all the codices).
77   Thucydides 5.66.3, 5.68.3; Xenophon *Lakedaimoniōn Politeia* 11, *Hellenica* 6.4.12.
78   Andrewes, *HCT* IV, 115; Cartledge 2002: 219.
79   Rhodes/Osborne 2003:, no. 88; van Wees 2006.
80   Thucydides 5.66.4.
81   Anderson 1970: 97; van Wees 2004: 99–100.
82   Xenophon *Lakedaimoniōn Politeia* 11.5–6.
83   Xenophon *Lakedaimoniōn Politeia* 11.8–10; Anderson 1970: 104–10; Lipka 2002: 198–201.
84   Xenophon *Cyropaedia* 2.1.22, 2.2.6–9, 2.3.21–2, 2.4.1–6; Anderson 1970: 94–104; Connolly 2006: 39–44.
85   Isocrates 12.180.
86   Herodotus 9.11.3; Thucydides 4.8.1; Xenophon *Hellenica* 3.5.7; 5.1.33.
87   On such units see Pritchett *GSAW* II, 221–5.
88   E.g. Lazenby 1985: 10–12; Lipka 2002: 143–5; and T. J. Figueira in Hodkinson/Powell 2006: 57–84.
89   Herodotus 6.56; Plutarch *Agesilaus* 17.2, 18.3; Isocrates *Letter to Philip* 1.6.
90   See further Anderson 1970: 245–7; Stylianou 1998: 291–3; Russell 1999: 116–21.
91   Toynbee 1969: 365–404; Anderson 1970: 225–51; Andrewes, *HCT* IV, 110–17; G. L. Cawkwell, *CQ* n.s. 33, 1983, 385–400; Lazenby 1985: 5–10, 41–58; T. J. Figueira, *TAPA* 116, 1986, 165–213; Cartledge 1987: 427–31; 2002: 217–20; Singor 2002; Lipka 2002: 257–64; van Wees 2004: 243–9; 2006: 155–61.
92   M. A. Flower in Powell/Hodkinson 2002: 191–217.
93   Herodotus 6.81, 120; 7.234.2; 9.10.1, 11.3, 14, 28.2, 29.
94   Aristotle *Politics* 1270a.

95   G. L. Cawkwell, *CQ* n.s. 33, 1983, 385–400; Hodkinson 2000: 65–112, 369–445; Cartledge 2002: 263–72.

96   Cartledge 1987: 139–59; Hodkinson 1997, 2000: 335–68, 399–445.

Chapter Two

1   **Croesus and the Battle of Champions** references for this section: Burn 1962: 36–45; Tomlinson 1972: 87–91; Kelly 1976: 74–6, 87, 137–9; Fitzhardinge 1980: 137–8; Hooker 1980: 112; P. B. Phaklares, *Horos* 5, 1987, 102–7; Robertson 1992: 179–207; Lazenby 1993: 40–1; Pritchett 1995: 228–62; Green 1996: 11; Cartledge 2002: 119, 121–3; Briant 2002: 31–8; Kôiv 2003: 125–33; Lendon 2004: 39–41, 51, 343 n. 18, 399–400; and How/Wells 1928 on passages cited.

2   Herodotus 1.83.

3   Herodotus 1.53.3, 69–70, 77.3–4, 79–84.

4   Herodotus 1.152.3.

5   Herodotus , 1.141, 152–3; Diodorus 9.36.1.

6   Herodotus 1.82.3–7.

7   Pausanias 2.20.7; 10.9.12; Herodotus 1.82.8.

8   Plutarch *Moralia* 306a–b; Palatine Anthology 7.430, 431, 526; Valerius Maximus 3.2 ext. 4; Suda under *Othryadas*.

9   Pritchett, *GSAW* II, 246–75; van Wees 2004: 136–8.

10   Plutarch *Moralia* 231e–f.

11   E.g. Xenophon *Hellenica* 4.7.2.

12   A. M. Armstrong, *G&R* 19, 1950, 73–9; Pritchett, *GSAW* IV, 16–21; van Wees 2004: 133–4; Dayton 2006: 33–51.

13   Herodotus 9.26.2–4; Diodorus 4.58.1–4; Pausanias 1.41.2; 8.5.1.

14   Thucydides 5.41.

15   **Assault on Samos** references for this section: D. M. Leahy, *JHS* 77, 1957, 272–5; Burn 1962: 173–4; Paul Cartledge, *CQ* n.s. 32, 1982, 243–65; 2002: 125; Salmon 1984: 243–5; Shipley 1987: 97–8; Bowen 1992: 117–20; and How/Wells 1928 on passages cited.

16   Herodotus 3.39, 44–9; 1.70.2–3; Plutarch *Moralia* 859b–60c.

17   R. Tölle-Kastenbein, *Herodot und Samos* (Bochum, 1978), 72–89; H. J. Kienast, *Samos XV. Die Stadtmauer von Samos* (Bonn, 1978), 12–42, 46–7, 56–64, 72, 91–3, 99–102; Müller 1997: 1012–24. Landing at the Heraeum: Herodotus 9.96.1.

18   Herodotus 3.54.1–55.2.

19   E.g. Thucydides 4.25.7–11.

20   Herodotus 3.39.3.

21   Herodotus 3.56; J. P. Barron, *The Silver Coins of Samos* (London, 1966), 17–18.

22   Plutarch *Moralia* 859d; compare 236d; scholion to Aeschines 2.77.

23   Diodorus 7.11; Eusebius *Chronica* I, 225; Schoene; compare Herodotus 5.30–31; J. L. Myres, *JHS* 26, 1906, 84–130.

24   Diodorus 8.32.1–2; Strabo 6.1.10; Justin 20.2.9–3.9; Pritchett, *GSAW* III, 21–2.

25   **Cleomenes** references for this section: Burn 1962: 166–8, 172–3, 198–9; Tigerstedt 1965: I, 89–91, 93; Stadter 1965: 45–53; W. G. Forrest, *GRBS* 10, 1969, 277–86; Tomlinson 1972: 91–100; Kelly 1976: 139–40; R. Sealey, *CJ* 72, 1976, 13–20; P. Carlier, *Ktema* 2, 1977, 65–84; Hooker 1980: 148–60; Rhodes 1981: 227–39; Legon 1981: 143–5; Joseph Roisman, *Historia* 34, 1985, 257–77; Dover, *HCT* IV, 317–37; L. A. Tritle, *Historia* 37, 1988, 457–60; A. Griffiths in Powell 1989: 51–78; N. G. L. Hammond, *JHS* 112, 1992, 143–50; Eric Robinson, *Liverpool Classical Monthly* 17.9, November 1992, 131–2; *Historia* 43, 1994, 363–9; G. Cawkwell, *Mnemosyne* 46, 1993, 206–27; Badian 1993: 116–17, 218–19; E. Millender in Powell/Hodkinson 2002: 11–21; Richard M. Berthold, *Historia* 51, 2002, 259–67; Cartledge 2002: 123–32; de Ste Croix 1972: 167–8, and in David Harvey and Robert Parker, eds, *Athenian Democratic Origins and Other Essays* (Oxford, 2004), 421–40; Piérart 2003; Scott 2005: 181–2, 306, 308–10, 332, 374–8, 546–52, 558–72, 575–9; and Macan 1895 and How/Wells 1928 on passages cited.

26   Herodotus 3.148; 5.49–51, 72.3 (a pun on Dorieus' name); 6.50.3, 76.2, 80, 108.2–3.
27   Herodotus 5.42.1, 6.75, 84.
28   Herodotus 5.39–48.
29   Herodotus 3.139–148.2; Plutarch *Moralia* 224a–b.
30   Herodotus 6.84; compare 6.40.
31   Thucydides 3.68.5: Gomme, *HCT* II, 358; Hornblower 1991: 464–6 (date).
32   Herodotus 6.108.2–3.
33   Pausanias 3.4.1.
34   Herodotus 5.48.
35   Herodotus 5.55–7, 62–63.2; Thucydides 6.53.3–59.4; [Aristotle] *Athēnaiōn Politeia* 18–19.4. Disarming the Athenians: Thucydides 6.56.2, 58.2; compare [Aristotle] *Athēnaiōn Politeia* 15.3–4; Polyaenus 1.21.2.
36   [Aristotle] *Athēnaiōn Politeia* 17.3–4, 19.4; Herodotus 1.61.4.
37   Thucydides 1.19.1.
38   *Papyrus Ryland* 18; D. M. Leahy, *Bulletin of the John Rylands Library* 38.2, 1956, 406–35; Plutarch *Moralia* 859d; Bowen 1992: 117–20; Griffin 1982: 45–7; Cartledge 2002: 120.
39   Herodotus 5.92a1; Thucydides 1.18.1; Aristotle *Politics* 1312b; Plutarch *Moralia* 859d; G. Cawkwell, *CQ* n.s. 43, 1993, 364–76; D. C. Yates, *CQ* n.s. 55, 2005, 65–76.
40   Herodotus 5.63.2–4; [Aristotle] *Athēnaiōn Politeia* 19.5.
41   Herodotus 5.63.3–4.
42   Greenhalgh 1973: 63–145.
43   Spence 1993: 1–9.
44   Herodotus 5.64.1–2; Frontinus *Stratagems* 2.2.9.
45   Herodotus 5.65.1.
46   Herodotus 5.64–5; [Aristotle] *Athēnaiōn Politeia* 19.5–6.
47   Herodotus 5.66, 69; [Aristotle] *Athēnaiōn Politeia* 20.1, 21.
48   Herodotus 5.70–73.1.
49   [Aristotle] *Athēnaiōn Politeia* 20.2–3; Aristotle *Lysistrata* 273–82 and scholion line 273. Compare Herodotus 6.75.3 and Pausanias 3.4.2 on the accusation that Cleomenes felled trees at Eleusis.
50   Herodotus 5.73.
51   Herodotus 5.89; 6.108.5–6; Thucydides 1.41.2.
52   Herodotus 5.74–5, 77; Meiggs/Lewis 1969: no. 15.
53   Herodotus 5.79–89; 6.49–50, 61.1, 73, 85, 87–93; 7.145.1; Thucydides 1.41.2.
54   Herodotus 5.75.2.
55   Herodotus 9.10.3, 53.3.
56   Herodotus 5.72.3, 90–3; 8.141.1; compare Herodotus 9.77; Thucydides 3.15.2; 5.30; Xenophon *Hellenica* 5.2.2.
57   Herodotus 5.97.2.
58   Herodotus 5.50.3.
59   Herodotus 5.49.8.
60   Herodotus 5.49–51, 97.
61   Herodotus 6.19.1, 77.2; Pausanias 3.4.1.
62   J. B. Bury, *Klio* 2, 1902, 14–25; Fontenrose 1978: 169–70; Piérart 2003; Scott 2005: 495–501.
63   Herodotus 6.76–77.2.
64   Herodotus 6.77.3–78.2.
65   Herodotus 6.79–82.
66   Plutarch *Moralia* 223a–b.
67   Herodotus 6.83.1, 92.2–3; 7.148.2; Pausanias 3.4.1; Plutarch *Moralia* 245d.
68   Pritchett, *GSAW* II, 146–60.
69   Plutarch *Moralia* 223b–c, 245c–f; Pausanias 2.20.8–10; Polyaenus 8.33; Socrates, *FGrHist.* 310 F6.
70   Herodotus 6.92.
71   G. L. Cawkwell, *CQ* n.s. 43, 1993, 164–78; D. C. Yates, *CQ* n.s. 55, 2005, 65–76.
72   Herodotus 6.48; 7.133–7.

73   Herodotus 6.49–51, 61.1.
74   Herodotus 6.61–70, 73–5.
75   Herodotus 6.85–6.
76   Herodotus 6.106.3.
77   E.g. Hesiod *Works and Days* 765–828.
78   Lazenby 1993: 52–3; Scott 2005: 615–18; but see Pritchett, *GSAW* I, 117–21.
79   Plato *Laws* 698e; compare 692d.
80   On this theory, see Cartledge 2002: 132–3 (on his third point see L. H. Jeffrey, *ABSA* 83, 1988, 179–81 and M. J. P. Dillon, *ZPE* 107, 1995, 60–8); Ogden 2004: 170–5; Luraghi 2008: 173–82.
81   Herodotus 6.105–6, 120; Scott 2005: 370–1, 404–5.

Chapter Three

1   Hignett 1963: 7–25. Similarly, the 'Themistocles Decree' (Meiggs/Lewis 1969: no. 23) is so problematic as to be unusable (see Burn 1962: 364–77; Lazenby 1993: 100–4; M. Johansson, *ZPE* 137, 2001, 69–92).
2   **Xerxes Marches, Greece Prepares, Summer 481–Spring 480** references for this section: F. Maurice, *JHS* 50, 1930, 210–35; H. D. Westlake, *JHS* 56, 1936, 12–24; Burn 1962: 313–63; Hignett 1963: 88–104, 345–55; N. Robertson, *JHS* 96, 1976, 100–20; T. C. Young, Jr, *Iranica Antiqua* 15, 1980, 213–39; Pritchett, *SAGT* III, 348–66; Lazenby 1993: 89–118; Borza 1990: 105–8; B. S. J. Isserlin, *ABSA* 86, 1991, 83–9; N. G. L. Hammond and L. J. Roseman, *JHS* 116, 1996, 88–107; Arthur Keaveney, *Eranos* 93, 1995, 30–8; Briant 2002: 161, 524–7, 528, 907; Cawkwell 2005: 89–91, 237–76; Wallinga 2005: 7–46; and Macan 1908, How/Wells 1928, and Green 2006 on passages cited.
3   Persian preparations and march: Herodotus 7.1–59, 100, 105–27, 132; Aeschylus *Persians* 69–70, 130–1, 723, 745; Thucydides 4.109.2; Lysias 2.27–9; Diodorus 11.1–3; Justin 2.10.
4   N. Sekunda, in John Hackett, ed., *Warfare in the Ancient World* (New York, Oxford, Sydney, 1989), 82–3, 84–5; N. Sekunda, *The Persian Army 560–330 BC* (London, 2002), 9–13, 15–18.
5   See Herodotus 9.18.1, 20, 22.3, 49.2, 69.2; G. S. Shrimpton, *Phoenix* 34, 1980, 32–5; J. A. S. Evans, *CJ* 82, 1987, 99–101, 104–6.
6   Herodotus 7.147.1, 173.3.
7   Herodotus 7.228.1.
8   Herodotus 7.21, 40–1, 60–99, 184–7; compare Aeschylus *Persians* 12–64, 115–42, 341–2.
9   Lysias 2.27; Isocrates 4.49, 6.100; Ctesias *Persika* 27; Diodorus 11.3.7–9, 5.2–3; Justin 2.10.18–20. Compare Thucydides 1.23.1; 6.33.5–6.
10   F. Maurice, *JHS* 50, 1930, 210–35; T. C. Young, Jr, *Iranica Antiqua* 15, 1980, 213–39 (but note wagons are attested in Herodotus 9.80.2, carriages in 7.41.1, 83, and implied in 7.187.1).
11   Morrison/Coates/Rankov 2000: 94–9, 100–20, 131–3, 210, 227–30, 238, 274; Gabrielsen 1994: 105–69.
12   Triremes, other galleys, and horse transports: Herodotus 7.21.2, 89–97, 184.1–85.1; compare Aeschylus *Persians* 341–2; Lysias 2.27; Diodorus 11.3.7–8 (3,000 transports, 850 horse transports); Isocrates 12.49; Justin 2.10.20. Sailing ships carrying grain: Herodotus 7.184.5; compare 7.1.2, 191.1.
13   Herodotus 7.32, 101, 146–7.1, 210.1, 234–7; 8.6.2.
14   Herodotus 7.234–7.
15   Herodotus 6.70.2; Xenophon *Hellenica* 3.1.6; *Anabasis* 2.1.3, 2.2.1, 7.8.17.
16   Herodotus 7.132, 138–71; 8.2.2–3.2; Thucydides 1.14.3, 18.2; [Aristotle] *Athēnaiōn Politeia* 22; Plutarch *Themistocles* 4; Pausanias 3.12.6.
17   Herodotus 7.132.2; Diodorus 11.3.3; Polybius 9.39.5; Pritchett, *GSAW* III, 232–3.
18   Herodotus 7.142–4; Thucydides 1.14.3, 93.3–7; [Aristotle] *Athēnaiōn Politeia* 22; Plutarch *Themistocles* 4, 10.2.
19   Herodotus 7.148.4–49.4, 158.5–62.1; 8.2.2–3.2; Thucydides 1.18.2.
20   Herodotus 7.138–43, 173, 175–8; 8.40.2, 108.3–4, 142.2; Diodorus 11.4.1.

21 Herodotus 7.172–4; 7.6.2; 9.1, 58.1–2 (the Aleuads); Diodorus 11.2.5–3.2; Speusippus, *Letter to Philip* 30; Damastes, *FGrHist.* 5 F4; Plutarch *Themistocles* 7.1–2, *Moralia* 864e.

22 **Leonidas at Thermopylae, Summer 480** references for this section: Burn 1962: 362–3, 378–81, 392–4, 406–22; J. A. S. Evans, *GRBS* 5, 1964, 231–7; Hignett 1963: 113–27, 142–8, 371–8; Lazenby 1985: 83–96; 1993: 117–18, 134–8, 140, 141–8; Green 1996: 111–13, 124–8, 134–43; N. G. L. Hammond, *Historia* 45, 1996, 1–20; M. A. Flower, *CQ* n.s. 48, 1998, 365–79; Cartledge 2002: 174–7; and Macan 1908, How/Wells 1928, and Green 2006 on passages cited.

23 Herodotus 7.177.

24 Herodotus 7.175, 177.

25 K. S. Sacks, *CQ* n.s. 26, 1976, 232–48; Nicholas Richer in Cavanagh/Gallou/Georgiadis 2009: 213–23.

26 Herodotus 7.138.2, 175.1, 206; Thucydides 1.141.2–5.

27 Herodotus 7.202–3.1; 8.1.2; Diodorus 11.4.6–7; Pausanias 10.20.1; Justin 2.11.2.

28 Herodotus 7.205.2.

29 Diodorus 11.4.2–5; Isocrates 4.90, 6.99; Ctesias *Persika* 28 (three hundred Spartiates, one thousand Perioecs, but at Plataea!).

30 Herodotus 7.229.2; 8.25.1; compare Herodotus 9.10.1, 11.3, 28.2, 29.2.

31 Herodotus 8.25.2.

32 Herodotus 7.132.1, 205.3; Diodorus 11.4.7; Thucydides 3.62.3–4.

33 Herodotus 7.203, 217.2; 8.1.

34 Topography: S. Marinatos, *Thermopylae: An Historical and Archaeological Guide* (Athens, 1951); A. R. Burn in G. E. Mylonas, ed., *Studies Presented to David Moore Robinson* I, (St Louis, Missouri, 1951), 480–9; W. K. Pritchett, *AJA* 62, 1958, 203–13; *SAGT* IV, 176–233; 1994: 248–93; 2002: 82–113; P. W. Wallace, *AJA* 84, 1980, 15–23; Müller 1987: 294–302, 369–85. See also 'The Leonidas Expeditions' website: <http://www.theleonidasexpeditions.com/theleonidasexpeditions.html>.

35 Herodotus 7.175.2, 212.2.

36 Herodotus 7.207–10.1.

37 Herodotus 7.210.1–2.

38 Herodotus 7.41.1, 55.2, 83.1, 211.1.

39 Herodotus 7.211.2–212.1.

40 Plato *Laches* 191c.

41 Herodotus 7.212–18.

42 Herodotus 7.219–25, 233.

43 Herodotus 7.100–5, 208.3, 209, 220, 226–32; Tigerstedt 1965: I, 93–100; but see E. G. Millender in Gorman/Robinson 2002: 33–59.

44 Diodorus 11.5.4–12.1; Justin 2.11; Pausanias 10.20.2. Night attack: Diodorus 11.10; Plutarch *Moralia* 866a; Justin 2.11.12–16.

45 Herodotus 7.220.3–4.

46 Parke/Wormell 1956: I, 167–8; II, 44; Fontenrose 1978: 77–8, 319.

47 Herodotus 7.220–2, 233; compare 7.100–5, 209; Plutarch *Moralia* 864b–65f, 866d–67b.

48 Diodorus 11.4.2–5 (king seeking death), 9.1; Justin 2.11.8–12 (oracle, honour); Plutarch *Moralia* 866b–c (Leonidas celebrates funeral games before leaving Sparta!).

49 Herodotus 8.40.2; 9.7β.

50 Herodotus 8.40.2, 71–2; Isocrates 4.93; Diodorus 11.16.3; Plutarch *Themistocles* 9.3; Wiseman 1978: 60–2; Müller 1987: 777–8.

51 Herodotus 8.24–6, 29–41, 50–5.

52 **Eurybiadas at Artemisium and Salamis, Summer 480** references for this section: N. G. L. Hammond, *JHS* 76, 1956, 32–54; W. K. Pritchett, *AJA* 63, 1959, 251–62; *SAGT* I, 94–102; Burn 1962: 381–92, 394–402, 423–75, 488–91; Hignett 1963: 149–247, 264–70, 386–417; P. W. Wallace, *AJA* 73, 1969, 293–303; Hdt. P. B. Georges, *CA* 5, 1986, 14–59; Müller 1987: 305–15, 329–31, 337–41, 406–13, 420–2, 692–713; J. F. Lazenby, *Hermes* 116, 1988, 168–85; 1993: 120–30, 138–41, 148–208; Green 1996: 201–17; A. J. Bowen, *CQ* n.s. 48, 1998, 345–64; 1992: 135–42; Briant 2002: 529–31; Wallinga 2005; and Macan 1908, How/Wells 1928, and Green 2006 on passages cited.

53　Herodotus 7.175.2–76.1, 178–83, 188–96.1; 8.1–23; Diodorus 11.4.1, 12–13; Nepos *Themistocles* 3; Plutarch *Themistocles* 7–8, *Moralia* 867b–68a.

54　Herodotus 8.24–82 (movements, preliminaries), 83–96 (battle); Aeschylus *Persians* 331–471; Meiggs/Lewis 1969: no. 24; Diodorus 11.13.5–19.4, 27.2–3; Plutarch *Moralia* 868a–71b, *Themistocles* 9–15, *Aristides* 8–9.2; Nepos *Themistocles* 4; Justin 2.12.

55　Late sources have the mole begun before the battle (Strabo 9.1.13; Ctesias *Persika* 30; Aristodemus, *FGrHist.* 104 F1), but this would have risked frightening the Greeks into premature retreat.

56　Herodotus 8.124.2–3.

57　Herodotus 8.4–5; compare Plutarch *Themistocles* 6.1, 7.5, *Moralia* 867b–c.

58　Herodotus 7.183.1, 192; P. B. Georges, *CA* 5, 1986, 44 n. 65.

59　Herodotus 8.49–50.1, 56–64, 70, 74–6, 79–82; compare Diodorus 11.15.2–17.4; Plutarch *Themistocles* 7.2–6, 11.2–13.3, *Aristides* 8.2–6, *Moralia* 869c–f; Justin 2.12.18–21.

60　Herodotus 6.7–17; Burn 1962: 209–14; Scott 2005: 90–112.

61　J. F. Lazenby, *G&R* 34, 1987, 169–77; I. Whitehead, *G&R* 34, 1987, 178–85; A. J. Holladay, *G&R* 35, 1988, 149–51; J. S. Morrison, *JHS* 111, 1991, 197–200; Morrison/Coates/Rankov 2000: 42–3.

62　Herodotus 7.96.1, 8.10.1, 60α; compare Herodotus 7.179–82.

63　Herodotus 8.10–11, 15–17, 84, 86, 89, 91, 93; Aeschylus *Persians* 386–432.

64　Herodotus 9.10.2.

65　Herodotus 8.96–125, 9.32; Aeschylus *Persians* 480–514; Diodorus 11.19.4–6; Plutarch *Themistocles* 16–17, *Moralia* 871c–d, *Aristides* 9.3–4; Justin 2.13.

Chapter Four

1　**Mardonius Takes Command, Autumn 480–Spring 479** references for this section: Burn 1962: 490–507, 509–12; Hignett 1963: 266–86, 291–8; Borza 1990: 108–10; Lazenby 1993: 204–20, 228; Green 1996: 211–16, 217–36; and Macan 1908, How/Wells 1928, Flower/Marincola 2002, and Green 2006 on passages cited.

2　Herodotus 8.100.5, 101.3, 113.2–3, 126.2, 129.3, 133; 9.1, 31–2; Diodorus 11.19.6, 28.4, 30.1; Justin 2.13.3; Plutarch *Aristides* 10.1.

3　Herodotus 8.126–9; Aeneas Tacticus 31.

4　Herodotus 8.133–6; 9.9.2, 11.2.

5　Herodotus 8.136, 140–4, 9.6, 7β1; Diodorus 11.27.2, 28.1–2; Pausanias 7.25.6.

6　Herodotus 8.141–2; Diodorus 11.28.1.

7　Herodotus 9.1–6; Diodorus 11.28.3–6; Plutarch *Aristides* 10.6; Justin 2.14.3.

8　Herodotus 9.6–11; Plutarch *Aristides* 10.6–8; Diodorus 11.28.5, 29.1–3.

9　Hyacinthia: N. Richer in Figueira 2004: 77–97.

10　Herodotus 9.10.2–3; M. E. White, *JHS* 84, 1964, 140–52; Lazenby 1993: 217 n. 4.

11　Herodotus 9.12–18; Diodorus 11.29.1, 30.1; Pausanias 1.40.2–3, 44.4 (story of Persian infantry killed by Megarians).

12　**Pausanias at Plataea, Summer 479** references for this section: Burn 1962: 509–46; Hignett 1963: 286–7, 289–344; Lazenby 1993: 217–47; Green 1996: 236–77; and Macan 1908, How/Wells 1928, Flower/Marincola 2002, and Green 2006 on passages cited.

13　Herodotus 9.19; Diodorus 11.29.1; Plutarch *Aristides* 11.3–9. Topography: W. K. Pritchett, *AJA* 61, 1957, 9–23; 1993: 294–5; *SAGT* I, 103–9, 119–21, II, 178–180, III, 289–294, IV, 88–102, V, 96–103; N. G. L. Hammond, *ABSA* 49, 1954, 103–22; Müller 1987: 491–3, 499–501, 505–11, 546–9, 577–9; Ober 1985: 118–26; Fossey 1988: 100–19.

14　Herodotus 9.15.3; Plutarch *Aristides* 11.2; Pritchett, *SAGT* I, 109.

15　Herodotus 9.20–25.1; Diodorus 11.30.2–4; Plutarch *Aristides* 14–15.1; Pausanias 1.27.1. The last two suggest that the Athenian 'Three Hundred' were cavalry (Pritchett, *SAGT* V, 121 n. 60), but this makes no sense unless the archers were as well.

16　Herodotus 9.25–32; Diodorus 11.30.4; Plutarch *Aristides* 12–13 (reports an abortive conspiracy among the Athenians at this time). Topography: Pritchett, *AJA* 61, 1957, 24–5, *SAGT* I, 111–15, II, 103–5.

17 E.g. Lazenby 1993: 227–8; Cartledge 2002: 150–1; W. Scheidel in Luraghi/Alcock 2003: 244–5.
18 Herodotus 9.61.2, 85.2.
19 Fort's location and capacity: Pritchett, *AJA* 61, 1957, 24; Müller 1987: 555–6; Burn 1962: 511; Connolly 2006: 29.
20 Herodotus 9.33–8; Plutarch *Aristides* 11.2, 15.1; Pausanias 3.11.5–8; A. S. Bradford, *AW* 23, 1992, 27–33; Flower/Marincola 2002: 164–78
21 Herodotus 9.38.2–40.
22 Herodotus 9.41–3; Plutarch *Aristides* 15.1.
23 Herodotus 9.44–6; Plutarch *Aristides* 15.2–5.
24 Herodotus 9.46–9; Plutarch *Aristides* 16.
25 Herodotus 9.50–52; Plutarch *Aristides* 16.6–17.1. The 'Island': Grundy 1894: 4–5, 22–30; Pritchett, *SAGT* I, 115–9, V, 117–20; Müller 1987: 562–3.
26 Herodotus 9.53.2.
27 Herodotus 9.55.2.
28 Herodotus 9.53–4; Plutarch *Aristides* 17.1–3; see also Connolly 2006: 35.
29 Herodotus 9.56–7; Plutarch *Aristides* 17.3.
30 Thucydides 1.20.3. See next section.
31 Aristotle F541 Rose, cited by scholion to Aristophanes *Lysistrata* 452–4; scholion to Thucydides 4.8.9; Hesychius s.v. *Edolos* and *lochoi*; and Photius s.v. *lochoi*; Kennell 1995: 167; van Wees 2006: 158–61.
32 E.g. H. T. Wade-Gery, *CQ* 38, 1944, 115–26; Jones 1987: 118–23.
33 Herodotus 9.58–61.1, 69; Plutarch *Aristides* 17.4–5, *Moralia* 872c–e.
34 Herodotus 9.61.2–62.1.
35 Herodotus 9.72; Plutarch *Aristides* 17.7.
36 Herodotus 9.62.2–63.2.
37 Herodotus 9.71.2–4.
38 Herodotus 9.61–8.
39 Herodotus 9.70.2 (both quotes).
40 Herodotus 9.70. See also Diodorus 11.30.5–32.5 (a simple, rationalised account); Plutarch *Aristides* 17.6–19.3; Justin 2.14.4–6.
41 Herodotus 9.69.2, 70.5; Plutarch *Aristides* 19.4–6; Diodorus 11.33.1 (10,000+ Greek dead).
42 Herodotus 9.71–85; Plutarch *Aristides* 20–1; Diodorus 11.30.1–3.
43 Herodotus 9.85.1–2.
44 D. H. Kelly, *GRBS* 22, 1981, 31–8; M. Lupi in Hodkinson 2006: 185–218.
45 D. Gilula in Derow/Parker 2003: 81–5; P. Brulé and L. Piolot in Figueira 2004: 151–78.
46 Hodkinson 2000: 256–9; Flower/Marincola 2002: 255–6. But see Andronike Makres in Cavanagh/Gallou/Georgiadis 2009: 187–94.
47 P. Hunt, *Historia* 46, 1997, 129–44; 1998: 33–9; van Wees 2004: 177–83.
48 Compare Herodotus 9.18.1.
49 Note that they needed a specially trained corps of hoplites to work with them; evidently light-armed men no longer fought in Athens' phalanx.
50 Herodotus 9.86–8; Diodorus 11.30.4.
51 Herodotus 9.2.1–2, 41.4, 77; Diodorus 11.28.3. Evidently *xenagoi* did not yet exist.
52 Symeonoglu 1985: 117–22 has only the Cadmea fortified at this time, but he fails to address the evidence of Herodotus, or the possibility that refined fourth-century walls replaced less-refined sixth-century ones.
53 Herodotus 9.31.5.
54 Herodotus 9.64.1.
55 **Leotychidas at Mycale, Summer 479** references for this section: Burn 1962: 500–2, 547–51; Hignett 1963: 247–59; Green 1996: 227–8, 277–83; and Macan 1908, How/Wells 1928, Flower/Marincola 2002, and Green 2006 on passages cited.
56 Herodotus 8.124.2–4, 131–2, Diodorus 12.27.2–3; Plutarch *Themistocles* 17.1.

57 Herodotus 8.131–2, 9.90–2, 95–6; Diodorus 11.27.1, 34.1–3 (250 Greek ships). Mycale: Hignett 1963: 255–6; Müller 1997: 606–34.

58 Herodotus 9.96–105; Diodorus 11.34.4–36; Justin 2.14.7–9.

59 Herodotus 7.139.

60 Plutarch *Cimon* 16.8.

Chapter Five

1 **Tensions with Athens, 479–464** references for this section: C. W. Fornara, *Historia* 15, 1966, 257–71; M. L. Lang, *CJ* 63, 1967, 79–85; Kagan 1969: 35–40, 50–2, 61–2, 377–9; P. J. Rhodes, *Historia* 19, 1970, 387–400; 1981: 291–2; Meiggs 1972: 38–41, 83–7, 465–8, 482; de Ste Croix 1972: 168–72, 178–9; J. F. Lazenby, *Hermes* 103, 1975, 235–51; A. S. Schieber, *AC* 51, 1982, 5–14; W. R. Connor, *TAPA* 115, 1985, 79–102; J. A. S. Evans, *Antichthon* 22, 1988, 1–11; P. A. Stadter, *GRBS* 34, 1993, 35–72 (at 43–7); Powell 2001: 103–7; Scott 2005: 280–4; and Gomme, *HCT* I, Hornblower 1991, and Green 2006 on passages cited.

2 Thucydides 1.23.6, 118.2.

3 Herodotus 9.106, 114.2–121; Thucydides 1.89.2; Diodorus 11.37.1–3.

4 Thucydides 1.89.3–93.2; Diodorus 11.39–40.4; Plutarch *Themistocles* 19.1–2; Justin 2.15.1–12; Nepos 2.6.2–7.6.

5 Plutarch *Aristides* 23.2–3. Thucydides 1.94–95.1; Diodorus 11.44; Justin 2.15.13–16; Nepos 4.2; compare Herodotus 5.104, 108–15.

6 Plutarch *Aristides* 23.2–3.

7 Thucydides 1.95 (especially 95.2, 7), 130; Herodotus 8.3.2; Diodorus 11.44.3–6; Plutarch *Aristid* 23, *Cimon* 6.1–3; [Aristotle] *Athēnaiōn Politeia* 23.2; Xenophon *Hellenica* 6.5.34; Isocrates 4.72, 8.30, 12.67.

8 Thucydides 1.95.7.

9 Diodorus 11.50.

10 Herodotus 5.23; Thucydides 1.128–34; Diodorus 11.45–6; Nepos, *Pausanias* 4.3–5; Justin 9.1.3; Pausanias 3.14.1, 17.7–9; Plutarch *Moralia* 560f, *Cimon* 6.4–6.

11 Herodotus 6.72; Pausanias 3.7.9–10; Plutarch *Moralia* 859d.

12 Diodorus 11.48.2; 12.35.4; M. E. White, *JHS* 84, 1964, 145 n. 21; Green 2006: 107 n. 182.

13 Thucydides 1.96–100.1; Plutarch *Cimon* 7–13; Diodorus 11.60–2; Herodotus 7.101; Gomme, *HCT* I, 272–95; Kagan 1969: 40–7; Meiggs 1972: 42–83; Blamire 1989: 110–53; Hornblower 1991: 143–54.

14 Thucydides 1.100.2–101.2; compare 1.58.1; Herodotus 6.46–7.

15 **The Great Earthquake and the Helot Revolt, 464–455** references for this section: A. Andrewes, *Phoenix* 6, 1952, 1–5; W. G. Forrest, *CQ* 54, 1960, 221–41; Kagan 1969: 54–5, 61–2, 71–4; de Ste Croix 1972: 173–80; J. Roy, *Phoenix* 26, 1972, 334–41; J. R. Cole, *GRBS* 15, 1974, 369–85; J. L. O'Neil, *CQ* n.s. 31, 1981, 335–46; Legon 1981: 181–2; Salmon 1984: 259–60, 262; R. K. Unz, *CQ* n.s. 36, 1986, 73–85; Blamire 1989: 167–73; Badian 1993: 89–96; P. A. Stadter, *GRBS* 34, 1993, 35–72 (at 63–5); Pritchett 1995: 5–81; *SAGT* V, 53–5; V. Parker, *Athenaeum* 81, 1993, 129–40; E. F. Bloedow, *AHB* 14, 2000, 89–101; Powell 2001: 110–12; Cartledge 2002: 184–91; Scott 2005: 306–8, 579–88; and Gomme, *HCT* I, Hornblower 1991, and Green 2006 on passages cited.

16 Thucydides 1.101.2.

17 Thucydides 1.128.1.

18 Diodorus 11.63.1–2, 4; Plutarch *Cimon* 16.4–5; Polyaenus 1.41.3; Pausanias 1.29.8; 4.24.5–6; Aristophanes *Lysistrata* 1137–44 with scholion; Aelian, *Varia Historia* 6.7.

19 Plutarch *Cimon* 16.6–7; Diodorus 11.63.4–64.1; Polyaenus 1.41.3.

20 Xenophon *Hellenica* 5.2.3.

21 Thucydides 1.101.2.

22 Herodotus 9.64.2; Flower/Marincola 2002: 220, 235–6.

23 Corinth: Plutarch *Cimon* 17.1; Thucydides 1.103.4; Diodorus 11.79.1–2. Elis: Herodotus 4.148; Thucydides 5.31.2; compare Pausanias 5.6.4, 6.22.4. Argos: Diodorus 11.65; Strabo 8.6.10, 19;

Pausanias 5.23.3, 7.25.5–6 (Mycenae); Herodotus 6.83; Aristotle *Politics* 1303a; Plutarch *Moralia* 245f; Pausanias 2.17.5, 25.8; 8.27.1 (Tiryns).

24 Herodotus 9.35.2.

25 Isocrates 6.99.

26 Xenophon *Hellenica* 5.2.3; 6.5.33; Thucydides 2.27.2; 3.54.5; 4.56.2; Plutarch *Cimon* 16.7–17.1; Aristophanes *Lysistrata* 1137–41 and scholion; Diodorus 11.64.2–3; Pausanias 1.29.8; 4.25.6. Only Plutarch reports Athens' first expedition, and Gomme (*HCT* I, 411 n. 1) and many others reject it, but it is easy to see why these abbreviated accounts would omit it or combine it with the one in Thucydides (N. G. L. Hammond, *Historia* 4, 1955, 377–9; Badian 1993: 89–91).

27 Polyaenus 2.10.3.

28 Thucydides 1.102.2.

29 Thucydides 1.102.1–3; Plutarch *Cimon* 17.2; Diodorus 11.64.2–4; Pausanias 1.29.8, 4.24.6.

30 Plutarch *Cimon* 15.3–16.3.8.

31 Thucydides 1.103.1; Diodorus 11.64.4, 84.8. I think Thucydides mentioned the end of the revolt out of proper chronological sequence so that he could include the Messenians among Athens' new allies in 1.102.4–103.4.

32 **The 'First Peloponnesian War', 460–445** references for this section: Kagan 1969: 80–1, 84–5, 88–97, 120–30; de Ste Croix 1972: 180–200; Meiggs 1972: 175–85, 417–18, 423; Tomlinson 1972: 101–15; A. J. Holladay, *JHS* 97, 1977, 54–63; *JHS* 105, 1985, 161–2; R. J. Buck, *CP* 55, 1970, 218–22; 1979: 143–7; Legon 1981: 183–99; D. M. Lewis in G. S. Shrimpton and D. J. McCargar, *Classical Contributions: Studies in honour of Malcolm Francis McGregor* (Locust Valley, New York, 1981), 71–8; Salmon 1984: 260–9; M. Philippides, *AW* 11, 1985, 33–41; Stadter 1989: 122–4, 214–16, 223–32, 308–9; Blamire 1989: 175–6; S. Hornblower, *HSCP* 94, 1992, 180–2; Badian 1993: 213 n. 50; I. M. Plant, *Historia* 43, 1994, 259–74; Pritchett 1995: 61–71; C. Falkner, *Historia* 48, 1999, 386–9; Powell 2001: 111–14; Conwell 2008: 37–64; Gomme, *HCT* I; Hornblower 1991; and Green 2006 on passages cited.

33 Pausanias 1.15.1–2; 10.10.3–4; Meiggs 1972: 469–72; Pritchett, *SAGT* III, 1–53, VII, 222–6; 1994: 1–25 (but *Hellenica Oxyrhynchus* 4.2 Chambers shows that this cannot be Orneae); L. H. Jeffrey, *ABSA* 60, 1965, 41–57; E. D. Francis and M. Vickers, *AC* 54, 1985, 105–15.

34 Herodotus 7.137.2; note Thucydides 1.105.1.

35 Thucydides 1.107.2.

36 Thucydides 1.93.3–7, 107–8.3; Herodotus 9.35.2; Diodorus 11.79.4–83; Plato, *Menexenus* 242a; [Plato] 1st *Alcibiades* 112c; Plutarch *Cimon* 17.3–5, *Pericles* 10.1–2; Pausanias 1.29.7–9, 5.10.4; Justin 3.6.10; Meiggs/Lewis 1969: nos. 35, 36. On the two battles in Diodorus see K. R. Walters, *AJAH* 3, 1978, 188–91; and A. Andrewes in J. W. Eadie and J. Ober, eds *The Craft of the Ancient Historian: Essays in Honor of Chester G. Starr* (Lenham, Maryland, 1985), 189–91.

37 Thucydides 1.108.5.

38 Tolmides: Thucydides 1.108.5; Strabo 10.2.5; Diodorus 11.84; Pausanias 1.27.5. Pericles: Thucydides 1.111.2–3, 115.1; Diodorus 11.85.1–2, 88.1–2; Plutarch 19.2–4. Naupactus: Thucydides 1.103.1–2; Diodorus 11.84.8.

39 Thucydides 1.109.2–3; Diodorus 11.74.5–6.

40 Meiggs 1972: 129–151, 487–95; G. L. Cawkwell, *Phoenix* 51, 1997, 115–30; 2005: 281–9.

41 Thucydides 1.114.2.

42 Thucydides 1.113–115.1; 5.16.3; Plutarch *Pericles* 22.2–3; Diodorus 12.5–7.

43 **The Thirty Years' Peace and the Outbreak of War, 445–431** references for this section: P. A. Brunt, *Phoenix* 19, 1965, 255–6; Kagan 1969: 170–8, 205–374; de Ste Croix 1972; Meiggs 1972: 190, 461–2; Legon 1981: 200–27; Paul Cartledge, *CQ* 32, 1982, 260–3; Salmon 1984: 281–305; Shipley 1987: 113–22; Stadter 1989: 232–59; Badian 1993: 125–62; E. A. Meyer in Hamilton/Krentz 1997: 23–54; Powell 2001: 114–29; Lazenby 2004: 16–30; Lendon 2007; and Gomme, *HCT* I, Hornblower 1991, and Green 2006 on passages cited.

44 Thucydides 1.115.2–117.3; 8.76.4 (Samos' revolt); 1.40.5, 41.2, 43.1 (Corinth's opposition at Sparta); 3.13.1 (potential allies); Diodorus 12.27–8; Plutarch *Pericles* 24–8.

45 Thucydides 1.58.1.

46 Thucydides 1.139.3.

47 Thucydides 1.24–45 (Corcyra and Corinth 435–4), 44.2–3 (Athens' motives), 45–55 (Athens blocks Corinth 433), 56–65 (Potidaea revolts and is besieged), 67–86 (embassies to Sparta), 87, 118.3, 119–25.1 (war votes), 125.2–126.1, 139.1–3 (negotiations). See also Diodorus 12.30.2–5, 31.2–33.4, 38–40; Aristophanes *Acharnians* 509–56, *Peace* 603–27; Plutarch *Pericles* 29–33.2.
48 Thucydides 2.9.2–3; Plutarch *Pericles* 33.4.
49 Thucydides 1.81.1, 141.6.
50 Thucydides 5.14.3; 7.28.3.
51 E.g. Homer *Iliad* 1.155–6; Herodotus 1.16–22.
52 Thucydides 1.79.2–85.2.

Chapter Six

 1 **Archidamus' War, 431–428** references for this section: A. W. Gomme, *HCT* II, III, and Hornblower 1991 on passages cited; P. A. Brunt, *Phoenix* 19, 1965, 255–80; Westlake 1968: 122–35; de Ste Croix 1972: 206–10; Kagan 1974: 19–24, 43–57, 62–3, 70–1, 77, 80–93, 95–8, 102–5, 132, 139–42, 148, 171–4, 193–5, 219, 223–4, 270–1; G. Cawkwell, *YCS* 24, 1975, 53–65; I. Moxon, *Rivista Storica dell' Antichita* 8, 1978, 9–12, 14–16; Legon 1981: 228–32; E. F. Bloedow, *Klio* 65, 1983, 227–49; Hornblower 1996: 157, 229–32; Powell 2001: 147–50, 154, 159–64; Lazenby 2004: 31, 32–5, 38, 40, 41–3, 49, 51–3, 55–6, 59, 70, 91.
 2 Thucydides 2.10–18; Diodorus 12.42.3–6.
 3 Thucydides 2.20.2.
 4 Thucydides 2.11.
 5 Thucydides 2.13.1, 19–23; Diodorus 12.42.6–7.
 6 Thucydides 2.47.2–3, 55.1–56.1, 56.3, 56.6–7.2; Diodorus 12.45.1, 3; Plutarch *Pericles* 23.2–24.1.
 7 Thucydides 2.47.3–54.5, 58.2–3, 59–65, 69.1; 3.87.1–3; Diodorus 12.45.2–5, 47.1, 52.2, 58; Plutarch *Pericles* 24.3–4, 35.3–4, 37.1.
 8 Thucydides 8.98.2–4; *Hellenica Oxyrhynchia* 20.3 Chambers.
 9 Thucydides 2.2–6; Diodorus 12.41.2–42.2; [Demosthenes] 59.98–101.
10 Thucydides 3.68.4; compare Thucydides 2.71.3.
11 Thucydides 2.71–4; Diodorus 12.47.1; [Demosthenes] 59.101–2.
12 Thucydides 2.18.1.
13 Thucydides 2.75–7; Diodorus 12.47.2; [Demosthenes] 59.102. Site of Plataea: Grundy 1894: 53–66; Fossey 1988: 103–9; V. Aravantinos, A. Konecny, and R. T. Marchese, *Hesperia* 72, 2003, 281–320.
14 Thucydides 2.78; 3.20–4, 52–68; Diodorus 12.47.2, 56; [Demosthenes] 59.102–3.
15 Kern 1999: 18–9, 52 (ramps), 60–1 (Persians), 101–7 (Archidamus' innovations at Plataea), but note Hamblin 2006: 226–36.
16 Thucydides 3.1 (spring 428), 3.15–16 (abortive autumn 428), 3.26 (spring 427), 3.89.1 (abortive spring 426), 4.2.1, 6 (briefly spring 425); Diodorus 12.52 (spring 428), 59.1–2 (abortive spring 426).
17 W. G. Hardy, *CP* 21, 1926, 346–55; Hanson 1998: 19–76 (attack), 79–128 (defence), 131–53 (Attica 431–425). Note how the damage claims in Thucydides 2.57.2, 65.2 are downplayed in Thucydides 3.26.3, 7.27.3–4.
18 Aegina: Thucydides 2.27; Diodorus 12.44.2–3; Plutarch *Pericles* 34.1. Potidaea: Thucydides 2.70; Diodorus 12.46.6–7. Megarid invaded: Thucydides 2.31; 4.66.1; Diodorus 12.44.3.
19 **Failures at Sea and Abroad, 431–426** references for this section: A. W. Gomme, *HCT* II, III, and Hornblower 1991 on passages cited; H. D. Westlake, *CQ* 39, 1945, 75–84; R. P. Legon, *Phoenix* 22, 1968, 200–25; B. D. de Wet, *Acta Classica* 12, 1969, 103–19; D. W. Knight, *Mnemosyne* 23, 1970, 150–61; Kagan 1974: 24–5, 27–42, 53–69, 72–80, 94–5, 107–17, 132–43, 146–53, 175–93, 195–7, 201–17, 265–9, 350–62; G. L. Cawkwell, *YCS* 24, 1975, 53–70; Lewis 1977: 61–9; A. J. Holladay, *Historia* 27, 1978, 399–427; T. Kelly, *Studies in Honor of Tom B. Jones: Alter Orient und Altes Testament* 203, 1979, 245–55; *American Historical Review* 87, 1982, 37, 25–54; Graham 1983: 38–9, 206–8; J. Ober in *The Craft of the Ancient Historian: Essays in Honor of Chester G. Starr*, J. W. Eadie and J. Ober, eds (Lanham, Maryland, 1985), 171–88; Wilson 1987: 97–106, 109–11; I. G. Spence, *JHS* 110, 1990, 91–109; B. Bosworth, *CQ* n.s. 42, 1992, 46–55; Malkin 1994: 219–27; Hornblower 1996: 180–4,

205–9, 220–8; Powell 2001: 149, 151–6, 161–2, 164–7; Briant 2002: 581–2; Lazenby 2004: 31, 32, 36–7, 39–40, 41, 44–51, 52–9, 61–6, 84.

20 431: Thucydides 2.17.4, 23.2, 25, 30–31; Diodorus 12.42.6–43.5; Plutarch *Pericles* 34.1–2. 430: Thucydides 2.56–8; Diodorus 12.45.3; Plutarch *Pericles* 35.1–3.

21 Pericles' strategy: Thucydides 1.141.2–44.1; 2.13.2, 55.2, 62.1–3, 65.7; Plutarch *Pericles* 34.1–2. The role of Athens' allies: Thucydides 2.7.3, 9.4, 25.1, 30.1.

22 Corinthian expedition: Thucydides 2.33. Zacynthus: Thucydides 2.66. Amphilochian Argos: Thucydides 2.68.1, 9.

23 Thucydides 2.80–2; Diodorus 12.47.4–5.

24 Thucydides 2.83–4; Diodorus 12.48.1.

25 Thucydides 2.84.5–92.7; Diodorus 12.48.

26 Thucydides 2.93–4; Diodorus 12.49.

27 Thucydides 3.2–18, 25–33, 69.1; Diodorus 12.55.

28 Thucydides 3.69–85.1; Diodorus 12.57.

29 Thucydides 3.94–8; Diodorus 12.60.1.

30 Thucydides 3.100–2.5; Diodorus 12.60.2–3.

31 Thucydides 3.102.5–7, 105–14; Diodorus 12.60.4–6.

32 Thucydides 2.7.2; 3.86.2; Diodorus 12.41.1.

33 Thucydides 3.86, 88, 90, 99, 103, 115–6; 4.1, 24–5, 48.6, 58–65; Diodorus 12.53–4.

34 Thucydides 2.7.1, 67; 4.50; Diodorus 12.41.1.

35 Thucydides 3.92–3; Diodorus 12.59.3–5; Athenaeus 461e.

36 **Pylos and Sphacteria, 425** references for this section: A. W. Gomme, *HCT* II, III, and Hornblower 1996 on passages cited; Kagan 1974: 219–56; Wilson 1987: 47–52, 62–95, 99–123, 127–9; R. A. Bauslaugh, *JHS* 99, 1979, 1–6; Lazenby 1985: 113–22; 2004: 67–81; R. B. Strassler, *JHS* 108, 1988, 198–203; Powell 2001: 166–72; Catherine Rubincam, *JHS* 121, 2001, 77–90; Loren J. Samons II, *Hesperia* 75, 2006, 525–40.

37 Thucydides 3.85.2–3.

38 Thucydides 4.2.1, 3, 11.2.

39 Note Thucydides 3.3.2–5, 97.1; 4.42.3; Herodotus 6.132; Plutarch *Pericles* 23.1.

40 Thucydides 1.142.3–4 (compare 1.122.1); P. A. Brunt, *Phoenix* 19, 1965, 268–70; H. D. Westlake, *CQ* 39, 1945, 78–9.

41 Thucydides 4.2.2, 2.4, 3.1–4.3, 5.2; Diodorus 12.61.1.

42 Thucydides 4.5.1, 6.1–2, 8.1–4; Diodorus 12.61.1–2.

43 Thucydides 4.8.3, 9.1.

44 Wilson 1979: 54–61, 118–9; C. J. Tuplin, *Liverpool Classical Monthly* 6.1, Jan. 1981, 30–31; and Pritchett, *SAGT* I, 6–29; 1994: 145–78.

45 Thucydides 4.9.2–13.1; Diodorus 12.61.3–62.7.

46 Thucydides 4.13.2–14.5; Diodorus 12.63.1.

47 Thucydides 4.8.9.

48 Thucydides 4.8.5–8.

49 Thucydides 4.15–22; Diodorus 12.63.2.

50 Thucydides 4.23, 26–29.1; Plutarch *Nicias* 7–8.

51 Thucydides 4.29.2–30.4. Aetolian use of fire against Demosthenes (Thucydides 3.98.2) suggests that the fire here may have been set deliberately.

52 A. Billinger, *TAPA* 77, 1946, 214–20; Anderson 1970: 120–1, 122–6.

53 Thucydides 4.38.3.

54 Thucydides 4.31–9; Diodorus 12.63.3; Pausanias 4.26.1–2; W. C. Compton and H. Awdry, *JHS* 27, 1907, 274–81; Pritchett, *SAGT* I, 28–29; Wilson 1979: 117–23; T. Leslie Shear, *AJA* 40, 1936, 188–203 (shields 189–90).

55 Thucydides 4.40.1.

56 Thucydides 4.38.5.

57 Thucydides 4.40.2.

58 Thucydides 4.36.3.

59 Thucydides 4.41; Diodorus 12.63.4–5.
60 Thucydides 4.42–8; Diodorus 12.65.5–7; Plutarch *Nicias* 6.4–6.
61 **Brasidas' Gamble, 424–422** references for this section: A. W. Gomme, *HCT* III, Hornblower 1991, and 1996 on passages cited; Westlake 1968: 148–64; Kagan 1974: 59, 111, 180, 229, 261–4, 270–93, 302–17, 321–49; Powell 2001: 175–9; Lazenby 2004: 36, 46, 56–7, 72, 83–92, 94–108.
62 Thucydides 4.53–7; Diodorus 12.65.8–9; Plutarch *Nicias* 6.4, 6.
63 Thucydides 4.41.3, 55.1, 80.2–4; 5.14.3.
64 Thucydides 4.80.3–4; Diodorus 12.67.3–5. Doubters: R. J. A. Talbert, *Historia* 38, 1989, 24–5; Michael Whitby in Powell/Hodkinson 2004: 97–9; Hornblower 1996: 264–7; Annalisa Paradiso in Figueira 2004: 179–98. Defenders: Cartledge, *Historia* 40, 1991, 381; Powell 2001: 252–6; David Harvey in Figuiera 2004: 199–217.
65 Thucydides 4.80–1; 5.14.3–4.
66 Thucydides 5.19.2, 24.1; A. Andrewes and D. M. Lewis, *JHS* 77, 1957, 177–80.
67 Thucydides 2.25.1–3, 85.1–3, 86.6, 93.1; 3.69, 79.3; 4.11.4–12.1; Diodorus 12.43.2–3, 62.1–5; Xenophon *Hellenica* 2.3.10 (ephor).
68 Thucydides 4.70.1, 74.1, 79.2–81.1; Diodorus 12.67.1, 3, 5.
69 Thucydides 4.66–74; Diodorus 12.66–67.1.
70 Thucydides 4.78–79.1; Diodorus 12.67.1.
71 Perdiccas: Thucydides 4.79.2, 82–3. Acanthus: Thucydides 4.84–8; cf. 4.108.5; Diodorus 12.67.2.
72 Thucydides 4.76–7, 89–101.2; Diodorus 12.69–70; G. L. Huxley, *Philologus* 135, 1991, 320–1.
73 Thucydides 4.102, 108.1; Pritchett, *SAGT* III, 298–323; D. Lazaridis, *Amphipolis* (trans. D. Hardy, Athens, 1997), 21–46, 60–1.
74 Losada 1972: 74–6; Graham 1983: 199–206.
75 Losada 1972: 107–13.
76 Thucydides 4.103–7; 5.26.5; Diodorus 12.68.1–3; Marcellinus, *Vita Thucydides* 23.
77 Thucydides 4.107.3, 108.3–6, 109; Diodorus 12.68.4–5.
78 Thucydides 4.110–16; Diodorus 4.68.6.
79 Thucydides 4.81.2–3, 108.2–6.
80 Thucydides 4.108.7, 117–19; Diodorus 12.72.5.
81 Thucydides 4.120–3; Diodorus 12.72.1, 7.
82 Thucydides 4.121.2.
83 Thucydides 4.122.4–6, 123.3, 129.2; Diodorus 12.72.6–8.
84 Thucydides 4.124–8.
85 Thucydides 4.132; 5.12–13.
86 Thucydides 4.129–30; Diodorus 12.72.7–9.
87 Thucydides 4.131; Diodorus 12.72.10.
88 Thucydides 4.135.
89 Thucydides 5.2–3; Diodorus 12.73.2–3.
90 Thucydides 5.6.1–2, 7.3–5.
91 Thucydides 5.6–11; Diodorus 12.73.3–74.4. Topography: N. Jones, *CSCA* 10, 1977, 71–104; Pritchett, *SAGT* I, 30–45, III, 323–46; but see Gomme, *HCT* III, 653 on the hill location.
92 Thucydides 5.14–19; Diodorus 12.74.5–6; Plutarch *Nicias* 9.2–7.
93 Thucydides 5.20, 24.2–25.1.

Chapter Seven

1 **Trouble in the Peloponnese, 421–418** references for this section: A. Andrewes, *HCT* IV and Hornblower 2008 on passages cited; Kagan 1981: 19–111; Salmon 1984: 324–9; Hornblower 1996: 415–17, 460–9, 493–500; James Roy, *Klio* 80, 1998, 360–8; C. Falkner, *Historia* 48, 1999, 385–94; Powell 2001: 179–81; Lazenby 2004: 100, 106–19.
2 Thucydides 5.14.4, 22.2–24.1, 25.1; Diodorus 12.75.2–4.
3 Thucydides 5.15.1, 17.1, 18.7, 24.2, 34.2; Diodorus 12.74.5, 76.1; Plutarch *Nicias* 10.1–2, 7; J. Ducat in Hodkinson 2006: 38–42.

4   Thucydides 4.134; 5.29.1.
5   Thucydides 5.16.2–3, 33; Andrewes, *HCT* IV, 31–4.
6   Thucydides 5.31.1–5, 34.1; Pausanias 5.5.3; Strabo 8.3.16–18; Herodotus 4.148; Pritchett, *SAGT* IV, 58–60.
7   Thucydides 5.49–50; J. Roy, *Klio* 80, 1998, 360–8.
8   Thucydides 17.2, 21–22.1, 25.1, 27–32, 36–8, 40–1, 46.5–48.3, 50.5; Diodorus 12.75.2–6; Plutarch *Nicias* 10.2, *Alcibiades* 14.3, 15.1.
9   Thucydides 5.21, 25.2, 35.2–9, 39.2–3, 42–8.1; Diodorus 12.77.2–3; Plutarch *Nicias* 10.3–6, *Alcibiades* 14.
10 Thucydides 5.52.2; Plutarch *Alcibiades* 15.3.
11 Thucydides 5.53–5; Diodorus 12.78.1–2.
12 Thucydides 5.35.6–7, 56.
13 Thucydides 5.57–58.1, 60.3; Diodorus 12.78.3; Xenophon *Hellenica*. 4.2.17 (Argives in 394); Andrewes, *HCT* IV, 78–80 (timing, *hamippoi*).
14 Thucydides 5.58–59.2; Andrewes, *HCT* IV, 80–2; Pritchett, *SAGT* II, 97–100 (topography).
15 Thucydides 5.59.2–60.3; Diodorus 12.78.3–5.
16 Thucydides 5.60.4–62.2; Diodorus 12.79.1–3.
17 **The Battle of Mantinea and its Consequences, Summer 418–Winter 418/417** references for this section: Andrewes, *HCT* IV, 94–149; Kagan 1981: 111–37; Lazenby 1985: 125–34; 2004: 119–28.
18 Thucydides 5.63–4; Diodorus 12.78.5–6, 79.3.
19 Topography: Andrewes, *HCT* IV, 94–8; Pritchett, *SAGT* II, 37–72; S. Hodkinson and H. Hodkinson, *ABSA* 76, 1981, 242–6.
20 Thucydides 5.65.2.
21 Thucydides 5.64.5–65.3.
22 Thucydides 5.65.3–66.2; see Andrewes, *HCT* IV, 99–103; Pritchett, *SAGT* II, 54–8; *GSAW* I, 127–33; Russell 1999: 10–15.
23 Thucydides 5.74.1.
24 Thucydides 5.33.1, 67.1, 68.3, 71.2; Xenophon *Lakedaimoniōn Politeia* 12.3, 13.6, *Hellenica* 5.2.24, 5.4.52–3, *Cyropaedia* 4.2.1.
25 Thucydides 5.67.1.
26 Thucydides 5.68.2.
27 Thucydides 5.68.1, 71.2, 74.1.
28 Thucydides 5.68.3.
29 Xenophon *Hellenica* 4.2.16–17. See Chapter Ten.
30 See Chapter One for sources. Defenders include G. Busolt, *Hermes* 40, 1905, 387–419; G. L. Cawkwell, *CQ* n.s. 33, 1983, 385–90.
31 Thucydides 5.75.4.
32 Thucydides 5.69. Speeches: Pritchett 1994: 27–109, 2002: 1–80.
33 Thucydides 5.71.1–2.
34 Thucydides 5.71.3.
35 Thucydides 5.72.1–3.
36 Thucydides 5.72.4–73.4. Quote: Thucydides 5.73.4.
37 Diodorus 12.79.6.
38 Woodhouse 1933; Guy L. Cooper III, *TAPA* 108, 1978, 35–40.
39 Thucydides 5.74–5.
40 Thucydides 5.75.3.
41 Thucydides 5.76–80.3; Diodorus 12.80.1.
42 Thucydides 5.80.3–81.1; Diodorus 12.80.2; Xenophon *Hellenica* 5.2.2.
43 Aristophanes *Birds* 149; Xenophon *Hellenica* 3.2.25; Simon Hornblower, *Phoenix* 54, 2000, 212–25 (C. Falkner, *Historia* 48, 1999, 393, suggests that Lepreum was not regained until the Spartans took Pylos in 410).
44 Thucydides 5.81.2; Diodorus 12.80.2–3; Plutarch *Alcibiades* 15.2.
45 **Sparta Returns to Open War with Athens, 417–413** references for this section: A. Andrewes, *HCT* IV, 152–5, 188–9; K. Dover, *HCT* IV, and Hornblower 2008 on passages cited; Kagan 1981:

138–42, 250–7, 288–92; Salmon 1984: 330–1; Powell 2001: 187–8; Lazenby 2004: 129, 130, 145–6, 153, 170.

46   Thucydides 5.82; Diodorus 12.80.3; Plutarch *Alcibiades* 15.2.

47   Pausanias 2.24.7.

48   Thucydides 5.83.1–3; Diodorus 12.81.1.

49   Thucydides 5.84.1; Diodorus 12.81.2–3.

50   Thucydides 5.115.1–2.

51   Thucydides 5.116.1.

52   Thucydides 5.115.3; 6.7.1–2; Diodorus 12.81.4–5.

53   Thucydides 6.1.1, 6, 8–26, 30–52, 62–88.6, 93.4; Diodorus 12.82–4; 13.2.1–2, 2.5–4.4, 6.1–6; Plutarch *Alcibiades* 17–18.2, 20.1–2, *Nicias* 12–16; K. Dover, *HCT* IV, and Hornblower 2008 on passages cited; Kagan 1981: 157–259; Powell 2001: 186–9; Lazenby 2004: 131–146.

54   Thucydides 6.73.2, 88.7–10, 89–93.1, 104.1; 8.2.4; Diodorus 13.7.1–2; Plutarch *Nicias* 12.1–2, *Alcibiades*17.3, 22.2, 23.1–2.

55   Thucydides 7.18.2.

56   Thucydides 6.95.1, 105.1–2; 7.18.3–4.

57   Thucydides 7.18.1–19.2, 27.1–28.4; Diodorus 13.8.8, 9.2; *Hellenica Oxyrhynchia* 20.3–5 Chambers; K. Dover *HCT* IV, 393–5, 400–8; Kagan 1981: 290–2; Ober 1985: 115, 141–2 (site); Hanson 1998: 153–66; S. Rusch in Gorman/Robinson 2002: 290–2.

58   Xenophon *Lakedaimonion Politeia* 11.4.

59   Xenophon *Hellenica* 4.5.12; 6.4.12, 17 with *Lakedaimonion Politeia* 11.4; Diodorus 15.32.1, 37.1; Polybius F60 B-W; Plutarch *Pelopidas* 17.2–3; Photius under *mora*.

60   **Gylippus in Sicily, 414–413** references for this section: Westlake 1968: 277–89; Dover, *HCT* IV, and Hornblower 2008 on passages cited; 367; Kagan 1981: 258–87, 294–353; Powell 2001: 190–3; Lazenby 2004: 146–66.

61   Assignment: Thucydides 6.93.2; Diodorus 13.7.2. Cleandridas: Plutarch *Pericles* 22.2–3; Polyaenus 2.10.1–2, 4–5. *Mothakes*: Aelian *Varia Historia* 12.43; Phylarchos, *FGrHist.* 81 F43 (Athenaeus 271e–f); Hodkinson 1997b: 55–61.

62   Thucydides 6.91.4, 93.2–3, 104.1–3; 7.1–2.2, 7.58.3; Diodorus 13.7.6–7.

63   Topography of Syracuse: H.-P. Drögemüller, *Syrakus* (Gymnasium Beiheft VI, Heidelberg, 1969); K. Dover, *HCT* IV, 466–84; and reviews in *Phoenix* 25, 1971, 282–5 and 26, 1972, 297–300.

64   Thucydides 6.94, 96–103; 7.2.1–4; Diodorus 13.7.3–6; Plutarch *Nicias* 17–19.1.

65   Thucydides 7.3.1–2 (compare Thucydides 6.69.1, 97.4, 98.3, 100.1); Plutarch *Nicias* 19.1–5.

66   Thucydides 7.3.4–4.5.

67   Thucydides 7.5.1–6.4; Diodorus 13.8.1–2 (confused); Plutarch *Nicias* 19.5–6.

68   Thucydides 7.4.5–6, 7–8, 10–15, 21–4; Diodorus 13.9.3–6; Plutarch *Nicias* 19.6–7, 20.2–3.

69   Thucydides 7.16.1–17.3, 18.1, 4, 19.3–5, 20.2, 27.1 (compare 7.58.1–4); Diodorus 13.8.3–6; Plutarch *Nicias* 20.1.

70   Thucydides 7.20, 26; Diodorus 13.9.2.

71   Thucydides 7.25–6, 31–41; Diodorus 13.10; Plutarch *Nicias* 20.4–5.

72   Thucydides 7.42–5; Diodorus 13.11.1–6; Plutarch *Nicias* 21.

73   Thucydides 7.46–50; Diodorus 13.11.6–12.6; Plutarch *Nicias* 22–3.

74   Thucydides 7.51–72; Diodorus 13.13.1–18.2; Plutarch *Nicias* 24–5.

75   Thucydides 7.72.5–85; Diodorus 13.18.2–19.3; Plutarch *Nicias* 26–7.

76   Thucydides 7.86–7; Plutarch *Nicias* 19.4–5, 28–9 (compare *Lysander* 16.1–17.1); Diodorus 13.19.4–33.1 (a fantasy piece).

Chapter Eight

1   **Revolts, Athenian Civil Strife, and Indecision at Sea, 413–411** references for this section: A. Andrewes *HCT* V, and Hornblower 2008 on passages cited; Westlake 1968: 290–307; D. Lateiner,

TAPA 106, 1976, 267–90; Rhodes 1981: 362–414; Kagan 1987: 1–225; C. Falkner, *Phoenix* 53, 1999, 206–21; Briant 2002: 591–7; Lazenby 2004: 171–98; Cawkwell 2005: 149–55.

2   Thucydides 8.3.1; compare Thucydides 3.93.2–3; 5.51–52.1; Xenophon *Hellenica* 1.2.18; H. D. Westlake, *JHS* 58, 1938, 31–40.

3   Thucydides 8.2, 3.2 (triremes), 5–8; Plutarch *Alcibiades* 24.1; Nepos *Alcibiades* 4.7; Justin 5.1.

4   Thucydides 8.1–2, 4.

5   Thucydides 8.7–11.2, 13.

6   Thucydides 8.11.3–12.3, 14.1–2; Plutarch *Alcibiades* 24.1; Nepos, *Alcibiades* 4.7; Justin 5.2.1–3.

7   Thucydides 8.12.3, 45.1; Xenophon *Hellenica* 3.3.1–4; Plutarch *Alcibiades* 23.7–8, *Lysander* 22.3–6, *Agesilaus* 3.1–5; Justin 5.2.5; Andrewes *HCT* V, 26–7; Shipley 1997b: 79–95.

8   Thucydides 8.13, 14.2–28.

9   Thucydides 8.29–36.1, 38–43.2.

10 Thucydides 8.24.2–6, 28.5, 30.2–31.1, 32.3–33.1, 38.2–4, 40, 55.2–56.1, 60.2.

11 Thucydides 5.22.2, 50.4, 76.3; Xenophon *Memorabilia* 1.2.61; Plutarch *Cimon* 10.6.

12 Thucydides 8.17–18, 29, 36.2–37.5, 43.2–4, 45–47.1; Diodorus 13.37.2–3; Plutarch *Alcibiades* 24.2–25.2; Nepos *Alcibiades* 5.1–3; Justin 5.2.4–14.

13 *Hellenica Oxyrhynchus* 22.2 Chambers.

14 Thucydides 8.44, 55–56.1, 60.2–3.

15 Thucydides 8.47–54, 56–59; Plutarch *Alcibiades* 25.3–5; Nepos *Alcibiades* 5.3; Justin 5.3.1–3.

16 Thucydides 8.61–63.2.

17 Thucydides 8.61–71; [Aristotle] *Athēnaiōn Politeia* 29–33; Plutarch *Alcibiades* 26.1–3; Diodorus 13.34.1–3, 36.1–4; Justin 5.3.4–6.

18 Thucydides 8.72–80.

19 Thucydides 8.81–8; Diodorus 13.36.5–38.4, 46.6 (treating Tissaphernes and Pharnabazus as same man); Plutarch *Alcibiades* 26.6–7; Nepos *Alcibiades* 5.4; Justin 5.2.14, 3.6–9; Xenophon *Hellenica* 1.1.27–31 (misdated to 410: Andrewes *HCT* V, 281–5; Krentz 1989: 102).

20 Thucydides 8.60.1–2, 89–98; Diodorus 13.34.2–3, 36.3–4, 38.1–2; [Aristotle] *Athēnaiōn Politeia* 33.1–2; Rhodes 1981: 410–14.

21 Thucydides 8.99–103; Diodorus 13.38.3–39.2.

22 Thucydides 8.104–6; Diodorus 13.39.3–40.5 (on which see A. Andrewes *HCT* V, 351–4; Lazenby 2004: 197–8).

23 **The Athenian Revival, 411–408** references for this section: I. A. F. Bruce 1976: 28–31; *AHB* 2, 1988, 54–6; R. J. Littman, *TAPA* 99, 1968, 265–72; A. Andrewes *HCT* V, 354–6; *JHS* 102, 1982, 19–25; H. D. Westlake, *Museum Helveticum* 42, 1985, 313–27; Tuplin 1986: 44, 48–9, 54–5, 60–2; Kagan 1987: 225–92; McKechnie/Kern 1988: 116–23; Peter Krentz, *AHB* 3, 1989, 10–14; 1989 on passages cited; S. Rusch in Gorman/Robinson 2002: 288–92; Lazenby 2004: 198–216; Hornblower 2008 on passages cited; Hale 2009: 210–20.

24 Thucydides 8.107–8.2; Xenophon *Hellenica* 1.1.1; Diodorus 13.40.6–42.3; Plutarch *Alcibiades* 27.1.

25 Xenophon *Hellenica* 1.1.2–7; Diodorus 13.45.1–47.1; Plutarch *Alcibiades* 27.2–4; Theopompus, *FGrHist.* 115 F5.

26 Xenophon *Hellenica* 1.1.8–10; Diodorus 13.47.3–49.2; Plutarch *Alcibiades* 27.4–8.1. Macedon: Andocides 2.11; Aristophanes *Lysistrata* 421–3; Meiggs/Lewis 1969: no. 91; Kagan 1987: 235; Borza 1990: 162–3.

27 Xenophon *Hellenica* 1.1.14.

28 Diodorus 13.47.2, 49.2–51.8; Xenophon *Hellenica* 1.1.11–19; Plutarch *Alcibiades* 28.3–6; Frontinus *Stratagems* 2.5.44, 3.9.6; Polyaenus 1.40.9; Justin 5.4.1–3; Aristides 1.237.

29 Xenophon *Hellenica* 1.1.25.

30 Xenophon *Hellenica* 1.1.20–26, 33–4; Diodorus 13.52.1–3.3, 64.2–4; Plutarch Alcibiades 28.6; Philochorus, *FGrHist.* 328 F139; Aristides 1.237; Justin 5.4.4; Nepos, *Alcibiades* 5.5.

31 On 410–406 chronology, I agree with Krentz (1989: 11–14) and N. Robertson (*Historia* 29, 1980, 282–301) in seeing Xenophon *Hellenica* 1.1.1 to 1.2.1 covering 411–410 (see Riedinger 1991: 11–15, 97–108), but I cannot believe that Alcibiades spent 408–407 scrounging funds in Caria, since paying his flotilla would have consumed his gains, or agree with Marcel Piérart (*BCH* 119,

1995, 253–82, at 276–7) that the sieges of Chalcedon and Byzantium lasted two war years, since Theramenes' preliminary raiding from Chrysopolis should have prevented long sieges. I think Lysander and Alcibiades held their high naval commands from summer 408 to winter or spring 406, for reasons explained in the text.

32 Xenophon *Hellenica* 1.1.8, 33–4, 1.2.1–17; Diodorus 13.52.1, 64.1; *Hellenica Oxyrhynchus* 1–3 Chambers (diversionary assaults).

33 Diodorus 13.64.5–7; Xenophon *Hellenica* 1.2.18. Meiggs/Lewis 1969: no. 84 lines 9–10 show that Pylos was not besieged before October 410.

34 Diodorus 13.64.5–7, 65.1–2; *Hellenica Oxyrhynchus* 4.1–2 Chambers; Plutarch *Alcibiades* 29.1–3.

35 Diodorus 13.54–62; Xenophon *Hellenica* 1.1.37; Justin 5.4.5.

36 Xenophon *Hellenica* 1.3.1–1.4.1; Diodorus 13.66–7; Plutarch Alcibiades 29.3–31.6; Polyaenus 1.47.2.

37 Xenophon *Hellenica* 1.4.8–21; Diodorus 13.68–9; Plutarch *Alcibiades* 32.1–35.3; Nepos, *Alcibiades* 5.5–6.5; Justin 5.4.6–18.

38 **Lysander and Callicratidas, 408–405** references for this section: Bruce 1967: 35–45; A. Andrewes, *JHS* 102, 1982, 15–19; Tuplin 1986: 49–50, 58–9; Kagan 1987: 294–379; Cartledge 1987: 28–9; McKechnie/Kern 1988: 125–9; Krentz 1989 on passages cited; Scott Rusch in Gorman/Robinson 2002: 285–98; Briant 2002: 600; Lazenby 2004: 217–37; Cawkwell 2005: 155–9; Hale 2009: 221–32.

39 Xenophon *Hellenica* 1.4.1–7, 1.5.1–9; Diodorus 13.70.1–3; Plutarch *Lysander* 3–4, *Alcibiades* 35.4; Thucydides 2.65.12; Justin 5.5.1.

40 Diodorus 13.72.3–73.2.

41 Xenophon *Hellenica* 1.4.21–3, 1.5.8–9(?); Diodorus 13.69.4–5; Plutarch *Alcibiades* 35.1–3.

42 *Hellenica Oxyrhynchus* 8 Chambers; Xenophon *Hellenica* 1.5.10–20; Diodorus 13.71, 73.3–4.4, 76.1; Plutarch *Alcibiades* 10.1, 35.4–6.3, *Lysander* 5.1–2; Nepos *Alcibiades* 7.1–3; Justin 5.5.2–8.

43 Xenophon *Hellenica* 1.6.1–12; Diodorus 13.70.4, 76.2–3; Plutarch *Lysander* 5.3–6.7.

44 Diodorus 13.76.3–5; Xenophon *Hellenica* 1.6.12–15.

45 Diodorus 13.76.6–79.7; Xenophon *Hellenica* 1.6.15–18 (abbreviates two battles into one). Mytilene's harbours: Strabo 13.2.2; Nigel Spencer, *ABSA* 90, 1995, 296–306, at 277–9.

46 Thucydides 8.23.5; Xenophon *Hellenica* 1.1.32.

47 Xenophon *Hellenica* 1.6.18–28; Diodorus 13.97.1–4.

48 Xenophon *Hellenica* 1.6.28–35, 1.7.29–30; Diodorus 13.97.4–100.4; Plutarch *Moralia* 222f.

49 Xenophon *Hellenica* 1.6.36–8; Diodorus 13.100.5–6.

50 Xenophon *Hellenica* 1.7, 2.3.32, 35; Diodorus 13.101–103.2; [Aristotle] *Athēnaiōn Politeia* 34.1.

51 [Aristotle] *Athēnaiōn Politeia* 34.1.

52 Xenophon *Hellenica* 2.1.1–5.

53 **Aegospotami, 405–404** references for this section: Christopher Ehrhardt, *Phoenix* 24, 1970, 225–8; Barry Strauss, *AJP* 104, 1983, 24–35; *AJP* 108, 1987, 741–5; Tuplin 1986: 59–60; Kagan 1987: 379–412; V. J. Gray, *Hermes* 115, 1987, 78–9; Krentz 1989: 171–92; Briant 2002: 615–16; Lazenby 2004: 237–50; Cawkwell 2005: 159–60; Hale 2009: 233–46.

54 Pasippidas: Xenophon *Hellenica* 1.1.32, 1.3.13, 17 (not actually called a navarch, but he gathered and left ships and was replaced by a navarch; his exile in 1.1.32 was probably after his time with Pharnabazus, since 1.1.32 is one of several syncronisms that become digressions; the preceding one at 1.1.27–31 concerns Hermocrates, another envoy). Cratesippidas: Xenophon *Hellenica* 1.1.32, 1.5.1; Diodorus 13.65.3–4.

55 Xenophon *Hellenica* 2.1.6–7; Diodorus 13.100.7–8; Plutarch *Lysander* 7.1–4.

56 Diodorus 13.104.3–7; Xenophon *Hellenica* 2.1.8–15, *Anabasis* 1.1.1–3; Plutarch *Lysander* 8.1–9.2; Polyaenus 1.45.1.

57 Xenophon *Hellenica* 2.1.15–19; Diodorus 13.104.8; Plutarch *Lysander* 9.2–4.

58 Barry Strauss, *AJP* 108, 1987, 741–5 (on the Hellespont at the beach between Büyük Dere and Kozlu Dere, and Karakova Dere to the south); Hale 2009: 356–9 (actually on the Propontis shore).

59 Xenophon *Hellenica* 1.5.17; Diodorus 13.74.2; Plutarch *Alcibiades* 36.2–3; Nepos *Alcibiades* 7.4–5.

60 Xenophon *Hellenica* 2.1.20–6; Diodorus 13.105; Plutarch *Alcibiades* 37.5–8.2, *Lysander* 9.5–11.1; Nepos *Alcibiades* 8.1–5.
61 Xenophon *Hellenica* 2.1.27–32; Diodorus 13.106.1–7; Plutarch *Lysander* 11.1–13.2, *Alcibiades* 38.2–3; Nepos, *Alcibiades* 8.6, *Lysander* 1.1–2; Polyaenus 1.45.2; Frontinus *Stratagems* 2.1.18; Pausanias 9.32.7, 10.9.11; Demosthenes 19.191; Justin 5.6; Isocrates 18.59–61; Lysias 21.9–11, and *Rylands Paypri* no. 489, lines 98–119. The last three sources show that more ships escaped than Xenophon or Diodorus state.
62 Xenophon *Hellenica* 2.2.1–23, 2.3.3, 6–7; Diodorus 13.106.6, 8, 107.2–5, 14.3.4–5; Plutarch *Lysander* 13.2–15.1; Pausanias 3.18.3; Isocrates 18.60–1; Lysias 13.8–42; Aeschines 2.76; P. Mich. 5796a, 5796b (R. Merkelbach & H. C. Youtie, *ZPE* 2, 1968, 161–9; Ariel Loftus, *ZPE* 133, 2000, 11–20); Justin 5.7–8.
63 Xenophon *Hellenica* 2.2.20.

Chapter Nine

1 **The Strategic Situation and Affairs in Greece, 404–399** references for this section: H. W. Parke, *JHS* 50, 1930, 37–79; William K. Prentice, *AJA* 38, 1934, 37–42; R. E. Smith, *CP* 43, 1948, 145–56; A. Andrewes, *Phoenix* 25, 1971, 206–16; C. D. Hamilton, *AJP* 91, 1970, 294–314; 1979: 78–81, 87–98, 109–11, 119–24, 128–9; 1991: 23–9; *AW* 23, 1992, 39–41; Wesley E. Thompson, *Rivista Storica dell' Antichita* 3, 1973, 47–58; Rhodes 1981: 415–22; Krentz 1982: 69–101, 131–47, 1995: 125–6, 139–56, 171–6; Ron K. Unz, *GRBS* 27, 1986, 29–42; Cartledge 1987: 86–98, 110–15, 248–53, 298–9; 319–20; P. Harding, *Hermes* 116, 1988, 186–93; Caven 1990: 80–4; I. Malkin, *CQ* n.s. 40, 1990, 541–5; Tuplin 1993: 45–7, 54–6, 201–5; C. Falkner, *Phoenix* 50, 1996, 17–25; Shipley 1997b: 79–95; James Roy 1999; Hodkinson 2000: 154–76, 423–32; Buckler 2003: 5–9,12–28, 31–4.
2 Xenophon *Hellenica* 2.3.7; 3.4.2, 7; Diodorus 14.10.1, 13.1; Isocrates 4.110–14, 12.66, 68; Plutarch *Lysander* 13.3–14.1, 19.2–3; Polyaenus 1.45.4; Pausanias 9.32.9; Nepos *Lysander* 1.3–2.3.
3 Diodorus 14.10.2, 17.5; [Aristotle] *Athēnaiōn Politeia* 39.2; Isocrates 12.67; Polybius 6.49.10; Rhodes 1981: 466.
4 Aristotle *Politics* 1271b11–15; Hodkinson 2000: 187–90.
5 Thucydides 1.141.2–5, 142.1.
6 Diodorus 14.12.1–9; Polyaenus 2.2.7. Xenophon *Anabasis* 1.1.9, 1.3.3–4, 1.6.1–5 omits the tyranny. See Sherrylee R. Bassett, *AHB* 15, 2001, 1–13; L. Tritle in Tuplin 2004: 325–39; Thomas Braun in Fox 2004: 97–107.
7 Diodorus 14.10.2–4, 70.3; Plutarch *Lysander* 2.5, *Moralia* 190e, 229a.
8 Xenophon *Hellenica* 3.5.5; *Hellenica Oxyrhynchus* 10, 19–21.1; Justin 5.10.12–13.
9 Diodorus 13.106.8–10, 14.10.1–2, 17.5; Xenophon *Lakedaimoniōn Politeia* 7.5–6; [Aristotle] *Athēnaiōn Politeia* 39.2 (Rhodes 1981: 466); Plutarch *Lysander* 16–17, 18.4; Cartledge 1987: 88–90; Hodkinson 2000: 154–76, 423–32; Buckler 2003: 23–5.
10 Xenophon *Hellenica* 3.3.4–11; Polyaenus 2.14.1 (a condensed, altered version of Xenophon in my view); Aristotle *Politics* 1306b34–6; E. David, *Athenaeum* 57, 1979, 239–59; J. F. Lazenby, *Athenaeum* 85, 1997, 437–47.
11 Xenophon *Hellenica* 2.3.13–14, 20; Diodorus 14.4.3–4; Justin 5.8.11; [Aristotle] *Athēnaiōn Politeia* 37.2.
12 Xenophon *Hellenica* 2.4.1–27; *Lysander* 12.53–7; Isocrates 18.13; Diodorus 14.32.1–33.5; [Aristotle] *Athēnaiōn Politeia* 37.1–2, 38.1–2; Nepos *Thrasybulus* 1.5–2.7; Justin 5.9.13–10.4; Ober 1985: 115–17, 145–7 (Phyle); Garland 1987: 8, 35–6, 144–5, 160, 162 (Munichia).
13 Xenophon *Hellenica* 2.4.28–9; Diodorus 14.33.5; Lysias 12.58–9; Plutarch *Lysander* 21.2.
14 Xenophon *Hellenica* 2.4.29–34; Diodorus 14.33.6. The tomb: LaRue van Hook, *AJA* 36, 1932, 290–2; Franz Willemsen, *Athenische Mitteilungen* 92, 1977, 117–57.
15 Xenophon *Hellenica* 2.4.35–43; [Aristotle] *Athēnaiōn Politeia* 38.3–40.4; Diodorus 14.33.6; Lysias 13.80–1, 18.10–12; Plutarch *Moralia* 349f.
16 Xenophon *Hellenica* 2.4.29; 31, 35–6; 5.2.3, 6; Diodorus 14.33.6; Lysias 18.10–12; Plutarch *Lysander* 21.3–4; Pausanias 3.5.1; Justin 5.10.7.

17 Pausanias 3.5.2; Athenaeus 550d–e.
18 Xenophon *Hellenica* 3.2.21–4; Diodorus 14.17.4–6; Pausanias 3.8.3–4.
19 Xenophon *Hellenica* 3.2.25–31; Pausanias 3.8.4–5.
20 Diodorus 14.17.4–12, 34.1.
21 Diodorus 14.34.2–5; Pausanias 4.26.2, 10.38.10.
22 Diodorus 14.38.4–5; Polyaenus 2.21.
23 Xenophon *Hellenica* 3.3.1–4, *Agesilaus* 1.5; Plutarch *Alcibiades* 23.7–8, *Lysander* 22.3–6, *Agesilaus* 2.2, 3.1–4.1; Pausanias 3.8.7–10; Nepos *Agesilaus* 1.2–5; Justin 6.2.4; Fontenrose 1978: 147–50 (Q 163).
24 R. E. Smith, *Historia* 2, 1953/4, 274–88; G. L. Cawkwell, *CQ* n.s. 26, 1976, 62–84; C. D. Hamilton, *AW* 5, 1982, 67–78; *AW* 8, 1983, 119–27; 1991; *AW* 25, 1994, 205–12; H. D. Westlake, *GRBS* 27, 1986, 263–77; Cartledge 1987; Michael A. Flower, *CQ* n.s. 38, 1988, 123–34.
25 **A Lukewarm War in Asia, 400–397** references for this section: Lewis 1977: 117–24, 136–41; Hamilton 1979: 102–9, 111–19, 187–8; 1991: 87–90; H. D. Westlake, *Historia* 30, 1981, 257–64; *Historia* 35, 1986, 405–26; Stephen Ruzicka, *CJ* 80, 1985, 204–11; P. Krentz, *AW* 15, 1987, 75–9; Cartledge 1987: 190–2, 209–12; Joseph Roisman, *AHB* 2, 1988, 80–7; Briant 2002: 616–35; Buckler 2003: 34–6, 39–58, 70; Thomas Braun in Tuplin 2004: 107–30; Cawkwell 2005: 160–3.
26 Xenophon *Hellenica* 3.1.1–2, *Anabasis* 1.4.1–3; Diodorus 14.19.4–5; Plutarch *Artaxerxes* 6.2–3; Justin 5.11.5–6.
27 Xenophon *Anabasis* Books I–IV; Diodorus 14.12.8–9, 19.1–30.3; Plutarch *Artaxerxes* 1.1–20.1; Ctesias (*FGrHist.* 688) *Persica* 59, 63–9, 71.
28 Xenophon *Anabasis* 5.1.3–4, 6.1.6, 7.1.2–7.2.9.
29 Xenophon *Hellenica* 3.1.3, *Anabasis* 1.1.6–7, 1.2.2, 1.4.2; Diodorus 13.104.5–6, 14.35.1–7.
30 Xenophon *Hellenica* 3.1.4–8, compare 3.2.6–7, 4.8.17–19; Diodorus 14.36.1–3, 38.2; Polyaenus 2.19, 6.10; Ephorus, *FGrHist.* 70 F71; Isocrates 4.144 (now, or 391?). Cyreans hired: Xenophon *Anabasis* 7.6.1–2, 7–8, 7.7.10–19, 57, 7.8.1, 7–8, 24. Larisa: Buckler 2003: 46 and n. 8.
31 Xenophon *Hellenica* 3.1.8–2.11; Diodorus 13.38.2–3, 6–7; Isocrates 4.144.
32 Xenophon *Hellenica* 3.2.12–20; Diodorus 14.39.4–6.
33 Diodorus 14.39.1–4; Justin 6.1.4–9; Ctesias, *Persica* 72–4; Plutarch *Artaxerxes* 21.1–3; Isocrates 5.62–3, 9.51–6; Nepos, *Conon* 2.1–2.
34 Xenophon *Hellenica* 3.4.1; *Hellenica Oxyrhynchia* 10.1 Chambers; Isocrates 4.142 (Conon 'blockaded' for three years before Cnidus, so his operations began summer 397); Didymus, *Demosthenes* col. 7.35–7 (Philochorus, *FGrHist.* 328 F144); Diodorus 14.79.4–5.
35 **Agesilaus in Asia, 397–394** references for this section: Bruce 1967: 50–6, 63–5, 72–5, 77–92, 122–39, 147–56; J. K. Anderson, *CSCA* 7, 1974, 27–53; Lewis 1977: 141–3; R. J. Seager, *LCM* 2, 1977, 183–4; Clive Foss, *CSCA* 11, 1978, 27–37; Vivienne Gray, *CSCA* 12, 1979, 183–200; Hamilton 1979: 129–34, 184–92, 203, 227–8; 1991: 29–39, 90–103; H. D. Westlake, *Historia* 30, 1981, 264–75; *GRBS* 24, 1983, 333–44; Cartledge 1987: 211–18; Lorraine Botha, *Acta Classica* 31, 1988, 71–80; James G. DeVoto, *Hermes* 116, 1988, 41–53; McKechnie/Kern 1988: 132–4, 137, 139–48, 170–83; Graham Wylie, *Klio* 74, 1992, 118–30; Krentz 1995: 186–94, 203–10; Shipley 1997b: 128–95, 200–3; Buckler 2003: 58–73; Cawkwell 2005: 163–5.
36 Xenophon *Hellenica* 3.4.2–4, compare 5.1.33, *Agesilaus* 1.6–8; Plutarch *Agesilaus* 6.1–6, *Lysander* 23.1; Pausanias 3.9.1–4; Justin 6.2.2–6; Nepos *Agesilaus* 2.1.
37 Xenophon *Anabasis* 3.4.35.
38 Xenophon *Hellenica* 3.4.5–6, 11–15, *Agesilaus* 1.9–22, 3.2.
39 Diodorus 14.79.4–8; Pausanias 6.7.6–7; Justin 6.2.1–2; *Hellenica Oxyrhynchia* 9.1–3, 10.1, 11.1–2 Chambers.
40 Xenophon *Hellenica* 3.4.13–15, *Agesilaus* 1.23–4, *Cavalry Commander* (n.b. 9.4), *On Horsemanship*.
41 Xenophon *Hellenica* 3.4.16–25; *Agesilaus* 1.25–35.
42 E.g. Xenophon *Anabasis* 3.3.6–4.5, 6.5.25–31.
43 Xenophon *Anabasis* 3.2.36, 3.3–5 passim.
44 *Hellenica Oxyrhynchia* 14.1–15.1 Chambers (*pot*[*amon*] in 14.3); Diodorus 14.80.1–4; Pausanias 3.9.5.

45 Xenophon *Hellenica* 3.4.25–6, *Agesilaus* 1.34–5, 4.6.6; Plutarch *Agesilaus* 10.4–5; Polyaenus 7.16; Diodorus 14.80.6–8; *Hellenica Oxyrhynchia* 15.1–16.2 Chambers; Nepos *Conon* 3.1–4.1; compare Justin 6.1.4–5.

46 Xenophon *Hellenica* 3.4.27.

47 *Hellenica Oxyrhynchia* 18.1–2, 22–3 Chambers; Justin 6.2.7–11; Isocrates 4.142.

48 Xenophon *Hellenica* 3.4.7–10, *Agesilaus* 1.32–3, *Anabasis* 6.5.7; Plutarch *Agesilaus* 7.1–8.4, *Lysander* 23.3–24.2.

49 Xenophon *Hellenica* 3.4.10, *Agesilaus* 3.2–3; *Hellenica Oxyrhynchia* 24.4 Chambers; Plutarch *Agesilaus* 8.3.

50 Xenophon *Hellenica* 3.4.27–8; Plutarch *Agesilaus* 10.5–6; Pausanias 3.9.6; *Hellenica Oxyrhynchia* 22.1, 25.4 Chambers (Cheiricrates).

51 *Hellenica Oxyrhynchia* 24–5 Chambers; Xenophon *Hellenica* 4.1.1–19, *Agesilaus* 1.35, 3.3–4; Plutarch *Agesilaus* 11.1–3.

52 Xenophon *Hellenica* 4.1.20–8, *Agesilaus* 5.4–7; Plutarch *Agesilaus* 11.1–7.

53 Xenophon *Hellenica* 4.1.29–40; Plutarch *Agesilaus* 12–13.

54 Diodorus 14.81.4–6; Justin 6.2.12–16; Nepos *Conon* 3.1–4.2.

55 Xenophon *Hellenica* 4.1.41, *Agesilaus* 1.35–6; *Hellenica Oxyrhynchia* 25.4 Chambers; Plutarch *Agesilaus* 15.1, *Moralia* 211a; Nepos *Agesilaus* 4.1.

56 **Haliartus, 395** references for this section: K. L. McKay, *CR* n.s. 3, 1953, 6–7; S. Perlman, *CQ* n.s. 14, 1964, 64–81; Robin Seager, *JHS* 87, 1967, 95–115; I. A. F. Bruce, *Emerita* 28, 1960, 75–86, and 1967: 56–63, 102, 109–14, 116–122; Hamilton 1979: 182–97, 201–8; Salmon 1984: 342–8; H. D. Westlake, *Phoenix* 39, 1985, 119–33; Strauss 1986: 42–63, 104–113; Cartledge 1987: 287–92, 358–9; McKechnie/Kern 1988: 132–6, 153–4, 161–70; J. E. Lendon, *Historia* 38, 1989, 300–13; M. L. Cook, *Eranos* 88, 1990, 69–97; Tuplin 1986: 53–4; 1993: 60–4, 98, 169–70; Buck 1994: 24–31; Krentz 1995: 194–203; Shipley 1997b: 208–10; Buckler 2003: 3–8, 75–82, and in Tuplin 2004: 397–411; Edouard Rung in Tuplin 2004: 413–25.

57 Xenophon *Hellenica* 3.5.3–5; *Hellenica Oxyrhynchia* 21.2–5 Chambers; Diodorus 14.81.1; Pausanias 3.9.9–12; Plutarch *Lysander* 27.1–4. The Locrian peoples would have aligned with each other and Thebes against Phocis after the Peloponnesian War, so they all will have participated in these events.

58 Xenophon *Hellenica* 3.5.1–2, 4.2.1, 4.4.2, 5.2.35; *Hellenica Oxyrhynchia* 10.2–5, 19.1, 20.1–2, 21.1 Chambers; Pausanias 3.9.7–8; Plutarch *Lysander* 27.1, *Agesilaus* 15, *Artaxerxes* 20.3–4; Polyaenus 1.48.3.

59 Xenophon *Hellenica* 3.5.18–19.

60 Xenophon *Hellenica* 3.5.6–25; Diodorus 14.81.1–3; Pausanias 3.5.3–6; Plutarch *Lysander* 28.1–30.1, *Comparison of Lysander and Sulla* 4.2–3, *Moralia* 229c; Justin 6.4.1–7; Nepos *Lysander* 3.4; Lysias 14.4–15, 16.13–14; Andocides 3.25; Demosthenes 4.17, 18.96; Aristides 1.274–5; Fossey 1988: 301–8 (Haliartus).

Chapter Ten

1 **One Decisive and Two Indecisive Battles, 395–394** references for this section: Anderson 1970: 142–54; Hamilton 1979: 211–31; 1991: 104–9; Salmon 1984: 350–3; Lazenby 1985: 135–48; Tuplin 1986: 51–3; 1993: 66–9; Cartledge 1987: 218–22, 360–2; Buck 1994: 40–7; Shipley 1997b: 196–240; Buckler 2003: 73, 82–99.

2 Xenophon *Hellenica* 4.2.1–8, *Agesilaus* 1.36–7; Plutarch *Agesilaus* 14.1–15.6; Diodorus 14.83.1; Justin 6.2.16–17, 6.4.8–10; Nepos, *Agesilaus* 4.1–4.

3 Diodorus 14.82.1–10; Xenophon *Hellenica* 4.2.1, 10, 17–18; Rhodes/Osborne 2003: no. 6. See Westlake 1935: 54–62; Pritchett, *SAGT* IV, 155–6, V, 167–71 on Ismenias' campaign.

4 Xenophon *Hellenica* 4.2.10–13; compare 7.1.14. Timolaus: *Hellenica Oxyrhynchus* 10.3–4 Chambers; Bruce 1967: 61–2.

5 Xenophon *Hellenica* 4.2.18.

6 Xenophon *Hellenica* 4.2.22.

7 Xenophon *Hellenica* 4.2.9–4.3.1, *Agesilaus* 7.5; Diodorus 14.82.10–83.2; Lysias 16.15; Demosthenes 20.52–3; Pausanias 3.5.7; Justin 6.4.11; Plato *Menexenus* 245e. Pritchett, *SAGT* II, 73–84 (topography).

8 Xenophon *Hellenica* 4.3.1–9, 4.3.15, *Agesilaus* 2.1–5; Diodorus 14.83.3–4; Plutarch *Agesilaus* 16.1–17.2; Nepos *Agesilaus* 4.4; Pausanias 3.9.12–13; Polyaenus 2.1.17, 31(?).

9 Xenophon *Hellenica* 4.3.15, *Agesilaus* 2.5–6; Plutarch *Agesilaus* 17.1–2; Lysias 16.16.

10 Xenophon *Hellenica* 4.3.10–12; Diodorus 14.83.4–7; Philochorus, *FGrHist*. 328 F144–6; Pausanias 6.3.16; Plutarch *Agesilaus* 17.2; Justin 6.2.15–6.3.12; Polyaenus 1.48.5(?); Nepos, *Conon* 4.2–4; Hale 2009: 251–2.

11 Xenophon *Hellenica* 4.8.1–6; Diodorus 14.84.3–4.

12 Xenophon *Hellenica* 4.3.10–15; Plutarch *Agesilaus* 17.2–3; Polyaenus 2.1.3, 18; Frontinus *Stratagems* 1.11.5.

13 Pritchett, *SAGT* II, 85–101; Buckler 1996.

14 Xenophon *Hellenica* 4.3.15–16; *Agesilaus* 2.7–9; Plutarch *Agesilaus* 18.1.

15 Xenophon *Anabasis* 5.3.6.

16 Xenophon *Hellenica* 4.3.16–18; *Agesilaus* 2.9–11; Plutarch *Agesilaus* 18.2; Diodorus 14.84.1.

17 Xenophon *Hellenica* 4.3.19.

18 Xenophon *Agesilaus* 2.12.

19 Plutarch *Agesilaus* 18.3–4; Polyaenus 2.1.19; Frontinus *Stratagems* 2.6.6.

20 Xenophon *Agesilaus* 2.14.

21 Xenophon *Hellenica* 4.3.19–21, *Agesilaus* 2.12–16; Plutarch *Agesilaus* 18.2–19.3; Nepos *Agesilaus* 4.5–8; Justin 6.4.13; Pausanias 3.9.13; Polyaenus 2.1.5, 23.

22 Xenophon *Hellenica* 4.3.21–3; Plutarch *Agesilaus* 19.3; Anderson 1970: 120–1.

23 **The War Around Corinth, 394–390** references for this section: G. T. Griffith, *Historia* 1, 1950, 236–56; D. Kagan, *Historia* 11, 1962, 447–53; C. D. Hamilton, *Historia* 21, 1972, 21–37; 1979: 229–74, 280–7; 1991: 111–12, 114; Lewis 1977: 143–4; C. J. Tuplin, *CQ* n.s. 32, 1982, 75–83; 1986: 56; 1993: 69–73; Salmon 1984: 25–6, 180, 354–67; M. Whitby, *Historia* 33, 1984, 295–308; Strauss 1986: 136–43; Cartledge 1987: 193–4, 222–4, 255–7, 293–4; 362–4; Buck 1994: 47–51, 52; Shipley 1997b: 258–71; J. Buckler, *CP* 94, 1999, 210–14; 2003: 101–9, 116–22, 139–52; Briant 2002: 645–6; Cawkwell 2005: 165–8.

24 Xenophon *Hellenica* 4.8.7–10; Diodorus 14.84.4–85.3; Nepos, *Conon* 4.5; Justin 6.5.6–11.

25 Xenophon *Hellenica* 4.4.1–5, 4.8.10–11; Diodorus 14.86.1–2; compare Andocides 3.26–7.

26 Xenophon *Hellenica* 4.4.6–13; Diodorus 14.86.3–4; Andocides 3.18; Wiseman 1978: 85–8; Anderson 1970: 121–2, 154–7.

27 Xenophon *Hellenica* 4.8.12–17; Diodorus 14.85.4; Nepos *Conon* 5.1–4; Isocrates 4.154; Lysias 19.39, 41; Andocides 3 *passim*; Anonymous *Argument to Andocides' On the Peace*; Philochorus, *FGrHist*. 328 F149a–b.

28 Harpocration, *Lexicon* under *xenikon en Korinthōi*; scholion to Aristophanes *Plutus* 173; Demosthenes 4.24; Parke 1933: 48–57; Anderson 1970: 121–3; Pritchett, *GSAW* II, 62–72, 117–25.

29 Justin 6.5.1–4; Polyaenus 3.9.2, 22, 31, 32, 35; Nepos, *Iphicrates* 2.1–2; Frontinus *Stratagems* 3.12.2.

30 Xenophon *Hellenica* 4.4.14–18; Diodorus 14.91.2–3; Polyaenus 3.9.24, 39, 45, 48, 49 (compare Polyaenus 3.9.54; Frontinus *Stratagems* 1.6.3), 52. Uncertain events: Nepos *Iphicrates* 2.1.3; Polyaenus 3.9.43, 57.

31 Xenophon *Hellenica* 4.4.19, *Agesilaus* 2.17; Plutarch *Agesilaus* 21.1; Diodorus 14.97.5; Andocides 3.27 (compare Thucydides 5.76.3).

32 Xenophon *Hellenica* 4.5.1–19, *Agesilaus* 2.18–19, 7.6; Diodorus 14.86.5–6, 91.2; Plutarch *Agesilaus* 21.1–22.4; Pausanias 3.10.1; Parke 1933: 53–5; Pritchett, *GSAW* II, 122–3; Anderson 1970: 123–6; Lazenby 1985: 148–50.

33 **Another War in Greece Ends in the East, 391–386** references for this section: Lewis 1977: 146–7; Hamilton 1979: 287–8, 292–8, 301–25; 1991: 116–19; Cartledge 1987: 194–9, 224–6, 366–7; Tuplin 1993: 73–5, 77–8, 172–5; Shipley 1997b: 271–9; Buck 1994: 56–9; Briant 2002: 649; Buckler 2003: 123–8, 152–83.

34 Xenophon *Hellenica* 4.8.17–19, 21–2; Diodorus 14.99.1–3.

35 Xenophon *Hellenica* 4.8.20, 22–30; Diodorus 14.94.1–4, 97.1–4, 99.4–5; Lysias 19.19–21; Rhodes/ Osborne 2003: no. 18, lines 7–8; Demosthenes 20.59–60.

36 Xenophon *Hellenica* 4.8.31–9; Polyaenus 3.9.44; Plutarch *Moralia* 219c; Frontinus *Stratagems* 1.4.7, 2.5.42; Diodorus 14.92.1–2; Cook 1973: 290.

37 Xenophon *Hellenica* 4.7.1 (quote). Campaigns: Xenophon *Hellenica* 4.6.1–7.1, *Agesilaus* 2.20; Plutarch *Agesilaus* 22.5; Pausanias 3.10.2; Pritchett, *SAGT* VII, 90–100.

38 Xenophon *Hellenica* 4.7.2–7, 5.1.29; Pausanias 3.5.8–9; Aristotle *Rhetoric* 1398b, Plutarch *Moralia* 191b, 209a; Fontenrose 1978: 18–19.

39 Xenophon *Hellenica* 5.1.1–24; Garland 1987: 40–1, 83–95.

40 Xenophon *Hellenica* 5.1.6–7, 25–9; Polyaenus 2.24; Rhodes/Osborne 2003: no.19(?); Tuplin 1993: 174–5.

41 Xenophon *Hellenica* 5.1.31.

42 Xenophon *Hellenica* 5.1.30–36, *Agesilaus* 2.21; Diodorus 14.110.1–4; Plutarch *Agesilaus* 23.1–3, *Artaxerxes* 22.1–4; Justin 6.6.1–4.

Chapter Eleven

1 **Sparta Tries to Dominate Greece by Land, 385–379** references for this section: R. P. Legon, *Historia* 16, 1967, 324–37; D. G. Rice, *Historia* 23, 1974, 164–82; Buckler 1980: 15; 2003: 190–212; Cartledge 1987: 156, 226–9, 258–61, 262–72, 296–7, 372–4; Hamilton 1991: 125–49; Tuplin 1993: 87–100; Buck 1994: 63–9; Dillery 1995: 207–27; Georgiadou 1997: 80–95; Shipley 1997b: 279–85; Stylianou 1998: 164–76, 184–93, 209–19, 221–6.

2 Xenophon *Hellenica* 5.2.1–7, compare 5.1.29; Diodorus 15.5, 12; Plutarch *Pelopidas* 4.4–5; Polyaenus 2.25; Ephorus, *FGrHist.* 70 F79; Strabo 8.3.2; Isocrates 4.126, 8.100; Polybius 4.27.6; Pausanias 8.8.7–9; 9.13.1–2. Topography: S. Hodkinson and H. Hodkinson, *ABSA* 76, 1981, 256–8, 267–8.

3 Epirus: Diod. 15.13.1-3; Caven 1990: 150-1. Glos: Diod. 15.9.3-5, 19.1; T. T. B. Ryder, *CQ* n.s. 13, 1963, 105-9; S. Dušanić, *ZPE* 133, 200, 21-30.

4 Xenophon *Hellenica* 4.2.16, 4.4.15; 5. 2.8–10, 5.3.10–17, 5.3.21–5; Diodorus 15.19.3; Plutarch *Agesilaus* 24.2. Topography: Pritchett, *SAGT* II, 96–111.

5 Xenophon *Hellenica* 5.2.11–24; Diodorus 5.19.1–3, 20.3 (note reversed order of Phoebidas and Eudamidas).

6 Xenophon *Hellenica* 5.2.25–36, 5.4.1, 46, 49; Androtion, *FGrHist.* 324 F50; Isocrates 4.126; Polybius 4.27.4; Diodorus 15.20.1–3; Plutarch *Agesilaus* 23.3–24.1, *Pelopidas* 5.1–6.3, *Moralia* 575f– 76a; Nepos *Pelopidas* 1.2–3; Aristides *Panathenaicus* 293, *Leuctricus* 1.10–11, 2.2, 3.2.

7 Xenophon *Hellenica* 5.3.9.

8 Xenophon *Hellenica* 5.2.37–3.9, 5.3.18–20, 28; Diodorus 15.21.1–3, 22.2, 23.2–3.

9 **The Boeotian War, 379–375** references for this section: G. L. Cawkwell, *CQ* n.s. 23, 1973, 47–60; Buckler 1980: 15–45; 2003: 205, 212–31, 233–40, 242–57, 270–8; Cargill 1981; R. M. Kallett-Marx, *CA* 4, 1985, 127–51; Tuplin 1986: 43 nn. 25–6; 1993: 125–30, 159–60; Cartledge 1987: 136–8, 156–9, 229–32, 299–304, 375–7; James G. DeVoto, *AHB* 1, 1987, 75–82; 1989; Hamilton 1991: 152–87; R. J. Buck, *AHB* 6, 1992, 103–9; 1994: 69–99, 104–11; Mark Munn, *CA* 6, 1987, 106–41; 1993: 136–48, 155–71, 210–21, 225–8; Dillery 1995: 228–35; Georgiadou 1997: 95–153; Shipley 1997b: 286–99; Stylianou 1998: 230–43, 249–59, 261–5, 279–80; 287–319, 351.

10 Xenophon *Hellenica* 5.4.1–13; Diodorus 15.25–7; Plutarch *Pelopidas* 6–14.1, *Moralia* 575b–98f (especially 578a, 586e, 598e–f); Nepos, *Pelopidas* 2–3; Polyaenus 2.3.1, 2.4.3; Dinarchus 1.38–9; Isocrates 14.28–9; Aristides 1.294. Topography: Symeonoglu 1985: 118.

11 Xenophon *Hellenica* 5.4.13–19 (compare 6.4.5); Diodorus 15.27.3; Plutarch *Agesilaus* 24.2, *Pelopidas* 13.1, 14.1; Isocrates 14.28–9; Grundy 1894: 3 (mud).

12 Xenophon *Hellenica* 5.4.20–34; Plutarch *Agesilaus* 24.3–26.1, *Pelopidas* 14.2–3; Diodorus 15.29.5– 6; Callisthenes, *FGrHist.* 124 F9.

13 Xenophon *Hellenica* 5.4.14, 52; Nepos, *Chabrias* 1.2; Diodorus 15.29.1–4.

14 Plutarch *Pelopidas* 18.1, 19.3; James G. DeVoto, *AW* 23, 1992, 3–19; Davidson 2007: 432–9.

15 Xenophon *Hellenica* 5.4.35–41, *Agesilaus* 2.22; Diodorus 15.26.4, 31.3–33.4; Demosthenes 20.76; Nepos, *Chabrias* 1.1–3; Polyaenus 2.1.2, 7, 21, 25; Plutarch *Agesilaus* 26.3–5; J. K. Anderson, *AJA* 67, 1963, 411–13; John Buckler, *Hesperia* 41, 1972, 446–74.

16 Xenophon *Hellenica* 5.4.42–6; Diodorus 15.33.5–6; Polyaenus 2.5.2.

17 Diodorus 15.28.2–4; *Inscriptiones Graecae* II² 34/35, 43; Rhodes/Osborne 2003: nos. 20, 22.

18 Diodorus 15.31.2.

19 Diodorus 15.28.4–5, 31.1–2; see also Xenophon *Hellenica* 5.2.21, 6.2.16; Cartledge 1987: 272–3; Stylianou 1998: 281–5; Buckler 2003: 232–3.

20 Xenophon *Hellenica* 5.4.47–56, *Agesilaus* 2.22; Diodorus 15.34.1–2; Polyaenus 2.1.11, 12, 24(?).

21 Xenophon *Hellenica* 5.4.56–7, compare 6.1.10; Frontinus *Stratagems* 4.7.19; Polyaenus 2.7.

22 Xenophon *Hellenica* 5.4.58–9; Plutarch *Pelopidas* 15.1–5, 25.5–6.

23 Xenophon *Hellenica* 5.4.60–1; Diodorus 15.34.3–35.2; Demosthenes 20.77, 22.15, 23.198, 24.180; Aeschines 3.222, 243; Dinarchus 1.75; Plutarch *Phocion*. 6.2–3, *Camillus* 19.3; Polyaenus 3.11.2, 11.

24 Polyaenus 3.11.3, 6, 15; compare 3.11.4, 10, 13, 14.

25 Xenophon *Hellenica* 5.4.63, 6.1.1, compare 5.4.46, 49, 55; Plutarch *Pelopidas* 15.1–5, 24.5–6; Isocrates 14.9.

26 Xenophon *Hellenica* 5.4.62–6; Diodorus 15.36.1–6; Polyaenus 3.10.2, 4, 6, and 12 (same anecdote), 13, 16, and 17 (same anecdote); Frontinus *Stratagems* 1.12.11, 2.5.47; Isocrates 15.109; Nepos *Timotheus* 2.1–2; Aristotle, *Oeconomicus* 1350a–b.

27 Plutarch *Pelopidas* 17.1–2.

28 Plutarch *Pelopidas* 17.3–4.

29 Diodorus 15.37.1–2, 81.2; Plutarch *Pelopidas* 16–17; Pritchett, *GSAW* IV, 103–22; James G. DeVoto, *AW* 23, 1992, 9–10; Buckler 1996.

30 **An Unsuccessful Peace, 375–371** references for this section: Westlake 1935: 67–83, 103–25; V. J. Gray, *CQ* n.s. 30, 1980, 306–26; Buckler 1980: 46–55; 2003: 251, 257–72, 278–88; C. J. Tuplin, *Athenaeum* 72, 1984, 537–68; 1986: 43 n. 27; 1993: 130–4, 160–2, 180–3, 185; Cartledge 1987: 306–8, 324, 377–80; Hamilton 1991: 187–204; Buck 1994: 99–103, 111–13; Dillery 1995: 164–71; Shipley 1997b: 310–15; Stylianou 1998: 320–29, 330–7, 346–60, 369–76, 382–8.

31 Xenophon *Hellenica* 6.1.1–19.

32 Peace of 375/4: Xenophon *Hellenica* 6.2.1; Diodorus 15.38; Dionysius of Halicarnassue *Lysias* 12; Philochorus, *FGrHist.* 328 F151; Isocrates 14.41, 15.109–10; Nepos *Timotheus.* 2.2. Thebans remain in league: [Demosthenes] 49.14–15, 21, 48–54; *Inscriptiones Graecae* II² 1607.50, 155.

33 Xenophon *Hellenica* 6.2.2–3; Diodorus 15.40, 45–46.3.

34 Xenophon *Hellenica* 6.2.3–39; Diodorus 15.47. Topography: G. S. Dontas, *Archaiologikē Ephēmeris* 1965, 139–44.

35 Xenophon *Hellenica* 6.3.1–20, 6.4.21; Plutarch *Agesilaus* 27.3–28.2, 28.5, *Pelopidas* 20.1; Diodorus 15.46.4–6, 50.1–51.1, compare 15.38.3–4; Dionysius of Halicarnassus *Lysias* 12; Pausanias 9.3.1–2; Nepos, *Epaminondas* 6.4.

36 Xenophon *Hellenica* 6.4.1–2; Plutarch *Agesilaus* 28.2–4; Diodorus 15.50.6, 51.2–4.

37 **The Battle of Leuctra, 371** references for this section: A. R. Burn, *ABSA* 44, 1947, 313–23; Anderson 1970: 192–220; Pritchett, *SAGT* I, 49–57; John Buckler, *Weiner Studien* n.s. 11, 1977, 76–9; *Symbolae Osloenses* 55, 1980, 54–64, 75–93; 2003: 287, 288–93; C. J. Tuplin, *CQ* n.s. 29, 1979, 351–6; *Athenaeum* 74, 1986, 321–41; *Klio* 69, 1987, 72–107; 1993: 134–5, 136–8, 186–7; Lazenby 1985: 151–62; Cartledge 1987: 236–41; V. D. Hanson, *CA* 7, 1988, 190–207; James G. DeVoto, *AHB* 3, 1989, 115–18; Hamilton 1991: 204–11; Georgiadou 1997: 172–9; Shipley 1997b: 315–22; Stylianou 1998: 381–2, 388–407.

38 Xenophon *Hellenica* 6.4.3–4; Diodorus 15.52.1, 7, 53.1–2; Pausanias 9.13.3, 7. Topography: A. R. Burn, *ABSA* 44, 1947, 313–23; Pritchett, *SAGT* I, 49–57; Buckler 1980: 57–9; 2003: 288–9.

39 Xenophon *Hellenica* 6.4.4, 6; Diodorus 15.52.2–3; Pausanias 9.13.6–7; Plutarch *Pelopidas* 20.2.

40 Diodorus 15.52.2 (Theban); Plutarch *Pelopidas* 20.1 (Spartan).

41 Xenophon *Hellenica* 6.4.7; Diodorus 15.50.1–3, 52.3–7, 53.4, 54.1–4; Callisthenes, *FGrHist.* 124 22a (=Cicero *De divinatione* 1.74); Pausanias 4.32.4–6, 9.6.5–6, 13.4–5; Plutarch *Agesilaus*

28.4, *Pelopidas* 20.3–22.2, *Moralia* 192f–193a; Polyaenus 2.3.8, 12; Frontinus *Stratagems* 1.11.6, 16, 1.12.5–7.

42 Xenophon *Hellenica* 6.4.4–6, 8–9; Pausanias 9.13.8; Polyaenus 2.3.3.

43 Xenophon *Hellenica* 6.4.10–15; *Agesilaus* 2.24; Diodorus 15.55–6; Plutarch *Pelopidas* 23; *Agesilaus* 28.5–6; *Moralia* 193b; Rhodes/Osborne 2003: no. 30; Nepos, *Pelopidas* 4.2; Polybius 12.25f.3–4; Pausanias 3.6.1, 9.13.9–12; Polyaenus 1.10; 2.3.2, 11; Frontinus *Stratagems* 4.2.6; Dinarchus 1.72–3; Arrian *Tactica* 11.1–2.

44 Xenophon *Hellenica* 6.4.10.

45 Xenophon *Hellenica* 6.4.11.

46 Xenophon *Hellenica* 6.4.13.

47 C. J. Tuplin, *Philologus* 130, 1986, 25–6 (*Hippeis* the emendation for *hippoi*).

48 Xenophon *Hellenica* 6.4.13–14.

Chapter Twelve

1 **From 371 to 369** references for this section: Westlake 1935: 90–102; Roebuck 1941: 27–41; Buckler 1980: 65–90; 2003: 301–11; E. David, *Athenaeum* n.s. 58, 1980, 299–308; Cartledge 1987: 232–6, 242–3, 383–6; 2002: 253–5; Hamilton 1991: 211–30; Tuplin 1986: 46–8; 1993: 114–115, 117–21; 139–44, 150–1; Georgiadou 1997: 179–84; Shipley 1997b: 336–50; Stylianou 1998: 408–18, 423–44; Luraghi 2008: 32–6 (Thuria), 209–48.

2 Xenophon *Hellenica* 6.4.16.

3 Xenophon *Hellenica* 6.4.18–26; Diodorus 15.54.5–7; Pausanias 9.14.1.

4 Xenophon *Hellenica* 6.4.27–32, 5.1–3, 23; Diodorus 15.57.1–2, 60.1–5; Pausanias 9.14.2–4.

5 Plutarch *Agesilaus* 30.4.

6 Plutarch *Agesilaus* 30.1–4, also *Agesilaus* 3, *Comparison of Agesilaus and Pompey* 1.2, 3.2, *Moralia* 191c, 214b–c; Polyaenus 2.1.13; J. Ducat in Hodkinson/Powell 2006: 42–4.

7 Xenophon *Hellenica* 6.5.2–9; Diodorus 15.58–59; Plutarch *Moralia* 814b; Isocrates 5.52; Dionysius of Halicarnassus *Roman Antiquities* 7.66.5; Aristides *Panathenaicus* 273, 311.

8 Xenophon *Hellenica* 6.5.10–21; *Agesilaus* 2.23; Plutarch *Agesilaus* 30.4; Diodorus 15.59.2–4, 62.1–2. Topography: Stylianou 1998: 417–18, 423–5; Tuplin 1993: 141–2, *Philologus* 130, 1986, 27–8 (*Eugaia*, not *Eutaia*); Pritchett, *SAGT* IV, 61–3 (Asea).

9 Diodorus 15.62.3; Demosthenes 16.12, 19–20; Aristides *Panathenaicus* 285D.

10 Xenophon *Hellenica* 6.5.19; 7.4.40; Diodorus 15.62.3; Plutarch *Moralia* 193c–d; Pausanias 8.6.2, 8.8.10, 8.27.2; Nepos *Epaminondas* 6.1–3.

11 Xenophon *Hellenica* 6.5.19, 22–5, *Agesilaus* 2.24; Diodorus 15.62.3–5, 81.4; Plutarch *Agesilaus* 31.1, *Pelopidas* 24.1–4.

12 Xenophon *Hellenica* 6.5.23–7; Diodorus 15.63.3–64.6.

13 Xenophon *Agesilaus* 2.24; *Hellenica* 6.5.25–32, 50; 7.2.2–3; Diodorus 15.65.1–6; Plutarch *Agesilaus* 31.1–33.1; Polyaenus 2.1.14, 15, 27; Frontinus *Stratagems* 1.10.3; Valerius Maximus 7.2 ext. 15; Aelian *Varia Historia* 14.27.

14 Diodorus 15.66.1–67.1; Pausanias 4.26.5–27.11, 9.14.5, 10.10.5; Plutarch *Agesilaus* 34.1, *Pelopidas* 24.5; Isocrates 5.49, 6.28; Dinarchus 1.73; Lycurgus *Against Leocrates* 62; Pausanias 10.10.5; Dio Chrysostom 15.28.

15 Plutarch *Agesilaus* 32.2, 8, *Pelopidas* 24.1–2; Xenophon *Hellenica* 6.5.50; Diodorus 15.66.1, 67.1; Pausanias 4.27.9.

16 Xenophon *Hellenica* 6.5.33–52; Diodorus 15.63.1–2, 65.5–6; Pausanias 9.14.6–7.

17 **From 369 to 362** references for this section: J. Wiseman, *Klio* 51, 1969, 177–99; Buckler 1980: 90–109, 151–60, 185–219; 2003: 312–38, 342–50; Salmon 1984: 374–81; S. Hornblower, *ABSA* 85, 1990, 71–7; Hamilton 1991: 230–51; Tuplin 1986: 46, 57; 1993: 121–4, 144–6, 151–7; Shipley 1997b: 353–9, 364–72; Stylianou 1998: 444–55, 457–64, 470–4, 480–3, 485–9, 490–2, 506–21; W. B. Caraher and T. E. Gregory, *Hesperia* 75, 2006, 326–56.

18 Diodorus 15.67.2.

19 Xenophon *Hellenica* 7.1.25.
20 Pausanias 10.9.5–6; *Palatine Anthology* 7.442, 512; Prtichett, *GSAW* IV, 134–6, 217–19; C. Vatin, *BCH* 105, 1981, 453–9.
21 Xenophon *Hellenica* 7.1.15–22, 25, 7.2.5–9; Diodorus 15.68.1–70.1, 72.1–2; Pausanias 6.2.2–3, 9.15.4; Polyaenus 2.3.9; Frontinus *Stratagems* 2.5.26; Plutarch *Moralia* 193f.
22 Xenophon *Hellenica* 7.1.41–3, 7.2.11–16; Diodorus 15.75.2.
23 Diodorus 15.70.2; Xenophon *Hellenica* 7.1.27.
24 Xenophon *Hellenica* 7.1.31–2.
25 Xenophon *Hellenica* 7.1.28–32; Diodorus 15.72.3; Plutarch *Agesilaus* 33.3–5, *Moralia* 219a; Polyaenus 1.41.5; Plutarch *Moralia* 219a. Topography: Buckler 1980: 106–8.
26 Xenophon *Hellenica* 7.4.20, 5.10.
27 Diodorus 15.72.3–4; Pausanias 8.27.1–8; Stylianou 1998: 471–4.
28 Xenophon *Hellenica* 7.4.22, 33–6; 7.5.3; Diodorus 15.62.2, 67.2; Ephorus, *FGrHist.* 70 F215; Pritchett, *GSAW* II: 223; Buckler 1980: 292 n.3.
29 Xenophon *Hellenica* 7.4.12.
30 Xenophon *Hellenica* 7.4.1–11; Diodorus 15.76.3.
31 Polyaenus 2.9. Compare Plutarch *Agesilaus* 34.6–8; Aelian *Varia Historia* 6.3: Epaminondas' attack should not have found Isidas at home oiling himself.
32 Xenophon *Hellenica* 7.4.25.
33 Xenophon *Hellenica* 7.4.19–27. Site: J. Roy, J. A. Lloyd, E. J. Owens in Sanders 1992: 190–4.
34 Xenophon *Hellenica* 7.4.33–5.9; Diodorus 15.82.1–4.
35 Xenophon *Hellenica* 7.5.9–14; Aeneas Tacticus 2.2; Diodorus 15.82.5–84.1; Plutarch *Agesilaus* 34.3–8, *Moralia* 346b–c; Polybius 9.8.1–8; Polyaenus 2.3.10; Frontinus *Stratagems* 3.11.5; Justin 6.7.1–9.
36 Xenophon *Hellenica* 7.5.14–27; Diodorus 15.84–89.2; Plutarch *Agesilaus* 35.1–2, *Moralia* 346c–3, 761d; Polybius 9.8.7–13, 12.25f.3–5; Pausanias 8.10–12; Aelian *Varia Historia* 12.3; Nepos *Epaminondas* 9.1–3; Arrian *Tactica* 11.1–2; Polyaenus 2.3.14; Frontinus *Stratagems* 2.2.12. Topography: Pritchett, *SAGT* II, 37–72.
37 Cartledge 1987: 325–9; Shipley 1997b: 375–97.
38 Piper 1986: 6–7; Cartledge/Spawforth 2002: 13–14.
39 C. D. Hamilton, *EMC/CV* I, 1982, 5–20; Buckler 1989: 15–24, 85–92, 97–8, 125; Cartledge/Spawforth 2002: 9–13.
40 Isocrates 6.73–84.
41 Paul Christensen, *JHS* 126, 2006, 47–65.
42 Compare Xenophon *Cyropaedia* 6.1.27–8, 50–5, 2.10, 15–18, 3.19–35, 4.16–18; 7.1.29–44.
43 Cartledge/Spawforth 2002: 14–15, 16.
44 E. Badian, *Hermes* 95, 1967, 170–92; de Ste Croix 1972: 164–6, 376–8; Cartledge/Spawforth 2002: 20–5.
45 Piper 1986: 14–23; Cartledge/Spawforth 2002: 31–7.
46 Piper 1986: 27–74; Cartledge/Spawforth 2002: 38–58.
47 Piper 1986: 91–116; Cartledge/Spawforth 2002: 59–79.
48 Tyrtaeus Fragment 12.31–2 West.

BIBLIOGRAPHY

Note that an author's name and the date of publication are used to identify works in the endnotes, except where abbreviations are used for journals or joint publications. Note that the stress is on books, due to space considerations. Many articles are referenced only in the endnotes.

Amyx, D. A. (1988) *Corinthian Vase-Painting of the Archaic Period*. University of California Press, Berkeley and Los Angeles.

Anderson, J. K. (1970) *Military Theory and Practice in the Age of Xenophon*. University of California Press, Berkeley and Los Angeles.

Andrewes, Anthony (1966) 'The Government of Classical Sparta'. In E. Badian, ed., *Ancient Society and Institutions: Studies Presented to Victor Ehrenberg on his 75th Birthday*, 1–26. Oxford University Press, Oxford.

Badian, E. (1993) *From Plataea to Potidaea: Studies in the History and Historiography of the Pentecontaetia*. Johns Hopkins University Press, Baltimore and London.

Blamire, A. (1989) *Plutarch. Life of Kimon*. Institute of Classical Studies, University of London, London.

Borza, Eugene N. (1990) *In the Shadow of Olympus: The Emergence of Macedon*. Princeton University Press, Princeton.

Bowen, A. J. (1992) *Plutarch: The Malice of Herodotus*. Aris & Phillips, Warminster, Wiltshire.

Bowra, C. M. (1960) *Early Greek Elegists*. Barnes & Noble, New York.

Briant, Pierre (2002) *From Cyrus to Alexander: A History of the Persian Empire*. Translated by Peter T. Daniels, Eisenbrauns, Winona Lake, Indiana.

Bruce, I. A. F. (1967) *An Historical Commentary on the Hellenica Oxyrhynchia*. Cambridge University Press, Cambridge.

Buck, Robert J. (1979) *A History of Boeotia*. University of Alberta Press, Edmonton.

—— (1994) *Boiotia and the Boiotian League, 432–371 B.C.* University of Alberta Press, Edmonton.

Buckler, John (1980) *The Theban Hegemony 371–362 BC*. Harvard University Press, Cambridge, Massachusetts and London.

—— (1989) *Philip II and the Sacred War*. Brill, Leiden.

—— (1996) 'The Battle of Koroneia and its Historiographical Legacy'. In John M. Fossey, ed., *Boeotia Antiqua VI, Proceedings of the 8th International Conference on Boeotian Antiquities, Loyola University of Chicago, 24–26 May 1995*, 59–72. Gieben, Amsterdam.

—— (2003) *Aegean Greece in the Fourth Century BC*. Brill, Leiden and Boston.

Burn, A. R. (1962) *Persia and the Greeks: The Defense of the West 546–478 B.C.* St Martin's Press, New York.

Cargill, J. (1981) *The Second Athenian League*. University of California Press, Berkeley and Los Angeles.

Carlier, Pierre (1984) *La royauté en Grèce avant Alexandre*. A.E.C.R., Strasbourg.

Cartledge, Paul (1987) *Agesilaos and the Crisis of Sparta*. Johns Hopkins University Press, Baltimore.

—— (2001) *Spartan Reflections*. University of California Press, Berkeley and Los Angeles.

—— (2002) *Sparta and Lakonia: A Regional History from 1300 to 362 BC*. Second edition of 1979 original with extra notes and bibliography, Routledge, London and New York.

—— and Anthony Spawforth (2002) *Hellenistic and Roman Sparta: A Tale of Two Cities*. Second edition with extra notes and bibliography, Routledge, London and New York.

Cavanagh, William, Joost Crouwel, R. W. V. Catling, and Graham Shipley (1996) *The Laconia Survey, Volume II: Archaeological Data*. British School at Athens, London.

—— —— —— and —— (2002) *The Laconia Survey, Volume I: Methdology and Interpretation*. British School at Athens, London.

—— C. Gallou, and M. Georgiadis, eds (2009) *Sparta and Laconia: From Prehistory to Pre-Modern*. British School at Athens Studies 16, London.

Caven, Brian (1990) *Dionysius I: War-Lord of Sicily*. Yale University Press, New Haven and London.

Cawkwell, G. L. (2005) *The Greek Wars: The Failure of Persia*. Oxford University Press, Oxford.

Christien, Jacqueline (1992) 'De Sparte à la côte orientale du Péloponnèse'. In M. Piérart, ed., *Polydipsion Argos. Argos de la fin des palais mycéniens à la constitution de l'État classique. Fribourg (Suisse) 7–9 Mai 1987*, 157–72. Bulletin de Correspondence Hellénique Supplement XXII, Athens, Paris, Fribourg.

Connolly, Peter (2006) *Greece and Rome at War*. Greenhill Books, London.

Conwell, David H. (2008) *Connecting a City to the Sea: The History of the Athenian Long Walls*. Brill, Leiden and Boston.

Cook, J. M. (1973) *The Troad: An Archaeological and Topographical Study*. Oxford University Press, Oxford.

Davidson, James (2007) *The Greeks and Greek Love*. Random House, New York.

Dawkins, R. M. (1929) *The Sanctuary of Artemis Orthia at Sparta*. Macmillan, London.

Dayton, John C. (2006) *The Athletes of War: An Evaluation of the Agonistic Elements in Greek Warfare*. Edgar Kent, Inc., Toronto.

Derow, P., and R. Parker, eds (2003) *Herodotus and his World: Essays from a Conference in Memory of George Forrest*. Oxford University Press, Oxford.

De Ste Croix, G. E. M. (1972) *The Origins of the Peloponnesian War*. Cornell University Press, Ithaca, New York.

DeVoto, James G. (1989) 'The Liberation of Thebes in 379/8 B.C'. In Robert F. Sutton Jr., ed., *Daidalikon: Studies in Memory of Raymond V. Schoder, S.J.*, 101–16. Wauconda, Illinois.

Dillery, John (1995) *Xenophon and the History of his Times*. Routledge, London and New York.

Ducat, J. (2006) *Spartan Education: Youth and Society in the Classical Period*. Translated by Emma Stafford, P.-J. Shaw, and Anton Powell, Classical Press of Wales, Swansea.

Figueira, Thomas J., ed. (2004) *Spartan Society*. Classical Press of Wales, Swansea.

Fitzhardinge, L. F. (1980) *The Spartans*. Thames and Hudson, London.

Flower, Michael A. (1991) 'Revolutionary Agitation and Social Change in Classical Sparta'. In Michael A. Flower and Mark Toher, eds, *Georgica: Greek Studies in Honour of George Cawkwell*, 78–97. Institute of Classical Studies, Bulletin Supplement 58, London.

Flower, Michael, and John Marincola, eds (2002) *Herodotus. Histories Book IX*. Cambridge University Press, Cambridge.

Fontenrose, Joseph (1978) *The Delphic Oracle: Its Responses and Operations, with a Catalog of Responses*. University of California Press, Berkeley and Los Angeles.

Fossey, John M. (1988) *Topography and Population of Ancient Boiotia*. Ares, Chicago.

Fox, Robin Lane, ed. (2004) *The Long March: Xenophon and the Ten Thousand*. Yale University Press, New Haven and London.

Gabrielsen, Vincent (1994) *Financing the Athenian Fleet: Public Taxation and Social Relations*. Johns Hopkins University Press, Baltimore and London.

Garland, Robert (1987) *The Piraeus from the Fifth to the First Century B.C.* Duckworth, London.

Georgiadou, Aristoula (1997) *Plutarch's Pelopidas: A Historical and Philological Commentary*. B. G. Teubner, Stuttgart and Leipzig.

Gomme, A. W. (HCT) *A Historical Commentary on Thucydides*. Five volumes, with volumes IV and V completed by A. Andrewes and K. J. Dover. Oxford University Press, Oxford, 1945–81.

Gorman, Vanessa B., and Eric W. Robinson, eds (2002) *Oikistes: Studies in Constitutions, Colonies, and Military Power in the Ancient World. Offered in Honor of A. J. Graham*. E. J. Brill, Leiden, Boston, and Cologne.

Graham, A. J. (1983) *Colony and Mother City in Ancient Greece*. Original 1964; revised and expanded edition, Ares, Chicago.

Green, Peter (1996) *The Greco-Persian Wars.* University of California Press, Berkeley, Los Angeles, and London, 1996 revision of 1970 edition *Xerxes at Salamis.*

—— (2006) *Diodorus Siculus: Books 11–12.37.1.* University of Texas Press, Austin.

Greenhalgh, P. A. L. (1973) *Early Greek Warfare: Horsemen and Chariots in the Homeric and Archaic Ages.* Cambridge University Press, Cambridge.

Griffin, Audrey (1982) *Sikyon.* Clarendon Press, Oxford.

Grundy, G. B. (1894) *The Topography of the Battle of Plataea: The City of Plataea. The Field of Leuctra.* John Murray, London.

Hale, John R. (2009) *Lords of the Sea.* Viking, New York.

Hall, Jonathan (1997) *Ethnic Identity in Greek Antiquity.* Cambridge University Press, Cambridge.

Hamblin, W. J. (2006) *Warfare in the Ancient Near East to 1600 BC.* Routledge, London and New York.

Hamilton, Charles D. (1979) *Sparta's Bitter Victories: Politics and Diplomacy in the Corinthian War.* Cornell University Press, Ithaca and London.

—— (1991) *Agesilaus and the Failure of Spartan Hegemony.* Cornell University Press, Ithaca and London.

—— and Peter Krentz (1997) *Polis and Polemos: Essays on Politics, War, and History in Ancient Greece in Honor of Donald Kagan.* Regina Books, Claremont, California.

Hand, Stephen (2005) 'Further Thoughts on the Mechanics of Combat with Large Shields'. In Stephen Hand, ed., *Spada 2: Anthology of Swordsmanship,* 51–68. Chivalry Bookshelf, Highland Village, Texas.

—— and Paul Wagner (2002) 'Talhoffer's Sword and Duelling Shield as a Model for Reconstructing Early Medieval Sword and Shield Techniques'. In Stephen Hand, ed., *Spada: Anthology of Swordsmanship in Memory of Ewart Oakeshott,* 72–86. Chivalry Bookshelf, Union City, California.

Hanson, Victor Davis (1989) *The Western Way of War: Infantry Battle in Classical Greece.* Alfred A. Knopf, New York.

—— ed. (1991) *Hoplites: The Classical Greek Battle Experience.* Routledge, London and New York.

—— (1998) *Warfare and Agriculture in Classical Greece.* University of California Press, Berkeley, Los Angeles, and London, revised edition of 1983 original.

Hignett, C. (1963) *Xerxes' Invasion of Greece.* Clarendon Press, Oxford.

Hodkinson, Stephen (1997a) 'The Development of Spartan Society and Institutions in the Archaic Period'. In Lynette G. Mitchel and P. J. Rhodes, eds, *The Development of the Polis in Archaic Greece,* 83–102. Routledge, London.

—— (1997b) 'Servile and Free Dependants of the Classical Spartan "Oikos"'. In Mauro Moggi and Giuseppe Cordiano, eds, *Schiavi e Dipendenti nell'ambito dell'Oikos' e della 'Familia'* (Atti del XXII Colloquia GIREA, Pontignano, Siena, 19–20 novembre 1995), 45–71. Pisa, 1997.

—— (2000) *Property and Wealth in Classical Sparta.* Duckworth and the Classical Press of Wales, London and Swansea.

—— and Anton Powell, eds (1999) *Sparta: New Perspectives.* Duckworth and the Classical Press of Wales, London and Swansea.

—— and —— eds (2006) *Sparta & War.* Classical Press of Wales, Swansea.

Hooker, J. T. (1980) *The Ancient Spartans.* J. M. Dent & Sons, London.

Hornblower, Simon (1991) *A Commentary on Thucydides. Volume I: Books I–III.* Clarendon Press, Oxford.

—— (1996) *A Commentary on Thucydides. Volume II: Books IV–V.24.* Clarendon Press, Oxford.

—— (2008) *A Commentary on Thucydides. Volume III: Books 5.25–8.109.* Oxford University Press, Oxford.

How, W. W., and J. Wells (1928) *A Commentary on Herodotus in Two Volumes.* Oxford University Press, Oxford, 1991 reprint.

Hunt, Peter (1998) *Slaves, Warfare, and Ideology in the Greek Historians.* Cambridge University Press, Cambridge.

Hutchinson, Godfrey (2000) *Xenophon and the Art of Command.* Greenhill Books, London.

Jacoby, Felix (*FGrHist.*) *Die Fragmente der griechischen Historiker.* Fifteen volumes, Berlin and Leiden, 1923–58.

Kagan, Donald (1969) *The Outbreak of the Peloponnesian War.* Cornell University Press, Ithaca and London.

—— (1974) *The Archidamian War.* Cornell University Press, Ithaca and London.

—— (1981) *The Peace of Nicias and the Sicilian Expedition*. Cornell University Press, Ithaca and London.

—— (1987) *The Fall of the Athenian Empire*. Cornell University Press, Ithaca and London.

Kelly, Thomas (1976) *A History of Argos to 500 B.C.* University of Minnesota Press, Minneapolis.

Kennell, Nigel M. (1995) *The Gymnasium of Virtue: Education & Culture in Ancient Sparta*. University of North Carolina Press, Chapel Hill and London.

—— (2010) *Spartans: A New History*. Wiley-Blackwell, Malden, Oxford, and Chichester.

Kern, P. B. (1999) *Ancient Siege Warfare*. Indiana University Press, Bloomington and Indianapolis.

Kõiv, Mait (2003) *Ancient Tradition and Early Greek History: The Origins of States in Early-Archaic Sparta, Argos and Corinth*. Avita, Tallinn, Estonia.

Krentz, Peter (1982) *The Thirty at Athens*. Cornell University Press, Ithaca and London.

—— (1989) *Xenophon. Hellenika I–II.3.10*. Aris & Phillips, Warminster, Wiltshire.

—— (1995) *Xenophon. Hellenika II.3.11–IV.2.8*. Aris & Phillips, Warminster, Wiltshire.

Lazenby, J. F. (1985) *The Spartan Army*. Bolchazy-Carducci Publishers, Chicago, Illinois.

—— (1993) *The Defence of Greece, 490–479 BC*. Aris & Philips, Warminster, Wiltshire.

—— (2004) *The Peloponnesian War: A Military Study*. Routledge, London and New York.

Lee. J. W. I. (2007) *A Greek Army on the March: Soldiers and Survival in Xenophon's* Anabasis. Cambridge University Press, Cambridge.

Legon, Ronald P. (1981) *Megara: The Political History of a Greek City-State to 336 B.C.* Cornell University Press, Ithaca, New York.

Lendon, J. E. (2005) *Soldiers & Ghosts: A History of Battle in Classical Antiquity*. Yale University Press, New Haven and London.

—— (2007) 'Athens and Sparta and the Coming of the Peloponnesian War'. In Loren J. Samons II, ed., *The Cambridge Companion to the Age of Pericles*, 258–81. Cambridge University Press, Cambridge.

Lewis, David M. (1977) *Sparta and Persia*. E. J. Brill, Leiden.

Lipka, Michael (2002) *Xenophon's Spartan Constitution: Introduction. Text. Commentary*. Walter de Gruyter, Berlin and New York.

Losada, Luis A. (1972) *The Fifth Column in the Peloponnesian War*. E. J. Brill, Leiden.

Luraghi, Nino (2008) *The Ancient Messenians: Constructions of Ethnicity and Memory*. Cambridge University Press, Cambridge.

—— and Susan E. Alcock (2003) *Helots and their Masters in Laconia and Messenia: Histories, Ideologies, Structures*. Harvard University Press, Cambridge, Massachusetts and London.

Macan, Reginald Walter (1895) *Herodotus. The Fourth, Fifth, and Sixth Books*. Two volumes. Arno Press, New York, reprint 1973.

—— (1908) *Herodotus. The Seventh, Eighth, & Ninth Books*. Two volumes. Macmillan and Company, London.

Malkin, Irad (1994) *Myth and Territory in the Spartan Mediterranean*. Cambridge University Press, Cambridge.

McKechnie, P. R., and S. J. Kern (1988) *Hellenica Oxyrhynchia*. Aris & Phillips, Warminster.

Meiggs, Russell (1972) *The Athenian Empire*. Oxford University Press, Oxford.

—— and David Lewis, eds (1969) *A Selection of Greek Historical Inscriptions to the End of the Fifth Century B.C.* Clarendon Press, Oxford.

Morgan, C. (1990) *Athletes and Oracles: The Transformation of Olympia and Delphi in the Eighth Century BC*. Cambridge University Press, Cambridge.

Morrison, J. S., J. F. Coates, and N. B. Rankov (2000) *The Athenian Trireme: The History and Reconstruction of an Ancient Greek Warship*. Second edition, Cambridge University Press, Cambridge.

Müller, Dietram (1987) *Topographischer Bildkommentar zu den Historien Herodots: Griechenland*. Ernst Wasmuth, Tübingen.

—— (1997) *Topographischer Bildkommentar zu den Historien Herodots: Kleinasien*. Ernst Wasmuth, Tübingen.

Munn, Mark H. (1993) *The Defense of Attica: The Dema Wall and the Boiotian War of 378–375 B.C.* University of California Press, Berkeley and Los Angeles.

Nielsen, T. H., and James Roy, eds (1999) *Defining Ancient Arkadia. Symposium, April 1–4 1998*. Acts of the Copenhagen Polis Centre 6, Copenhagen.

Ober, J. (1985) *Fortress Attica: Defense of the Athenian Land Frontier 404–322 B.C.* E. J. Brill, Leiden.

Ogden, Daniel (2004) *Aristomenes of Messene: Legends of Sparta's Nemesis.* Classical Press of Wales, Swansea.

Parke, H. W. (1933) *Greek Mercenary Soldiers: From the Earliest Times to the Battle of Ipsus.* Clarendon Press, Oxford.

—— and D. E. W. Wormell (1956) *The Delphic Oracle.* Two volumes. Basil Blackwell, Oxford.

Piérart, Marcel (2003) 'The Common Oracle of the Milesians and the Argives (Hdt. 6.19 and 77)'. In P. Derow and R. Parker, eds, *Herodotus and his World: Essays from a Conference in Memory of George Forrest,* 275–96. Oxford University Press, Oxford.

Piper, Linda J. (1986) *Spartan Twilight.* Aristide D. Caratzas, New Rochelle, New York.

Powell, Anton, ed. (1989) *Classical Sparta: Techniques Behind Her Success.* University of Oklahoma, Norman, Oklahoma.

—— (2001) *Athens and Sparta: Constructing Greek Political and Social History from 478 BC.* Revised second edition, Routledge, London and New York.

—— and Stephen Hodkinson, eds (1994) *The Shadow of Sparta.* Classical Press of Wales and Routledge, Swansea, London and New York.

—— and —— eds (2002) *Sparta: Beyond the Mirage.* Classical Press of Wales and Duckworth, London and Swansea.

Pritchett, W. K. (*SAGT*) *Studies in Ancient Greek Topography.* Eight Parts. Parts I to VI published by University of California Press, Berkeley and Los Angeles, 1965–89; Parts VII and VIII published by J. C. Gieben, Amsterdam, 1991 and 1992.

—— (*GSAW*) *The Greek State at War.* Five volumes. University of California Press, Berkeley and Los Angeles, 1971–91.

—— (1993) *The Liar School of Herodotos.* J. C. Gieben, Amsterdam.

—— (1994) *Essays in Greek History.* J. C. Gieben, Amsterdam.

—— (1995) *Thucydides' Pentekontaetia and Other Essays.* J. C. Gieben, Amsterdam.

—— (2002) *Ancient Greek Battle Speeches and a Palfrey.* J. C. Gieben, Amsterdam.

Raaflaub, Kurt A., and Hans van Wees, eds (2009) *A Companion to Archaic Greece.* Wiley-Blackwell, Chichester, West Sussex.

Rhodes, P. J. (1981) *A Commentary on the Aristotelian* Athenaion Politeia. Oxford University Press, Oxford.

—— and Robin Osborne, eds (2003) *Greek Historical Inscriptions 404–323 BC.* Oxford University Press, Oxford.

Rich, John, and Graham Shipley, eds (1993) *War and Society in the Greek World.* Routledge, London and New York.

Riedinger, Jean-Claude (1991) *Étude sur les Helléniques: Xénophon et l'histoire.* Les Belles Lettres, Paris.

Rihll, Tracy (2007) *The Catapult: A History.* Westholme Publishing, Yardley, Pennsylvania.

Robertson, Noel (1992) *Festivals and Legends: The Formation of Greek Cities in the Light of Public Ritual.* University of Toronto, Toronto, Buffalo, and London.

Roebuck, Carl Angus (1941) *A History of Messenia from 369 to 146 B.C.* University of Chicago, Chicago.

Roy, James (1999) 'The Perioikoi of Elis'. In M. H. Hansen, ed., *The Polis as an Urban Centre and as a Political Community,* 282–320. Acts of the Copenhagen Polis Centre 4, Copenhagen.

Rusch, Scott M. (1997) 'Poliorcetic Assault in the Peloponnesian War'. 1997 PhD dissertation, University of Pennsylvania, Philadelphia.

Russell, Frank Santi (1999) *Information Gathering in Classical Greece.* University of Michigan Press, Ann Arbor.

Salmon, J. B. (1984) *Wealthy Corinth: A History of the City to 338 BC.* Oxford University Press, Oxford.

Sanders, J. M., ed. (1992) *Philolakon: Lakonian Studies in Honour of Hector Catling.* British School at Athens, London.

Schwartz, Adam (2009) *Reinstating the Hoplite: Arms, Armour and Phalanx Fighting in Archaic and Classical Greece.* Historia Heft 207, Franz Steiner Verlag, Stuttgart.

Scott, Lionel (2005) *Historical Commentary on Herodotus Book 6.* E. J. Brill, Leiden and Boston.

Sekunda, Nicolas V. (1998) *The Spartans.* Osprey Publishing, Oxford.

Shipley, D. R. (1997b) Plutarch's Life of Agesilaos: *Response to Sources in the Presentation of Character.* Clarendon Press, Oxford.

Shipley, Graham (1987) *A History of Samos 800–188 BC.* Oxford University Press, Oxford.

—— (1997a) '"The Other Lacedaemonians": The Dependent Perioikic *Poleis* of Laconia and Messenia'. In Mogens Herman Hansen, ed., *The Polis as an Urban Centre and as a Political Community: Symposium August, 29–31, 1996*, 189–281. Acts of the Copenhagen Polis Centre 4. Copenhagen, 1997.

Singor, Henk (2002) 'The Spartan Army at Mantinea and Its Organisation in the Fifth Century BC'. In W. Jongman and M. Kleijwegt, eds, *After the Past: Essays in Ancient History in Honour of H. W. Pleket*, 235–84. Brill, Leiden.

Snodgrass, A. M. (1999) *Arms and Armor of the Greeks.* Second edition of 1967 original, Johns Hopkins University Press, Baltimore and London.

Spence, I. G. (1993) *The Cavalry of Classical Greece: A Social and Military History.* Oxford University Press, Oxford.

Stadter, P. A. (1965) *Plutarch's Historical Methods: An Analysis of the Mulierum Virtutes.* Harvard University Press, Cambridge, Massachusetts.

—— (1989) *A Commentary on Plutarch's Pericles.* University of North Carolina Press, Chapel Hill and London.

Strauss, Barry S. (1986) *Athens after the Peloponnesian War: Class, Faction and Policy, 403–386 B.C.* Cornell University Press, Ithaca and London.

Stylianou, P. J. (1998) *A Historical Commentary on Diodorus Siculus Book 15.* Oxford University Press, Oxford.

Symeonoglu, Sarantis. (1985) *The Topography of Thebes from the Bronze Age to Modern Times.* Princeton University Press, Princeton.

Tigerstedt, E. N. (varied dates) *The Legend of Sparta in Classical Antiquity.* Three volumes (I: 1965, II: 1974, III: 1978). Almquist & Wiskell, Stockholm, Gothenburg, and Uppsala, 1965–78.

Tomlinson, R. A. (1972) *Argos and the Argolid: From the End of the Bronze Age to the Roman Occupation.* Ithaca, New York.

Toynbee, Arnold (1969) *Some Problems of Greek History.* Oxford University Press, London.

Trundle, Matthew (2004) *Greek Mercenaries: From the Late Archaic Period to Alexander.* Routledge, New York.

Tuplin, C. J. (1986) 'Military Engagements in Xenophon's *Hellenica*'. In I. S. Moxon, J. D. Smart, and A. J. Woodman, eds, *Past Perspectives: Studies in Greek and Roman Historical Writing*, 37–66. Cambridge University Press, Cambridge.

—— (1993) *The Failings of Empire: A Reading of Xenophon Hellenica 2.3.11–7.5.27.* Historia Einzelschriften Heft 76, Franz Steiner Verlag, Stuttgart.

—— ed. (2004) *Xenophon and his World: Papers from a Conference Held in Liverpool in July 1999.* Historia Einzelschriften Heft 172, Franz Steiner Verlag, Stuttgart.

Van Wees, Hans, ed. (2000) *War and Violence in Ancient Greece.* Duckworth and the Classical Press of Wales, London and Swansea.

—— (2004) *Greek Warfare: Myths and Realities.* Duckworth, London.

—— (2006) '"The Oath of the Sworn Bands": The Acharnae Stela, the Oath of Plataea and Archaic Spartan Warfare'. In Andreas Luther, Mischa Meier, and Lukas Thommen, eds, *Das Frühe Sparta*, 125–64. Franz Steiner Verlag, Munich.

Wallinga, H. T. (2005) *Xerxes' Greek Adventure: The Naval Perspective.* Brill, Leiden and Boston.

Westlake, H. D. (1935) *Thessaly in the Fourth Century.* London, 1935; Ares Publishers reprint, 1993.

—— (1968) *Individuals in Thucydides.* Cambridge University Press, Cambridge.

Whitehead, David (1990) *Aineias the Tactician: How to Survive Under Siege.* Clarendon Press, Oxford.

Wilson, J. B. (1979) *Pylos 425 BC: A Historical and Topographical Study of Thucydides' Account of the Campaign.* Aris & Phillips, Warminster.

Wilson, John (1987) *Athens and Corcyra: Strategy and Tactics in the Peloponnesian War.* Bristol Classical Press, Bristol.

Wiseman, J. P. (1978) *The Land of the Ancient Corinthians.* Paul Aström, Gothenburg.

Woodhouse, W. J. (1933) *King Agis of Sparta and his Campaign in Arkadia in 418 B.C.* Clarendon Press, Oxford.

INDEX